CELEBRATE!
Young Poets Speak Out

Michigan – Spring 2006

Creative Communication, Inc.

CELEBRATE!
Young Poets Speak Out
Michigan – Spring 2006

An anthology compiled by Creative Communication, Inc.

Published by:

CREATIVE COMMUNICATION, INC.
1488 NORTH 200 WEST
LOGAN, UT 84341

Copyright © 2006 by Creative Communication, Inc.
Printed in the United States of America

ISBN 10: 1-60050-048-X
ISBN 13: 978-1-60050-048-0

Foreword

Welcome! Thank you for letting us share these poems with you.

This last school year we surveyed thousands of teachers asking what we could do better. We constantly strive to be the best at what we do and to listen to our teachers and poets. We strongly believe that this is your contest. Several changes were made to this anthology as we adapt to what was requested.

In this and future editions of the anthology, the Top Ten winners will be featured on their own page in the book. Each poet that is included in this book is to be congratulated, however, the Top Ten Poets should receive special recognition for having been chosen as writing one of the best poems. The Top Ten Poems were selected through an online voting system that includes thousands of teachers and students. In a day and age where television programs use viewer voting to determine which contestant is the winner, it is appropriate that our poetry winners are chosen by their peers.

Over the years we have had many parents contact us concerning the privacy of their children. The comments focus on the fact that publishing a poet's name, grade, school name, city and state with each poem is too much information. We want to address these concerns. In the Fall 2005 edition of the anthology, we made the decision to only list the poet's name and grade after each poem. Whereas we received many calls and letters concerning the issue that we were publishing too much information, we received thousands of calls and letters requesting that we again publish more information to include a student's school name and state with each poem. Therefore, for this and future editions we will publish each student's name, grade, school name and state unless specifically instructed not to include this information. Just as this information is included in a school yearbook, we provide this information in this literary yearbook of poetry. This decision hopefully makes it easier to find classmates in the book and brings appropriate recognition to the schools.

We are proud to provide this anthology. In speaking to the poets in our anthologies we have found that our anthologies are not stuffy old books that are forgotten on a shelf. The poems in our books are read, loved and cherished. We hope you enjoy reading the thoughts and feelings of our youth.

Sincerely,
Gaylen Worthen, President
Creative Communication

WRITING CONTESTS!

Enter our next POETRY contest!
Enter our next ESSAY contest!

Why should I enter?

Win prizes and get published! Each year thousands of dollars in prizes are awarded in each region and tens of thousands of dollars in prizes are awarded throughout North America. The top writers in each division receive a monetary award and a free book that includes their published poem or essay. Entries of merit are also selected to be published in our anthology.

Who may enter?

There are five divisions in the poetry contest. The poetry divisions are grades K-3, 4-6, 7-9, 10-12, and adult. There are three divisions in the essay contest. The essay division are grades 4-6, 7-9, and 10-12.

What is needed to enter the contest?

To enter the poetry contest send in one original poem, 21 lines or less. To enter the essay contest send in one non-fiction, original essay, 250 words or less, on any topic. Each entry must include the writer's name, address, city, state and zip code. Student entries need to include the student's grade, school name and school address. Students who include their teacher's name may help the teacher qualify for a free copy of the anthology

How do I enter?

Enter a poem online at:
www.poeticpower.com

or

Mail your poem to:
Poetry Contest
1488 North 200 West
Logan, UT 84341

Enter an essay online at:
www.studentessaycontest.com

or

Mail your essay to:
Essay Contest
1488 North 200 West
Logan, UT 84341

If you are mailing your poetry entry, please write "Student Contest" at the top of your poem if you are in grades K-12. Please write "Adult Contest" at the top of your poem if you are entering the adult division.

When is the deadline?

Poetry contest deadlines are December 5th, April 5th, and August 15th. Essay contest deadlines are October 17th, February 15th, and July 17th. You can enter each contest, however, send only one poem or essay for each contest deadline.

Are there benefits for my school?

Yes. We award $15,000 each year in grants to help with Language Arts programs. Schools qualify to apply for a grant by having a large number of entries of which over fifty percent are accepted for publication. This typically tends to be about 15 accepted entries.

Are there benefits for my teacher?

Yes. Teachers with five or more students accepted to be published receive a free anthology that includes their students' writing.

For more information please go to our website at **www.poeticpower.com**, email us at editor@poeticpower.com or call 435-713-4411.

Table of Contents

Spring 2006
Poetic Achievement
Honor Schools

* Teachers who had fifteen or more poets accepted to be published

The following schools are recognized as receiving a "Poetic Achievement Award." This award is given to schools who have a large number of entries of which over fifty percent are accepted for publication. With hundreds of schools entering our contest, only a small percent of these schools are honored with this award. The purpose of this award is to recognize schools with excellent Language Arts programs. This award qualifies these schools to receive a complimentary copy of this anthology. In addition, these schools are eligible to apply for a Creative Communication Language Arts Grant. Grants of two hundred and fifty dollars each are awarded to further develop writing in our schools.

Abbott Middle School
West Bloomfield
Mitra Dunbar
Sandy Feldman*
Ellen Seiss

Addison Middle School
Addison
Kathy McClure*
Christy Sumner

Cadillac Jr High School
Cadillac
L. Dahlquist*

Cass Technical High School
Detroit
Sergent Arline
Lasumitra DasGupta*

Central Middle School
Iron Mountain
Grace Laydon*

Centreville Jr High School
Centreville
Andrea Justus
Maryjane Pinney

Clarkston High School
Clarkston
Ryan Eisele*
Erin Houston
Laura Mahler
Nancy Nankervis
Lori Yegge

Columbia Middle School
Brooklyn
Barb Dagenais*

Dwight D Eisenhower High School
Shelby Township
Andrew Bulat
Kelly Coval
Lisa Packan*

Erma Henderson Upper Campus
   Detroit
      Crystal Gant
      LaDonna Hosey*
      Mr. White

Flynn Middle School
   Sterling Heights
      Wilda Nance*
      Diane Okun*
      Mrs. Setlak

Gesu Elementary School
   Detroit
      Judy Kuzniar*

Grand Blanc Middle School
   Grand Blanc
      Stacey LeSage-Slaga*
      Pat Nelson
      Deborah Perry*

Grosse Pointe Academy
   Grosse Pointe
      Lawrence DeLuca
      Wendy Demartini

Grosse Pointe South High School
   Grosse Pointe Farms
      Harry Campion
      Mary Collins*

Guardian Lutheran School
   Dearborn
      Karen Turgeon*

Hally Magnet Middle School
   Detroit
      Francene Ambrose
      Karen Careathers
      Irene Robinson*
      Ms. Thomas
      Nicole Walker

Hilbert Jr High School
   Redford
      Michael Sophiea*

Jefferson Middle School
   Monroe
      Gary L. Boudrie*

Kingsley Area High School
   Kingsley
      Kelly Knight
      Mrs. Krygier

Lakeview Middle School
   Lakeview
      Kathryn Nerychel
      Colliene Willison

Ludington Magnet Middle School
   Detroit
      Karin Brown
      Lisa Jenkins
      Michelle Morden

MacDonald Middle School
   East Lansing
      Mimi Cecil*

Manchester High School
   Manchester
      Kevin Mowrer*

Manistee Middle School
   Manistee
      Mary Hunter*

Mercy High School
   Farmington Hills
      Jan Mordenski*

Mona Shores High School
   Norton Shores
      Heather Hall*

Montague Nellie B Chisholm Middle School
   Montague
      Jennifer Szegda*

North Rockford Middle School
   Rockford
      Greg Crowe
      Lori Watters

Oakland Christian School
   Auburn Hills
      Patricia J. Eastman*
      Nancy Kwik

Paw Paw Middle School
   Paw Paw
      Annette Markovich*

Posen Consolidated High School
   Posen
      Mary Misiak*

Roseville Jr High School
   Roseville
      Mr. Borse
      Mr. Branant
      Jennifer Rose
      Kathryn Tasich*

Ruth Murdoch SDA Elementary School
   Berrien Springs
      Philip Giddings*

St Ann Elementary School
   Cadillac
      Mae Purrenhage*

St Anthony of Padua School
   Grand Rapids
      Mary Beth Westby*

St Gerard Elementary School
   Lansing
      Shelly Piecuch*

St John Lutheran School
   Fraser
      Susan Machemer*

St John Vianney Catholic School
   Flint
      Judy Gansen
      Elizabeth Petrides*

St Thomas More Academy
   Burton
      Phyllis Cory*

Troy High School
   Troy
      Megan Alef
      Meagan Foster
      Donna Guith
      Linda A. Pavich

West Middle School
   Plymouth
      Nicole Lerg*
      Marjorie Palmer

Language Arts Grant Recipients 2005-2006

After receiving a "Poetic Achievement Award" schools are encouraged to apply for a Creative Communication Language Arts Grant. The following is a list of schools who received a two hundred and fifty dollar grant for the 2005-2006 school year.

Acushnet Elementary School – Acushnet, MA
Admiral Thomas H. Moorer Middle School – Eufaula, AL
Alta High School – Sandy, UT
Alton R-IV Elementary School – Alton, MO
Archbishop McNicholas High School – Cincinnati, OH
Barbara Bush Elementary School – Mesa, AZ
Bellmar Middle School – Belle Vernon, PA
Bonham High School – Bonham, TX
Cool Spring Elementary School – Cleveland, NC
Douglas Elementary School – Liberty, KY
Dumbarton Middle School – Baltimore, MD
Edward Bleeker Jr High School – Flushing, NY
Emmanuel/St. Michael Lutheran School – Fort Wayne, IN
Floyds Knobs Elementary School – Floyds Knobs, IN
Fox Creek High School – North Augusta, SC
Friendship Jr High School – Des Plaines, IL
Gibson City-Melvin-Sibley High School – Gibson City, IL
Hamilton Jr High School – Hamilton, TX
John F. Kennedy Middle School – Cupertino, CA
John Ross Elementary School – Edmond, OK
MacLeod Public School – Sudbury, ON
McKinley Elementary School – Livonia, MI
Monte Cassino School – Tulsa, OK
New Germany Elementary School – New Germany, NS
North Beach Elementary School – Miami Beach, FL
Paradise Valley High School – Phoenix, AZ
Parkview Christian School – Lincoln, NE
Picayune Jr High School – Picayune, MS
Red Bank Charter School – Red Bank, NJ
Sebastian River Middle School – Sebastian, FL
Siegrist Elementary School – Platte City, MO

Language Arts Grant Winners cont.

Southwest Academy – Baltimore, MD
St. Anthony School – Winsted, CT
St. John Vianney Catholic School – Flint, MI
St. Paul the Apostle School – Davenport, IA
St. Rose School – Roseville, CA
St. Sebastian School – Pittsburgh, PA
Sundance Elementary School – Sundance, WY
Thorp Middle School – Thorp, WI
Townsend Harris High School – Flushing, NY
Warren Elementary School – Warren, OR
Washington High School – Washington Court House, OH
Wasilla Lake Christian School – Wasilla, AK
Woodland Elementary School – Radcliff, KY
Worthington High School – Worthington, MN

Young Poets
Grades 10-11-12

Note: The Top Ten poems were finalized through an online voting system. Creative Communication's judges first picked out the top poems. These poems were then posted online. The final step involved thousands of students and teachers who registered as online judges and voted for the Top Ten poems. We hope you enjoy these selections.

Top Poem Grades 10-11-12

My Hero

Those doctors came like a thief in the night;
Ready to steal that joy you held so tight.
They said, "According to what our tests have to say,
Your child's brain has developed the wrong way."

"We suggest an abortion would be right.
This child's future does not seem too bright,"
You heard them tell you with little regard.
You knew deep in your heart life would be hard.

Yet you still decided to let me stay,
Despite what those evil doctors had to say.
My life was precious to God and to you.
You knew that God had something for me to do.

His way is perfect you always told me,
Even though things aren't what we'd have them to be.
You have taught me so much about God's love,
And how our mind should be on things above.

You loved me when no one else could care.
You lived through the pain that was hard to bear.
Therefore, you are my hero above anyone,
Because you loved me when all was said and done.

Janae Anderson, Grade 12
Prairie Baptist School

Top Poem Grades 10-11-12

Existence

I am curious
I wonder about the humanity of our race
I wonder why good is smothered by evil
I wonder about honor and integrity, valued as dirt
I wonder about Satan's grip upon our world, and I weep: I am despair
I imagine a land of castles and green plains
I imagine a cool breeze consuming my being
I imagine all that will live; I imagine all who have died; damned and saved
I imagine those forgotten, and I recall: I am memory
I see death and torment feasting upon the world
I see a hypocrite preaching; I see fault lain at the feet of others
I see my two hands, committing foul deeds
I see a broken man, and I too fall: I am darkness
I dream in anguish, yet I dream that all is not lost
I dream of the holy past, and of the bright future
I dream not of the present, dark as night
I dream of renewed life, and I rejoice: I am hope
I hear a song; I hear birds calling in the trees
I hear the rustle of their branches
I hear a babe's voice, crying
I hear two lovers laugh, and I smile: I am life

Jonathan Bartnik, Grade 12
Troy High School

Top Poem Grades 10-11-12

In My Closet

In my closet
Are lots of things.
Many different shirts
And tons of blue jeans.

But if you look deep down
Way down deep inside,
You will find so much more
That I try to hide.

Maybe some old shoes,
Belts and holey socks,
Even some old watches
That no longer go "tick-tock."

Below all of the good
Are the broken dreams
Things that went wrong
And weren't all that they seemed.

Some stuff in my closet
Is old, rugged and torn
Even the love and the hope
That was pushed to the floor.

Ashley L. Breden, Grade 12
Ross Beatty Jr/Sr High School

Top Poem Grades 10-11-12

Boarded Up

A house bent apart
Apart from the road
Standing alone amid the gleaming land
Splinters of woods and rusty nails
Strewn about like shattered glass
The poplar tree in the yard
Once lush
Emanating a scent of home
Now drooping with old age
Wilting slowly in the vindictive heat
The house itself
Battered and tattered over years
Forbidding boards
Fitted and nailed upon the windows
Upon the decrepit door
Shutting out all
Spiteful, wretched, vile
Only darkness remains here
A house bent apart
For what reason, what cause
One can only ask

Hyunje Cho, Grade 10
Grosse Pointe South High School

Top Poem Grades 10-11-12

The Dark

It seems I'm living
In a land full of pain
Where there's nothing to lose
And nothing to gain
Sometimes I wish I
Wasn't here
Wishes constantly killed
By fear
Lost in the dark
Where no one is near
Screams in the dark that
Nobody hears
Lost in this dark
I am all alone
Lost in this dark
This dark is my home

Chris Lewis, Grade 11
St Johns Schools

Top Poem Grades 10-11-12

As I Look into the Mirror

As I look into the mirror,
I'll tell you what I see,
Something twisted and contorted
Something that is no longer me
Something I never wanted to be.

As I look into the mirror
My thoughts begin to race
My anger starts to build
Against my tear-stained face
How did I get here
And become this grotesque disgrace?

As I look into the mirror
My thoughts begin to change
The person staring back at me
Indeed is not so strange

As I look into the mirror
I slowly cease to cry
I start to crack a smile and my face begins to dry
I realize life is what you make it
And the limit is the sky.

Dave McKenna, Grade 10
St Johns Schools

Top Poem Grades 10-11-12

The Quilt

Her breaded hands stitched it for me
Loving palmed patches a mark
Luminous reds and superfluous violets scampered a star
The daybreak she spent with a silver thumb
Knowing what quilted squares might become
Frivolous heart and wrathsome speed
Racing down Indy 500 threads
Shuddering bodily eye weights
Getting workouts in a back room gym
Until it was completely swallowed in her pride.
The hands sluggishly drooped
The tongues dry with chamomile tea
Made it feel wonderfully pretty tied up in ropes
And locked it into my smooth hands
With a combination that smiles.
Though fairy days now vanished
And tea stingingly cold
Bland strings hanging nonchalant
Merely sticky notes of daft gray hands
Inscribing a pin cushion of an amorous patched heart
And simply what she had written here.

Jessica McLean, Grade 11
Southfield Christian School

Top Poem Grades 10-11-12

Never Too Old

Six faces it had upon itself, with a mailing tape-like smile.
To an adult this was just a packaging box, but to me it was more worthwhile.

The delivery man would drop it off, a strange something inside.
But as my mother opened it I urged her to hurry! This one I could fit inside!

For this box was a toy like no other, with endless hours of fun.
It was there I would play, from night until day, or until its seams came all undone.

This box it was my clubhouse, or my castle by a moat.
It doubled as my racing car, and my perfect rowing boat!

A house, a cave, a fort, a plane, it was all these things to me.
One time it was a pirate ship, and I, the captain of the sea.

The delivery man still brings today, boxes with contents inside untold.
And as I sit and stare at its cardboard walls, I wish I wasn't so old.

For I miss those days that I lived in a castle, and thought that I was a beautiful queen
But as I look back now, I've recently discovered, that you're never too old to dream.

Carole Polan, Grade 12
Dwight D Eisenhower High School

Top Poem Grades 10-11-12

Picture Perfect

Somewhere,
in a high clearance government building,
in the middle of Maryland,
there is the Department of School Photography.
For a study made long ago
revealed that teenage egos
are simply much too large.
To make room for the sludge of
dates and equations
essential for future career success,
it is deemed necessary
to un-cramp our skulls from our blimp-like
self-esteems.
Meticulous clerks
concoct foul smelling Uglification Solutions.
Picture negatives are dipped in
the liquid and are horrifically transformed.
When perfectly nice looking
boys and girls
open up their school picture packets,
their egos never fail to shrink five sizes.

Dan Riggins, Grade 10
Traverse City West Sr High School

Top Poem Grades 10-11-12

Simplicity

Simplicity.
A word.
Common yet uncommon.
Hard to comprehend.
Even harder to put into perspective.
Why?
The root of the word explains it, simple.
What is simple anymore, not much.
How sad that the word has become so complicated, cynical.
Very rarely do people take the time to enjoy things, simple things.
They are taken for granted, forgotten.
Pushed aside for something bigger and better.
What will become of us when complicated things are gone?
If complexity ever ceases to exist.
Will people realize what simplicity is?
The thing they have ignored in their fast-paced lives.
Ignored in their ignorance?
Or, will we cease to exist, because we are too blind to see something so easy?
Something so uncomplicated.
Something so simple.

Brittany Sharp, Grade 10
Byron Center High School

Dear Mom

Dear
Mom I　　　Know
I have done wrong but
your little boy wants to
come home so I can
sit　back　with
you　and
watch TV
and
cuddle
Christopher Matejovsky, Grade 11
St Johns Schools

Seventeen

The in between age
That almost there stage.
A year that means nothing
But in the middle of something.
Just another birthday
Adulthood only a year away.
Sixteen you can drive
At eighteen your alive.
Still to school you go
With even more info to know.
Can't seventeen be that good
Only if it could.
And when you get older
You'll wish it was bolder.
The in between age
That almost there stage.
Kelsey Gordon, Grade 12
Ross Beatty Jr/Sr High School

Our Love

As the sun rises
As a new day begins
We fall in love all over
As the sun sets
As the day ends
Our love grows stronger
As our love grows
Our hearts are closer
As our hands touch
Our blood rushes
As our eyes meet
The more we become attached
Our love is more powerful than ever
Our hearts are wide open
As the sun rises
As a new day begins
We fall in love all over
As the sun sets
As the day ends
Our love grows stronger
Fatima Ali, Grade 11
Star International Academy

Your Love

Your love is my first and last thought,
to me it is always priceless so I can't determine the cost.
The feelings I experience are happy and sad,
without your love is like writing without a pen and a pad.
Your kiss is a wish so I fix my lips,
for that one brief moment that is like a solar eclipse.
Your full lips touching mine, my mind hard to find,
it is like seeing after for so long being blind.
They say love can be seen at first sight,
sometimes you spend your whole life going by twice.
Constantly looking for a smile that is bright,
hoping to jump the broom while throwing rice.
Just make sure that the love is true,
because if you mix the wrong colors you just might be blue.
I look before I leap, so I don't have to weep,
your love is like food without you I don't eat.
Sometimes I have doubt it's hard to believe,
your love is like air without I don't breath, and drown in this lonely sea
Lance Young, Grade 10
Powers Catholic High School

A Father's Undying Love

I visited the hospital room of a very young mother today.
She held her newborn closely in her arms as she began to pray.
Tears streamed down her cheeks as she thought of that heartbreaking day
When news came from the battlefield that her husband had slipped away.
She realized that her baby boy would never see his dad;
There would be no fishing, playing catch, or hugs when he was sad;
But as she lay there thinking, a new thought crossed her mind —
Her husband was a hero of the good and lasting kind!
Because of his dear sacrifice, her baby would be free
To strive for his utmost potential and to learn on bended knee.
I visited the hospital room of a very young mother today,
And left with many emotions that I had stowed away.
I realized the great sacrifice of a father's undying love
And the importance of being thankful to those who are now above.
May we never forget those men who gave their lives so we could be free,
And may we stand behind America as she fights for victory.
Mary Boggess, Grade 12
Prairie Baptist School

Let's Come Together

Let's come together everybody you see,
and make the world a better place for you and me.
There is too much killing in the world nowadays.
Can we have a decent place for our boys and girls to play?
I mean really, who wants to wake up scared thinking they might get shot.
Scared some stupid fool might roll through blowing up the block,
with an AK-47 or a Glock.
We need to all come together and start thinking you see.
It makes no sense how we can just hate each other.
We should listen to the Bible, it says love one another.
Life is too short for arguing and feuding.
So, let's teach our kids how to love instead of the shooting.
Sandra Dickerson, Grade 11
Advanced Technology Academy

Change

Come share my world,
It's not different from yours.
It's filled with pain, hate, and violence,
We have no open doors.
I wish things could change,
All for the better.
I really wish that we could just
All come together.
We need to stop fighting,
It's the wrong thing to do.
You ask why children act so wild,
Well, they obviously get it from you.
Change is the only way,
To make things right.
But it's going to take some time,
Because change doesn't happen overnight.

Jasmine James, Grade 11
Advanced Technology Academy

The Looking Glass

The waves, the waves, they ride East 'tis said.
The western winds these waves are fed.
Oars in tow, regress to weave,
Shrouds of glories upon their leave.
Gallantly poised, up in arms,
The very same that oft' bring harm.
Perchance discard the Alcatraz for a time,
Though do come again to Cain's crime.
Tidings sent o'er waves, with lightning come,
Merely spawned to form clouded dome.
Fogged lens make shallow sighted
The populace left so benighted.
The fish swim swiftly to the west,
Though few do pass the current's test.
Scour lowly estuary to vast offing distant,
Futile to encounter not inscrutable instant.
How can veracity think to stand a chance,
When none find Atlas's burden within cognizance?

Jeff Wong, Grade 12
Andover High School

Beautiful Girl

I dated the most beautiful girl today
With looks and a voice that will never decay.
Her hair is like gold that shines so bright.
Her eyes are like diamonds; a beautiful sight.
Her voice is angelic when used to sing;
Like doves in the air and church bells that ring.
Our features, however, are of interest to find.
I think she's too wise, and she thinks I'm too kind.
But alas our differences bring us close.
If it was a potion, most powerful its dose.
My heart has gone in an unending twirl
For I am with the most beautiful girl.

Kevin Taylor, Grade 10
Hastings High School

The Victorious Fightin' Irish

The Fighting Irish never give up
Because of all their former luck,
They never miss or drop a ball
Because the players give their all!
Their record was really great this year
To me it brought some happy tears,
If they lost it would be like a sin
Hopefully they'll gain a win!
They always seem to earn the crown
When one of their players scores a touchdown,
As they add six points to their score
All the fans from the stands let out a roar!
Players are strong and always stay tough
Even when it seems the goings are rough,
As in their name they fight, fight, fight
And they play their best with all their might!
Here come the fans galore
All wanting more and more,
For to win the game the players strive
To do their best is how they thrive
Watching them makes me glad I'm alive!

Therese Maher, Grade 10
St Thomas More Academy

Fly Away

Sometimes when I feel no one cares I dream I can fly
I imagine flying high above the sky into the clouds
some might call it running away from my problems
but I, I call it clearing my head and freeing my heart
the song "break away" is my favorite song
the words reflect on my life

when I try to speak up it does feel like no one can hear me
it makes me want to break away from the pain
it's not all that bad sometimes
my mom is sometimes there for me when I need her
she tries to comfort me the best she can
I love her for trying and not walking away.

December DeGlopper, Grade 10
West Michigan Academy of Environmental Science

Hate

We cry, we let out tears, we yell and think.
The feeling is hate, and why do we hate.
Hate can go, but returns in single blinks.
Hate comes any time it's never too late.
Hate is dark, very hard to overcome.
Hate means tears, and a shredded tiny heart.
Hate makes you feel depressed, and very dumb.
You always feel there is a missing part.
Hate is lonely, and has no friends.
Hate spreads and creates a confrontation.
Hate is hideous, but it still makes big trends.
Hate is hate, and it's no exaggeration.
We hate because we all discriminate.
We hate because we underestimate.

Jamilah Kaid, Grade 10
Edsel Ford High School

Dreams

Dreams exist in many ways
They exist at night and during days
Dreams sail through many minds
They sail from places out of time
Dreams join together many hands
They join together lives and lands
Dreams give hope to many lives
They give people wings to fly
Dreams are many different things
They help people spread their wings
Erica Hayes, Grade 10
Kingsley Area High School

Winter Rose

Red ragged rose,
Prickled with thorns
Disposed of beauty,
Now ugly and torn

Left in the cold,
As winter prevails
Frozen and stifled
Once the snow turns to hail

Painted with frost,
Covered all white
Awaiting the spring
When all will be bright

Soon melting away
The sculpted mask
Unleashing wildly,
Blooming on task
Kaitlin Mulka, Grade 12
Posen Consolidated High School

Bedtime Prayer for a Troubled Soul

As I lay me down to sleep,
I pray that you watch over me.

Protect me from this place of fear.
Dry the endless stream of tears.

Keep my guardian angel at my side.
Block the anger from my mind.

Keep me close, through the night.
Tell me I will be all right.

Lord, please make it stop,
Or mute my ears to block it out.

All the yelling, all the fighting,
A troubled soul keeps on crying.
Lauren Thomas, Grade 10
Cass Technical High School

Enough

Have you ever felt as if something was too much?
As if you wanted to stop it, but it was hard to clutch?
We have no peace worldwide, and I say enough
Enough of all the racism against all people: from dark to light
Enough of all these arguments that escalate to fights
Enough of all these fights that escalate to war
Another "War on Terrorism," but tell me, what for?
And just because you caught Saddam with no bomb, do we still have to be hated?
Or does 'Iraq' and 'weapons' sound anything related?
Come to think of it, they probably do now; now that America's invaded
Now can you see how much hate the war created?
I say enough of what we're doing in Iraq
All day, every day, bombs and gunshots
Enough with Iraqi children waking up in fear
Enough killings every day, bringing oceans of tears
Now enough is enough but it doesn't stop here
Let's go to Palestine; tell me what do you hear? (BOOM!)
It's a suicide bomber!? Or do we call him a terrorist, too?
But, when the Palestinians get killed, what do we call the Jews?
I'm just a Muslim-Arab-American with poetry that can be lethal
And I'm trying to explain what's really happening; really happening to my people
Ahmad Hasan, Grade 10
Central Academy

Jill

It was a Saturday night she was by herself
Driving back to college without a seat belt
She was thinking about her life her heart was tore
Because she didn't get to spend enough time with her family the night before

She had a great life school was easy and life was fair
She had lots of friends and always good memories to share
This was the kind of person who loved to live
If you needed help on anything she'd have advice to give.

But on this very night on her way back to C.M.U.
She had to leave this world she left me and you.
She was thrown from her car after swerving past a deer
So many people are still in shock even though it's only been a year

I don't know the pain she felt but I know her life is not done.
Because she's living in Heaven now where for pain, there is none.
Why her? Everyone wonders, she did nothing but good.
They don't know who could replace her because no one ever could.

Now that she's gone we know it's not fair she died too young
What did she do to deserve this? Her college life had just begun.
Don't be sad that she's gone in your heart she lives still
And when you're driving, wear your seat belt in memory of Jill.
Aleashia Capogna, Grade 12
Oxford Area Sr High School

Everyday Evil Doer

I feel its pounding
unsteady, and unsure
the faltering beat resounding
for the lack of breath no cure.

This must be like drowning
vision and clarity obscure
the anxiousness is mounting
I don't remember when beats of my heart were fewer.

The lump in my throat isn't downing
I don't feel warm sand's lure
the world around me is clouding
stress is an evil doer.

As things spin surrounding
I long for the moor,
happiness and light hearts there abounding
I wish for a mind that was newer.

The buzz and ticks are loudening,
where are skies e're bluer?
I feel my conscious less proudening
lost in the depths of this sewer.

Brianne Walsh, Grade 12
Grand Ledge High School

Biker Boys

His bike will never be faster than mine.
We shift from first, second, third, fourth, and fifth,
I'm sure I will kick his slow green behind.

Blue, white, and silver that great beauty's thine,
I will not lose no matter what the cost
His bike will never be faster than mine.

He says he is faster than all bike kind
He thinks he is badder than all bikers,
I'm sure I will kick his slow green behind.

His chrome pipes may be shinier than mine
He wears his bags for aerodynamics,
His bike will never be faster than mine.

He knows he's slower than bikers divine
While even though his motor is bigger,
I'm sure I will kick his slow green behind.

Faster than lightning they always do say
That is my bike and bright shining armor.
His bike will never be faster than mine,
I'm sure I'll kick his slow green behind.

Leland Ross, Grade 12
Centreville High School

My Rock

Here before you is a rock,
Mom you are always there on the clock.
The rock is like you it will not break,
Only there sometimes to give me a shake.
The way it sparkles, is like your smile.
If only I could make it last for awhile.
The colors deep inside,
Are nothing you can hide.
For your feelings are deep.
Pleasure having you makes me weep.
Taking the snow, wind, and rain,
You never show me any pain.
Even when the skies are gray,
You always find a way to show a sunray.
Mom your love is like a rock, everlasting, and strong.
Helping me with every wrong.
There for me in every way,
I never ever want you to go away.

Amanda Waterman, Grade 12
Clarkston High School

Mice

Why couldn't Noah leave those two
Really what good do they do?
They always mess up stuff
Which makes cleaning very tough.
I hate hearing their little paws
Scratch away at the insides of my walls
And the little presents they leave under the sink
Are surely starting to stink.
I try to get them in a trap,
But somehow my fingers always get snapped.
They eat poison like an M&M
Yet still I can't get rid of them.

Scott Hartsell, Grade 12
Ross Beatty Jr/Sr High School

A Mother's Love

My mother is a woman that I love and admire
My love for her burns like an unrelenting fire
She's a person that accommodates me with love as God Himself
My goal in life is to treat and love her better than myself
She's a woman of compassion and love
And I will always put her above
She's a woman of strength and can endure to the end
She's a woman that will never give in
My love for her is so inexplicable
And for me to hate her is so terrible
I will never hate her and that's a promise to the end
My love for her will always abide within
I will never let anyone erode at our love
My love for her is as pure as a holy dove
My love for her is so elusive
And this is the conclusive.

Tylon Risby, Grade 10
Cass Technical High School

Sunshine

Sunshine falls
It rains down magic
It makes me happy
I feel so ecstatic
I love the world
It is so great
Tomorrow's another story
Then I will hate

The world turns cold
Like a stone
It makes me feel bold
But I'm still all alone
Now I am
A sad little lad
But don't feel bad
Everybody get glad

Matt Szczerowski, Grade 12
Posen Consolidated High School

Poetry

Poetry is your thoughts
Put down on paper,
Poetry is everything you've ever dreamed
Expressed in this meaningless scribble.

Poetry is a swirl of colors
Said instead of painted,
Poetry is the song of crickets
And the silence of your deepest secret.

Poetry is everything
And nothing all at once,
Poetry is everywhere
Even when you don't see it.

Jessica Hamacher, Grade 10
Whittemore Prescott Area High School

Deranged Blackout

A repose of life's cessation
What happened to your essence?
Drowned out of memoirs
Empty holes remain
Leaving you in contempt
Can the gashes be healed?
Sewn and stitched back into place
Can broken wings be mended?
Cast in love's embrace
Are there lacerations on the heart?
Left behind in wake of casualty
Are there memories lingering?
Causing despondency
Wake soon and alter life's outcome
An obtainable deliverance

Sara Manley, Grade 12
Comstock Park High School

Night Life

The sun may have set
For some though, the day isn't over yet
There is a whole new world unveiled in the dark
A whole group of people looking for a chance to make their mark.
In society they look for a place
All they really want is to set their own pace
In the dark they do thrive
In the light they don't feel as alive
Everything lies in the music and the beat
It brings along a chance for friends to meet
They look for those with whom they are alike
But strive to be different, these people of the night.

Maegan Payne, Grade 12
Manchester High School

Freedom

We fight for our liberty;
We fight for what is true;
We send our men overseas
To defend the red, white, and blue.

We fight in wars and give our lives
So that we may be free;
And now we freely fly the flag
For every man to see.

Our nation was built on God
And His promises true;
In hopes that we may tread,
In the way our forefathers once knew.

Men went to war being courageous, honorable, and brave;
And many of them passed on and are lying in the grave.
They gave their lives for our country, and they linger in our hearts;
Now let us do what we can do, and give our every part.

James Boggess, Grade 11
Prairie Baptist School

I Hate You

I hate you because of this, and I hate you because of that.
I hate you because it's easy to,
All of those times you made me mad.
I hate you because of the way you are,
Even though it's what made me fall.
I hate your ways, your acts, your reasons, but your words most of all.
I hate the sense I feel, when I run away from you
Sometimes it's good, sometimes it's bad, but either way — it's what I do.
I hate the way you look at me as if you did nothing wrong
I hate the way that just for once, your emotions can't be strong.
I hate everything I take in, and everything that I don't
I hate everything I make you do for me — even if I know you won't.
I hate all the words that I write down —
the "I love yous" and the "I miss yous" make me sore
Every word doesn't have the same meaning anymore.

Amber Dilley, Grade 10
Franklin High School

The Secret

The secret was kept and hidden from me
Like the treasure of a mischievous pirate
My anger crept up like a killer
Striking me in the heart
Exploding into neglect
Why treat one better than
The treatment put on oneself,
The devastation, the humiliation,
The grimy boots of your disrespect
Trampling all over my trust
Counterfeit is what you are to me now
False and phony

Joel Parrish, Grade 12
Clarkston High School

A Strong Mother

A strong mother,
The one who has been beside me.

A strong mother,
The one who never gave up on me.

A strong mother,
The one who loves and cares for her child.

A strong mother,
The one who taught me right from wrong.

A strong mother is a mother who does not stop loving her child.
My mother is a strong mother.

Orlando Acosta, Grade 12
Thomas More School

Colors

All the colors
Overwhelmed me when I left you
So many sides, so many stories
Every day a new one in a different color
You know you did one of the worst things
You can do to a person
But for that I'll walk away
Rip apart
Forget all the memories etched into my skin
It's time for me to do it again
Grant me this one favor
And stay out of my life forever
Oh, and you can even keep your colors
The colors haunt me
Jumping out at the last moment
Tackling me to the ground
And smothering me
I thought I left it all behind me
But I guess I was always wrong
Twisted and crying in a pool of lies

Sarah Moore, Grade 12
Clarkston High School

Misguided

My brain is on overdrive, yet I'm absent minded
Realizing the true character he is hiding
An exposed secret to my reality
A danger to our society
Extending an interest and a loving hand
Resembling a player in the band
Behavior of a typical human being
Forgotten, unlike a fiend
Wanting for this to be different than the rest
A need for it to be the best
A disaster to every persons dream
This life is nothing as it seems
Like a kick in the face, or getting sprayed with mace
I need to wake up and open my eyes
Discover what is happening under each disguise
But it's all hidden and locked away
With eyes wide shut here I lay
Time slowly ticking by
Awaiting useless secrets to die
Pausing for the perfect ride

April Willis, Grade 12
Inland Lakes High School

Captain's Spirit

I'm a pirate who's never sailed that horizon.
Why now, my rogue heart?
Wandering the deep, I search the still waters,
that which disguise the turmoil raging below, for my soul.
Water untraveled, untouched, uncrossed…until now.
Treacherous, stormy waters beneath placid glass,
left alone for their want to devour me.
To see beyond the surface is to delve into the unknown.
But what will I find?

Nikki Fisher, Grade 10
Kingsley Area High School

Truth

I've been down this road before,
I don't want to go back,
You're pushing me to be with you,
I'm trying not to fall for you,
It's too late,
I fell for you again,
I want you back,
Maybe all will be better,
Maybe I can forgive you,
I kiss your sweet lips,
Long and hard,
I'm still hurt by your dishonesty and betrayal,
I decide we can never go back,
You've broken my heart for the last time,
I clutch your picture as I fall to the floor
I lay there crying
I made the biggest mistake of my life
I shouldn't have let my one true love go,
It's too late and I can't turn back now.

Kylie Bray, Grade 10
Escanaba Area Public High School

Strength, Truth, Life
You gave me love, you gave me life.
You believed in me before I was born.
I cried and you heard me, I was cold and you clothed me.
I called on you and you came to my rescue and told me it was ok,
I was blind and you gave me sight, I was weak and you made me strong.
I was thirsty and you gave me water, hungry you gave me food,
in need of shelter and you put a roof over my head.
All these things you give to me and yet I take for granted,
never let me out of your sight, nor let me stray away from you.
You are my truth, strength and light.
I will live through you and let you handle me and my problems.
I will follow in all of your ways with all my strength and all my life.
I love you.

Chris Giannola, Grade 11
Dwight D Eisenhower High School

Why Is This?
Why is this: I want to go home.
Why is this: My soul don't want to go on.
Why is this: I listen to the same song.
Why is this: I want to be free, but better yet I can't see
I wrote this poem with my heart.
Why is this: You want to see me fall apart,
But the words are talking to me,
Why is this: When I get angry I feel an evil soul come over me.
I write 'til my hands fall off, but you love to see a person like me fall off.
It's not what I saw that healed me.
It's what my heart felt that's healed me.
That's why.

Joseph Green, Grade 11
Thomas More School

Life (Soon a Paradise)
In life you learn a lot about yourself
You learn a lot about other people

You learn that things are not always what they seem
You grow up doing things that you do not want to do but you have to!

Most of the time, it is for the best
What can you say — life is hard

You have responsibilities and obligations to yourself
All these things make you a better person

There is pain and joy, smiles and frowns
But soon those frowns will eventually turn upside down
There will be nothing but smiles and no pain
You will only gain life

You don't have to roll the dice
Because soon Earth will be a paradise
Don't play with your life and take that chance
Just listen to His commands.

Cody Spearman, Grade 10
Cass Technical High School

The Match of My Life

Here I sit on the cold, hard mats
Thinking about how to win
This intensive most important match
It's the championship meet and finals are near
It is most definitely my favorite time of the year
I'm listening to my music
Headphone blaring with the rhyme
The rhyme that gets me going
Gets me pumped up every time
The announcer calls my name
It's my time to shine
I don't care what it takes
That gold medal is mine
I'm going to get out there
And work off my behind
To prove what I'm made of
Right now is the time
Sweaty and exhausted, my fans cheer me on
One minute left, being the champion is where I belong
The ref raises my hand and I have won
Dedication and hard work had paid off in the long run

Josh Newville, Grade 10
Kingsley Area High School

Changes

I found myself in my backyard,
Staring through the trees,
Noticed something I almost forgot,
The place where my dog used to be.

I found myself at the same coffee shop.
The place we used to resort to.
Different faces behind the counter,
Not the same regulars I'm used to.

I found myself at the house.
Where my favorite summer occurred.
I realized I wasn't fourteen anymore,
And that it will be awkward with her.

I found myself in the middle of your problems.
It never used to be this way.
I think you like being miserable.
I believe this is how it will stay.

I found myself watching everything shift.
All the things that surround me.
Faces, stories, people, and places,
Change is all I can see.

Jessica Dehring, Grade 11
Posen Consolidated High School

Thou Should Not Love

Love in young hearts is always forsaken.
Marriage is just for the foolish hearted.
All your strong emotions will be taken.
It would be wise to not get them started.

Love turns into depression that lasts long,
Seems as if these feelings won't expire.
So those who are smart will stay very strong,
And avoid the feeling of hot fire.

So consider keeping your heart always.
Stay clear of the plague that conquers others.
Take my advice and you will live long days,
Unlike many other foolish lovers.

Our bodies are revered so always care.
The feeling of commitment will not fair.

Ashley Montgomery, Grade 12
Belleville High School

Leaving

Quietly waving in the wind,
I stand calm and peaceful.
Since my beginning, I have stood here
watching my surroundings and feeling alone.
My other companions are starting to leave me
as autumn has started to approach.
My youthful days are gone
and the end of my journey is coming.
The wind keeps blowing,
and I fall to my death.
My color has faded dark.
My time has come.

Trisha Alexander, Grade 12
Mona Shores High School

In the Fall

The leaves fall from the trees
Many different colors
Red, orange and brown

A light breeze
Leaves blowing around
The sound of trees

Small animals gathering food
Hunting starts
People in the woods

Days are shortening
Nights are getting cold
Winter is coming

All in the fall
Till the end of us all

Matt Styma, Grade 11
Posen Consolidated High School

Optimistic

I don't have a yellow brick road,
Or diamonds and pearls
Or a fairy godmother —
All I have is a
Dream,
And the
Hope to
Conquer.

Raven Jones, Grade 11
East Grand Rapids High School

Remedy

Years ago, when you stumbled,
and scraped your knee,
you'd scamper to your mother, who,
acting as a shaman, a magic healer,
which she was back then,
patiently dried the tears,
and kissed the hurt away;
unfortunately,
the more years you pile onto your back,
the deeper the hurt burrows,
the harder it gets
to kiss the pain away,
and soon the epiphany reaches you,
like the sting of a scraped knee,
only far worse,
that even something as magical
as kisses
cannot truly heal.

Lauren Myrand, Grade 11
Mercy High School

To My Love

Compassion was how I felt
When we first hooked up
Now it seems like it kills you
Just to pick the phone up

"Sorry, I was busy"
That's always your excuse
Now I'm the one that's "BUSY"
Sorry, game over, you lose

Hope there's no hard feelings
Because it's you I will always love
No one will ever know how much
Except for the Lord above

Yes, you told me you love me
I'm not saying that it doesn't matter
I felt you really meant it
If only you could have shown me better

Marlena Hill, Grade 11
Cass Technical High School

A Feverish Hamlet

"Ay, madam, it is common."
You harlequin at the parade of morality! A mistress clad in scarlet robes.
There she dotes, nay — shames.
Not love at all, but a regular plebeian display
And yet her bosom bares no ignominy.
O, the foul disgrace, what a hackneyed contessa.
As shameful an act as spring birthing winter,
That bitter snow should disgrace the fresh green and mark the newborn buds.
The following of the tablets bids us honor our origin,
(And yet the exulted Book doth spurn the insidious act). The path is forked.
Fear I I'll not partake in any joy, for never can mine eye seem to lay gaze
Upon a pax romana, now that this has fallen pat.
Perhaps mine own self be blamed, my quarrelsome thoughts.
For who creates anger but the affected soul?
It is not, as most suppose, the provocative —
The provoked are only so as much as they allow
Themselves to glance into the glass of spite.
The fox may nip at the heel of hound, but the hound may choose not to bellow.
But still, I cannot from my mind remove, this burning and scorching wound.
It scars my heart and hinders my patience.
Out stain! You damned spot! O, that I may ever be at peace!

Maren Fischer, Grade 12
West Bloomfield High School

The Struggle of a Mother

The struggle of a mother is one of the biggest struggles to endure,
Feed your child, pray awhile, to keep your children pure,

It is the biggest pain ever felt,
When a mother is all alone,
She's looking for help,
No one to call on the phone,

A mother prays all day, and cries all night,
Trying her hardest to continue this fight,

She holds up the house with all her might,
Teaching her children to hold on tight,
Showing them what's wrong, and what's right,

A mother must be wise,
And know how to compromise and sacrifice,
Strong enough to fight for her children,
While drugs, sex, and violence are on the rise,

A mother is like a soldier,
In a lifelong war,
I can't think of anything tougher,
Than the struggle of a mother.

Arielle Johnson, Grade 10
Cass Technical High School

Shopping

Let's go! Get in. It's time to go shopping.
Delight invades. The car leaps forward letting
the road lead. Excitement quickening
ideas for impulsive ways of getting

absolutely all the stuff we can.
Impressive clothing in the stores arouse
desires. Wallets open as was planned.
One down, all others left. Unfazed we browse.

Go in. Spot perfect item. Dressing room.
Glimpse image. Just right. Pay cashier. Make dash
to prey on next option. Naught nil can ruin
the passion in shoppers till they collapse.

Lets go! I want to leave this place so cursed.
Delight subdued. Regret stuffs full the purse.

Leona Mullett, Grade 12
Centreville High School

Save Yourself and No One Else

When I was young I wanted to save everyone
Then one day I realized I couldn't and cried
But I moved on with life
Recently I realized I wanted to save the one I loved
But realized I never could
And I bawled and tried to move on
Today I realized throughout all of this I wasn't saving myself
And I cried 'cause I didn't know how
So I was kind of hoping
That maybe you would finally step up
And save yourself
So I could save myself
'Cause despite how much I love you
I know I can't save you
So why did you ever expect me to
Why did I ever believe I could

Angelica Ariana Singleton, Grade 12
Mona Shores High School

A Four Letter Word

As I walk I see it
As I watch television I see it
As I dream I see it
When I talk I hear it
Let's face it, it's everywhere
What's everywhere?
Love is everywhere
It's like an old show tune stuck in your ear
It won't go away
It's like the old man at the corner store
He's never going away
Love…Love, it's like you, it's not going away
And the love I have for you will always stay the same!

Courtney Bates, Grade 10
Cass Technical High School

The Divorce

When mom left,
we thought it would be better.
In time things got worst,
parents, screaming,
yelling, fighting, arguing.

The divorce was filed,
that's when all the pain started.
First it was about the son,
and then the house

Late phone calls into the night.
Dad steaming like a tea pot,
you can see the sweat beads starting to form.
Having the black cordless phone slam onto the receiver,
as a hammer strikes wood.

After two years,
we all rest in peace,
some were hurt,
and moments will never be forgotten.

Darin Plinski, Grade 12
Clarkston High School

The You in You

The moment that leaves you shaking in your shoes,
What of the second you forget that you're not you?
Realizing, tasting, wondering, what you would do,
In this mere moment if you were not you?

Everyone around you asking has something changed,
Do you dare tell them the about the strange?
Hoping, feeling, guessing if you're not the same,
When these people ask, who do you blame?

It is not but the blaming, that is but the whole truth,
The secret is not but a mere question of who?
Dreading, fearing, knowing they found out you,
But blame can't be placed if you are not you?

Now that the secret is out and now that everyone sees,
Have you become a someone that everyone can be?
Sharing, believing, seeing, misconcepted easily.
Was it the lies that kept it so no one could see?

In this mere moment that has you shaking to your shoes,
Are you willing to be that "person" that shakes inside "you?"
Understanding, trying, being, that someone to look up to.
Now in this mere moment have you found the you in you?

Bionca Doers, Grade 10
Kingsford High School

I Didn't

I didn't see you
Behind the corner
I didn't know you were so close by
I didn't expect to meet you
in such a time like this
I didn't know you would come so soon
You surprised me
I didn't feel your presence at first
I didn't acknowledge you at first
But now I see you
Behind the corner and I recognize
that you were never far
You were just taking your time
to come to me
Cashia Thomas, Grade 11
Grosse Pointe South High School

Nameless Death

I don't know you,
but your death hangs
like a cloud over my heart.
My sister sighs with relief.
It's no one we know.
Everything is okay.
Our lives move on,
no more than a minute spent
on this young girl's lost life.
But it's *not* okay.
A life has ended
and for many the pain will never fade.
It makes me hope for
one more day to say
"I love you."
Death is a part of life,
but it creates a darkness
over which no victory can be held.
And that causes me
to take your death to heart
when I don't even know your name.
Lila Frikker, Grade 12
Troy High School

Buster Brown

A young boy
very adventurous
no care in the world
just the love of his parents
fueling him for success

Not prepared for the life he leads
only being there for what he needs
grasping to the soft teddy bear
he slowly drifts off to sleep
breathing in the nightly air
Dillon Wirgau, Grade 12
Posen Consolidated High School

Death to Rebirth

As the lost soul of a young boy walks through the valley of death
He feels no evil, nor speaks no evil but dies with no intent in living
He is reborn with new hope and new thoughts, a fresh soul
He is ready to bear the burden of living in a world that does not want him
He shall take on that challenge and succeed with no hate just happiness
No one can touch him for he is on his own plateau high above the thoughts
He walks as if no one can touch him, as if a bubble surrounds him
He wakes still in the class that mocks him and laughs when he speaks
Constant fear runs through his veins
For these voices have taken hold and will not let go
I do not have a dollar to my name
He's in frequent shame for he knows his life is wrong
He should not be living this life
If he ends it will anyone care?
Who will attend his funeral?
For it shall be full of black and white shame
Alec McCleskey, Grade 11
Clarkston High School

I Am My Number One Fan

I refuse to be sad or mad at the way I've been played
I'm going to wake up and look around at what mistakes have been made
I will not forget what was done to me
I'll cover the hurt with a smile and put it in my memory
I'm alive and well, never to hurt again because I refuse to go back to where I've been
I gave my kisses, said my goodbyes, and wiped my tears from my big brown eyes.
I held you close, held you near thought you were everything through my fear.
Now I'm finished, the curtain can fall
Because in the end I'm the one standing tall.
I can finally say that I am proud of who I am
Because in the end, I Am My Number One Fan
Alexandria Lewis, Grade 10
Melvindale High School

The Bracelet

It sits undisturbed, in the top drawer of my faded wooden dresser
Locked in the long purple box
With the glistening white Christmas bow still attached
Just like when you gave it to me, on that icy winter day a year ago.

Where it will stay for now
Untouched, worn and scratched.
Filled with the memories of us together; both happy and sad.

All the times we spent together,
All the times we spent apart,
All the times we cherished,
Pain and heartache we will only know.

In pictures it's just an accessory, something to complement a necklace.
To me it's a constant reminder of all the lies, sorrow, and deception.
The small silver heart, shimmering like diamond in the sun
Engraved with our initials, surrounded by a gold heart.
I'll never forget.
Catherine Cichon, Grade 12
Clarkston High School

Hole 11

We had strolled at least a mile,
From the front clubhouse,
past the heavily secluded brown halfway house,
to the sacred spot we always seem to get.
As we plop open our Blue and Green lawn chairs;
the oak trees behind us shade our backs
like a giant green canopy.

As the stogies are lit,
the smell of cigar smoke fills the air
as if we were in a tavern,
and the men behind us
begin hacking it up.

Across the way,
the crowd at hole 17
is beginning to arrive and gather,
which means that beer sales are mounting,
and the sober are few!

As the time passes,
and the day grows older,
players start to arrive,
and the fun of the Open really begins.

Patrick McIlrath, Grade 12
Clarkston High School

Everlasting Feelings

I have everlasting feelings I can't bear to tell
I have secrets that I have not told

One feels like bursting in the air
Another like running in heaven
And the last dreadful feeling like I'm in ashes

I have everlasting feelings I can't bear to tell
I have secrets that I have not told

Whispers hide my feelings
Most of my secrets will be kept
But one I do tell
Anger inside is burning up
It will one day burst but not earlier than scheduled
This is the only feeling I do not let out

I have everlasting feelings I can't bear to tell
I have secrets that I have not told

Until I open the door to my everlasting feelings

Jeana Brown, Grade 10
Cass Technical High School

Ode to My Aunt

I heard from a dreadful call
You had passed with a sudden fall
Sadness and good memories overflowed me
Your face was the only thing I could see
The wise words you would always say
Now I wonder if I will ever be okay
Your smile spread to everyone around
You made people laugh without making a sound
I remember the gifts you gave every year
It's hard to say this without shedding a tear
Your warmth was always felt
So strong it could make others melt
It wasn't too long ago you received my last visit
It's hard to say this
But I'm really going to miss it

Amanda Pieczynski, Grade 12
Posen Consolidated High School

Eternal Fixation

I love you,
but do you truly exist?
I feel like I need you,
you're my breath of air.
My flaming heart,
inextinguishable,
causing my eternal fixation.
Why must we be apart?
Am I being protected
from your being deceitful?
There's just something about you,
drawing me closer.
My heart would say "yes,"
my conscience, "no."
And here I sit,
thinking of you.
Always on my mind,
making you my life's suicide.

Ashley Wright, Grade 11
Franklin High School

We Delved into Obliteration

We delved into obliteration
as we held hands —
Into the obscurity we sauntered,
through the mist of unforeseen dolor —
foretold truths have risen to the challenge,
yet the impetuousness is deceiving.
The final flight of our being —
everyone dies forsaken
She has never mistaken
hope arises in the eyes of the unborn
as it abates from the hearts of the noble past.
The annihilation of tomorrow
Pray my last breath lasts.

Wendy Xiao, Grade 12
Andover High School

Dawn of Fire

From a hill
came slanting sunlight,
Screaming like
savages in the night.
A glossy white image
with acres of smoke,
Like the invisible
friendship between old town folk.
With officious cries
and grotesque yellow flames,
This great blazing
beast was becoming untamed.

Eric Simone, Grade 10
Kingsford High School

Driving My Truck

I hop in my truck
And turn the key
It fires right up
The motor runs free

I push in the clutch
And grind it in gear
I give it some gas
And begin to steer

I back out the drive
And on to the road
I shift out of reverse
And away I go

I go down the road
And make some turns
Every time I stop
My tires I burn

Isaac Kowalski, Grade 12
Posen Consolidated High School

Peaceful Day

Sitting out in the sun,
Waiting for what may come
Flowers and fruit,
In bloom all around
Loving mother earth,
So tender and soft
The clouds overhead,
Gliding through the sky
Dark corners exist not,
Because light shines everywhere
And the wonderful music,
Drowns out all the voices
As this perfect day,
Seems more and more beautiful.

Justin Bending, Grade 12
Franklin High School

Ode to India

Your sunlight plays on the bright silk
Saris laid out on the padded tables
The rich silk floating through my fingers
Sari after sari made with your own silk
Proud to call such a creation your own
But this beauty is nothing compared to you
Pride in my India

Marriages on your soil are truly blessed by the Trinity
The countless handfuls of fresh jasmine woven in the bride's hair
Give her a scent reminiscent of a goddess
The groom's car speeding off in a cloud of dust
Finally the groom reaches for the mangalsutra
Three knots around the bride's neck and its over
Another marriage blessed by your favor
Pride in my India

An ancient country steeped in tradition
It is as if nothing has changed since the beginning
Women still wrapped in the saris of the past
Your farmers of the old, still tilling with oxen and buffalo
Lastly the giant date trees forever swing in your sweet evening breeze
Pride in my India

Neeharika Kalakota, Grade 12
Midland High School

All You'll Have Left

You can climb to the top of a hill,
but when you fall you'll only see stars flying about your head
and it'll only hurt for a short time.
You can climb to the top of a cliff,
but when you fall you'll see the stars flying about your head again
and it'll hurt a little longer and harder.

But when you climb to the top of the world and you fall,
you'll forever fall into the stars soaring through space and the hurt will go away.
All you'll have left are the knots on your head.
It's like falling in love.
The first time you hope you climb high enough.

So when you fall you don't fall and get hurt,
but if you do it only hurts for a short time.
The second time is a little higher, hoping you won't feel the hurt again.
But if you do it hurts a little more and a little longer.

But when you climb to the top of the world and fall,
you'll forever fall into the stars and eternal love.
You'll never be hurt again.
All you'll have left from the ones before are the tears in your heart.

Jessica Kelley, Grade 10
Centreville High School

Divorce

Divorce, divorce, he left without a trace.
Why can't you see what you have done to me?
I cannot look into his eyes or face
Now our family will no longer be.

We wait and wait for you to come back here
I tire of waiting and begin to sleep.
I dream of where you are; I know you're not here.
Why did you do this Dad, why do I weep?

After a month we begin to forget,
All the anger and all the pain drift away.
You come back, and soon a table is set.
Now I keep all father figures at bay.

You broke my heart and I frantically cry.
I hope you have found a good reason why.

Marcie Clark, Grade 11
Waldron Middle/High School

Trife Life

Born yesterday, gone tomorrow.
This man's life is full of sorrow.
He walks through the streets on the verge of death,
Trying to get a dime bag before his last breath.
She uses her body as an idol to men.
They use and abuse her so she'll never win.
She thinks it's a helpful benefit,
Because a better life, she could only dream of it.
It's a pain for these ones,
The refugees of the forbidden sun.
All in the spin of life,
They didn't have to live so trife.
Dangered with the fear of the end.
No one will support or lend,
A helping hand or someone to encourage,
The strength that wasn't there or the least bit of courage.

Sydney Searls, Grade 12
Martin Luther King High School

They Say It's a Better Place

All was going very well up to the age of three
I was taken away from my mother
And they say it's a better place…
I was taken away from her for three years
Going through some of the worst things people could ever do.
And they say it's a better place…
When it's truly the worst place you could ever be
All alone
And they say it's a better place…
Away from the one person you love the most
And they say it's a better place…
Finally, at the age of six I was leaving with my mom
Truly that's the better place!

Anthony Gulledge, Grade 10
Tri County Area Schools Alternative Education

The Letter

The letter gleamed in the warm sunlight
on the table,
and demanded attention like a queen.
Its flap grinned coyly
at the fuss it was creating.

It unclenched its mouth,
to reveal the damage:
"You have not been accepted."

The letter sat on that table for weeks or months.
Then finally,
the weary receiver picked it up,
stomped on it,
until it was a tattered mess,
then burned it,
and buried the charred remains
in the backyard.
And it seemed it had never existed.
But the receiver mourned his loss,
and laid lilies on the cold, toiled ground
every day.

Until a new letter came.

Rachel Hyde, Grade 11
Clarkston High School

Education's Doors

It made many doors,
And made me feel no sores.
Like a weapon that opened a brighter door,
And never made me poor.
Made my mind grow with ideas,
And Kept many ideals.
Love that appeared with care,
And made it so rare.
Knowledge that came forward,
And never will go backward.
Improvement that contrived intelligences,
And had a number of experiences.
Attitude that made a key,
And ignoring the disrespectfulness way.
Tested many experiments and never failed one,
And made it all alone.
Encouragement was always made, but arriving so late,
And always on a wrong date.
But accepting from my mate,
Knowledge that made it worth wide,
And made it spread worldwide.

Azhar Shobatee, Grade 10
Universal Academy

Living S.O.L.

As we live our Soap Opera Lives, we tend to become S.O.L.;
Because "All My Children" although they are "The Young and the Restless," they seem to be "Trapped in the Closet." Some may
claim to be, way more than they aim to be, claiming to be…"The Bold and the Beautiful." Though their "Guiding Light" points
them in the right direction, instead of following their passions, and being apart of that "Dynasty" that they want to be, they just
sit there and think, but "As the World Turns" and there is no stopping it, some people just wind up in a "General Hospital"
because they have just swallowed something that they can't handle…the truth! I am that conscience in your mind…yes I am, I
am that "Guiding Light" I am that one who can discombobulate all "The Days of Your Lives" with a thought. I am Muhammad
Ali, yes "I can float like a butterfly, and sting like a bee." Just watch me, I am the last of a dying breed, because people fail to
see that they may fulfill their fantasies and begin to live their dreams. I am your worst nightmare, because there is no telling
when "I'll be back" from terminating you terminators. I am like R. Kelly because I believe I can fly, and I'm glad I made it, I'm
the world's greatest. I am like Martin Luther King, because I too have a dream. I too dream of equality, but what has gotten
into me? But even though the "Knot's Landing" and sometimes it seems like it's "Another World" I told Toto "I don't think
we're in Kansas any more" because even in "Dallas" "there is no place like home" and that is why we live S.O.L.

James Moody, Grade 12
Detroit Academy of Arts and Sciences

I Don't Want a Forced Love

If you don't love me from your heart, don't love me at all.
If you don't really care, then I'll let my tears fall.
If you don't think about me when you're gone, then leave and go away.
Unfortunately most people think, "I love you" is just an everyday phrase to say,
Although I love you and I need you, I don't want a forced love from you.
I want someone to love me in return, something that's real and true.
I want someone who really cares and someone who wants to be there for me, can't you see,
It's been a long time now, and I'm finish playing this hurtful game.
I'm letting you go, and making it very simple and plain.
It has been five years since I've heard your voice.
It's time that you think about me and make that choice,
The choice if you love me or not, because only you know.
You'll hurt me more if you stay and your heart wants to go.
I don't want you to love me with half of your heart or kind of.
So please let me be, because I don't want a forced love.

Amani Andrews, Grade 10
Franklin Road Christian School

Misery Loves Company

I hurt myself because you won't hurt me.
I've abandoned myself because you've declined to desert me.
No matter how many tears I cried or obscenities I yelled, I couldn't make you stay.
Looking up to the sky for a blessing I've realized that I lost my way.
I've fallen off the path of righteousness in your eyes.
And for that I feel as though I'll soon die.
My heart begs for your pain and hurt.
My soul feels incomplete without feeling the sorrow I'm accustomed to because of your devious dirt.
I write your name a thousand times on the walls of my heart hoping you'll come back home to break it.
When I had you I was ungrateful for the pain but now that you're gone I'm more than willing to take it.
I can't breathe without knowing where you are or think about the love you're giving another.
I can't concentrate knowing that you've sold me away for some other lover.
I want the pain; will you please give it to me? I want to cry in your presence; will you please oblige me?
But you won't because like all the rest, you've denied me.
Come home and break my heart again. Come home to unhappiness one more time.
Come home and make the saddest memories in my heart chime.
Will you agree to hurt me just once more?
Will you agree to letting me fall helplessly as you walk out my heart's door?

Jhazmin Slay, Grade 10
Cass Technical High School

Windows

Whenever I looked out
The windows were the same
No matter what I saw
The windows gave it gleam
No matter what went on
The windows saw no pain
Now I wish for my old place
Now I stare in vain

I hoped one day I would look out the same windows
As a different girl
But the windows went before I came
To realize it's gone
I never thought it'd be
Now the windows that I have
Are still so white to me

But green windows are in my heart
Even though we are apart
Now when I see the windows
It's from the outside
Windows of then
Will I look out again?

Christina Abdo, Grade 11
Dwight D Eisenhower High School

No Excused Arrival

She waits outside just to see if he will arrive,
The sun is high, and her mother wonders why,
She won't come back inside.

But she waits and waits, for his sudden arrival,
As the sun goes down and the weather is mild.
With a heavy sigh, she sits back and wonders,
Why he hasn't come yet.

The sun is setting and dinner is waiting,
Yet she sits on the steps and wait for a promise he had made.
The heat has cooled, and the birds have cooed,
Yet he is no where to be found.

The sky is dark, the stars are out
And yet, he is still no where to be found.
But upon the steps, she no longer sits,
With tears in her eyes, she goes back and wonders why.

The telephone rings, excuses are made,
But she smiles to herself, and hangs up the phone
With a satisfied smile.

Jennifer Steffens, Grade 12
Mona Shores High School

The Place I Know

There's a place up north I like to go
Sometimes it's sunny; sometimes it snows.
Are we there yet, are we there yet?
No, we still have a while to go
We like to pass the time with song and radio
It's a place we've gone since I was born
And is as comfortable as those old shoes that are worn.
We gather together with our family and friends
Because that is what is important in the end.
Through the years, we've watched each other grow
But we always come back to what we know.
I love this place so much
Where we play and swim and such
The place I know and where we go
This is where I grew up.

Allyson Way, Grade 10
Manchester High School

On Viewing a Bridge

To flames you go with mast in full and blaze,
so man can scare away from rosy whine.
To glory you go with mast in heightened gaze,
so man can strive for light to fill the time.
The eyes, the eyes, they know of what they see.
And beneath the towers of mind and painted stone,
she flows with grace of simple supreme beauty.
How can one know but what he is shown?
The words they deceive the eyes who sing so free.
From sea to land and space we man have flown.
She stands alone to take from her the earth.
He stands alone to take from him the truth.
Oh! but Man, you are so great
You built the bridge that leads to fate.

Aaron Jacobowitz, Grade 12
Andover High School

I Give You My Heart

I give you my heart mind, body, and soul
I give you my love for you make me whole
I give you this promise the promise to try
I give you each breath and the tears I cry

I give you my past my future and now
I give you my thoughts my hope and this vow
To give you my voice and the music I sing
I give you forever I give you this ring

To give you my world all the pain and strife
I give you my hand learn to share my life
I give you this kiss and these words I say
"I'll cherish you always as of this day."

I give you my faith that these words are true
For today, I swear, to spend my life with you.

Larenda Allore, Grade 10
Woodhaven High School

Bull Riders

The bulls have big horns
They stick in you like thorns
Most cowboys wear hats
Some cowboys wear chaps

The bulls are there to buck
They're brought there by a truck
Sometimes the fall hurts
You will rip many shirts

Bull riders wear a vest
It helps protect their chest
You hold onto your bull rope
And all you do is hope

Craig Niedbala, Grade 11
Posen Consolidated High School

Wishing to Fly

From where I fly, what will I see?
Heavens above shedding tears
Gently it touches my fragile frame
I stand firm, though maybe I'll fail
For the Earth below is not hell
Fire burns and saying otherwise
Red is the color of vengeance
Of that no tears could remedy
Is there something beyond the cloud?
Or these tears only a mirage
Flying between the sky and Earth
Filled with fears — unspeakable
For when the wind carries me high
My existence is compromised
My fate is put into thy hand
To help me lift this cross I bear
Blow me up high into the sky
So I can catch a glimpse of thee
Though if there's nothing I will find
I'll float with memories within

Steven Hanrahan, Grade 10
Grosse Pointe South High School

True World

Here trapped inside this world
Of never-ending hunger,
The endless struggle for power
People killing people,
Nations killing nations
An endless vortex of agony
And madness, moving like a
Bloodstained hurricane
Never stopping,
Relentlessly progressing
In this world
Of infinite darkness

John Wilson, Grade 12
Clarkston High School

I Thought I Saw the Sky

I thought I saw the sky today in a vast abyss of regret
Once, under that sky we laid in the stillness of a spring night observing the stars
Oh, how they sparkled and shone with a glint as if only to say "nothing lasts forever"
Once, under that sky we trembled in the coldness of winter
Once, under that sky we ran a race, a race of a summer morning
through the woods and we rested in the sunlight side-by-side next to the tree
our tree which thrived in the heat of our burning passion
our passion which has since ceased
I thought I saw the sky today
as my world grows colder without you
I thought I saw the sky today reliving memories
memories of you standing in the golden tones of autumn
memories of sunlight in my life fading, fading away
I thought I saw the sky today
I thought I saw the sky

Johnny Vicencio, Grade 10
West Ottawa High School

Every Woman's Nightmare

Woke up this morning feeling rather low
Only God knows why I stay because I don't even know
As I stare at the reflection of a woman I don't even know;
A woman who is internally dying
I can't fathom staying here another night
I know this ain't really love
I don't want to repeat this cycle the second time around
The hitting, cursing, and the screaming is more than I can bear
I can't keep feeding into this sorry excuse you call love
When I know in the bottom of my heart, it is nothing more than discontent and hate
I made up my mind, I am leaving
But, where will I go and who will I run to when my mind is so confusing?
But I gotta go, I can't stay
The promises to change are no longer enough
So it's over

Alycia Berry, Grade 10
Cass Technical High School

Innocent Pride

The blue sky looks upon the moon of unrest
As the entanglements of soothing twains of reassurement resist
My body knows no borders thin as paper
Rather my body can't stop the borders of brick and mortar
Once the walls of the enemy collapse my heart whispers numb
As for the river of innocent blood does not stop the hate
I wish the breeze of guilt could reverse the door of hell
But as long as the souls of the raven exists
Then the pride of the eagle will be lost
And as long as my conscience shows me not what I want to see
Then my heart will have to overcome the moment of peace
As the thought of being lost and being lost forever
Catches the attention of the people that shall not be lost
Then once more the thoughts of fighting for freedom is dispersed to the proud few
Therefore making the cry of normalcy is necessary
Not only for the ones that fight but also for the ones that believe

Warren C. Eakes, Grade 10
Belleville High School

Love...Hah, There Is No Such Thing

People say you are in or "hot" and I am not
You say you love me, but I know it's not true
'Cause when I'm gone u say to hell with you
I know I'm not that sweet or suave
But I could be the one for you if you'll let me follow through
They mock and humiliate me while they praise you
I know you think I'm weird but I thought we were true
And since you know how I feel now how about you
Therefore this anime, skateboard, physics loving nerd is through

David Billingslea, Grade 10
Cass Technical High School

America

America — the greatest place on Earth...
Home of a democracy that's always blinding me and you,
And in addition to them, the media and our neighbors are doing it too,
Using their propaganda, and spin-doctors, keeping us guessing with their lies,
We were shocked to see the truth back then, but now it's no surprise.
America: a place where we are free,
Free to get strip-searched for bombs,
Free to stay home from school, and yet they put the sentence on our moms,
Free to get discriminated; whether it be sex, race or religion,
Free to get our homes searched, without a warrant, by the police division,
The government grants them permission; so they can take apart your kitchen,
Only if they smell one HINT of suspicion.
America, a place where several cities remain divided,
Even after fifty years; which was when we all decided,
That "Everyone was born equal" as Martin Luther King recited,
Yet in America today, these rights are still not always provided.
Come live the "American Dream,"
We are the nation supreme,
Where we're all on the same team,
Yet things aren't as they seem.

WELCOME...TO AMERICA.

Adam White, Grade 10
Dakota High School

To Sing, or Not to Sing

To sing, or not to sing. That is the question
Whether it is noble or not. To let your mind suffer
To let the lights and crowds overwhelm you
To take your life at risk yet again
And to step aside? To live, to play
No more; and to sing is to be a star
The heartache of life and lost of love
To sing is a life, it consumes me
The fans beg and wish. To live, to play
To sing is just a dream ah there's the rub
So on the stage of music where dreams may be
When the lights and crowds have gone
You stopped to think — that's what life has come to be
So have drugs and alcohol crowded the mind. No?
So who bears the name of music and time.

Kayleigh Conley, Grade 11
North Branch High School

A Man of Fortune

The pirates life is the life for me,
There's nothing else I'd rather be.
Not a doctor or a lawyer,
But a swash buckling destroyer.

Pirating for the likes of me,
Pirating on the western seas,
I'd be a Captain through and through,
Captain of a cutthroat crew.

All for one and one for all,
Just like a Musketeer.
The pirates call, that enthralling call,
To be a buccaneer.
Greg Donajkowski, Grade 11
Posen Consolidated High School

Red Nail Polish

Necks stretched,
eyes squinted in hope,
you can nearly hear them say,
"Pick me. Please pick me."

But the hand is extended
to the red dominatrix,
an old favorite, and she
is escorted across the marble floor.

The disappointed crowd watches eagerly
as her sultry shoulders
slowly twist to reveal her
tired, bleeding heart.
Courtney Williams, Grade 11
Mercy High School

Kiss

We stare into each other's eyes,
body temperatures start to rise,
as all our emotion flies,
I've never felt like this…
this moment will not be lost,
the moon reflects off her lip gloss,
I move in and skip the cost,
this chance will not be missed…
I move in and take the chance,
I pucker up and hold my stance,
hoping that you will advance,
awaiting that pure bliss…
a moment passed, I start to stop,
the chance is gone, my shot is blocked,
but you move in and our lips lock,
now we've shared our first kiss.
Stephan Phillips, Grade 11
West Bloomfield High School

One Last Line

One last line to walk.
One more memory to hold.
Hate; spite; controversy.
Imaginative.
Blindness bright and brilliant,
Mind's maker now turned militant.
Contemptuous; tortuous; melodic.
Sad.
One more sigh to breathe.
One more crescent moon of charcoal.
I leave it up to interpretation,
But these are my intentions, laid dead
On the throne of the sun on the sweet blue horizon.
Bitter; pitiful; rhapsodic.
Please.
Silver, gold, clay and ivory
Make the chains that hold Reality.
I brush my side against Guilt's black robe
And find the embodiment is gone;
The robe is my own.
Forever.

Katherine Leach, Grade 10
Heritage High School

Repentance

There is a quiet groaning deep within me today
I detest the dust and filth that define me
I am overwhelmed by the dark chasm
between who I am and who You want me to be

I sit across the table
from the woman who has become familiar
with the dirtiness in my closets and the tear stains on my cheeks
I hoped that she would see right through my face, my eyes, my words
to the raging battle beneath
But we talk with normalcy
Don't you feel it?
My desires my calling my crushes my dreams my history my weaknesses my worth
my convictions my hopes my fears my enslavements
blend into quiet struggle… muffled anguish

You pull my longing up from my heart
And my cry pierces the silence
"I want to change!" "I want to be new!" "I want to be Yours!"

When grace comes, it is almost painful
A long-closed door in the darkness begins to creak haltingly open
Light creeps around the edges
And lays its hands, gentle but firm, upon the edges of my blackness

Claire Bates, Grade 12
Andover High School

Illusions

Soft green grass
Under my bare feet
White puffy clouds
High above my head

Chickadees chirping
Fills my ear
Water rushing at the shore
Splashes up onto my face

Someone comes and takes my hand
Guides me along the soft, warm sand

We walk and we talk
Reminiscing about how it used to be
Laughing at the crazy things we used to do
Playfully attacking each other in the sand

Then, with a flash, it's gone
It was all only a dream
But such a wonderful illusion

Kaylin Shultz, Grade 11
Alpena High School

Inside My Heart

Inside my heart blood flows,
Windows open and feelings form.
I try to teach myself to think from the heart.
That's where we all should think from.
Some of us make wrong decisions.
It is up to us to make them right.
Touch my heart, O' Lord, for my decisions
Seem to be slipping and sinking like quicksand.
Make a way for my decisions to meet my heart's desires.
Make a way for your angels to lie in my heart,
So that I may make pure decisions.
This is why it is important to look deep inside
Your own heart, 'cause I have to take the time
To look inside my heart.

De'Angelo Wheeler, Grade 11
Blanche Kelso Bruce Academy

Eternity in a Bottle

You are an inch away from heaven,
two years too late,
angelic whispers in the night.
No words describe the length of eternity.
I will save time in a bottle; memories in my heart.
I will think not with my brain, but with my instinct.
Once we were friends;
now I wish to give you hope,
I wish to bring you joy,
I wish to shield you from the pain.
I would bring that all to you and make the days last forever,
a moment's not too soon,
let me show you.

Samar Coyle, Grade 11
Cranbrook Schools

One Rose Never Withering

One last rose pierced the snow
One final chance to feel love's glow
One last call to he who listens
One unnoticed whisper from cold lips risen.

One last rose, sacrificed
Since words when unspoken never suffice
One final offering, draped in red
Hope amongst the path where he might tread.

One last breath frozen in air
One last flurry through tangled hair
One final glance at a velvet sky
Walking away forever on this night.

But another's slow footsteps come behind
Slow hands caress what he knew he'd find:

One final rose slips inside his coat
Beside the undelivered letters he wrote
Opposite her footprints, he then parts
Wishing to follow the girl with the lonely heart.

Allise Noble, Grade 12
Midland High School

The Fork in the Road

What happens when new becomes old,
and old becomes a trend?
Can a broken heart find the will to mend?

I left my heart out in the open —
Against my conscience, I held your end
My life was on trial;
you were the judge that would determine the rest
So while I played friend,
you kept me close enough
that your life might not go bust
But you've raised yourself high now,
And my stair-step has yet to receive commend

Finally, we somehow find ourselves here —
at this fork in the road
With differing views,
we've gone by what we know
But our knowledge was like a trick
Perceived in different shades,
It's not always the same;
And so the old trend
will again take its reign.

Danielle Emerson, Grade 12
Dwight D Eisenhower High School

Following

The moon is following me
It is shining high in the sky
It must be lonely if it's looking at me
I turn around it's still there
It's following me
Day after Day
Night after Night
It's watching and waiting for me
It looks out for me
Does the moon look out for you?
Day after Day
Night after Night
It watches me

Katrina Katcher, Grade 12
Dwight D Eisenhower High School

Cats

There was a cat sleeping on my leg
My leg was starting to get numb
I should be mean
And kick him in the bum

The cat is so cute, I have no choice
So I just let it sleep
Now I'm momentarily paralyzed
And I lose the use of both my feet

And then another cat arrives
So gorgeous and appealing
The purring gets so loud
I lose my sense of hearing

Then she jumps upon my lap
And rests her head on my arm
Further paralyzing me
With her charm

So each day I spend my life
Like some disabled fool
Thank you God for inventing the cat
I didn't know you could be so Cruel

David Karschnick, Grade 12
Posen Consolidated High School

My Grandpa

My grandpa was a great man,
He loved God with his all.
Now he is in Heaven with his God,
And I will meet him again.

Some glad day that will be.
I shall see him again.
When that day shall come,
Oh what joy in Heaven will be.

Heather Owen, Grade 12
Juniata Christian School

My Life

The problem with me is plain and simple.
I have too much strife and pain to live through.
Most people think I am sane and peaceful.
But that is a false statement. An act you can't see through.

Yes, people like me. I have lots of friends.
I'd have even more if I owned a Bentley or a Benz.
It's a shame how shallow people are. They are quick to make amends.
Especially when your corporation pours out dividends.

From the way I write this poem you'd think I was rich.
A couple diamonds in my ears and some karats on my wrist.
But no, I'm not wealthy. My income is fixed.
$20 every two weeks and at least 10 bucks spent.

Well I'm just your average teenager. Nothing more, nothing less.
Other than I'm happily loved and thankfully blessed.
My room, my friendships, and my grades are a mess.
But ironically, they have nothing to do with my never-ending stress.

Jonathan Conway, Grade 10
Cass Technical High School

Childhood

What I remember about my childhood
Is running barefoot through the sprinkler in the green grass
And playing hide and seek, hoping to be the last one found
And swinging from my tire swing grabbing the leaves as I glide by
And laughing with my neighbors.
Drawing pictures with chalk on the sidewalk
Excited to show my mom.

Nothing about ten years from then,
Nothing about the world around me.

Thomas Stowers, Grade 12
Troy High School

Hunters of the Night

Monsters in the ancient times, legends of the timeless night
We are always lurking in the shadows, but we stay out of the light

In the dark, you hear the screaming, as we stalk our prey
When you sleep, we're in your dreams, you just can't keep us away

As silent as the grave, they don't hear us coming
It's your blood that we crave, there is no use running

In your neck, I'll sink my teeth, as I draw the life from you
I'll feel you shudder underneath, your dead body, stiff as a statue

We are faster than you can imagine, and stronger than you believe
We spread though the land like famine, you won't be safe until we leave

We will never stop feeding, with our burning desires
You'd better start screaming, for we are the VAMPIRES!!

Micah Harris, Grade 10
Advanced Technology Academy

The Beauty of a Storm

The rain falls to the ground
As I watch with great virtue
The storm rushing in
The clouds filled with anger

The lightning strikes
Leaving the Earth in great awe
Causing the woodland creatures to scurry
As if paying reverence to the Almighty Heavens

Pouring down from the sky
The drops of water fall
As if diamonds sprinkled into the sky from God
Settling in puddles that accumulate upon the muddy Earth

The furious storm shows its exasperation
As its wrathful thunder sounds
Almost stopping your heart with fear
As the loud blast echoes

Although the powerful storm
Continues to enforce its rage so passionately
Although appearing to be hopeless and gloomy
It leaves behind wondrous beauty and tranquility
Amanda L. Novak, Grade 11
Posen Consolidated High School

A Walk to Remember

A walk to remember
all the way to the end.
This is something
even you cannot mend.
No longer there to endure
you cannot construct my roads.
Always taking control, without asking my consent.
Two under the same roof? You do the math.
Trying to just deal was enough
without the frequent comments.
Not one breath was taken
without you getting bent.
My own path carved
deeply in the earth.
The route set for my walking
since the day of birth.
A walk to remember
all the way to the end.
This is something
even you cannot mend.
I am my own.
Kayaser Ahmed, Grade 10
Cass Technical High School

Fair Apollo

Oh sweet Apollo from heaven above,
Whose skin glows from time spent in golden light,
All swoon, struck by Cupid's arrow of love,
And seek to be the lone Venus in sight.
His noble face is perfection divine.
His eyes are deep like a forest at dusk,
He moves like night, and his dark spirals shine;
A living David, the object of lust.
But my love stems not from sinew and bone,
Not from brute strength or golden looks so fair.
My love springs from the heart and mind alone,
His kindness and passion is uncompared.
Fair Apollo I give my heart to thee,
And though you search no truer love there be.
Stephanie Baker, Grade 12
Waldron Middle/High School

Journey

For it was my mistake
To start a journey that would never
Make it through the night.
We tried to mend the cannon holes
But our little boat had not hope
The lies started small
But grew beyond repair.
A wave to big to overcome
Took our friendship to the bottom of the ocean
Whatever hope we started with
Died not long ago
But the hope began a journey that we knew
Would never make it through the night.
Amanda Weiss, Grade 12
Ross Beatty Jr/Sr High School

A Student's Peace of Mind

Peace of mind is in the eyes of the beholder.
The sweet peace of mind,
is something we all seek to find.
This sweet, sweet peace of mind.
To students it comes down to this,
another early morning, more books, and another day at school,
and many years that we will all miss.
The peace we receive
from a teacher's point of view.
Is something to cherish
our whole life through.
The peace that we receive
from a long day at school
is something most rewarding,
And something like a dream.
While ending our senior year
we feed upon the moment,
and dream of our future.
Another day and another year.
Krystal Terpening, Grade 12
Franklin High School

Out of the Sand

The sun lights up his whole surrounding, lush green grass great oak trees glistening waters in the shining of the sun.
The heat bakes the area around him.
Yet he's focused on only one thing he focuses his attention on the round white object with the back drop of almost white sand.
It's smoothed out all around him with nothing but the size 12 footprints in the sand.
Slowly readjusting his footing he stares at his target with the eyes of a lion on its prey.
His hand twitches with readiness on the black grip then,
He slowly pulls back the iron club and smoothly comes through.
A shower of sand erupts in slow motion from where he stands and rains down on the short green grass.
Only a second later a white ball pounces onto the green and roles towards a thin pole and stops only a foot before it.
The crowd explodes into a loud series of claps and cheers in honor of the great shot.
The tall man climbs from the sand pit he puts up his hand clinched with the iron club in recognition of the crowd.

Barak Thomas, Grade 12
Clarkston High School

Let the Truth Be Told

Living in a harsh environment that we call reality
Full of traps, consequences, and sometimes rewards
Racial profiling in the underground stream of society
Students that have potential to get caught up in a pregnancy and drop out
Gas prices rise and people going bankrupt from greedy Republicans
Lives senselessly taken away by a losing war with no exit plans
Where the rich get special treatment while poor communities struggle with debts.

And where is our money going? To a country that we bombed
And given more attention than the disaster from Mother Nature in New Orleans
The leader trying to "protect us" by taking our freedom of speech away
If you didn't like him in the first place, why did you vote for him? Twice!
But y'all want to complain about him like we got stuck with a president, that nobody voted for.

How much debt does the president need to be in to see that we are getting nowhere.
Because of all this, have we caught Osama yet? No!
And there are still corrupted cops that go after innocent African Americans
Then kill them, and quick to sprinkle "crack" on them.

Derron Davis, Grade 10
Cass Technical High School

It's Her Picture on Your Wall…

I can't find myself in your beautiful eyes anymore. I can't look into them and see the shining sun.
Instead I see clouds of regret and a veil of secrecy.
There is something changed about you, but I can't seem to find it yet.
You just flash one of your smiles that make me melt to pieces, and act like nothing's changed.
But I can see it in your gorgeous, once warm and happy eyes.
I can sense it in the way you talk. Your voice, once so strong and confident, is now full of fear.
You're hiding something, and I'll soon find it out. I look at you once again, but you're hiding well.
It's a game we both know how to play and I can't seem to guess what is changed.
I look up to see the sun, and see her arrogant face staring down on at me,
And I can't stand your pleasant smile anymore; it makes me want to throw you out the window.
I just wish to get away from you.
I can't find myself in the dazzling eyes that once made me feel so safe and happy.
Not because I tried and failed, but because I don't want to look at them.
Don't call my house! Don't ever bother to talk about me and the dear moments we shared!
Erase me off your mind! If it's her picture that you want, you can have it, but I shall not stay around.
It's her picture on the wall you desired and now you've got it.
I hope you two make each other extremely happy!

Dimana Chaneva, Grade 10
Chippewa Valley High School

On the Field

Running my legs are like an Amtrak locomotive,
each speedy pump of my legs faster than the last.
It is almost an instinct.
When I whip the white lacrosse ball,
the play accelerates to the next level.
Teammates coordination plays
quick as electrifying lightning in a spring thunderstorm.
The ball is shot fast as a fiery cannon ball
being blasted from a jet-black Civil War cannon.
The weightless net billows in the wind like
A bed sheet on a line drying outside.
The shot echoes out in the distance,
not from a gun, but from a lacrosse ball.
The billowing net is struck by the heavy ball.
The vibrant crowd rejoices in a roar of excitement.
Minutes go by that feel as if they were seconds.
Another well-deserved win pinned on the charts.

Nick Fantin, Grade 11
Clarkston High School

Perfection

In His eyes; perfection
Sins made, are simply forgave
Breath of each soul, looked upon equally
Everyone's stance is the same

Our precision is made to leave impact
Such as a blooming flower in the sun
Or like the stars guiding the lost
Always remember to remain at optimism level

It is our job to be apt in ourselves
Therefore, we can then shine our light on others
Just like the moon on a pitch black night
As long as excellence is present always, life will live on

Brittany Twining, Grade 12
Mona Shores High School

First Kiss

The gentle clutch of his hand swiveled around
My delicate fingers.
I could feel the warmth of his body
Start to lean up against me
The touch of his morning shavened face
Fell against my rosy pink speckled cheek,
Making a grin pop up across my face.
Just being together filled my body up
With warmth and comfort.
He looked at me and I at him,
Our eyes glistened at one another.
His lips crept up against mine,
As the butterflies rose up twinkling around
In my stomach.
The cozy sensation trickled up and down my body,
As once again you took my breath away
With your simple heartfelt touch.

Michelle Raetzke, Grade 12
Clarkston High School

Time

Time is precious
When it is here
Time is priceless
With the one you hold dear

What would you do?
If their time ran out
What would you do?
Would you scream and shout

If the one you loved was lost
What would you feel in your heart?
If they left you right here tonight
Would you know where to start?

So cherish every smile
Welcome every embrace
Adore all the laughter
And every time and place

So if it feels so short
Like it wasn't their time to fall
Always remember it is better to have loved and lost
Than to have never loved at all

Megan Pieczynski, Grade 11
Posen Consolidated High School

Hurt

Why do you hurt me?
You hurt me once.
You hurt me twice.
I'm still with you, but scared to be hurt again.
Have I hurt you?
Once?
Ask yourself this.
Do I care for you?
Do I love you?
Would I do anything for you?
Ok now stop asking, I'll answer those questions for you.
They are all Yes.
Now I'm asking myself.
Do you care for me?
Do you love me?
I don't know if you want to answer those questions,
Because I think I know the answer.
Baby, I can't believe you've done this to me.
I gave you a second chance.
You ruined it.
You ruined us.

Jason Ri, Grade 11
Centreville High School

Out There

The Earth
is like God's playground.
An experiment
of curiosity.

The Planets
are like the lost.
Moving around,
always the same routine.

The Sun
is a glowing fire,
that settles the people
as it rises and sets.

The Stars
are the deepest wishes
you feel at heart,
too far away to come true.

The Universe
is one huge family.
Everything related,
yet so far away.

Courtney Umbras, Grade 10
Dwight D Eisenhower High School

I Wish

I wish I could go inside your mind
to know what you wanted to do
I wish you could just make up your mind
to what's to become of me and you

I wish you didn't need more time
to tell me what's to happen next
I always figured that you would be mine
but I guess that was too much to expect

I wish I didn't have to feel so much pain
It hurts to see you every day
I wish things could just be the same
but I know it won't work out that way

I wish we could just go into the past
to fix what we had done wrong
I wish there was a way to make this last
It hurts so much to hear love songs

I wish the things that I say
could change the way you feel
I wish my feeling for you would go away
so I'll know the end is real

Emily Perrault, Grade 12
Posen Consolidated High School

All of Me

My breath falls heavy from your stare that has awakened me.
Let me watch your every move and return the favor.
Your smile that heals every broken wound in me
Is the weakness that makes me fall.
Hold onto my presence and share what I have, my all.

Danielle Turner, Grade 11
Cass Technical High School

My Angel in the Form of a Human*

It is dark outside
The snow continues to fall and the ground can no longer be seen
The cold air swirls
I can feel it on my skin and somehow I can feel it inside of me
A cold creeping air goes through my body
Through the foggy window I see her there
An angel in the form of a human body
Gasping for air, she rests in her bed
I walk to the window and I call out to her
I beg her to forgive me for not being there for her, for not loving her enough
Tears trickle down my face as I send a prayer to heaven for her
In an instant she is gone from me and I can no longer see her
My heart skips a beat
Just as I begin to fall, I feel warm loving arms around me
It is her
She catches me before I can fall
I turn to find my angel, in the form of a human, standing in front of me
In the window, I see the sun begin to rise
The storm stops
"I love you grandmother," I turn and say
"I love you too," she whispers, "and I always will"

Stephanie K. Taylor, Grade 10
Renaissance High School
*In loving memory of Mae Audrey Taylor

To: Erica

You were there in my darkest hour
and when my mom would scream and shout
You stood by me when my life was all shaken up
So many times we have had together
You were there when my faith almost disappeared
you stood by me when the cops brought us home
and when I needed just to vent, you were always there
we were together at Grandpa's death
we huddled around and told old stories.
We were together when my dad went to prison for robbery,
and my family was crying in doubt
that everything would be all right soon again
and soon enough our lives were back to normal —
as normal as it was going to get.
When we fought soon after we were laughing —
being angry served neither of us.
Right now I just want you to know that we'll be together forever this time
I'm hoping that we never again part over the usual petty things
But we both know we will soon be laughing it off, like nothing ever happened.

Shareena Carpenter, Grade 11
Centreville High School

Summer Lovin'

Soft, cool breeze brushes against the face
Pink, orange, yellow and red
Peak over the mountains like bleeding watercolors
It's time to start another day
Throw on the chaps
Cowboy boots and a cowboy hat
Walk down the winding path
Watch the wildflowers sway in the wind
Down at the barn, everyone's lively
Catch the energetic horses
Black, grey, brown colors rushing by you
Simply another day at work
Saddle up the horses
Out the gate for a lovely two hour ride
Beautiful scenery
Back inside the dusty gate
As the day closes
Release the wild spirits
Back home to relax, waste the dark night away
After a long night sleep
It's another summer lovin' day

Alex Willemain, Grade 10
Grosse Pointe South High School

The Gift of Grandma

The gift of grandma,
One which is so sweet,
One who is always strong,
And always on her feet.

I have the gift of grandma,
To give me advice,
One who is always there,
And tells me to think twice.

Generation after generation,
She is never at a scare,
Grandma, Grandma,
Who tells me the Lord will always be there.

Grandma always told me,
"Child He will work it out,"
Grandma always told me,
To never have a doubt.

She has been through so much,
And always I will love her,
Grandma, Grandma,
There is no one like her.

Brandii Halliburton, Grade 10
Cass Technical High School

What Is Wrong? What Did I Do?

You pick me up.
It is right then and there where
I have to deal with the depressed
Agonistic screech of your voice giving me attitude.
And for what?
What is wrong? What did I do?

I ask you a question, you ignore me.
I tell you something, you don't care.
What is wrong? What did I do?

You don't smile until 8 pm, when you are getting drunk.
You're alone, there's no one to drink with,
but you do it anyway.
You're loud, crazy and obnoxious.
The taste of five o' clock must make you happy.
You have kids that don't like what you do.
They're not even teenagers yet, that's not right.
Put away the alcohol.
What is wrong? What did we do?

Steve Jones, Grade 12
Clarkston High School

Spring

Life and beauty stirs hearts that are torn,
And gives sweet grace to those who mourn,
So they, again, can sing.
Like a rainbow after a dull, gray storm,
The birds awake and flowers form.
Rejoice! Here is the spring.

Kelly Crittenden, Grade 10
Grattan Academy High School

Friends Forever

I am so glad that we are friends
I hope our friendship never ends
We survived our brothers trying to make us fight
When life sucked you let me know things would be all right
And all the times that I was sad
You made me think life's not all bad
There are many times you saved my life
Just by helping you took away my strife
You've done so much to help me out
Now it's my turn to listen if you need to scream and shout
I know things can get hard and tough
And it can feel like you've had enough
Now it's my turn to let you know things will be okay
Things will get better for good one day
Just know I'm always here for you
If anything happened to you I wouldn't know what to do
Just always stay strong
And let me know if something is wrong
You are the greatest friend ever
I hope we stay best friends forever

Erin Schriedel, Grade 10
Utica High School

My Sounds

When I beat the drum
I become one with it
I make music to the world
When I spin the mallet
Which becomes a twirl

I love to play outside
When to the crowd becomes live
I jump when I play
I swing and sway

This is my style
Just look around
At what I do
Maybe this could be you

Devin Easley, Grade 10
Cass Technical High School

Year of Changes

Eighteen the year of changes
Not fitting the clothes or
Keeping the food down my
Life has changed all around.
Cries of sadness and then joy
Left only the thought
Of no more parties or
Late nights out and
How in nine months
It will be all about
Warm bottles in the night,
Stinky diapers and
Getting up without a fight.

Britney DuVall, Grade 12
Ross Beatty Jr/Sr High School

Picture

A picture
A moment
A memory
Good times
Bad times
For all to see
A greeting
A parting
A long lost love
A funeral
A wedding
All of the above
A dog
A cat
A flock of birds
A win
A loss
A million words

Lindsay Jarosz, Grade 12
Rochester High School

Fifteen

I know many of my peers are really quite mean,
Some of them say things that are quite obscene.
There are some girls that make drama to be the center of the scene,
And there's people held back by drugs, I call it a smoke screen.
With so much pressure I feel I need someone on which to lean
There's times I feel everyone's black and I'm a green bean.
There's so much to do; I feel like a spinning machine
Sometimes school and friends, you must choose between,
And it's really annoying when parents intervene.
Sometimes it's so hard being fifteen.

Paige Aldrich, Grade 10
Troy High School

The Unstoppable Team

When I look in the locker room, what do I see?
I see a team that is well able to contend for the big prize,
It does not matter of the circumstances, nor the odds against them,
It is the strength this team carries even when they seemed to have fallen,

That same strength can only be found in the heart of the team,
Where there is dedication, proficiency, constant-determination, and unselfish play.
Which by the way are keys to what makes this team a dominant force,
Why? We learn from each other, help each other, and renew a player
from their mistakes, helping them to avenge their teammates,

As a matter of fact, this team I represent takes a great pride in its purpose,
To explain on the ice why they or should I say we, carry to unstoppable power
that only can be shown and seen in all of hockey,
in the Bloomfield Corporation,
As of the team, concentration is at all time high, differences are resided,
and regardless of the team we face, ultimate power and courage
is what connects this team to the golden prize.

Samuel Lumpkin, Grade 12
Andover High School

I Remember

I remember the good times when I had my first love
I remember I thought you were an angel sent from above
I remember when you asked me out and I was filled with joy
I remember everyone's reaction when I told them you were my boy
I remember falling in love when everyone said I could do better
I remember telling you that we'd be together forever
I remember our first kiss, that one warm day
I remember being in your arms and having nothing to say
I remember all the fights over stupid little things
I remember all the words when putting each other to blame
I remember all the tears you made me cry
I remember all the times I thought I would say good bye
I remember you always came back holding me so tight
I remember my dad telling me NO boy is worth a fight
I remember that day it was warm outside
I remember it as the perfect day until I almost lost my pride
I remember it was the day I had to let you go
But I still have love for you and that's all I want you to know

Courtney Squirewell, Grade 10
Romulus Sr High School

Ode to My Bug

I hate all bugs,
Except mine.
It's a green one,
Not olive but lime.
As the engine roars,
I feel a power surge.
From my center out it pours.
When I drive alone,
At the days end,
In the dark,
My mind out zones.
Alas I realize I must park.
Now impatiently I await the up coming day,
To start my bug,
My Lime Green Bug.

Megan Palco, Grade 12
Clarkston High School

A Work of Art

You are an ivory sculpture, beautiful and slim.
You are a dominant flower in a single cyme.
Your iris the painted sky inside pearls washed in milk.
Your tongue drips honey, your skin textured silk.
Your walk a graceful dance that none can copy.
Your speech a melodious song making others talk sloppy.
Your breath…a fresh crisp autumn breeze.
Your scent like lavender, relaxing me with ease.
Your thoughts are a tapestry, filling me with wonder.
Your presence is capturing, blotting out all others.
You are my solar plexus, my world's heart.
You are an authentic, beautiful work of art.

Demetrius Richardson, Grade 12
Blanche Kelso Bruce Academy

You Are My Life

You walked into my life as a lovely surprise,
Not knowing what to do with myself,
I was lost in your eyes.
Time was passing by with you,
I was myself for once,
I loved you, and you did too.
I always try to tell you what you mean to me,
What my heart says,
And how I want us to be.
It never comes out right,
You never seem to know what it is I want to say,
All my feelings for you, I will write.
I always want to hold your hand,
Make you feel the love,
Falling in love with you was never planned.
I will always be by your side,
Helping you along life's course,
With me, you'll never need to hide.
So kiss me and tell me what consumes your soul,
You are my life,
My love and heart is what you stole.

Audrey Laga, Grade 11
Richmond Community High School

Adventure to a Foreign Land

The waters are big and blue they say,
Of a land that exists far, far away.
Blue is bluer than the sky,
And ocean waters tower high.

They cover land that is lush with green,
And filled with vibrant colors no man has seen.
The flowers bloom each dawning day,
And by the night, they die away.

The animals there are peaceful and kind,
And evil is not even a speck in one's mind.
And riches flow from towers high,
Gold and gems stacked to the sky.

Yet, no one has had a chance to see,
All the glories explained to thee.
They do exist, but once one goes
We are told they never return, and no one knows,
Just what will a person see in this land so fair,
And all the adventures waiting there.

But a warning to all those who seek this land,
For to all humans this world is banned!

Marisa Strimpel, Grade 12
St Mary Catholic Central High School

Coincide

Taste of lemon, taste of lime
That, my friend, is the bitter, the sour
Lick a bit of sugar; take a little time
To notice how sweet the sweet is.
My father was killed when I turned nine
Simply to make up for his own mistakes.
He covered the wound and said it was fine
As long as the little girl lived.
Through years of hard work only to fail
To find cures for the spreading disease
But a month or two later I received in the mail
A conquering letter confirming defeat over sickness —
I once thought that I'd find true love
Without too many broken hearts made,
In time I would find from the guy up above
That it was, is, and will be on its way.
So, to sum it all up, I'm here to say
You can't have the best without the worst
Nor can night exist without day
It's the bitterness I desire,
Because life just isn't sweet without it

Alexis Rocha, Grade 12
Heritage High School

My Life

My life is average
It's average because I'm not spoiled
I'm not neglected
Just guided and protected

My life is goal-oriented
It's goal-oriented because I'm not letting
Anything stop me
Considering I'm here trying to be
All that I can be

My life is crowded
It's crowded because I have a lot of
Friends and family
While other people in my face
Because they want to be in my space

My life is different
I say different because even
Though it's only average and very
Much crowded
I am still loved and have a great head
On my shoulders.

Azure'D Foster, Grade 10
Advanced Technology Academy

Allusion*

To be or not to be.
That has always been the question,
On everyone's eyes.

But for once, a rose by any other name
Does not smell just as sweet,
As the sewers beneath our feet.

For whom the bell tolls,
It does not toll for thee.
Rings rung out by society.

Water, water everywhere,
And every one is drowning,
On the ads of TV.

You can call me Ishmael,
But the price is not right,
For an innocent will die tonight.

But remember, my captain,
Before you're cold and dead,
It's only society, ringing in your head.

Kaitlin Cole, Grade 11
Chippewa Valley High School
With thanks to Shakespeare

Pain and Sorrow

I felt your pain like the flower felt the light.
Your pain really hit me like a plane hitting the ground.
Your tear of sorrow flows through me like the Detroit River.
Your heart beats louder than a marching band parade.
Your heart hit flat-line like on a hospital monitor,
But the closer you get,
The closer the river flows over.

Kerryl O'Bryant, Grade 10
Thomas More School

The Brown-Eyed Boy

The brown-eyed boy
He slaughtered my soul and butchered my heart with harsh and niggardly words
Pierced my skin with the rays of his eyes
He hid his true colors behind a golden disguise
His eyes told me they cared
On the outside they were as bright as the sun on a summer day
On the inside all that brightness goes away
Bloodshot red is all you see when you look internally
It was just a cover-up
All that beauty would soon cease to be
Acting as if he loved me when he really didn't care
Telling me lies like he would always be there
Now he's out of my sight as far as I can see
I never thought he would become the boy he became to be
He tried to ratify and make me realize that when I looked
Into his eyes that there was nothing to despise and no reason to cry
Much more lie in the eyes than many will ever realize.

Sughraa Abdullah, Grade 10
Cass Technical High School

The Boy Next Door

Don't leave me as I left you before.
It was the biggest mistake — walking out that door.
I've tried to live with thoughts of you left behind —
But there is nothing I want more than to rewind.
My heart it aches when I hear your name.
It bends. It breaks. I go insane.
To look out to the street and through the trees —
Just knowing both of our windows caught the same breeze.
But they did not catch what I failed to put down —
My life. My heart. My knees on the ground.
There's nothing I want more than to hold you again.
Can't you see my heart is in pieces?
Shattered from what could have been.
How could I not have seen you changing when I was there all along?
Was it something I missed? Where did we go wrong?
I still remember the night you dropped the hint.
I knew what you meant, but I would never admit.
I acted as if I had no clue —
When inside I was screaming, "I need you."
Now it's too late to say what should have been said before.
I will always love the boy next door.

Erin Smolinski, Grade 10
Troy High School

Sunny Meadow

Sunny Meadow,
Dappled Sunshine.
Illuminating buzzing bees,
Swarming over buttercups.
As I approach the droning grows louder.

Hundreds of tiny little bees,
Busily flying hither and thither,
Happily pollinating yellow flowers,
Flowers as yellow as the stripes on their back.

Return to the hive,
Where they dance a message.
Deliver their harvest,
To feed the young,
And make the amber liquid
That slowly flows through the honeycomb.

Carefully approach the hive.
Droning grows fiercer.
Look inside to see the laborers.
Ouch!
Giving life to better the hive.

Sarah Zakshesky, Grade 11
Posen Consolidated High School

What You Are to Me

Roses are red
Violets are blue
But never mind that poem,
Let's talk about you,
From your head to your toes,
You're perfect like
The ocean's mystical flow.

Or like the sunrise
When it brings its sunshine.
So I gotta thank the sunrise,
For bringing me my sunshine.

You bring me an abundance of happiness
And that's the truth.
Without you my world would be dark
And all my thoughts would be blue.

Your voice is like a harp.
It soothes my soul.
When I think about you at night,
My heart turns gold.

Anthony Winbush, Grade 11
Blanche Kelso Bruce Academy

The Voice of the Mind

The voice of the mind,
speaks of many things,
and they are all different, never once the same.
It speaks of love, warmth, comfort, and trust.
It speaks of hate, pain, imperfection, and insanity.
It speaks for itself,
and stands alone, alone in the world,
yet sharing its infinite wisdom.
The voice of the mind,
speaks of many things,
and they are all different, never once the same.
It speaks of hunger, lust, anger, and temptation.
It speaks of the heart, emotion, stillness, and betrayal.
It speaks of greatness, pride, honor, and loyalty.
It speaks of life,
and it's never once the same…never once the same.
The voice of the mind,
speaks of all.

Eric Blough, Grade 11
Clarkston High School

Why?

Sitting in my room
Waiting for the phone
Why won't it ring?
I've been waiting for an hour
I close my eyes, and start to dream
A tear spills through my closed eyes
I quickly wipe it away
This is so stupid
Me laying down on my bed
Waiting for this stupid phone
It won't ring
He won't call, why would he call?
I drift to sleep with tears streaming down my cheeks
Never hearing the phone ring softly in the background.

Rachel Jablonski, Grade 12
Mona Shores High School

If We Had Time

If we had the time to really live,
To accomplish all
In accomplishing, give.

If we had the time to really dream,
To hope for
In hoping, scheme.

If we had the time to really love,
To feel for
In feeling, think of.

Imagine the things we could achieve
By living for, dreaming of, and loving what we believe.

Faith Frederick, Grade 12
Munising Baptist School

Confusion

People in this day and age
Are so confused and don't know which way,
They should go to find themselves.
Men liking men and girls liking girls,
They are badly messed up in this corrupted world.
It's a shame on how you don't know who you are,
While you are gambling your life like a deck of cards.
Some people are both and kiss each other.
It's easy to get lost, some feel alone,
Some just don't know right from wrong.
Why are the confused ones telling people how to live?
And they don't realize what they did.
I realize sometimes things happen where you are lost,
It might have come from loved ones you have lost.
Either with marriage, love, or death,
People get lost by being upset.
People just have to talk or have some personal time within them,
So they can remember who they are and leave confusion behind them.
The world is corrupt and it also has a black heart,
But don't find yourself in the dark.

Chantel McCutchen, Grade 11
Advanced Technology Academy

15 Lines of Freedom

The red, white, and blue
Represents us as a whole.
To look up at that flag pole,
I feel joy in my heart to be free.
Then when the sun shines through it
I remember those who died for it.
The fathers, brothers, mothers, and sisters,
They gave their lives for their country.
No monument, no statue, or honor
Will ever replace the sacrifice they gave.
The hearts and souls of these soldiers will never die,
For they will live on through history.
This flag will always stand for those Men and Women
Who did their duty to keep this flag up high.
That is what I think and feel when I see those gracious colors in the air.

Richard Kroll, Grade 12
Posen Consolidated High School

What Is Compassion

A nose two lips all are the same
But are they?
They have a life force of their own.
Love, hate, have compassion
for the things you do in life make life worth living.
Take time to nurture what has been given to you,
Else die in fire and ash.
A life is a precious gift.
You can have so much love for a person, and so much hate.
But you need to have compassion for those who are different than you.
Show your kindness to all then one day peace shall reign on Earth.

Andrew Barnhart, Grade 12
Airport Sr High School

The Snow Has Melted

The snow has melted all around the yard,
Water lies where there once was this white snow.
The once frozen land is no longer hard,
It will stay wet until the warm wind can blow.
In the early spring plants begin to awake,
Orange and yellow irises will bloom,
And other flowers will rise at daybreak.
The wilderness no longer looks with gloom.
The beautiful songs of the birds now play
With melodies as sweet as choir hymns.
Each has their own new song to play each day
As they sit on the tips of budded limbs.
When the winter ends and the spring begins,
It is a beautiful sight to see each year.
It is as if the world is without sin,
There is no longer need for intense fear.
This only comes around once in a while,
This vision is now in my mind's eye file.

Emily Knapp, Grade 12
Waldron Middle/High School

Stereotypes

The way I walk
The way you look at me
I know you can't talk!
Do you know what you see?

I am wise on the inside
Oh! I know about you!
What I am doesn't have to be explained on the outside
But my body is private too!

Stereotyping isn't right
It hurts others and me
Look into the light
Now tell me what you see!

Makenzie Moss, Grade 10
Cass Technical High School

Truly Beautiful

I'm sure you wonder why I love you,
Or why I think it's true.

But let me explain, it is quite plain, but I,
Feel that around you I can touch the sky.

We met and befriended two years in the past,
I felt like our friendship was going to last.

In ninth grade you showed me the way when I was confused.
Tenth grade, you lifted my spirits when I was used.

Who knew that day that I'd realize my feelings for you?
I didn't know my heart would find its way to you,
The only one who's made me feel truly beautiful

Aly Davis, Grade 10
L'anse Creuse High School North

The Sea

I'm like a great, grand, sea,
big and deep.
Not some insignificant
rain puddle.

I cooperate with others,
usually letting them sail to their destinations.

Most of the time I'm soft spoken,
just like the sea
you hear my voice softly
whispering in the sea shells,

But other times

I lash out violently
leaving behind, misery and destruction
shutting others out while I
release my anger.

Eventually, I will settle down
and once again become
the great majestic, magnificent, peaceful
Sea.

Ryan Smith, Grade 11
Clarkston High School

Red

Easily mistaken for love and yet often perceived as anger
It can be categorized as good or bad
Red can be death, evil, fire, scared and mean
Red can be festive, exciting, bright, safe and assured.
Red is the color on the face of one who's embarrassed
Blacks partner on a young child's checkerboard
The round nose of a clown
The fire truck that drives by at full speed
The heat lamps that keep you warm
It's Valentines Day all over the world
Stop lights that stay red for minutes
A fire hydrant in a yard of green grass
Apples that shine and peppers that sizzle
The seven out of thirteen stripes on our American flag.
Red is infrared, red oak, red cell, red carpet
It is pigment, blooming, cherries and rust
Scarlet, maroon, glowing and burgundy
Red is a color that resembles a ruby
It is vibrant and beautiful
It is red, redder, and reddest
It is redness.

Victoria Zegler, Grade 11
Lahser High School

Into the Darkness

If I disappear,
No one will notice.
If I'm consumed by fear,
No one will save me.

Tied up in this lie,
I watch my life pass by.
I scream, but no one hears,
I'm drowning in my tears.

Hidden behind the hollow stare,
A girl longs for someone to care.
If I keep saying it's okay,
Will the pain just go away?

I get back up only to fall,
Lonely and broken.
I have lost it all,
Into the darkness.

Marissa McKee, Grade 10
Manchester High School

Where to Go

Where has the boy gone?
Sometimes I miss him.
Longing to run around,
Just to have fun in the sun
Where has the boy gone?

Where has the man gone?
I miss him most.
To be more than nobody,
Having a sense of pride.
Where has the man gone?

Where has the soul gone?
To Heaven I hope.
To wander around a cloud,
Looking back at those below.
There is nowhere else to go.

Brandon Hentkowski, Grade 11
Posen Consolidated High School

I Seem

I seem so alive
You would think I was full of life
I seem so happy
But I cry myself to sleep
I may never be alone
But I feel so lonely
I'm sometimes slow
I don't seem to care
But deep down
I'm deeper than you'll ever know

Alex Machasic, Grade 11
Dwight D Eisenhower High School

Tired of Being Tired

Why is it that I'm so young yet so old?
Serious at times, mature in most circumstances
Kept to myself when I want, I could even be
Grown if I wanted…but only mentally.
Finally when I came to the end of the cornfield past the scarecrow
I have traveled in a perfect circle only to be where I began.
Such a wise mind and I fall and get back up only to fall again in the same place
Where the passage says entrance!
So where is the exit exactly?!
When is it my turn to lay back and be satisfied?
I carved this especially for you in sugar…in return I get nothing,
Not even some appreciation.
Can't even place myself on a pedestal.
Why should I, what's so good about little old me?
Hmmm that makes no sense, hurt by the same soul
Just different bodies, names, people.
I'm tired of it. Sick and tired.
I deserve that happiness in the picture window of that store!
Too old to be caught up and too young to be tired.

Briana Hess, Grade 10
Cass Technical High School

A Dream

To dream in peace, and not awaken, with thoughts and fantasies forsaken
Of lives and worlds time has forgotten, with flights of fancy I've begotten.

When I drift off, into sleep soft and slow, I try to prepare for the end of the show
As I view the plot with no hint of regret, played out by the colors of an autumn sunset.

Wisdom, truth, for I have dreamt, of a winter's day often misspent
Lasting expressions of eyes often cold, icy visions my mind cannot hold.

Mindless imagery of demons abound, distorted reality in which I have found
Spring rains, in which they flood, flowing fast in a river of blood.

The fiery passion of a lover's kiss, feverish temptations in a summer of bliss
The endless seduction of pleasure unseen, it's hard to remember, it's all but a dream.

A mother's voice as I awake, gives a haunting yell for me to awake
I open my eyes in a fit of fright, I felt a year of emotions in the course of a night.

Jordan Purol, Grade 11
Posen Consolidated High School

No Longer

The past is behind me, the future is near,
and no longer do I sit but now I care.
No longer do I fear the dark and stormy nights of temptation,
because God said He'll always protect me, and I know He's right.
No longer do I look through the crowds and select my friends,
but now they come to me 'cause I got Jesus on my risk band.
I want to bust down the wall of temptation kill all my enemies,
but God said keep them close to me.
Love thy neighbor for this is right,
you will never go wrong praising the man upstairs day and night.

Trina Rogers, Grade 10
Advanced Technology Academy

Winter

The leaves are colored in red and orange
They begin to fall
The temperature begins to drop
The weather is about to change

Birds are flying south
Bears begin to hibernate
Rabbits turn their color white
Plants all start to wilt

White flakes falling from the sky
It covers the land
Without any green to be seen
Killing all of the flowers that were once there

Children now playing in the snow
Adults shoveling their driveway
Some waiting for this white to disappear
For the warm weather to come back

The birds start to reappear
The leaves begin to grow
Temperature begins to fall
The flowers begin to bloom

Jennifer Ciarkowski, Grade 11
Posen Consolidated High School

To Mr. November Ago

A face
Much chiseled like that of a statue's
And like a statue you stand tall and strong
Yet like lady liberty, you too oxidize
You are far from being stainless steel
You always will be

A heart
Much like a sponge soaking in vitality
And taking in grains of salt
Yet, never enough to dry

An excess
Of this love, warmth, and glowing aura
But like anyone exposed to excess
I have taken your face
Your heart
For granted

Forgive me for the days I have that
Obvious, unenthusiastic demeanor

Sarah Bourgoin, Grade 11
Fruitport High School

Sister to Sister

Well, sister, let me tell you:
Love has its major ups and downs.
It's like a roller coaster,
And it could be a train wreck,
And it could be a car accident,
And it might be all three at once —
Separate.
But while it was happening.
I moved on fine,
And regained strength,
And recovered courage,
And mended my broken heart
So someone else can have it.
So sister, don't give up.
If it fails make sure you know
That it's hard to believe but, there are other fish in the sea —
I've made it through sis,
I've made it through,
And love for me is a roller coaster.

Lindsey Seabolt, Grade 10
Troy High School

Run with Me

Run with me, far away from here;
Take with you, all the things you hold dear.
Hold my hand, and never let go;
This path will take us to a better unknown.

Run with me, and never look back;
Look at me, and say it was just an act.
Pick up your feet, and run forever;
Where we're going we can be together.

Run with me, and this will end;
All these things, that have been bad.
Trust in me, and it will be all right;
Run with me, until we're out of sight.

Sara Richards, Grade 10
Divine Child High School

The Love That Never Was

The love that never was
Left unnoticed, forgotten
Pushed aside like an old toy, but all the same spoiled rotten
Cherished, valued
Viewed as one of a kind
For each and every its own, once in a lifetime
But the language of life changes and all at once love is revised
Trusting nothing
Dodging hope
Losing will to survive
Hitching rides that lead to nowhere but a true and honest place
Nothing like a living man's look upon his face
When realization kicks in…
Love never was
Not a drop for human race

Cortney McGee, Grade 11
Cass Technical High School

Empty

Feeling empty
Soul is lost
My love is gone
Heart is cold under the frost

Missing what is not here
Confusing reality with nothingness
Or are they the same?
Can't go on living like this

There's nothing here to see
Drenched in sorrow, the wind
Blows pain in my face
Waiting for anything to begin

Wasting time on everything
No point in doing anything
My love, not here to hold me
My love, not here to hold

Looking for hope
To grasp and to hold
I reach for the light
And fall back into cold

Christopher Zoldos, Grade 12
Dwight D Eisenhower High School

Emotion

Looking deep
Deep inside
Looking at the things
That have made the eyes cry.

Searching for that
Feeling within
Makes you wonder
If it was just a sin
Just searching, thinking,
Fills me with doubt
Having a thought
But not figuring it out
Not sure
Of what it may be
Just trying
Driving me crazy.

What I feel, I don't know
Can't even think of a notion
I'm all mixed up, deep inside
With this crazy emotion.

Sara Wisniewski, Grade 11
Posen Consolidated High School

Master of Fate

The master of fate has closed the door of calming whispers
calling no more of closed doors and shattered dreams
when a dove flies from an open window
and catches the winds of fate
and floats through the illusions of life and flight.

Ashley Nicole McCoy, Grade 12
Ross Beatty Jr/Sr High School

Communication

I stand out on the sidewalk
Because I know you will see me and come out.
We never call one another,
There is no need for words.
Everything we do is through silent communication.

At first, it did not seem as if our friendship could last like this.
However, it has been nine years and we still work the same way.

It has been fun being your neighbor and friend.
But now we must move on to the next chapter in our lives,
College.

No more Barbie Pool Parties.
No more Michael's Little Sister.
No more Winnith.
All of our childhood fancies have disappeared.
But we will always have our own private world of communication.

Brianna Slater, Grade 12
Troy High School

Each Wave Has a Life

Each wave has a life, a never-ending goal
To reach the distant shore
Or a far-off moor
A forever want to follow the current wherever it lead
To follow no matter what the speed
Yet they do not know that when they reach their goal, their lives will end
That all the time they had to spend
Leads to death
As I listen to the surf,
I think about our goals' worth
And I think of waves
Who lead their lives so that they might,
Reach the end
So when you're down my friend,
Look to your path and do not fret
Think of the waves who live for that one glorious moment
Reach for the sky
And never forget,
That like us,
Each wave has a life

Adam Parker, Grade 11
Bentley Sr High School

What's Above
The Dawn is my blanket of dark secrets as I hide from my true self
As it fades to a lighter shade of color
I start to reveal more and more

Black is the background with stars that sparkle in my eyes hinting that I need a friend
Purple to *Pink* is the color of my lips whispering "help me" in your ear
Blue is the tears that I shed with sadness

Navy Blue is the middle color of fear that fades to *Black* with passion
Skin pale *White* with eyes wide open and I see you drifting far away as if you are
The Dawn turning to the early morning

When I awake I see your face again

Angylica Larson, Grade 11
Dwight D Eisenhower High School

November to January
It's cold around this time of year, cold like the ice mountains of the Arctic.
Chills pierce my body like a needle stings my skin.
The breeze pinches my face; the tension freezes my fingers and toes.

       my   a
   sculpts   hair   of   r
The wind   into a form   t.
November to January
I know you can feel it!
Just once you experience this time of the year, you'll understand.
Every now and then, when you stand outside on the front porch and listen to the wind, you hear a flute in a harmony, like you've stepped into a fairy tale of some kind.
Unexpected thoughts flow through your mind as the wind and
the air   beneath you.
      move
Like the wind beneath you when your father picks you up by your hands and swings you around the room.
      the air.
    flying into
   airplane
Like an
The Earth rotates, and the season caresses your body. Imagine. I know you understand this feeling.
November to January

Bianca Harris, Grade 10
Martin Luther King High School

My Hero
A man whose flaws seem nonexistent
Whose intellect and smarts impress me every time I
read about him
Whose character was so pure and good that even his
enemies could never speak ill of him
Whose days were constantly spent in prayer, and fast
and in sheer love and care for others
Who always made anyone feel as though they were the most important person in the world
Whose warm, gentle, smile lit up not only the Earth, but the heavens as well
Whose pious character no one could match
Whose sincerity, honesty, and love proved to others that the "perfect man" did exist
That man is my hero

Azfur Ali, Grade 10
Troy High School

Escape or Remain

The dark whining breeze
Flushes upon my face
As a sheet of ice
Moving in a frozen lake

My heart beats calmly
My brain thinks swiftly
But my body moves like a rock
And my look's as pale as milk

I try to move
But my body says no
So still I remain
Upon this cold night

The flakes fall down
Like little fluffy masses
My mind is stale
And my body remains
Lonnie Leigh Burgess, Grade 12
Posen Consolidated High School

Captivating Eyes

Full of color
Yet so dark and cold
Numb to the surroundings
The soul grows old
Heart stops beating
Look of lost
Pain starts steaming
All these feelings that are shown
Through his captivating eyes
Danielle Smith, Grade 10
Freeland High School

Freedom

In years past
    Armed forces have promised
That safety and liberty will last,
    And enemies will vanish.
Men have died
    Protecting our land.
People have cried
    Watching their stand.

The people will mourn
    When loved ones are gone,
But the land will never be torn
    Because of the brave fight.
So praise and thanks
    To the women and men,
Who in their boots won't shake;
    Who will honorably fight
When our freedom is at stake.
Caitlin McKinney, Grade 11
Prairie Baptist School

He'll Never Know

He'll never know the clutch of his hand on the back of his bike
Or how to use a compass on one of those long hikes.

He'll never know how it feels to fall asleep
To one of his stories of heroism and the courage so deep.

He'll never know all that he planned to teach him
About laying down his life and going out on a limb.

He'll never know the regular smell of his shirt
When he wrapped him in his arms of comfort.

He'll never know how we felt that day we got the news
That he wasn't returning from that rescue.

He'll never know how I cried and fell apart
And felt like I'd lost half of my heart.

But today he'll know that his Daddy was one of the bravest men he never met
And the flag from his funeral he'll someday get
Because his bravery and selflessness reigned
And many people from the flames he saved.
Beth Julian, Grade 12
Posen Consolidated High School

Conformity

A kaleidoscope of dead leaves smother beneath countless feet
Feeling no pain, no more torment of the longevity of life
An obscure despondence runs over one's thoughts
How I wish that I could live as though I were a dead leaf
Nothing unique, no knowledge of pain resulting from merely being.

A thick layer of transparent glass is crushed under so much weight
Scarred by their thoughtlessness, yet feeling no grief
One feels a deep lethargy falling over their cold, stiff limbs
How I wish that I could live as though I was a glass floor
Smooth and icy, and happy, knowing that my purpose has been duly served.

Thin ripples of water touch the different shapes of innumerable soles
None realize the miracle, which they perform so carelessly
Don't look down, or you'll break the spell of nonchalance
How I wish that I could be different than those who walk on water
Creating my own miracles, without standards to follow.
Elizabeth Kepsel, Grade 12
Inland Lakes High School

I Walk Within a Shadow

The sky is dismal with a contorted heart.
It forever endures lifelessness in the shadows of a greater plane,
Never fulfilling, empty with disillusion.
Its own gleam turned dull, shattered, lying in the shallow waters.
Katherine Trahan, Grade 12
Hastings High School

Hardships

Secrets lie where our hands have clasped,
And questions have formed from unrecognizable fear,
Apprehensive to what will come,
Dreams will come with progress,
The beauty that was once obvious has slipped,
Into a fog, white, misty,
And has been lost,
To find our love again has been hard,
Crying, yelling, and fighting,
Hating and loving,
Now we are strong,
Like the bond between a mother and her child,
Everlasting,
The best kind of love,
Ours

Jacquelyn Siska, Grade 12
Hastings High School

Is This Life?

Heavy with regrets,
I sluggishly open the stout door.
I step into the frigid, grim world.
The whistling wind is taunting me,
telling me to turn back.
The icy breeze is smacking my face,
turning my cheeks into a burgundy blistery blend.
There is nothing left to do,
but carry on, leading one foot ahead of the other,
keep gazing at what is promised ahead.
For if you turn around,
the past will catch up,
and bite at your stilted ankles.
Leaving you infected with its unforgettable disease.

Sandra Chrisman, Grade 11
Clarkston High School

Airport

You open the eyes with a jerk,
Check whether your bags are still there.
Crowds around you seem to be running amuck.
All of them in a hurry to go — don't know where.

The young couple in the distant chair,
Seem to be in a passionate embrace.
The mother with two infants to care,
Is looking for deliverance or God's grace.

Continental journeys continue to be an enigma.
You reach your destination ever before your start time.
Distance of separation appears an anathema.
Division of people by countries is certainly a crime.

Some people run here with smiles of jubilation,
Some people take steps as if on an edge of a knife.
With so many meetings and so many a separation,
Airports really are reflections of life.

Dinesh Banda, Grade 11
Troy High School

But I Remember Him

Oh, the kid all them stared at.
Pants sagging down to his ankles,
The deep aroma of contraband,
Hair strands placed strategically,
In every possible position.
The rugged terrain his face consisted of.
Yes, the way he trudged through
With all the intensity and authority.
The way his body melted into the seat.
Another rebel without a cause,
Another that just didn't care.

Never did he walk with anyone else.
With his head held high,
He seemed desiring of solitude.
No one dared question it.
It's just the way the pieces fit.
He had his pride; he had his way.

Just an ordinary day, if ordinary can be defined,
He had been killed, killed by himself.
And they all just said, "I didn't know him."
But I remember him.

Tina Ro, Grade 12
Troy High School

Differences

Captivated by the shared memories of pain,
We stare at each other, our eyes begin to strain.
We remember the times we put each other to shame,
And all the hurt we received at the end of each game.

Our hearts deceived by every lie,
Our souls repent as we both cry,
With every emotion and the strength to try,
We began to learn the difference between you and I.

I followed my heart, you followed your mind,
We met in the middle and left our doubts behind,
We both took for granted what we had was hard to find,
We didn't open our eyes to see that we were blind.

I hated to be wrong, you loved to be right,
So all of our conversations would end in a fight,
I'd let you win to be polite,
And that's how it ended every night.

I know things will get better as the days go by,
But the pain and hurt will be with us 'till we die.

Jaclynn Marie Vanier, Grade 12
Cheboygan Area High School

In His Eyes

There used to be a bright spark of wonder in his eyes that simple curiosity in every child as they grow. There used to be a perpetual question upon his lips, "What is that? What is that?" Where is it now? Where have those few words gone? I know: they've gone to a reclusive world a place where he sinks slowly into darkness. The bright spark within his eyes has dimmed. Dulled by the multiple drugs, his skeletal body, droopy eyes, their effect becoming increasingly evident. Was it worth it? Losing that spark for a facade of normalcy?

My brother, he's approaching that age, where people being to ask, "When is he going to a home?" A home? He has a home. We will not send him off to a some wasteland, a forgotten place. I will not abandon him! I want to believe that he can do so much more than this, more than spending the rest of his life with menial tasks. Leaving him vulnerable to ridicule and blatant stares, to energies concentrating solely on the purpose of avoiding him, afraid that by a single touch they will be infected. He only means to play with you, to interact with a world not his own. He does not understand and we apologize profusely. We shouldn't have to. We shouldn't have to. Yet, you never forgive, you never understand. He is only a baby, unaware of his grown body. I want him to experience life.

And maybe he does experience it all in the little things he enjoys. He beams with joy, when autumn approaches and the best toy he ever received was a six dollar rake to gather all the leaves. He glistens with sweat, when our driveway is covered in swirls of chalky greenish blues and tints of pink. He glows with pleasure, when he dives into a pool and feels the water envelop his body in comfort. His eyes shine with delight, when we sing our songs, and dance our dances to say our good nights.

Blythe Kim, Grade 12
Andover High School

My Contemplation with God

Am I wrong for loving? Am I wrong for missing? Am I wrong for longing? Am I wrong for my contemplation? God am I wrong? If so I don't mean to. You know how I can be so sad and blue, living my life like I don't have anything to do. But Lord I see your clues, and I sense your presence, I hear you talking to me through my every move. I'm sorry how sometimes you have to repeat things over to me and I know I need to be listening attentively. Nevertheless, am I wrong for every wrong that I do? Lord you know everyone makes mistakes but this one I don't wanna make because I don't want another heart break. So I'm asking you, "Do I love this dream girl of mine?" I'm contemplating on was she really made to be mine. Even though I'm asking you I'm scared of the truth. I'm scared I might mess up something you made and gave to me. I just can't stop thinking about them. Seeing them puts me on a new high. Hearing their name drives me insane. It just seems excruciating sometimes the way a woman can put you on cloud nine and change your game. Lord I know "Life is Hard" and You and the devil is playing them cards. And you know I could never doubt anything you send to me especially this beautiful woman you have presented to me. I just had to ask You was she meant for me? I have one final question contemplation as brought to my mind. Am I wrong for questioning the love I want to call mine. Am I wrong?

De'Andre D. Woods, Grade 10
Pontiac Northern High School

Push Crash Cry Repeat

As I watched him running on the field and begin counting down the final seconds, I realized what was happening. I saw it and I understood it, and I knew that there was nothing I could do to stop it.
So tears began to slide down my face.
I had finally picked up my heart from where I had dropped it the last time, and as I stood on this turf under these shining white lights, I felt it slipping through my fingers again. When it was over and I saw a sea of purple flood the field, I heard it crash to the ground and shatter into pieces.
That night, I vomited; as though my body thought that that way, it could cleanse itself of the feelings of empty sorrow and rage, and pain that were running through my blood.

I tried to run from it, but I only ran towards it.
I tried to hide from it, but it already lurked in every place I tried to hide. So finally,
I tried to kill it. And I found that the only way to kill it was to accept it.

I had just blown my second shot at it
I had just learned now that what doesn't kill you truly makes you strong. And,
I had just found that losing will take everything from you, except
The will to go on
So Push It.

Annie Shepard, Grade 10
Grosse Pointe South High School

Living Shadow

It all started out, when I was three.
My little shadow came to be.
He would copy my actions. He'd repeat all my words
When I pointed to the sky, he'd point to the birds.
I have a shadow, a living shadow, a shadow like no other.
By the time I was five, my shadow was two.
Why he was following me, I still had no clue.
Wherever I went, he'd follow in suit.
Some thought it was funny. Some thought it cute.
I have a shadow, a living shadow, a shadow like no other.
When I turned nine, my shadow was six.
Now add similar clothing into the mix.
When I wore a red shirt, he wore one as well.
That he was my shadow, anyone could tell.
I have a shadow, a living shadow, a shadow like no other.
I'm 16 now, my shadow, also, a teen.
He imitates me less, but it still can be seen.
I guess that I'm lucky, whether the sun's up or down.
I can count on my shadow to always be around.
I have a shadow, a living shadow, a shadow like no other.
I have a shadow, a living shadow, that shadow is my brother.

Jonathan Shin, Grade 10
Troy High School

Breath of Innocence

You have all the power
Power among such great force
Like a distance between you and instinct
But still facing this becomes an issue

Establishing your sense of well-being
Innocence brushed with a child
A child's whose only concern, to be loved
Effort and ingenuity compiled in a lifeless role
Fighting for those, whom you love so much

Desperate measures, hiding behind such corrupt excuses
Fighting for a freedom, fighting for a belief
Smothered around notorious characters
Apologies beyond sorrows for some relief
We all share the countless actions that threaten our identity

You are, what you are
Dreams can miraculously change the world
If only those who succeed use the strength to control
History is made each day

Take experiences as prized possessions of gifts
And resist from living, just to live.

Christina Masters, Grade 12
Dwight D Eisenhower High School

Tears

A tear I cry when I hurt you.
A tear I cry when I desert you.
A tear I cry when you have lost my trust.
A tear I cry when you have been crushed.
A tear I cry forever more,
A tear I cry to let you know,
I will be strong,
To show you I'm done with doing wrong.
From now on the tears I cry,
Will be tears of joy,
Until the day I die.

Justin Frederick, Grade 11
St Johns Schools

Shopping

Shopping is my favorite thing to do.
If I could, I would go every day.
Whether it is a hoodie or a shoe,
"I want to go shopping!" is all I say.

From American Eagle to Wal-Mart,
They are all very wonderful and great.
Shopping to me is like a form of art.
Sometimes when I go, I am on a date.

I am not sure why, but it is so much fun.
My love of going shopping at the mall
Comes from the stores' signs shining like the sun
No matter where I am, I love it all.

Shopping is the greatest pastime ever.
As long as I live, I won't stop. Never.

Megan Clark, Grade 11
Waldron Middle/High School

Baby Boy

When he laid on top of me, I didn't know,
That your father would be one of those no shows,
We rushed into it, not thinking of our aftermath,
That you would come and pass our path,
We probably should have used protection,
Then I wouldn't be here with this infection.
Not saying that you are a disease baby boy,
I planned on making you my life and my joy.
When I told him about you, I blamed me,
As if I climbed on top of me.
Eight months down the road had finally came,
I sit at home alone figuring out who to blame,
He caused you to not be here with me today,
The man who gave me you and took you away,
A punch to the stomach and a push down the steps,
I lie in the hospital and look at your broken chest,
A young life taken so very quickly,
He said his last words to you ever so swiftly.
You were my blessing, my hope, and my joy,
My beautiful and special baby boy.

Adrienne Kilgore, Grade 10
Cass Technical High School

The Future

My future is fast approaching,
Another journey, about to begin.
But, my life and times, with friends,
Could soon come to an end.

All of us, going our separate ways.
A new beginning,
And things about to take place.

Some days I am terrified,
And shy away, from the truth.
Some days, I'm ok with this,
But on other days,
I'm not.

Its best, to just stay in the moment,
And see, all that I have.
Not everyone is as lucky as I,
And for them, I feel sad.

For now, I need to stay confident,
Mostly in myself.
The future could be an amazing thing.
But for now I must just wait and see.

Amber Siero, Grade 12
Manchester High School

I Am

I am he who lives within you,
and dies like childhood innocence.
I am he who you fear,
and he of all you trust.
I am he who lives on genius,
and he who gives-in to common sense.
I want to be he who reigns supreme,
but still follows in Their footsteps.
I want to be he who never quivers,
but cannot lose nerve.
I am he who wages war,
and he who kills the innocence of peace.
I am he whom you seek,
and he whom you will never find.
I will be the one who decides your fate,
and tell of your deeds.
I will be the one who ends the war,
and only because I let it begin.
"Who am I?" you ask?
The answer is quite simple:
I Am You!

Daniel Tincknell, Grade 12
Oxford Area Sr High School

My Soldier

Soldier
Strong, loving, brave, daring
Who feels the pain of the country,
Who needs support from his family,
Who fears not coming home,
Who loves the children he had to leave behind,
Who thinks we can stop the terrorism if we stand together,
Who believes God is watching over him,
Hero

Melissa DeGrandis, Grade 11
Dwight D Eisenhower High School

Reflecting on Life

Reflecting on Life
Makes you look at the ups and downs
Reflecting on Life
Makes you appreciate what you have
Reflecting on Life
Makes you see everything clearer
Reflecting on Life
Makes your decisions harder
Reflecting on Life
Gives you a sense of hope
Reflecting on Life
Lets you learn from your mistakes
Reflecting on Life
Makes you realize that things can change
Reflecting on Life
Makes you see that life goes on
Reflecting on Life
Makes you realize that everything is worth fighting for
Reflecting on Life
Makes you realize that it's the small things that truly count in the end

Rebecca Long, Grade 12
Manchester High School

Strength

The only way a man can prosper is if he destines himself to succeed.
And the only man who's weak is one who plans for defeat.

At times a man's flesh becomes a burden to his bones.
It's not 'cause he's physically weak — it's just 'cause he isn't mentally strong.

Humility and respect is courage at its finest.
No need to fear the world when Jesus is behind us.

The mask of a man's face hides everything beneath.
To express those compressed emotions can become the great of all reliefs.

An eclipse can darken the day as lightning brightens the nights.
A real man can walk away 'cause there's no victory in a fight.

Days may seem hard, but days don't last long.
Just think of every day gone as a day close to your way home.

Travell Collins, Grade 12
Blanche Kelso Bruce Academy

Days Go By

I watched the clock tick down the days
How did this happen, it's all been a haze
I got busy and things got out of line
Schedules filled up and I ran out of time

Now I am late and I smell like drugs
My hair is greasy and likely full of bugs
Why did I do that, what a stupid decision
Something else I should've done, I had a vision

My interview is over and my parents are fuming
I can't reschedule, is what I'm assuming
So many consequences for one wrong choice
Why didn't I listen to that other voice

Now I am cold and without shelter
My life is turned upside down and all helter skelter
Now I am wishing that I could just die
As I sit here, lonely, watching days go by

Connor Tuck, Grade 11
Harper Creek High School

Who Are You

I'm thinking of the reasons why I can't sleep at night,
And only your illusion comes to mind.
I see the moon gleam so vividly,
But in its presence it's you I find.
Persistently pondering potential passion,
Could it possibly be love?
It makes no difference,
My thoughts fly high like a falcon hunting prey.
My mind races of our future together,
I can never keep it in one place.
You control my mind,
Wreaking havoc on me
You obstruct my thoughts.
Those eyes
The way you look at me
Making me feel high,
I've lost control of thinking,
Oh, your elegance,
Still it is only a dream.
As my alarm clock shatters the silence,
Clouds of infatuation dissolve into darkness.

Candace Holstine, Grade 11
Clarkston High School

Best Friends

I wished for a best friend like you,
And you came into my life,
So my wish came true,
I met you and we became best friends,
Me and u will always be best friends,
Until we go to heaven our friendship will never end,
If anything it will just begin.

Candace Everage, Grade 10
Cass Technical High School

Nature

The sky turns dark
rain falls to the ground.
The white snow melts
it turns into water puddles.

The weather turns hot —
plants begin their growing.
Green grass comes up;
birds chirp a welcoming song.

The leaves of the trees start to turn color.
The sky remains bright blue
flowers are pretty
the ground is full of colors.

Leaves begin to go away
the grass is covered
snow falls from the sky
the ground is now colored white.

It is very cold
the flowers begin to die
water turns to ice
the temperature is cold.

Roxann Hincka, Grade 11
Posen Consolidated High School

Little

Precious little poem book
Filled with thoughts unheard
Holding all my secrets
Only holding them in words
Precious little poem book
Keep them locked up safe
You hold my many feelings
Anger, grief, and hate
My secrets are for no one
Only your pages know them all
You have helped me through the moments
Times I thought I were to fall
You hold all my happiness
My love, and my life
My precious little poem book
Your words are always pure and true
You remind me of the silliness I once confided inside of you
Precious little poem book
Don't you ever tell
You've gotten me through my moments
You are my heaven in a shell

Erin Cook, Grade 12
Mona Shores High School

Fatherhood

What does it mean?
I am afraid.
What should I do?

She will be so small.
She will need me to take care of her.
What should I do?

I will care for her!
I will love her!
I will be a father to her!
Forever!
Edward LaLonde, Grade 12
Cheboygan Area High School

Life

This is the time for learning,
From your old mistakes.
So stop your life from turning
And you will lose your aches.

It's also time to be at your full potential,
Even if you have regards.
It is very essential
So be right on guard.

Don't look behind
And don't turn your head.
You're not completely blind
Just listen to what your peers have said.

You will not fail if you are strong,
Just be patient and it won't take long.
Brittany Chojnacki, Grade 11
Posen Consolidated High School

Forever Lost

Here I lie in shame,
You were the only one to keep me tame.
Your soft lips,
And mile white skin,
Kept me sane within.
You've left, you're gone,
And I wonder,
How my life goes on.
Can you feel it in your veins?
It will always be there,
Burning, running free, with no vaccine.
I hope it rips you apart inside.
Just like you ripped apart my heart.
I can't even pick up the shattered box,
That once held my love for you.
Here I lie in shame,
You were the only one to keep me tame.
Matt Sharrow, Grade 10
Freeland High School

I Wish That...

I wish we won in '04
I wish we won in '05
I wish I could run
I wish I was able to play the sports I loved.

I wish there was a way to see the stars up close.
How about a way to see the world in a day.
To see the world in peace,
or to see myself in that world of peace.

A time to stop and enjoy the moment,
a time to put down whatever you are doing and smell the flowers.
Time to relax, time to tell someone, I love you.

You wish so much,
and never get what you wish for
then you wish some more.
That you don't really know what you want,
then you never accomplish your goals;
To see the stars,
smell the flower, or see the world in peace.

Megan Goldberg, Grade 12
Clarkston High School

Because of You

Sixteen months ago I could not answer the question "What is love?"
Until one month later my God sent him to me from the sky above
He makes me feel like I'm the only one that matters in his life
And told me that one day he would make me his wife

After my last boyfriend I was ready to die
Until my baby DeAngelo came to me from the sky
His love is like the sound of the rain
So quick and easy to ease my pain

If I could I would stay with him all day long
And be with him and know that nothing would go wrong
Is it just in a kiss
That our fences turn to dust in a kiss
Oh we must in a kiss
Promise there's tomorrow

I looked at him, and as he looked at me I told him: my heart is in your hands
Thank you so much for giving love a chance

And as I look in the sky I realize that the clouds are white
The sky is blue; I can't believe this dream came true
I wrote this poem because of you
Because you'll never miss a good thing until it leaves you

Madina C. Mathis, Grade 10
Cass Technical High School

One More Day

I had a wish for one more day
That our time would just stand still
But our time together has run out
It was out of our hands…this was God's will

I will be strong, and you will be proud
For my strength has come from you
Unconditional was love
The kind only known by few

Together we weep as one
Your tears fall from my eyes
You whispered the day had come
It was time to say, "good-bye"

A picture of your face
In a frame within my mind
Timeless are the memories
Of the love, you left behind

I had a wish for one more day
That our time would just stand still
I realize now, in the love you gave
My wish has been fulfilled.

Bianca Pope, Grade 10
Cass Technical High School

Cost of Battle

A Savior brought up
An Angel cast down
Jesus hit clouds
Lucifer the ground
The Holy One whose life was given
So our sins would be forgiven
The Evil One, Satan by name
Putrid Lord of demon and flame
There they are, in the ring
fighting for all eternity
for it is such a great thing
Yet the Holy will win the war
Ending the battle forever more
Evil gone, hatred lost
Forever joyous, but what the cost?
So many martyrs, so many races
So many people from many places
They are gone, some must carry on their goals
Whoever they are or were
God rest their souls…
   — Amen

Zac Castle, Grade 10
North Branch High School

Could You Sing Once Again?

I'll play that symphony softly upon your neck,
If you whisper its notes softly in my ear.
I'll play it back for you,
If you whisper me the rules

We composed the best bars
But we never finished the song —
We could get lost in the phonetics,
You mouthed out the words so perfectly.

Trial and error, we're only just beginners,
Trying to find the spot where the song fit just right —
Crying out the high notes when you're almost at the end
Of the song, we fit together.

If I played with these instruments,
Tried to harmonize, we could finish.
I'll play it oh so softly if you wish…

Are we there yet?

Zoë Berkery and Emma Williamson, Grade 10
Grosse Pointe South High School

Forever Zero

The inescapable
The eternal
The inexorable force of the Juggernaut, charging forward,
Catching all without fail nor error in its misanthropic grasp.
Clasping all the living and forcing all to insentience.
The unrelenting final woe of life.
The last salience of the living.
The ethereal fear, born from the cradle.
The final truth of perpetual darkness.
The individual Ragnorok with the same outcome for all.
The everlasting peace spawned from a void, nothingness.
The end of the king, the peasant, and the vagrant.
The ultimate end.
The ruthless eternity where nothingness reigns supreme.
Perpetually Forever Zero.

George Starr, Grade 12
Blanche Kelso Bruce Academy

Little Willie

The steer I remember so well.
It seems just like yesterday.
I had you when I was 9 years old.
You weighed probably 20 times more than me.
You were the gentleness kind.
You pawed when people came near.
You were like my watch dog.
When I took you to the fair
You were the best steer there
And you won the trophy on show day.
I still have that trophy
And even though you're not here
I still remember you so well

Sara McIntyre, Grade 12
Ross Beatty Jr/Sr High School

Shadows

She stands hidden in the shadows
Of a room filled up with light.
You'll never see her standing there,
She's just out of your sight.

She watches you with tears in her eyes,
Wishing she were dead,
As she replays in her mind
All the things you never said.

The band plays a love song
Words she wrote for you,
But you wouldn't listen to the truth,
You broke her heart in two.

You thought you were too good for her,
You thought you were too cool,
But when it came to the game of love
You'd broken all the rules.

You'll get yours she thinks out loud
And someday I'll get mine.
What you give is what you get,
Oh, I can't wait for that time.

Caitlin Sweeney, Grade 12
Mason High School

Go Back

It looks like someone
shook a snow globe.
All the flakes falling
spiraling, swirling, and spinning down.
Covering everything
like a thick white blanket.
Put on snow gear to step out
and deal with the cold.
Making sure I have enough layers
I don't want to freeze.
By now the snow is up to my knees.
My body goes numb
as I lay in the snow
watching all the different flakes
covering my body as they fall.
I remember when I was little
playing outside all day
sledding, snowball fights and snowmen.
I wish I could go back
to stay out in the snow longer.
And appreciate it better.

Audrey Spencer, Grade 11
Clarkston High School

Pain

The feelings I'm having.
I've never had them before.
It's like a hole in me,
That's ready to grow deep inside me.
I'm hurting, but my facial expressions will not show it.
I feel like my heart is beating to the rhythm of my emotion.
And I try to cry, but my barrier overcomes me,
As I look deep down the road.
My eyes get blurry,
As I give up hope.

Derek Thomas, Grade 11
Thomas More School

Internal Affliction

I travel a desolate path ever winding and never ending,
Walking to and from upon the face of the Earth,
Trying to find a purpose, however, I find my life uncontending,
Like a phoenix rising from the ashes towards rebirth.

Attempting to curse away misdirection by never asking why or what for,
Throwing my cares aside into the depth of the seas and horizon,
I find myself once again examining this world of lore,
Searching my soul, trying to discover what lies within.

Now I see between the clouds of dust,
Rising out one by one like the rhythmic beating of my heart,
More than fear, anger, love, or lust,
These feelings paint a picture on my soul like a work of art.

Finally, I start to contemplate and view a clearer picture,
The thoughts askew are now separated from fact and fiction,
They are engraved in stone like that of a scripture,
Thus brings about the end of my internal affliction.

Tom Hentkowski, Grade 11
Posen Consolidated High School

Leave Me Alone

I wish you would just leave me alone.
I wish I could have seen the future so I would've known,
I would have known the pain I feel every minute of the day lately — then.
Every time I hear from you, the wound you made reopens
And begins to infect itself all over again.
And I am left with the lonely and painful job of cleaning up the shredded emotions
And feelings you left behind for me to attempt to put back together.

So I kindly come to you to ask you,
Ask you would you please just leave me alone.
I need to do this on my own!
I have to clean up the mess we made, alone.
So please continue living the life that causes me so much pain!
Enjoy the laughs and good times; I will learn to tolerate my goodnight cries.
Please don't stop learning to love.
Because I will soon learn to not be hateful and understand how to become grateful!
So please, leave me alone.

Ryan Justice, Grade 12
Blanche Kelso Bruce Academy

Snow at the End of the Road

White fluffy flakes fall over the world
like powdered sugar on a cake.
Joy and excitement come from those who love
while rage and anger come from those who hate.
Higher and higher rises the sea of snow,
no one knows what to do or where to go.
Has the time come for the end to be now?
Is this the way it's supposed to be?
Hands in hands, hearts to hearts,
families cling together like magnets on a refrigerator.
Bodies start to fill up with fear and chill
as windows get covered with frost and ice.
The clock light is dimming, preparing for sleep,
when an angel of glow shows its face.

Rhonda Dazell, Grade 12
Ross Beatty Jr/Sr High School

The Person You Used to Be

The past it seems so different
Than it once used to be
Looking back at all the times
Wondering what happened to you and me.

You say that I am worthless
That all I've done is failed
But don't you see in my eyes
You're the one who has now bailed.

You used to bring me down
But I've opened my eyes and finally see
The time for freedom has come at last
And it is now time for me to leave.

I used to think you were right
I now know that can't be true
I miss the person you used to be
But I don't miss you.

Eleisha Perrault, Grade 11
Posen Consolidated High School

Decay

I'm sorry that I can't express the way I feel.
For when you are unhappy all my joy you happen to steal.
I'm unsure if I'll ever be able to speak,
For maybe one day I'll actually find the words I seek.
You never, ever consider my feelings.
You never think about if your words will leave a scar.
It's so bizarre,
How I can care so much and you care so little.
Sometimes I just cry, asking God for some type of reply.
Why must I be treated like this.
All these bad memories my heart must reminisce.
Happiness my soul does truly miss.
So now, I will allow you to continue to treat me the same way.
Maybe soon you'll realize that every harsh word you say,
Is causing my body to decay.

Ja'Nise Washington, Grade 11
Renaissance High School

United

Madness is all over the world,
And at times it gets hard.
And I'm ready to stop the madness.
And the time is now.

Let freedom ring is what he said.
Underestimated by whites,
But he was a good man.
The truth is here now.
Please hear him out.
Everyone needs to know the real truth.

King was a really good man.
See, he was an ordinary man with a good soul.
Now it is time when Martin Luther King, Jr.,
Joins hands with God,
And the two of them went and talked about the past.

Just now, we have to stop the madness without him.
Just remember him and what he said.
This is to all white and black people.

Jeremy Douglas, Grade 10
Thomas More School

Monday Morning

If you are a student you know what I mean,
Getting up on a Monday is just plain obscene.
As you lie in your bed, all cozy and warm,
Your alarm clock goes off, sounding out like a horn.

You begin to groan, your mother starts yelling,
When you'll get up there's no way of telling.
Just ten more minutes, your mind starts to plead,
Just ten more minutes that's all I need!

You look at your clock, thinking it's only seven,
That can't be right, it's ten past eleven?
You try to get up: you give such a heave,
Just one little problem, your body won't leave!

You fall back asleep; your mother comes in!
You're out of that bed and gone like the wind!
You look out the window, while trying to flee,
The school bus is leaving? That just can't be!

You can't find your clothes; your breakfast's not ready!
Your dog ate your homework instead of his teddy!
As you fervently pray, "I'll pay any cost!"
You wake up, and find that all is not lost.

Kyle Cusick, Grade 10
St. Thomas More Academy

You can't be serious…(about that)

Many people do not take the time to notice
All of the people that are homeless
They don't appreciate the little things in life
Not even a housewife
They take for granted their hearing and sight
Even the sight of daylight
A spouse's affair
Doesn't compare, to being in a wheelchair
They don't appreciate the United States
When people risk their lives, just to migrate
Mad because a car cut them off
People's water in Africa just turned off
They lose their jobs and subside
Try being involved in genocide
They're stressed out because stocks are down, and they can't seem to find the right answer
There's also nine million people living in America with cancer
Many people give up on life because they're "lost"
Six million people fought for their lives in the holocaust, and lost
Don't take things too seriously that are not
And remember to appreciate the things that you've got

Lindsay Balgooyen, Grade 12
Mona Shores High School

When Gold Turns Gray

Lights of bright red and gold shine through a stained glass view. A star of fire has brought a new day. In a secluded corner the music of an idle soul plays, while enticing fingers dance across "Ivorine" keys. To an unseen crowd it is a gentle melody across coarse fingertips. With unbound beauty circling Ivory blossoms amongst white golden flames. For it is an unspoken tune that falls on deaf ears and whose magic is only witnessed by blind eyes.

Bianca Jones, Grade 10
Cass Technical High School

A Day in the Life of a Teddy Bear

Every day I sit on her bed and wait for her to come home.
I am quiet and patient, there's not much for me to do here while she's gone away.
But here I am again, sitting upon her pillow. I look over at the alarm clock. She'll be home in only a matter of minutes. I hear the door, and then it shuts. She stops by the living room to tell her mother about her day. Step, step, step — I hear her footsteps coming towards her room, her only hideaway.
She closes the door behind her. Her eyes well up with tears.
She sits down on the foot of the bed. No movement. No sound, except for the tears that fall freely onto her lap.
It is quiet — too quiet.
For the first time today she looks back at me. I stare blankly at her.
My cheesy bear mouth is sewn up into a small smile, but there are no smiles from her today.
Her tears fall faster. She picks me up. I am so little in her hands.
I stare up at her — no eyelids to blink, no tears to cry.
I am a simple fluff and stuffed teddy bear. She squeezes me close to her heart. I'm being rained down on.
Her tears soak through my red fur and seep into the fuzzies I'm stuffed with. She whispers about him. I am his gift to her. He is a part of her, and so am I. My fur has been stained many times with salty, bitter tears — the tears he makes her cry.
Besides the fuzzies that fill my interior, I am full of secrets and the pain, the memories and the feelings, the hopes and the dreams. She is forever showing how deeply she cares for him. He makes me angry.
But what can I do, I am just a teddy bear, full of fluff, full of stuff. Full of love, and she thinks I don't hear her.
She is asleep now. Her face is tearstained. And now I wait again. Soon enough she'll need me. And I will be here.

Lindsey Ellavich, Grade 10
Dwight D Eisenhower High School

Did You Know?

You want to know my mind, my heart and my soul
In due time, I will tell you all there is to know
I will oblige myself to be complaisant
If you will promise to be patient
As I put into practice that very same virtue
For it to me, just recently, has only been accrued

So, you asked me what it was you know
My unabridged answer, I'd rather not compile
But if you spare me a minute or two, I think that I can show
What it is you seek without sacrificing flair or style

You know my heart and know it well
You knew me better than I knew myself
You know the truth and it has set you free
Through me you see, transparently
For these reasons, I belong to you
Forever and ever; through and through
My love for you is true
But you already knew that, didn't you?

Sam McNamara, Grade 11
Light and Life Christian School

Moving On

High School is almost to its end.
I'll miss all of my family and friends.
I don't want to leave this little town.
Afraid of what will come around.

No more endless talks on the telephone.
I will just have to get used to being alone.
I don't need to gain anymore knowledge.
Besides, what's the use in college?

I'll miss going to all of the games.
This seems to be such a shame.
I do not want to go, you can't make me!
Can you not hear my sobbing plea?

No, no, no…
I feel so down and low.
This is really going to blow.

Rachel Beach, Grade 12
Posen Consolidated High School

My Teacher and Friend

You were my teacher.
That's all that will count.
The things you've taught me,
No other teacher could ever amount.

You told me jokes; you make me laugh.
You read my love letters in front of the class.
You were my mentor.
You were my friend.
You helped me through a struggle
Until the very end.

Matt Miller, Grade 10
Blanche Kelso Bruce Academy

Quilt

From the first whispers of sunlight
to the dark monologues of the moonlight
she waits for me

waits to feel the beat
of my unsteady heart against hers
to feel my unsure hands holding onto her
as I wander off to sleep.
Mostly, she waits to be needed.

Silent, she speaks more than words ever could.
Dry, she takes in every tear I've cried.
Generous, she is the keeper
of every dream I've ever had.

Ragged, coming apart at the seams,
she's nevertheless the only one
whose devotion is worn on her sleeve
stitched with pink thread.

Maureen Gruley, Grade 11
Mercy High School

The Octis Incident

How do I explain this legend of mine
It started with a leap of faith which turned out fine
The drudgery which I extended my arm in
Only closed its doors to me and left me blind

The pool of loss which I dove into
Only dried up, and left me in shivering ice
How easily will I dupe myself this time
The matter is grave and risk is high

I look from the aspects of a rival of mine
He simply laughed and smirked at me and took off his mask
"What can I say, you felt wrong, when you felt right"
His words ring with anger in my mind

The time between now and then brought trouble to my mind
I was going to run, but my strength held my feet to the ground.

Ankit Mehta, Grade 10
Troy High School

Love Is Like

Love, like a river, will make a new path
whenever it meets an obstacle
There is only one happiness in your life
to love and be loved
When you love someone
all your wishes start coming out
As we sit side by side in the morning light
we look out at the future together
Love is like a mountain, not easy to climb
but once you get to the top the view is wonderful
To the world you are one person
but to me you are the world

Arielle Wells, Grade 10
Cass Technical High School

Beyond a Window

Before my eyes I see,
A window opening wide,
The heavens embracing me,
The wings of my heart sprouting inside.

I yearn to be free,
But I won't forsake those I love.
I shall glide over land and sea,
Like a serene white dove.

I come towards the window.
I gaze at the starlit sky,
But not at what is below.
I gain my courage to fly.

Out that window I soar.
For the sky I am bound.
That window is a door
Where all the unknown can be found.

Natalie Bohay, Grade 12
Warren Mott High School

Rain So Sweet

The clouds are gray
Lightning is in the distance
Making it from dark to day
The trees begin to sway

Slow glistening rain falling down
Trickling softly from the sky
Sparkling like white diamonds
Touching the flower petals gently

Dark clouds drifting apart
The bright yellow sun peeking out
Warming up the wet earth
A faint rainbow appears

Melonie Roznowski, Grade 11
Posen Consolidated High School

Flats

An old stage flat
stands against the others
in a tattered forest of carved trees
that sway gracefully and fall silently.

It is so old
that its rough, parched bark
comes off easily when you pick it.

Saw it in half to tell how old it is
by counting the layers
from years
of endless productions.

Michelle Dimuzio, Grade 12
Mercy High School

The Debate

Brown and tan, specked with red.
Bits of town, through country spread.
Fighting, killing, all for what's right,
How is blood revered in God's sight?
Stop the violence and the war,
End the mindless massacre.

Men fight for freedom, protection, democracy.
Thankful citizens' appreciation shown,
Hearts poured out
By a roadside bomb.

And so the debate rages on.
Stay and fight? Tuck tail and run?
Is life more precious because it holds
American blood — red, white and gold?
Or is all life worth fighting for?

We must stay, we must leave.
For freedom spread, because of mortars shed.
So now with fractured shattered views,
It is at last time to choose.
For violence in the name of peace, for tolerance and sweet relief.

Kelly Seidl, Grade 12
Ferndale High School

Abortion

Approximately 1,500,000 babies are aborted each year,
One of those million could of wiped a tear,
One of those million could of cheered you up,
And when you have fallen one of those million could of lifted you up,
When you were weak, one of those million could of made you strong,
When mourned, one of those million could of sang you a song.

Head, toes, fingers, and feet,
When does the baby's heart start to beat?
Between the eighteenth and twenty-fifth day,
The electrical brain waves start to function as early as forty days,
Yet you say they're not alive?

The baby is a gift,
It is given inside,
The baby is a blessing,
Just give it a try.

Think before you act,
Treat yourself with respect,
Don't let yesterday's choice,
Be tomorrow's regret.

Brianna Clarke, Grade 11
Flint Southwestern Academy

Season

With new appearing beauty,
Like spring's bright reoccurring life,
When winter moods pass,
A forgotten friend forgives.
Enchanted, much like honey will the flood dissolve,
Great foreseen friends they will become,
As recovering fauna prosper again.

Jessica Stema, Grade 12
Posen Consolidated High School

Inside Myself

Lost, uncertain, confused and dead.
These are all thoughts inside of my head.
I want out now, yet I can't find my way,
These are my frustrations of every day.

Please oh God, let me go home.
I'm distraught and so tired, I feel so alone.
No person understands me, these feelings inside.
No one could care, if today I died.

I didn't ask, not for this pain.
I'm no longer with myself, no longer sane.
Inside my body, there's a heart made of stone.
That is the reason why I'm so alone.

Nothing I do, can change my past.
I've lost my will, I'm done at last.
I'll go away forever, putting my life on a shelf.
I'll never come back, from hiding inside myself.

Phillip Cuti, Grade 10
Hudsonville High School

Sisters

When you are young,
a sister is someone you look up to,
who you want to be just like,
unless she is younger,
then you want to be as far away as possible.
As life goes on you all grow older.
You start to share things.
Talk about relationships and crushes.
Even though the fighting hasn't stopped,
the love has surely grown.
When you are living on your own you start to miss the fights.
You would give anything just to go back to those times
you were elbowing each other,
singing as loud as you could with the car radio,
sitting in your rooms talking about life.
Oh how you long for those days,
and what you all know is that those memories are priceless.
The memories to come
will be the ones you take with you forever.

Alyssa Crager, Grade 10
Kingsley Area High School

I Feel Sorry for Old Ladies

I feel sorry for old ladies,
with stringy gray hair that falls out in clumps,
stuffed up ears that make them rasp "EH!"
creamy eyes and meter thick glasses,
creased and folded faces, sunburned by time,
worn voices, harsh like crow calls, that scrap and grate,
false teeth that fall out into their laps when they chew,
perfume that smells of old shampoo and little dogs,
sagging skin that no longer fits their frame,
hands that can't grasp and arms that can't lift,
squeaky knees and knotted shoulders,
crinkled backs and swollen joints,
who can't stand straight and must limp with a cane,
stiff leg muscles that send them tumbling down stairs,
knobby feet that don't fit in real shoes,
bones that crack and make them sore.

People always say they wish they were older.
I wish I was younger.
I have no wish to be swollen, stiff, and old.

Lauren Dedow, Grade 12
Clarkston High School

These Apartments

Outside of my window are stacked
one atop another
a library of appealing books.

In one, an old woman sits knitting
dreaming about the day she was in love.

The apartment above her
holds the story of two treasure-hunting children
who find gold under the couch.

To the right, an aged man
blows smoke rings into a cloudy abyss;
his journey is almost through.

These apartments
with their endless stories
have taken the place of my childhood reading.

Megan Pryce, Grade 11
Mercy High School

Medicate

I stand up, and speak out loud
Against the people, in the crowd
I feel my heart racing fast
Talking about, what I've felt in the past
The lies that I've heard
The hearts that have been burned
This pain I have seen
I want to wipe the slate clean
I want to medicate my life
From the toxin, and the sin
It comes from below, much deeper than skin

James Sterling Jr., Grade 10
Waldron Middle/High School

Mistakes of the Heart

Stay dear heart,
Don't beat too fast.
Lest ye repeat mistakes
Of your past

Be steady and strong,
Don't skip a beat.
You must be prepared
If met with defeat.

Falling for love too hard
And too quick,
Without putting much thought
Into the ones that you pick

It is said love has no reason
And love has no rhyme,
But one thing you'll find
Is that love does take time.

So stay dear heart
And don't beat too fast,
And let your mistakes
Remain in the past.

Abbey Ravert, Grade 11
Faith Baptist School

What Is Love

What is love
is it a start to something new?
I think love is made for two
something strong and something true,
it's a bond between me and you,
something special that lasts forever.
No matter what, through thick or thin,
our love keeps getting better and better.
Love is your best friend
the one you can trust,
the one that won't leave you
behind in the dust.
Love is always there for you
no matter what's up.
Year after year love will age,
but year after year
love never grows old.
Love never ends
even after death do us part,
because no matter what happens
you're still in my heart.

Brad Haske, Grade 11
Posen Consolidated High School

Resentful Pain

A game of the heart's desire,
A sudden shock,
At the beginning of a beautiful day with you,
I have cried for the love that you give
Only because of my resentful pain,
Of the ending, unconditional love that he gave.
Sighing to think,
We could just not yet be facing a fake period of feeling,
I will try to forget,
And let mine be yours.

Holly Donner, Grade 11
Kingsley Area High School

Dead Hope

ViCAREious heroin existence
Monotone numbness
Gray insipid world
Bleed into me my nothing
Pour your heart out
Until the meaty flesh of your past coincides with the corpse of your future
Then tell me to do nothing to save you
Put the needle down
Smile at the black and white picture hanging above the sink in your bathroom
A vaguely familiar reflection of dead hope
There's a hole the size of my fist next to Apt. 8703
Another mistake is made downstairs at room 2205
And I see you drowning in the flickering ambiance of city streetlights
That glow like the AbSynthetic denial of your youth
You could have been someone, you could have listened
But instead you've turned into a polyester loved one
A shriveled hologram of what used to be brilliance
You are killing yourself
Sadistically aware that each pill that slides down your throat
Ends up in the pit of my stomach.

Chrissie Bingham, Grade 11
Clarkston High School

The Wheels on a Wagon

Young children are like the wheels on a wagon, they never stop.
They're full of energy, and love to run, skip, jump, and hop.

Young children are like chocolate cake, super, super sweet.
They are topped with lots of frosting and can be quite the little treat.

Young children are like extra weights, they always drag behind.
They seem to always throw a fit and they sure do love to whine.

Young children are like pizza, there is not one that is alike.
There are a lot of different toppings and flavors,
but each one in their own way are liked.

Young children are like your favorite pair of shoes.
Even with all the holes and stains, they are the pair that you cannot bare to lose.

Stephanie Talan, Grade 10
Dwight D Eisenhower High School

Ambition

You always were
So ambivalent towards me.
It was because of one thing,
But it was ambiguous.

My life was always set by my goals,
Which I failed plenty of times,
But have gotten back up.
Your love gave me strength like a horse.
But I ran like a duck. why?
Ducks don't run.

My life has one MEANING.
That meaning is success. Why?
'Cause I'm blessed.
When I come to realize my wrong-doings,
I thought to myself, my…
Ambition?…All I wanted out of life was
Richness, fame, and wealth.

Marcus Thornton, Grade 11
Blanche Kelso Bruce Academy

Youth

When life was simple and thoughts so pure.
When time was perfect and faith so sure.
When play time was endless,
and hugs were like a drug of joy.
Oblivious to harsh people.
Unaware of reality and its cruel ways.
Safe and protected.
Happy and blissful.
Tasks were easy, chores were small.
The house but a castle,
containing a hall of dreams and desires.
The bed a basket filled with fairy tales,
awaiting to be released throughout the night.
When life was fair and love was true.
When death was unspoken of,
and money was not an object.
When greed and lust did not exist,
and the world was but the backyard.
Youth, how simple, desirable, looked for within all.

Mallorie Cooper, Grade 11
Allegan High School

Suspense

S tanding in the moment
U nable to move a muscle
S tomach full of butterflies
P reparing for the moment of truth
E veryone is watching
N o one makes a sound, counting down the
S econds…tha thump, tha thump, tha thump
E ruption of applause as the winner is announced

Tabitha Sawyer, Grade 12
Ross Beatty Jr/Sr High School

My Mind

I am a black, talented 15 year old boy.
I wonder if God sleeps.
I hear 4 orange cats meowing.
I want 5 million dollars.
I see the homeless secure.
I am a black, talented 15 year old boy.

I pretend to be a rich celebrity.
I feel 19 baby horses running free above my house.
I touch the crystal clouds above.
I worry about our country.
I cry when a loved one dies.
I am a black, talented 15 year old boy.

I understand the cycle of life.
I say what is needed.
I dream of being in the hot bright sun of Georgia.
I try to give it my all the first time.
I am a black, talented 15 year old boy.

Marc Brown, Grade 10
Cass Technical High School

Take My Soul

My blood has run cold, I am no longer bold.
My bones are chilled as my thoughts are stilled.
In this frame of mind that is not kind
my vision blurs, as nothing stirs.
My blood from my wound seeps as I weep.
I'm going to die. So let me let go of my last sigh.
I'm near the end. Let the grim reaper descend
to take my soul that is out of control.
I hope there is no pain that will drive me insane
when I go. Now everything seems slow
as the grim reaper comes and takes my soul

Jenny Dachtler, Grade 10
Laingsburg High School

Tell Me…

Why have you led me on
Allowing me to think you cared
To think you actually considered my feelings
I can't believe I trusted you
Letting you into my world
And told you how I truly felt
For the first time I allowed my true feelings to show
Believing my heart was safe with you
Were you truly sincere in telling me that you cared
Or was it all just a joke
I gave you my heart and you just ran with it
How dare you
Hurt someone who you claimed to have loved
It's all said and done now
And it's time to start anew
So, I'm leaving you behind
No more calls
Only an exchange of a simple glance

Kaletah Flowers, Grade 10
Cass Technical High School

My Love

I have a love, he's from above;
(Or so the poets write.)
But I'm not sure, for if he were
He'd be a better sight.

His face is dear, but not, (I fear;)
So perfect as my own.
He is not tall, and worst of all,
He cannot write a poem.

I hear his voice, but not by choice,
(I sing a better tune.)
He sings a song, and before long,
He's howling at the moon.

His eyes are fine, but I think mine
More charming than the sea.
He is all right, but in good light,
(I'm more in love with me.)

Natalie Libka, Grade 10
Juniata Christian School

Impossibility

Impossibility is a reality
Life so confusing in itself.
Once ago, happiness reside
Forgotten once myself.

Fears of belonging,
Tears of sorrow,
Deep within one body
Hiding from tomorrow.

Hidden from a lost pain,
Sickened by all the lies.
World has repeated itself,
And happier time dies.

Pieces are falling,
With no available hand
As they see a death.
This is no dream land.

Lauren M. Flewelling, Grade 11
Posen Consolidated High School

Desire

The   hearts
Desire   is love,
    and   friendship.
    Peace and joy.
    Time   is   the
    Only master
    Of   the
    Heart

Troy Montie, Grade 10
St Johns Schools

Tell Me It's Half Past Six

tell me it's half past six, time for day
tear-soaked midnight eclipses my will to stand
I forfeit to the calendar page, then arise
I ask the skies how the day will be
the answer comes in heavenly fire
rising, hanging, looming in a dull suspension
beautiful, albeit obscured by rainclouds.
my father told me that God paints the sunrise,
the sky His limitless canvas, its view perfection
the sun's visage blinding, I must see His face through the sunrise
I look for Him in the skies, yet can't see past her
it's just not sunrise without the light of her face
no warmth comes in the absence of her spirit
I placed my dreams in her radiant glory
but she turned her eyes to the moon,
she couldn't bear waiting for the sunrise
storm clouds filled her place when she left
and rain erupted at midnight.
God paints the morning sunrise, for certain,
a vision of love and hope, salvation and glory,
yet my eyesight can fixate only on storm clouds.

Nate Reynolds, Grade 12
Walled Lake Central High School

All That Is Left

It smells of broken dreams,
All you can hear is a mother's cry and screams.
Here lies an ocean that has run dry,
Why do we seem to sit and watch, not even try?
Have we lost all compassion for those in need?
All that will come from this is misery and death from this poison seed.
It's the blood that runs through our soul,
Somewhere we have forgotten and now it's left an unbearable hole.

The pain of those who have suffered can be seen through their eyes,
For too long we have sheltered a history of lies.
Now the question is, where do we go from here?
The answers we seek are on the scars that we bare.
We cry and pray for some kind of sign,
We seem to always want to cross that unbearable line.
Expect to see us broken, weakened by our soulful cries,
From a past that's rooted in pain, the dreams and hopes shrivel as it dies.

We face the fall of our redemption and the weakness of our shame,
It seems they find comfort on the souls that they blame.
What they don't want to know they cannot see,
The innocence of a child is the reflection of what will come to be.

As we shall forever walk this Earth eternally blind.

Maria Bojaj, Grade 12
Dwight D Eisenhower High School

Fake Friends

They come they go, what they may say, you'll never know, the truth, the lies, the tales tall and deep like wells, sink in deep, the hits repeat, every time I think the fun times we shared, the laughs we made, the late nights, pillow fights, but now an end, everything ends, and soon you'll find, where are your friends now? No smiling faces in sight, you fall and fall until you hit ground and the bottom of this pit is cold with mounds, of cries and all the lies come crashing down, until you realize just to appreciate the one truth you have, the true friend inside, the only one you need, who will always be there whenever you need, and that's the one you have, so be true to yourself, and keep your head high, yes all the words will fall like rain, but if you look past it they will fall hard behind, and cause you no pain, the real is real is real is fake, but even to your grave, you're the only one you take

Angela M. Thompson, Grade 10
Advanced Technology Academy

Puppet

A real live puppet am I
Complete with strings that pull me to attention
Strings that manipulate me through life's play

Yes, those tenacious strings are like many prison bars
Their very design is to hold me back from life's freedoms
Though a part of me, I sometimes ignore my strings and navigate my own path
Then I find I clash with others and become entangled with their own undesirable strings

But as it turned out, my strings proved to be patient
They were always there to pull me out of my entangled messes
Once, I actually broke free from my strings
I then found that I was alone and very frightened
I could not even move and wanted back the security that my strings provided

I then realized that my strings really love me
My strings would always be there to guide me through life's play
I began to see that my strings were not made of rope or wire
But actually the teachings, expectations, and arms of my Mother

I have come to believe that a day will come when I will guide the life of my own child
As my mother guided me
But now with the "strings" of my own conscience

Savannah Anderson, Grade 10
Newaygo High School

Werewolf

The wind blows through my hair as I walk up the hill near my house
I can feel an electric current coursing through my body
It's not the wind that has got me riled up
It's the shift that makes me so eager for this one time each moth
I look up at the bloated moon shining with its cold light
I get down on my hands and knees preparing for the change as the moon shines on me
I can feel the beginnings as black fur crosses over me starting from my back
I can feel my joints popping and my back arches as my tail grows from behind me
My tail id quickly covered by the dark hair still racing across my body
My hands fold themselves and form club-like paws
Claws sprout from my newly formed paws replacing my worn and dull human ones
Tiny daggers cut my tongue as my human teeth are lost and new lupine ones are formed
Finally the change has completed and I lay panting on the cool green grass
I eventually raise my head and howl to the moon
I say to it, "I am werewolf, hear me howl!"

Kristan Lanctot, Grade 10
Troy High School

Ephemeral Dreams

It's the eleventh dream day,
and I'm dreaming of fulfillment and a world beyond reality.

Across the vacant walls of my room,
the clock casts an ominous red glow.

2:22…make a wish!
I wish behind veiled eyes for eternal bliss. Don't wake or the wish is lost.

It appears in my violet dreams on the stems of thorny roses.
Where all is unrestricted. Where realities conform to the will of the imaginative mind.

I reach between the thorns to rescue my rose wish.
One prick and I'll be rejected into the abyss of individual nightmares.

It cuts so swiftly. The pierce is deep, defined by this rose-colored liquid, which soon floods my dream.
Dismembering all hopes of liberation.

I've failed.
My wish is lost, and so must I be with it.

Cast into the darkness of immoral desertion, I lay in silence waiting for the next dream day.
Where I dream of new beginnings.

Brittany Jones, Grade 10
Cass Technical High School

Affection

Affection is the color of rosy pink cheeks blushing as you're caught kissing
It has the sound of two hearts beating in sync with one another
The taste is as sweet as chocolate slowly melting in your mouth
Affection smells like spring, wonderful smells of newly growing plants
When you look at it, it looks like two people walking hand-in-hand only looking at each other
Affection makes me feel needed

Affection is the color of lips that haven't gone unkissed
It has the sound of a light puff from a kiss to the forehead
The taste is of the best tasting freshly picked strawberries
Affection is the smell of that certain someone's cologne as you hug him
To look at it, it looks like an elderly couple sharing a candle lit dinner
It makes even the toughest person feel weak in the knees

Affection is the color of bright red, sweaty palms from holding hands too long
It has the sound of a softly whispered, unwanted good-bye
The taste is like a big piece of chocolate cake your own little slice of Heaven
Affection smells like flowers that you received for absolutely no reason at all
To look at it, you'd see two people cuddled together underneath the stars
Affection makes life worthwhile

Affection is how two people
Share their love for one another

Jessica Jackiewicz, Grade 10
Central Montcalm High School

Your Baby Girl

You took one look into my eyes and said I was the most beautiful baby girl you had ever seen. Then I got home and you started drinking again and all of a sudden you hated me. About a year went on and you drank more and more each day. I grew older not knowing who you were. Everything I heard about you was bad. Never once did I know the real you, nor did I know if I did something to make you leave. It's been 15 years now and I still don't know you or have any memories of you. Yet each day I sit and think about you, and how many memories we could have had together, and what all I missed out on with you not being here with me.

Loni Sparks, Grade 10
Truman High School

Elegy of the Cupcake

A day like no other
Was the day I made cupcakes with my mother
Putting liners in the pan
Watching the batter expand

Taking it out of the oven with ease
It is making me hungry, oh please
Setting it on the rack to cool
The smell of it is making me drool

An hour for the frosting to melt
Mmm, all the cupcakes to be dealt
Spreading on the cool topping
For me there is no stopping

Once I pick it up
Put milk in my glass cup
One bite and all is gone
Goodbye cupcake, so long

Meranda Mulka, Grade 12
Posen Consolidated High School

The Rocking Chair

Sheets of dust do collect
Amid the Tartan plaid.
Rick rock, tick tock,
The clock shifts swiftly along.
But no longer do you hear the birds' broken melodies,
Although sweet in their harmonic tone.
And no longer do we sway into the rhythmic slumber
As we did in the rocking chair.

Changes here and there,
The path never again the same.
Frequently filled as it once was,
Empty only remains.
Mesmerizing mazes, the challenge at our tortured physiques.
But no longer do we proceed together,
Hands tight in the tangling embrace.
And no longer do we venture into the world of perplexity
As we did in that rocking chair.

Sara Moroz, Grade 12
Ross Beatty Jr/Sr High School

My Window

As I look out my window,
    A thousand thoughts cross my mind.
There are so many questions whose answers I don't know.
Due to this ignorance I am confined.
The window it is taunting me,
    Showing me what I can't obtain.
I want so badly not to be
In this position of disdain.
Although you may find this queer
The window through which I look is my eyes,
And I'm confined due to my fear.

Zach Riggs, Grade 11
St Johns Schools

The Big Dance

The biggest game of the football year,
Will be played on the Detroit frontier.
Detroit will be the place to be,
On this, friends, we can agree.
People will come from east to west,
Many will come just a little bit stressed.
All the fans will come for the same reason,
Hoping that this is their team's miracle season.
The game will feature two great teams,
One will leave with shattered dreams.
The teams will battle throughout the game,
Some for glory and others fame.
Coaches urge their messages to be conveyed,
So when the time comes big plays can be made.
The offense and defense must work to perfection,
So their team will head in the right direction.
Players have worked their whole lives for this chance,
Because of it they're at the Big Dance.

Gabe Egan, Grade 10
St Thomas More Academy

Eyes

If we looked into everyone's eye
We would see things differently
Not their color
Or their clothes
We wouldn't hear them speak
We would only see.
It's like walking in someone else's shoes
Looking into their eyes is when we really see
That we are all the same
All alike
In some way.
We all need and want
And if we looked into their eyes
We would see our reflection
We would see ourselves
And that's ironic to me
We are so busy trying to stand out
Separating us from the pack
But when you look into someone else's eyes
We see ourselves.

Kelly Ferrari, Grade 12
Dwight D Eisenhower High School

Orange Leaves

Your fire burns bright,
but briefly;

soon sparks, flickering to the ground,
are swept away by the wind.

Once your flames are extinguished,
smoke drifts along the road into darkness.

Katherine Hoff, Grade 12
Mercy High School

The Black and the Gold

The wind from the Ohio River rushes in
rushes over the sea of black and gold.
Terrible towels twirling
People screaming.
It never gets old,
The Black and the Gold.
An Arsenal unlike any other.
An unfazed Sophomore leader.
A smile that lasts the full 60 minutes.
And a human school bus.
It never gets old,
The Black and the Gold.
They're welcomed to the Motor City
the bus has made the final stop.
The "Road Warriors" find themselves at the finale.
A sea of black and gold outnumbers the blue and green
and outmatches them on the field as well.
That one for the thumb.
It never gets old,
The Black and the Gold.

Jeff Mallison, Grade 12
Clarkston High School

Young Poets
Grades 7-8-9

Note: The Top Ten poems were finalized through an online voting system. Creative Communication's judges first picked out the top poems. These poems were then posted online. The final step involved thousands of students and teachers who registered as online judges and voted for the Top Ten poems. We hope you enjoy these selections.

Top Poem Grades 7-8-9

Four Different Worlds Making One Different Family

Come on and take a trip with me and through my eyes you will see
What I think my ancestors would be, to make a different family

Traveling to Mexico far back years ago, a Latino man with light brown wavy hair
Who mostly grows crops but who also has fun, Salsa dancing under the sun

African American mostly makes me, it's how my family was raised
And who I'll always be, I think of a small black woman who always picks cotton
Keeping her head up and never stoppin, little does this woman know what lies in her future for her
That one day she will be free

Going up north to the Indian village where a Native American woman sits
She combs her hair that goes to her knees and skins fish in order to feed
She makes clothing of buffalo skin and puts it on for the later fire dance
Chanting and singing, her people have fun
While the king of the village watches, looking down on each individual one

Germany is where I see a man struggling every day for his family
For him hard times will come and hard times will go, black hair and brown eyes
That's how this man looks, he wishes for a better life to take foot by foot
One day he'll make it to America where his struggles will die down

Now that you know of my family, did this help you to look down deep to see
What would you do or what would you say, if to you we look a funny way
But we don't, it's all inside, it runs through our blood like water through a vine
We're regular but now you know what makes my family no ordinary Joe.

Jason Beavers, Grade 7
Ludington Magnet Middle School

Top Poem Grades 7-8-9

The Little Things

Time flies by like butterflies,
Always floating on the breeze.
Life is short and drifting,
Like water on the shore.
Memories are forever,
Like a youth long since past.
Cherish the little things,
While they last.

Samantha Clark, Grade 8
Whitmore Lake Middle School

Top Poem Grades 7-8-9

Why Are There Trials?

Why are there trials?
Does God not really care?
He says He wants to see smiles,
But how can I when the pain is still there?

My heart is so hurt.
My emotions are mixed.
I don't want to be mad at God,
But I will until this problem is fixed.

Why are there trials?
And things in such a mess?
Why, if God loves me
Would He leave me in such stress?

What did I do to deserve all of this?
What did I do to be put on God's naughty list?
I know I should talk to Him, and that's what I'll do.
I hope He will listen and show me through.

Why are there trials?
Because God really cares.
He wants me closer
When He thinks I don't care.

Ashley Cooper, Grade 9
Juniata Christian School

Top Poem Grades 7-8-9

Words

Made up of letters
Simple fact
Some handle them with anger
Some handle them with tact

They hold us spellbound
They drive us away
They have within them the ability
To make or ruin our day

They create unions
They cause fights
They force us to make decisions
Fight or flight?

We hold their power
Within us all
The only way to abuse them
Is to not use them at all

Cassandra Flores, Grade 8
St Gerard Elementary School

Top Poem Grades 7-8-9

Soldier's Song

There she is, lying down drenched in her own tears.
Here we are once again, as we were last year.
The ground is cold; she's all alone except the memories in her head.
She's looking at a dark tombstone of her loved one dead.

In her hand, yes, she holds a flag of a soldier.
Someone had the painful task; someone had told her
He was brave; yet he died for the cause so true;
Died for the cause of the red, white, and blue.

Andrea Gibbs, Grade 9
Juniata Christian School

Top Poem Grades 7-8-9

Brands

I'm sick of these burn marks
Upon my back
And that I blindly come back for more
After every attack.
Called in by the tender healings
Brought about by the hand,
That cruelly twisted,
And pressed upon the brand.
I'm sick of these brands that read
Things like: freak, loser or jerk
I'm sick of these brands that we give one another,
I'm sick of the tears that these foul marks bring,
Of the pleasure we take to see the sizzle of skin.
I remember the feeling of the burning brand,
Even as I take one up in my own hand.

Tanner Isaac, Grade 8
Oakland Christian School

Top Poem Grades 7-8-9

Moonlight Shows All

Rain is drenching, pouring, thundering on,
Tatatatatatat. Rings are forming, water rising,
Icy cold dropping to endless bottom.

A crunching, a creaking in the endless plinking.
Plink, plink. Clouds are parting.
Moonlight shows all.

A figure, lonely, on the dock is sitting.
Moonlight shows all.
Swoosh, the rain blows back plinking, plopping, never-ending.

Pounding, and thundering on.
Crash! The bright lightning flashes.
Splish, glug, paddling in the lake.

Figure on the dock watches all.
Wissh, rain is gone, clouds are parting.
Dock is empty, lake is smooth.
Moonlight shows all.

Cassie Pettus, Grade 7
Grand Blanc Middle School

Top Poem Grades 7-8-9

The Miracle

She stared down deeply at the sand-brown floor.
She wiped the tears from her eyes, but there only came more.
She could only hope for the best…
"How did this happen?" she asked herself mumbling,
But she knew there was no answer to stop her tears from coming.
She could only hope for the best…

Even the world's best doctors could not make things bright,
But she would not give up hope, not without a fight.
She could only hope for the best…
When she did stop crying a nurse came in.
She let her last tear roll down her soft white chin.
She could only hope for the best…

The question was posed; she nodded her head.
She would have to wait and see what the future holds ahead.
She could only hope for the best…

So the nurse shut off the oxygen flow in the glass box,
And gave the petite baby to her mom.
She held her baby in her arms, hoping it wouldn't die.
She still had all the hope in the world, even when the doctors told her otherwise.
All odds were against the premature child, but she fought them one by one.
She opened her eyes and her mouth, and she was the miracle.

Nick Somoski, Grade 7
Roseville Jr High School

Top Poem Grades 7-8-9

My Mom

My mom is like the morning
So bright like the rising sun
My mom is like a peach
So gentle on the inside and out

She has a heart of gold
So beautiful and bright
As she drifts off to sleep
Her spirit takes flight

As I grow up with her
She keeps me safe from harm
And though I don't believe in luck
She's my lucky charm

Her love is that of an enigma
Impossible to describe
No matter what she says or does
She always feels alive

She's a soft and gentle voice
Guiding me through the path of life
My mom is caringly tender
So full of God's nurturing light

Joshua White, Grade 8
Iroquois Middle School

Top Poem Grades 7-8-9

The Love of God and Man

Did you hear the whisper I whispered in my heart?
Did you see the cares of mine, though we are apart?
Did you come to rescue me from my untold pain?
Could you take my deepest loss and turn it into gain?

Though you love me, could human ever see
Everything about my life, the way God sees me?
He knows when I need a hand to lift me off my feet;
He knows when I have victory, and when I have defeat.

God knew when in this life I could not stand alone,
So He put you into my life, together we are sewn.
I thank you now for using God's wisdom and grace
To try and see each of my cares shown upon my face.

Olivia Winter, Grade 9
Juniata Christian School

Something

He said something was missing
Something I couldn't make
It's something you can't find
It's nothing you can create
I know I'll never forget
There must have been something there
I just wish I could find it
As I cry out in despair
She holds his heart somehow
I watch with envy and regret
I should be used to it by now
I should have known how this would end
But I watched and waited softly
I knew what I wanted to be
As she let go of his hand
He decided he would leave
I hugged him gently and I know
I have one more chance to see
To my surprise he did not let go
But instead he said he loved me

Ashley Micallef, Grade 8
Muir Middle School

One Day

One day
One day is nothing much
But could be:
Your life
The beginning
The moment that you'll remember
FOREVER
A dream come true
The longest hours
An adventure
A tragedy
A time of peace
A time of chaos
When time stops
And when time begins
When tears are shed
Or when a laugh is heard
This moment
This day,
Treasure it
For it could be your last.

Anna Schulte, Grade 9
Grosse Pointe South High School

Ryan

Hi my name is Ryan
If I don't see you I'm cryin'
Let's eat I'm buyin'
Ryan I think you're real sweet
Let's go grab a bite to eat

Elizabeth Mazorowicz, Grade 7
West Middle School

My Grandma Shepherd

She rocks in her soft rocking chair lots of big curlers in her hair
As she sits here talking to me college football plays on TV
She has always taught me great things before she grew her gentle wings
Her cold hands holding on mine tightly as tears slide down, oh so slightly
She looks deeply in my eyes as she says her final good-byes
Memories engraved in my heart just knowing that soon we must part
She had shared her life with me Grandma, you gave me surety
Our love for each other was pure I know I can always be sure
She told me to always do good and try my hardest like I should
Your breathing now become so slow please I ask you do not go
The tears are now coming fast as I remember our past
She said she loved me forever I will forget her face, never
She has now taken her last breath Grandma sees her angel of death
With her knitting wrapped around me I know I can finally see
As the seraphim's face appears the sadness starts to disappear
Grandma's love will always last the future, present, and the past.

Kelli Lehman, Grade 8
Richardson Elementary Middle School

Through a Mother's Eyes

Madonna, please hear my prayer.
Of my own sake, I do not care.
I care only of my son, whose life was spent.
My heart is not yet broken, but only bent.
Please bless the boy that my daughter has loved.
Guide his soul from your place above.
And do not forget that poor gang leader, who burned with such a hateful fever.
Please forgive these little men, who never knew what they could've been.
Forgive their sins, for their mothers, and don't forget their sisters and brothers.
I know that we mothers have to agree that we all blame ourselves to a certain degree.
Please wash this guilty feeling away, and for my family, keep my tears at bay.
These children, I will not hate, because it's in the past and it's too late.
Please let my, and their, family see it this way, to throw out the pain and smile one day.

Mallory Estepp, Grade 9
Riverview Community High School

Cherokee Morning

The great sun rises slowly,
As the children wake,
To the promising scent of roast duck,
Fresh from last night's hunt.

The native family laughs, plays, and feasts,
In the peaceful tranquility of the wilderness.

Deer begin their usual day playing and grazing in the golden fields,
Fish swim happily in the lush, clean rivers.

The native Cherokee wake,
With the deer and fish,
With the forests and fields,
With the spirits.

It is a new day.

Ben Schauder, Grade 8
Beach Middle School

The Sky

Soaring gracefully,
in the sky.
A falcon soars,
way up high.

Humans have always pondered this,
the strange concept of flying.
When, in reality, if you jump off a cliff,
you would just be dying.

The sky is an open space,
where clouds roll by.
And if you wish to explore it too,
you have just the same dream as I.

Looking through the window of a plane,
feeling trapped and lonely.
I would rather be soaring through the clouds,
finally being set free.

Andrew Dolehanty, Grade 8
St Gerard Elementary School

Football

Football is a sport that takes some skill.
You must have a lot of will.
The players' bodies are abused.
And then they're of little use.
All the others, the team must trust.
When the victory is driven by lust.
A football player's life is driven.
That is how they make a livin'.
It is hard to run with the ball.
When the enemy is trying to make you fall.
The guy with the ball must be pretty slick.
Or will have to pull some fancy trick.
Players are always getting hurt.
When their bodies are being shoved into the dirt.
When football players are smashing.
You can hear their helmets clashing.
The road to victory is tough.
Especially when you've had enough.
When every player helps his team,
The Super Bowl is the ultimate dream.

Jeffrey Raths, Grade 7
St Thomas More Academy

Falling into Spring

Fall
Chilly, colorful
Changing, dying, falling
Trees, leaves, flowers, vacation
Planting, growing, blooming
New, warm
Spring

Destiny Wilde, Grade 7
Montague Nellie B Chisholm Middle School

Faith

Faith is like a seed
Jesus is your seed
You need Him to start to grow
The Bible fills you with the holy word
The Bible is your water
You need it to grow
The Lord is your Father, Son, and Holy Spirit
The Lord is the sun
You need Him to shine on you so you can grow
When you have all these things you are a flower
Your body is the holy temple

Kalena Shaw, Grade 7
Oakland Christian School

Coach

When we first met we barely knew each other
After some time he was like my brother
He was my new softball coach
The first day of practice he made the approach

We always practiced really hard
His reputation was unmarred
No matter what we always had fun
We felt like winners even if we hadn't won

With each practice he helped me out
With him I had no doubt
He had never put me down
If around him you could not frown

Everything was going great
Until that day with his terrible fate
It is because of that one thing
That now I miss the laughter he used to bring

But now I know why God needs him
Because without him Heaven is dim
I hope he knows he is missed very much
With him my life was touched

Janice Ciarkowski, Grade 8
Posen Consolidated High School

Teacher

Math, math, math, what is this rather silly creation?
Who invented this educational form of frustration?
Will I ever be able to use it in real world situations?
Will I ever be forced to use it on a vacation?
Will I ever use it outside of work?
Can I ever use it to prove that I am not a jerk?
Will math ever keep me from going crazy?
Will I ever do math when I am not feeling lazy?
I have so many questions, but no solutions.
Who shall help me find a resolution?
Ohhh, it's no fun being a math teacher.

Kabir Sodhi, Grade 9
Troy High School

Lonely House

There's a lonely house
It sits on a hill
It rains all the time
For some reason
Raspberries grew all around it

There's a lonely house
No one lives in it
It's completely empty
You could see into a cellar
No trace there either

There's a lonely house
It vanishes at night
There's no sight till daylight
No walls in sight
All there is
is purple — stemmed raspberries.

Alyssa Wint, Grade 7
Columbia Middle School

Dirty Ant in Space

A dirty ant flies quietly through space,
off to another place.
You can tell his race,
by looking at his grim, grim face.

Cody Hurl, Grade 7
Grand Blanc Middle School

Mice

Mice like to run
Mice like to scurry
Why are they always
Such in a hurry?

Maybe they're running
To find cheese
I bet it's the cheddar
That they want to seize

What if they were allergic
But didn't know
I bet their coughing
And sneezing would show

But I don't think
That mice are allergic to cheese
I think that they love it
And probably wouldn't sneeze

Even though mice
Really love cheese
I bet they would share some
If you ask please

Meloney Rocke, Grade 7
Roseville Jr High School

Pillows

You know me as your secret punch bag and
headquarters where dreams are formed.
My mother is the bed mattress, she holds me every night and day.
My father is the case I lie in, he protects me from my frights.
I was born in a factory; they feathered, sewed, and sold me.
I live in your bedroom; it is my job to soothe you.
My best friend is Teddy the bear,
Because he tells me of his nights with you.
We like to think about life in each other's shoes.
My enemy is the blanket, all frilled and dressed with lace,
Because he brags and boasts about how he keeps you nice and warm,
and all I do is lie there like a big useless boulder.
I fear the washing machine,
Because it tumbles me all about.
I love it when you sleep on me,
Because I feel I have fulfilled my destiny.
I dream and wish only to please you,
For always and forever.

Katie Kiehl, Grade 7
Verona Mills School

My Place

My place is calm, my place is scary.
It's even extraordinary.
This place of mine is a sanctuary.

This place is blue with light shining through.
It's where I go when I'm sad and chaotic too.
This place of mine, you'll never find, maybe one day you'll see things like I do.

My place is not dark. My place is not light.
I live in the shadows of fear or fright.
I've never been alive. I've never been free.
That's why my place is a sanctuary.

This place shields me from my fears and worries.
My place heals me from my sadness and fury.
It's nice to know there are others like me
Who talk, walk, and act like me.
But aren't me because they're free to be.

My place heals me of my depression and jealousy.
All I want is to be me to fly free
With my secret daydream.

Laura Taylor, Grade 7
Hopkins Middle School

Nature

As the butterflies fly from flower to flower
And the grasshoppers hop through the green blades of grass
And the green frogs croak upon the water lilies in the green water
Lies the beautiful golden sunshine
On a beautiful early summer morning

Jacquie Cummins, Grade 7
Columbia Middle School

School Spirit

Rah, rah, rah
Cheering our teams
Waiting…'til someone scores
The crowd goes wild
Butterflies in everybody's stomach
Waiting to see who will score the next point
When they tie, it goes into overtime
Even more people are nervous
Half an hour passes, the score is tied
Whoever gets the next point wins
The crowd is going crazy
The school's team makes it
Everybody in the stands is standing
With joy and excitement in their body
The team in a circle telling each other "good job"
Everybody comes out onto the floor
Congratulating the teams
Some people are screaming and some are crying
The students cheering the school song
And the band playing the tones

Jacy Hagelgans, Grade 7
Centreville Jr High School

The Ocean

The ocean flows like blood through my veins
It moves like the beating of my heart
Giving so much life
Taking so much life away
Bound by gravity
And I, bound by myself
Its beauty, rich as my soul
It reaches far and wide
Like my love for you
So deep
So dead
So alive

Emily Smolinski, Grade 9
Posen Consolidated High School

Summer Days

A new day is often heard,
With the singing of a bird.

Their melodies so light.
Like stars in the night.

I listen to the croaking of frogs,
And think of them leaping off logs.

I can't wait for the day,
All the adventures just waiting astray.

The pool entices me with its gleaming blue glisten,
Just as I look to see the clouds kissin'.

Kathryn Nowicki, Grade 7
St Anthony of Padua School

Colors

Where do colors come from
Why are there colors
Colors like brown that make you frown
Pink makes you wink
When you have the flu you are feeling blue
When you are red you should stay in bed
The color black just makes me want to yak
Yellow makes you mellow
Those are some of the colors that I like.

Andrew Andonian, Grade 7
Columbia Middle School

Katelyn*

Katelyn, Katelyn,
Innocent angel, God's masterpiece.
Christ's love radiated from your face.
You left this world while you were still young
To see our Heavenly Father above.
But why you died I still debate.
My gentle tears in the solitude of the dark
Have brought no healing
To the bottomless hole in my heart.
Yet light streamed into the hopeless abyss,
Scattering the sorrow,
And bringing me hope.
My hope and joy
That one day,
Someday soon,
I will see your smiling features
Waiting for me at Heaven's doors.
But, for now, you have sent a butterfly,
One to help my aching soul,
To give me hope, peace and joy,
To heal my hurting heart.

Lauren Merz, Grade 7
Grand Haven Christian School
*Dedicated to my friend who died of leukemia.

Frosty Winter Air

Frosty winter air
     knocks down branches from all trees
          nipping children's ears

Big fields of flowers
     bright skies, warm wind, but cool nights
          finding Easter eggs

Long, hot summer days
     swimming at the beach feels good
          faces are sunburned

School is back again
     gray, plaid jumpers and book bags
          jumping in the leaves

Lauren Zamiska, Grade 7
Peace Lutheran Church & School

Fall

A wind blows softly
Branches swaying with grace
A calm and cool fall day
Evan Bachteal, Grade 8
MacDonald Middle School

Love Never Dies

Some people lie
But love never dies
In my heart
We'll always be apart
I can see
How things should be

Love can hit you like a brick
But that is always the trick
We are both knowing
Our cups are overflowing
You'll always be in my heart
Till death do us part
Garrett C. Quick, Grade 9
Posen Consolidated High School

Life as a Basketball

People bounce me,
People shoot me,
People pass me,
But me,
I love to fly through the air
And smack against the backboard.
Tyler Knudsen, Grade 7
Manistee Middle School

Queen of the Hall

There she goes,
Flipping her hair,
There she goes
All the boys stare.
Here she comes
Looking at me,
Here she comes
Why can't I be
Just like her
Pretty and tall,
Just like her
Queen of the hall.
She seems so perfect
Blonde hair and blue eyes
She seems so perfect
She gets all the guys.
I just want to be
Part of her posse,
I just want to be
Gorgeous and glossy.
Heather Cooper, Grade 8
Beach Middle School

Don't Change

Don't change for anyone,
Not even your mom,
Don't change at all,
'Cause you are the bomb,
Act like you are,
Not like you are trapped,
In a jar,
Wear what you want and,
Don't feel shame,
Even if it's a little lame,
Don't change to be cool,
'Cause you'll just be a fool,
Don't change for anyone,
And go to school,
Say what you want,
If it comes from your gut,
Don't change for anyone,
Don't change at all.
Don't change.
Kyle Engel, Grade 8
Hilbert Jr High School

The Wonderful World

I may never be able to detect,
The wondrous sights I always neglect.

The flowing current of a river,
Oh how the Earth is such a giver.

The swaying patterns of a tree,
Ceaselessly waving back at me.

The towering heights of a mountain high,
Making me dream of flying to the sky.

I gaze upon the canyons below,
The sight makes my mind flow.

Now I see the world as a gift,
Look before it begins to shift.
Justin Anderson, Grade 7
St Anthony of Padua School

Time

It goes by fast
Sometimes slow
It's nonexistent
When you need it most

Maybe someday
We could control it
Until that day
I shall say
Time has been on my side
Tyler Krajniak, Grade 9
Posen Consolidated High School

Slave

Who are you, old woman?
Why are you here?
Are you a slave,
Hiding in fear?

Who are you, old woman?
A slave running away?
Running from your master,
But instead here to stay?

Who are you, old woman?
A spirit from the dead?
Who had nothing to give,
But all to dread?

Who are you, old woman?
Is the earth what you've become?
Or are you the eagle,
Full of freedom?
Meghan Jordon, Grade 7
Columbia Middle School

To Be Seen or Not to Be

The path unseen
Is a future unknown
The path now seen
Is a future now known
Rowena Jackson, Grade 9
Detroit International Academy

Doves and Crows

A dove so beautiful the sign of life,
Cutting through the air like a knife.
A dove so beautiful what a sight,
Every morning in its flight
in the air with no despair

Now a crow so dull and black
always sitting in the back
only flying in the air
when filled with despair.
Brent Mitchell, Grade 9
St Johns Schools

War

Permit me to tell you about war
For I have fought Goliath
The agony on the battle field,
The sound of a soldier screaming,
The cannons flashing before my eyes,
Yet the war I remember the most
Left me sad and alone
As I walked away
From the cries of pain
Matthew Stanley, Grade 8
Grosse Pointe Academy

My Race Car

I bought my first car
When I was only 12 years old
It was a Mustang too
And it was blue

Put in a roll cage
It was all the rage
I painted it black
Then I raced around the track

My dad was in the stands
Cheering with my fans
My car is roaring every Friday night
Right in the center of light

It was my first racing season
And for that reason
The best summer I ever had
Racing and working with my dad.

Garry Scharphorn II, Grade 7
Montague Nellie B Chisholm Middle School

I Am

I am good at basketball and smart
I wonder what I will do when grown up
I hear people talking
I see people together
I want to go to college
I am good at basketball and smart
I pretend to act dumb
I feel happy and excited
I touch something rough and bumpy
I worry about my mom's back
I cry when I think about my old dog Blaze
I am good at basketball and smart
I understand that people in this world are different
I say I will live my dream
I dream about getting a scholarship
I try to be the best
I hope to pursue my dream
I am good at basketball and smart
I will do what it takes
That's how I am

Jenna Paytas, Grade 7
Roseville Jr High School

S-h-a-T-a-r-a

S is for the sweetness I have inside of me.
H is for my big heart to share with others.
A is for all the ones I care about.
T is for time that I spend with my family.
A is for attitude that is sometimes good, and sometimes not.
R is for respect that I have for myself and others.
A is for accepting other people just the way they are.

ShaTara D. Simmons, Grade 7
Oakland Christian School

Why

One fall night during the full moon
I sit on my bed in silence
Wondering why
WHY…did we break up?
WHY…am I hurt so badly?
WHY…doesn't he love me?
WHY…do I feel so much pain?
WHY…can't I get him off my mind?
WHY…do I still love him?
Why…why…why…
Then there's a break in the silence
Tap went a rock on my window
I look out, it was him
I rush to the door, run out and ask you why
Then all the sudden we were hugging…turning in circles
It felt like we were together for the first time
All the thought came rushing in
If we loved each other so much
WHY are we in such a great amount of pain?
I no longer knew, all I knew and all I still know…
Is how much I really love you.

Jessica Grubb, Grade 7
Perry Middle School

Family

F is for family a great thing to have.
They will always love you even when you've done bad.
They will always support you because it's you they love most.
F is for family a great thing to have.
When you and your family are in a bind just remember
You will always go through it together until the end.

Morgan Page, Grade 7
Camden Frontier Middle School

Spring into Spring

Spring is the early time of year
Little bunnies running around with big, floppy ears
Spring is lovely and nice
Easter comes and here it has begun
Baby animals all around
Making a huge, loud sound
Easter eggs and candy
Baskets full of treats
Fresh new green grass
Water like liquid blue glass
Sky clear blue, with fluffy white clouds too
Trees swinging in the wind
When growing flowers do begin
Spring is a wonderful season to have
But it comes on way too fast
You can't miss it, and if you do
You'll be sorry you did
Just to be sure you get to enjoy it
You have to *spring* into spring!

Becky Ray, Grade 7
Ruth Murdoch SDA Elementary School

Tsunami Terror

Sitting on the sandy beach
Feeling the wind
Brushing through your hair
Smelling the sweet saltwater
Sitting there like a beached whale
Then seeing something terrifying
The huge wave building up
Out in the ocean blue
Far from shore
It comes crashing down
The wave is a bomb,
Exploding on the dry land
You can smell the fish,
Dead or alive
Everything is wiped out
Soon it will be over
Nothing left to see
Joey Thornton, Grade 7
Addison Middle School

Basketball

Got a basketball game tonight,
have to do my best, because
we're playing against the best.
Passing the ball to the open player,
taking the outside shots.
Making baskets and losing the ball,
final minute of the game,
all tied up, one last shot.
Looking for the open player,
everyone is blocked.
Going for the drive…
5…4…3…2…shoot…
…1…buzzer goes off,
the ball goes in, we won the game.
Brandon Schuch, Grade 8
Posen Consolidated High School

The Four Seasons

A cold chill of snow
Freezing, keeping out the warmth
Until the sun comes

The dangerous wind
Combined with thunderous light
If of spring weather

The sun, so scorching
beating down on the dry earth
After pouring rain

Leaves of all colors
Falling, falling to the earth
Colors all around
Megan Green, Grade 8
Peace Lutheran Church & School

A Man's Best Friend

"Sit," said the old man as he gave food to the dog
"Stay," said the old man as he walked away
The little dog stayed
After a while the man came back and gave the dog more food
This went on for three weeks
Then one day he again told the dog to stay
And the dog did as he was told once again
Soon a day went by then two days and so on for a month
But the dog still stayed right where he was
He sat through winter and summer
His only food was scraps thrown to him by children and caring people
After only two months the dog was thinner than before
He sat with big solemn eyes watching where the man had last said stay
Soon new buildings were built around him
But still he stayed
The dog sat and listened and waited
He grew old and became blind
But he still listened for the old man
Then one day as he lay there
He saw the man and realized he was with him
In Heaven.

Sean Sullivan, Grade 7
Centreville Jr High School

Not Enough Time

Not enough time,
good ideas I have none.
Not enough time,
good ideas I have none.
What do I do? What do I write?
It's effortless for my classmates, but not for me.
How do I think when the clock's deafening ticks pierce my thoughts.
I do not have the courage to look as the minutes pass.
Why can't I do it? Why can't I concentrate?
Who do I ask for ideas, so as to begin?
Where do I go in my mind for thoughts?
When do I know when my time has ceased?
Not enough time,
good ideas I have none.
Not enough time,
good ideas I have none.
Cody Normington, Grade 7
North Rockford Middle School

Water

Swoosh, I dive into the pool.
Glistening in the shimmering, shining sun
the water on the side of the pool goes drip drop, drip drop.
Beneath the dazzling water I swish and swoosh around in every move.
I approach the separation of the water
and the air above and spring up from underneath.
Soaking up the sun
I swoosh down in the water
and start all over again.

Alissa Solberg, Grade 7
Manistee Middle School

Inspiration

Inspiration comes from the heart
It is beautiful, unique, and art
Inspiration can be people, places, or things
Grasping you and me by its inspirational wings
Holding you and me tight
So don't give up your inspiration without a fight
It can be the sky
Maybe the many clouds passing you by
Even if it is your imagination
Your inspiration is your sensation

Samatha Hutchens, Grade 7
Hally Magnet Middle School

What I Thought Was Hard

There's many places I haven't been,
I'm always stuck in a house.
My dad's really mean and strict,
My sister's always on my head.
I thought my mom was never there,
And my brother had forgotten me.
Everyone didn't do what I asked,
I thought everyone hated me,
And my dad had previous alcoholic problems.
I realized I had an easy life.
So what if my dad's mean,
Or my sister's on my head.
My mother has always been there.
I'm not always going to get my way.
My brother was busy with school and work.
My dad has gotten over his problems,
And I have gotten over mine.

Robert Dumas Jr., Grade 8
Erma Henderson Upper Campus

Basketball, Basketball

Basketball, basketball
Down the court we go
It's the fourth quarter
And Jefferson is down by two

#30 shoots for a three and makes it
There is a foul on that play
#30 gets one shot
And makes it

Jefferson is up by two
The other team goes, shoots, and misses it
Jefferson going down the court
And the other team steals it and makes it

Now it is a tie game with two seconds left
Jefferson shoots really quick and makes it
Jefferson Wins and still *Undefeated*
And the crowd goes *Wild*

Megan Volker, Grade 7
Jefferson Middle School

Stay

My love is pure
It's wholesome; true
All my life I've been searching for you
For who thought I would meet someone with your grandeur?

When I set my eyes upon you
My heart does sing with love
For before you came to be with me
True love I never knew

Please stay and protect me
From the harshness and the pain
I need to you here to be
So my heart won't break again

Drake Carr, Grade 7
Grand Blanc Middle School

School

There's a place where all kids go,
to keep building on what they know.
You learn math, science, English, and so much more.
Sometimes it's a big huge bore.

There's a place where gym is fun.
All you do is scream and run.
You get good exercise there's a plus.
If you get mad you start a fuss.

There's a place where you learn discipline too.
Like tucking in your shirt and tying your shoe.
It's the principal's office you try to avoid.
If Mrs. Slattery sees you often, she gets pretty annoyed.

There's a place that starts in the fall.
You better be ready with books and all.
It comes to an end in the summer.
When it's time to go back it's quite a bummer.

There's a place that's really cool.
It's a place that I call school.

Ana Guerra, Grade 8
St John Vianney Catholic School

Smooth

Smooth as warm water at the beach running over my tan legs.
Smooth as sunlight tanning my back.
Smooth as ice cream dripping down my face.
Smooth as the watermelon seed I spit out.
Smooth as sleeping rocking gently in a hammock.
Smooth as the warm wind blowing my face.
Smooth as my legs running with my friends.
Smooth as the lap of the ocean.
Smooth as the whispering of the trees.
Smooth as summer.

Lucilla Chalmer, Grade 8
Beach Middle School

I Remember

I remember when you got picked up from my house.
When you closed the door you yelled, "we'll have plans next weekend, I promise!"
I remember seeing you the next weekend.
Not at my house, nor yours. We didn't play…you couldn't play anymore.
I remember the bad news:
The salty tears were pouring down my wet face like a rainy day.
I remember the darkness.
I remember seeing you through the hospital window. A deep sleep that seemed to last forever.
I remember the green lines on the screen that jumped, then ran, and then jumped.
Just like in the movies…Beep…Beep…Beep…
I remember waiting; I remember hoping; I remember praying for a miracle.
I remember the good news…the miracle.
I remember the enormous smiles and the warm tears that tasted like honey.
I remember the blissful relief.
I remember you in the hospital window, smiling.
I remember you breathing. Breathing in and out the fresh air of life.
You finally woke up. You kept those green lines jumping. You kept your promise, thanks for not breaking it.
I remember…How could I forget?

Jacob William Diskin, Grade 8
Hillel Day School

The Big Day

As the bride comes down the aisle everyone stands with a smile
Some people start to cry as if someone has died
But those aren't tears of sadness they are tears of joy and gladness
After the priest gives his speech the bride and groom can hardly speak
They slip the rings on each other's fingers and then that question begins to linger
Will they stay together as promised or will their marriage be demolished
Then those big words come up "I do, I do" and then the couple's dreams have come true
You may kiss the bride, is what is done then they embrace with a kiss and a hug
Next is the reception in a dining hall where they throw a party and have a ball
Last comes the honeymoon which is a special time, for the bride and groom
Hopefully they live a long and happy life together as husband and wife

Selena Smolinski, Grade 8
Posen Consolidated High School

I Won't Need You

Can you tell me what's going on?
I need to know what it is you're thinking.
Am I even on your mind?
Do you see me every time you close your eyes?

Do you go to bed thinking of me, fall asleep and dream of me, or wake up calling my name?
And I know it's my fault for trying to pull you close but really push you away.
I've been trying to say I'm sorry, but you just don't seem to hear me.
Do you wish we ever met, or do you wish I were dead?

I need you in my life, right beside me.
And I just can't sleep at night because I know you won't be there when I wake.
All I wanted was you to call my own.
But all I got was a broken heart to call mine.

So don't worry I'll make it through.
Because soon I won't need you.

Lyndsie Fuller, Grade 8
Mendon Middle/High School

Dreams

I am a woman,
With many dreams,
I dream big
And sometimes
I dream small.
But either way, I still have dreams.
I am a dreamer
Who has dreams beyond my beliefs.
I may have some dreams that others might not see,
But in my eyes, I see them clearly.
Dreams do not have to be perfect,
Dreams do not have to make sense,
But dreams do express how you feel inside.
Everyone has dreams
No matter how much money you have,
Or how much money you don't have,
Everyone has dreams.
Anyone's dreams can come true
You just have to work hard to get it.
Just don't forget that everyone is a dreamer,
And that your dreams can come true.

Mariah Taylor, Grade 8
Gesu Elementary School

The Guinea Pig Tree

There was once a Guinea Pig sitting in a tree
Looking at me as if he was sad,
That he could not eat a thing,
Glaring at anyone who passed by that tree,
While he was looking at lettuce and peas,
That guinea pig looked at me,
We exchanged looks of anger and fate,
We somehow understood what was wrong,
That day we met we knew everything,
That was my day the guinea pig in the tree.

Amelia Erbel, Grade 7
Manistee Middle School

When Daddy Went Away

Why is he leaving?
Is he coming back?
Why are they screaming?
He's starting to pack.
Out of the door,
And down a long street,
When again will Beth and Daddy meet?
"Daddy don't go!
I am only seven!"
He replies, "Sweetie I'll see you when we get to Heaven!"
"But Daddy that's too long!
The memories we've had!"
He walked out the door,
Beth fell to the floor,
And that was the last time she saw Dad.

Stephanie Lambert, Grade 7
Columbia Middle School

I Am

I am a curious girl who wants to make people proud
I wonder why
I hear screaming
I see tears
I want to impress people
I am a curious girl who wants to make people proud
I pretend to fly
I feel the rain
I touch the ground
I cry because I am not good enough
I am a curious girl who wants to make people proud
I understand that you have to work hard
I say practice makes perfect
I dream of water
I try to concentrate
I worry that I will fail
I hope that I succeed
I am a curious girl who wants to make people proud

Alexa Ritter, Grade 7
Roseville Jr High School

I Am

I am a child with her head in the clouds.
I like the idea of magic around us.
I feel the need to be among the trees, with
their stories.
I hear the rustle of the leaves as they speak to me.
I see the good and evil in all.
I am a child with her head in the clouds.

I wonder if the legends are true.
I know the people think me weird; they may be right.
I care what people think, but dismiss the negative.
I wish I could see a dragon, just once.
I am a child with her head in the clouds.

Meghan Slocum, Grade 7
Paw Paw Middle School

Athleticism

Just because I'm athletic
Don't call me dumb
Doesn't mean I don't have a life
Doesn't mean I watch sports

Just because I'm athletic
It doesn't stop me from studying
It doesn't make me popular
It doesn't make me a jock

Just because I'm athletic
Doesn't mean I'm mean
Doesn't mean I'm snotty

Just because I'm athletic — it doesn't make me stupid

Nathan Snooks, Grade 8
St John Lutheran School

The Storm Is Coming

The storm is coming.
Waters turn tempest.
Seagulls screech.
As they fly for shore.

The storm is coming.
Rain pelts the Earth.
The land is losing its battle.
The skies reign has begun.

Roaring waters.
The sky's anger is upon us.
We seek redemption,
for what we have done.

The storm is coming.
Lightning tears open the heavens.
The angels sing,
of sorrow and lost hopes.
We feel the wrath,
of those above us.
The storm has COME.

Jacob Forstat, Grade 7
Grand Blanc Middle School

The Cottage

We wake up early
and pack our bags to leave.
When we get to the cottage
the sun is reflecting in the lake
sparkling red and orange.
Ducks are having babies
the mother duck
shows the baby ducks how to swim
and she says follow me
in a straight line.
Rose runs down to the dock
and takes a picture of the duck family.
Night comes
we eat
then dad and me go down to the dock
and look at the stars.
The next day we go fishing
I catch a big fat blue fish.
Dad cleans it
we eat the fish for dinner.

Geoffrey Smith-Woollams, Grade 8
Beach Middle School

The Truth

From ourselves we try to flee,
Then cover it up with fake glee.
Running in circles; 'round and 'round,
Afraid our inner self may be found.

Brianne Richardson, Grade 8
Oakland Christian School

The Last Days

As he lie in that hospital bed,
Tons of visions ran through his head, like a train circling around his bed.
He did not know what was going to be,
It could take a cycle for the worst, just maybe.
Family members appeared to see him,
And the curtain of night began to grow dim.
Then the day had officially come,
To be with God, the Chosen One.

Rodney Kosters, Grade 8
St Anthony of Padua School

The Big Show

I walked into the stadium I seemed to be doing fine
I was with my friends we were waiting in line
We came to see the show everyone was here
The band finally came on stage and we all gave a cheer

There was the plump drummer his sticks were a flash
I didn't want to be hit by one they were so fast they'd leave a gash
I had just started drums half a year since I got my set
I will never be that good or at least so I bet

But here I am, ten years from that fateful day
Well am I that good I shrugged because I may
I started with a simple beat then the guitar came
I knew this was the real deal and not another game

I felt the sweat drip down my chin my big solo was coming up
My arms were feeling wobbly as useless as a newborn pup
Then everything stopped but that's just what I felt
Less than a second had passed than my first note was dealt

I sat back and closed my eyes I kept the beat flowing
I finished and heard applause boy my face was glowing
That was the best day of my life

Scott Carpenter, Grade 7
West Middle School

Deficient

Ancient lipstick stains on all your pillow cases
I keep forgetting how far away your place is
States all cut up with imaginary lines
I told you love knows no miles but that disagrees with these traffic signs

You were my beginning so can't you please stay till the end
I won't stop tearing out these stitches, I don't want my heart to ever mend
Just this once can't you please come over
So I can tell you how much I miss you with my head on your shoulder

Memories of us have become silhouettes in my mind
Your voice stays in my thoughts but I might as well be blind
As much as I hate this it's the best anyone could wish to find
Apparitions of you and I will be forever entwined

Connor Crank, Grade 8
MacDonald Middle School

Superstar

As he dribbles up the court,
He is playing his favorite sport.
He looks around to see his team,
And passes the ball through the smallest seam.
His teammates give it right back to him,
Because he's the best player in the gym.
You shouldn't let him shoot the ball,
Because he is going to make them all.
Another great thing is that he is quick,
He will definitely be a number 1 pick.

Scott Couture, Grade 8
Posen Consolidated High School

Rachel Joy Scott

Rachel was kind. Rachel was caring.
Rachel was a loving person.
Rachel was sweet. Rachel was fun.
Rachel was great.

Rachel was a spiritual influence.
Rachel was a great Christian.
Rachel put her all to God.
Rachel was unique.
Rachel accepted everyone.
Rachel wanted to be everyone's friend.

Rachel loved God.
Rachel wanted everyone to be treated equally.
Rachel helped others when they needed help.
Rachel was there when nobody had friends.
Rachel was beautiful in her own way.
Rachel was loved by all people.

We should all be like Rachel Joy Scott.
Rachel was a person that we all want to be like.
Everybody loved her, and I do too.
Rachel Joy Scott is my role model.
Is Rachel your role model? Do you want to be like her?

Faith Nielsen, Grade 7
Hudsonville Christian Middle School

Journey Down the Never Ending Road

I think that I must stop and ask for directions
My map is messed up and needs many corrections
I look around the green, green forest
Down the dusty golden road to as far as I can see
I don't know if I could ever reach my destination
It's further than my wildest imagination
So I travel on not knowing when to stop
I think I will sit down for a minute
Where am I to go what am I to do
Who am I to meet I haven't a clue
But all I know is that someday
I will reach my destination

Autumn Reese, Grade 9
Posen Consolidated High School

Spring

Spring,
Colors, leaves, the birds and the bees,
all come out in the spring.
Flowers show their faces, and come out of
their dark places in the spring.

Now I have to rake,
that's something I just can't fake.
We do that old spring clean,
Sometimes it makes me very mean.

I throw the leaves into the compost,
this part I like the most.
Sometimes I rake them into a pile,
this part always gives me a smile.

Now that my chores are done,
I am going to have some fun.
I can play some baseball,
I haven't played that since the fall.
Spring…

John Fisher, Grade 8
St John Vianney Catholic School

Wishing

Wishing is dreaming.
Wishing is playing.
Wishing is all about thinking.
In class, at home, in bed, anywhere is wishing time.

Wishing is when the sky is light,
The trees are warm and the night is soft.
Wishing is when you lay in bed and stars glow.
Wishing brings joy to all with a wish in mind.

Melissa DeMorrow, Grade 7
Montague Nellie B Chisholm Middle School

Big Buck

I once was in the woods
Walking my uncle's dog
He was a chocolate lab
His name was Hunter
I was back by his pond
It was behind his house and pasture
Then I saw the deer
There was a big buck
The others were does
The buck had the biggest ears
It was in the green grass grazing
When they saw me
They ran so fast
It was a nice beautiful sight
Watching them run through the misty woods
In the morning

Michael Ellis, Grade 7
Addison Middle School

Rain Drops

I like looking at the rain
Outside on my porch
Rocking in my tall chair
Rain sounds like drip-drip
And plunk on the ground
When it rains
The sky is crying just
Like a baby at night
I like to swim while
It's raining
So I can
Feel the raindrops
Slide down my face
Rain is a waterfall;
Falling beautifully and free
I love everything about
The fresh, misty rain.

Carissa Clemons, Grade 7
Addison Middle School

Flowers

Flowers are as purple as plums,
Flowers are as yellow as the sun.

Flowers are grace,
Sweeping across your face.

Flowers are peace,
To fill the bare crease.

Flowers are sweet,
Unlike my feet.

They are at times very tall,
And also are really small.

They light up the room,
When they're in full bloom.

Allison Veneklase, Grade 7
St Anthony of Padua School

Ski Race

The day has come
My first race
A beautiful day
No time to waste
The day has come
My first race
Going down the hill
At a steady pace
The day has come
My first race
A perfect day
I took first place.

Scott Fuller, Grade 9
Cadillac Jr High School

Hope for Love

Can you see the warmth on a cold winter's night?
It seems almost impossible to be like that in a way.
Like hope will never become more than those poor naked trees
And love will never be because of those sad, sad, memories,
Of winters past being all alone
Never warmed by your love.
My hope still stays kindled
For the hope that may be
That someday I will be warmed by somebody.
Somebody who cares, somebody who knows.
Someone like you, so special and gentle.
Someone who's fun, quirky,
Yet sweet.
So happy.
Someone like you to make great memories.
My heart leads
And I follow right into your arms,
So that I will be warmed on a cold,
Cold, winter's night.

Sarah Strozeski, Grade 7
North Rockford Middle School

Soup

Today we are going to make
The world famous awful soup
First we add the sewer water
Boil it for ten minutes until the room reeks
Then cut up some wild onions,
garlic, and five month old spinach
then mix it with Tabasco sauce and a bottle of prune juice
pour the mixture in
then liquefy some blue cheese with the egg plant
cook it for thirty minutes then serve it to who ever didn't evacuate the building

Sean Glassford, Grade 8
Ruth Murdoch SDA Elementary School

Change Is Good

As she walked every eye was on her, her footsteps sounding like explosions.
The first day in her new school, would never be like the old ones.

She didn't want to move, for her parents were splitting up.
This next year would be a tough time for her, and she couldn't give that up.

She wished she had a friend. Someone who she could trust
Someone to laugh and cry with, and never leave her in the dust.

She stepped into homeroom, eyes searching for an open seat.
When she spotted a familiar face, who she already happened to meet.

Her best friend from Georgia, sat there staring back in awe.
She had moved away so long ago, she couldn't believe what she saw.

At that moment, all her worries seemed to disappear
From that morning on she knew it would be a great year.

Danyelle Cummings, Grade 7
Grand Blanc Middle School

Just Because I Am a Girl…

Just because I am a girl
Doesn't mean that I am weak.
I don't have to depend on other people.
It doesn't mean that I can't stand up for myself.

Just because I am a girl
I don't have to cry over boys
I don't have to know how to sew or knit.
I don't have to major in home economics.

Just because I am a girl
Doesn't mean I have a subscription to Teen People.
Doesn't mean that my room is pink.
Doesn't mean that I am always organized.

Just because I am a girl
Doesn't mean that I have to love all the boy bands
Doesn't mean that Jessica Simpson is my idol
Doesn't mean that I worry about my looks.

Because I am a girl everyone should treat me equally!

Alyssa Pontti, Grade 9
Iron Mountain High School

Reese's Peanut Butter Cups

They like me for the chocolate and I don't know why
They should like me for my peanut butter, that's inside

I'm little and round but no one cares
It only matters to them, if I am theirs

They say I'm sweet, they love me of course
But I hate when they bite me, 'cause they do it by force

Nobody wants to get eaten up
Especially me, a peanut butter cup

Jonathon Wolfer, Grade 8
Ruth Murdoch SDA Elementary School

Hands

God gave us hands to help each other,
No two are the same as another.

Each hand has its own fashion,
To do what is our own passion.

We all hold hands with each other,
Because everyone is our sister or brother.

We all come in different sizes or tones,
Because He didn't want us all to be clones.

God gave us all our own special trait,
That is why we are all so great.

Jenna Rood, Grade 7
St Anthony of Padua School

My Love

I love to cuddle,
not to fight,
be with you day and night.
My love for you will continue to grow,
give it time and it will show.

I wanna know you,
I want to find out,
I want to see you,
and figure you out.

I want you to be there for me,
I want you to be right there while I breathe.
And I want to know that
you are all for me.

I love you truly,
without a doubt,
stay with me
to complete my heart.

Amber Spratt, Grade 8
Davis Middle School

War on Terrorism

On September 11th the Iraqis attacked,
And this to the Americans seemed like a slap.
President Bush sent for General Kevin,
He sent for divisions one through seven.
Bush gave Iraq 48 hours to respond,
Before he would start to attack and bomb.
They started their attack with the F1-17,
At night this bomber was virtually unseen.
Without Bush's law to protect,
There might be another terrorist attack.
The first month went well with few casualties,
They even caught a few refugees.
The next year was hard and the fighting was fierce,
In a few more the defenses would be pierced.
The Americans were using the M-16,
And the Iraqis were using the RPG.
The Americans moved into Baghdad and took the city,
This to the Iraqis was truly a pity.
War ended and there was a lot less killing,
Soon there would be no blood for the spilling.

Mark Foster, Grade 8
St Thomas More Academy

Nature

It's fun running through a field of plains,
and flying a kite down the lane.
When you hear the ocean, the water calms you always.
Just like, when the trees would sway.
I love mother nature, and nature loves me.
It's like we're a happy family.

Joshua Gavin, Grade 9
Detroit City High School

How

How can I make him understand?
How can I make him see?
How can I make him realize?
How much he means to me!
Ashlyne Ball, Grade 8
Central Middle School

On the Battle Field

Here on the battle field
I run for saving grace
The chaos behind me
Has destroyed the town all through
I keep running
A Hawk with a machine gun
Ceases to stop
I keep running
There is no shelter here
So I keep on running
Louder and louder
The roar of the chopper is heard
And I keep running
My back starts to get warm
My sight in a blur
And I keep running
For the sake of my country
I keep running
Ryan Lawrence, Grade 8
St John Vianney Catholic School

A Football Player's Dream

A football player dreams
of becoming great.
He may join a team
that might achieve.

Players young and old
try to succeed
but some rarely ever achieve
their dream.

Some in college dream
of a National Title.
They work all summer
for a goal
that they may never know.

All in the Pro's
have one goal
to win the Super Bowl.

Goals are achieved
while goals are lost.
This is what makes
Football the best game of ALL.
C.J. Nightingale II, Grade 8
Mendon Middle/High School

Drop

The drop of water
Clings
To the cold metal.
But as more collects,
It loses strength
And falls.

The tear clings
To the damp eye.
But as more collect
Behind it,
The weary woman
Loses strength
And it falls.
Marie Bloem, Grade 8
Cutlerville Christian School

To My Grandfather

I will always remember you
And that beautiful smile
I wish that you were still here
Even for just a little while

But I know that you were suffering
So God has called you home
Please know that I will miss you
And that you surely aren't alone

My mama is with you
Your son Dennis too
Your mother and father
Just to name a few

May they watch over you
And the angels up above
So Papa please know
That you are surely loved.

Love your
Little Ree-Ree
Sharita Williams, Grade 7
Roseville Jr High School

Nothing

Nothing to write about,
Oh nothing to write.
My mind has gone blank,
So I have nothing to write.
If I had something to write
I'd write it right now.
Oh nothing to write,
Oh nothing at all.
This is the poem about nothing,
Nothing at all.
Scott Devine, Grade 7
West Middle School

Cold

Winter's icy breath envelopes me.
Rips my heart,
Freezes my tears.
Blue frost,
Covers my nose.
Fog chokes me.
I'm cold.
Mary Margaret Fessler, Grade 8
West Middle School

A Place Within Me

There's a place within me
A place I visit often.
Where I wonder only
If I could be someone
Else wondering what
It would be like.

There's a place within me
Where I can't be myself
Because I'm afraid
To let anyone else
Really see me
For whom I am.

There's a place within me
Where I begin to die
Very slowly, very painfully
They break me down
Every day, every moment
I pretend not to be me.
Jessica Millender, Grade 7
Gesu Elementary School

School

Too much to do
Getting bored doing work
Trying to stay awake
Keeping up with grades
Straining to study and not play
Focusing on paper and not thinking of 3 o'clock
Waiting for 8th hour to get over with
Ready to leave any time
Watching the clock constantly
Hurry clock hurry

School

Hanging with friends
Goofing off all day long
Having a great time
Waiting for hilarious jokes to come up
Relaxing while we can
Hoping the weekend is as good as this
Ready to come back any time
Watching the clock constantly
Stop clock stop
Nick Allen, Grade 7
Centreville Jr High School

Muddy Fun, Playful Run
Puppy
Cute, playful
Growling, sleeping, running
Bed, toys, mud, farm
Rolling, jumping, squealing
Ugly, noisy
Pig

Taylor DeBrot, Grade 7
Montague Nellie B Chisholm Middle School

Fluffy
Fluffy is my adorable cat
She tries to eat little rats

She looks like a big ball of hair
With all of the fur that she wears

She likes to run outside
She even likes to hide

But, I wouldn't trade her because she's like no other
And besides I am like her mother

On my couch is where she likes to sit
And it's my hand, which is sometimes bit

When she runs away it's me who's scared
But, she always comes back because she cares

It's her who is the spoiled one
Always likes to have fun

But, still I wouldn't trade her
And all of her Fluffy fur

Stephanie Shuman, Grade 7
Montague Nellie B Chisholm Middle School

Mail
I don't have a constant home,
I travel from here to there.
I have one lip to lick and stick,
and four pointy paper corners.
I can be first class, priority, or fragile,
Depending on what you fill me with.
On my left side is a stamp,
My decorative cheap passport.
On my right is where I am from,
In the middle is where I am going.
I fly a lot, but sometimes I ride,
Until I get where I am going.
I'm shoved in a damp, dark, and cold box.
And tore open the next morning,
My contents are read, and I am thrown away,
Never to travel again.

Hilary Edwards, Grade 8
Verona Mills School

Curiosity
Dearest passerby,
   hold your soul dearly
   lest you become weak and weary
   a warning written sincerely —
sincerely — to you — from I

Along this path dank and dark
where no person hath tread far
into its lonely regions
don't go into its dark legions

Wilt thou heed — thou visitor
you are a mere guest
let it manifest
that this path should not be disturbed
and all you crush — the flowers and grass
hear them whispering you won't be back?

Everything you never knew
will never get to you —
there's nothing left to do
that can save you —
from the abominable doom,
that you consumed

Josh Shrum, Grade 9
Roseville Jr High School

Passion
A complicated matter
unpredictable in part
may leave you speechless
planning for more
you may know it's wrong
but it feels so right
devastating you and rejuvenating you
at the same time
different every time
leaving you waiting for surprise
changing you every time
for good or bad you'll never know
it's addictive
watch out for your passion

Aqueelah Akbar, Grade 9
Cass Technical High School

What Is Love?
What is this thing called love? I do not know.
Involving foe or friend or both?
Unexpected or right in front of you.
Opposites or alike in every way.
Out of the blue, whispering, "I love you."
Together or apart, the love we share.
Old-fashioned lovers, you know me better.
Have I found love for you? I cannot tell.

Kathleen FitzGerald, Grade 8
Grosse Pointe Academy

If I Had a Time Machine

If I had a time machine
I could travel to lands unseen

I could look upon the Earth
As it was at its birth

I could see things never seen
By any other human being

But one thing I really fear
If I travel back through the years

I might run into Genghis Khan
Before he was dead before he was gone

Yes I think I would be frightened
Of that man of that tyrant

So I guess my time machine
Will have to stay a wonderful dream

Dave LaPonsie, Grade 8
St Anthony of Padua School

Would You

Would you laugh,
If I got burnt?

Or would you cry,
If I got hurt?

Would you love me,
If I loved you back?

Or would you hate me,
If I couldn't react?

Would you help me,
If I needed help?

Or would you leave me,
To sit and yelp?

Would you comfort me
If I needed to cry?

Or would you leave
And say good-bye?

Elizabeth Juncaj, Grade 7
Flynn Middle School

Nature

Trees swaying gently
Singing sweet melodies
Birds chirping in the sun

Molly Petersen, Grade 8
St Gerard Elementary School

Grief of Death

I saw a rose and thought of you.
I saw a raindrop and thought of you.
I saw an old paperback and thought of you.
I saw a dance and thought of you.
I saw a morning dove and thought of you.
I saw the stars and thought of you.
I saw a prayer and thought of you.
I saw a storm and thought of the day when you thought for the last time.

Hannah Lesniak, Grade 8
St William School

My Life Is Meaningless to Me

Every day isn't the best, worst doesn't even come close to its meaning.
My life is meaningless to me…
Every day is a day of torture, but no one cares…
You'd cry the tears of a thousand oceans, just to feel sick and dehydrated.
You feel a hug of another, just to think that someone cares.
You pray to God who is not there, just to feel that someone is listening.
My life is meaningless to me…
You feel trusted, then find out that they never trusted you.
You can never trust anyone, because no one will trust you.
My life is meaningless to me…
You fall in love, you put your heart on the line, and your life on pause.
Then get your heart broken into millions of pieces.
Then you're left all alone…scared…afraid of life…wishing someone was there…
but you're not trusted…you'd never trust…and no one cares…

Meagan Sayer, Grade 8
Basic Christian Education

Broken Picture

You're like a page in a book never knowing when your drama will end
I'm fighting for you but we lost it all
Stare into my eyes once more because now I'm full of hate
Forget the stupid love notes
So paint me a pretty picture, make it just you and me

One more heart break
Your smile makes me weak every time
I'll save the memories, I'll keep them close, close to my heart
Keep me away from the torment, take me back to the beach
So paint me a pretty picture, make it just you and me

Sitting on the floor I dream of your face that I almost had erased
I know the phone calls past one were breathtaking
I'll make my own love song and push it in your face
I see you every now and then things never felt so flawed
So paint me a pretty picture, make it just you and me

Love was never my thing, but you talked me into it
I remember when my heart was whole but that was before I met you
And times like these make me fall in love with you all over again
I'll cross out your name and only mine will remain
So paint me a pretty picture, make it just you and me

Alyse Lindley, Grade 9
Churchill High School

California Dreamin…

I'm dreamin of California,
   that's where I want to be;
      It has oceans, many fun things,
         and Yosemite.
            It has good temperatures
               and that satisfies me!
                  You can hike, rock climb,
                     and surf at the beach.
                       California is bright, sunny,
                         and doesn't really rain.
                           But for right now I will
                             stay dreamin in my bed.

Laura Douglas, Grade 7
Flynn Middle School

Before It's Too Late

Turning my head, what do I see?
Injustice, hate, and cruelty
Why has mankind darkened so?
Not trusting a soul, sunken so low
No care, no share of thought or love
Always superstitious of everything
Beneath and above
We must unite under God's light
Before it's too late
To change or better our fate
Then as the Day will befall upon us
No one shall forgive
For no one shall live
Mankind will die
Dark black, due to all the treason and lies
So love and unify under the One Almighty,
To dignify as a devoted mankind
Together let us love and bind
Let's come together, live and tether
Come before it's too late,
To change or better our fate.

Zainab Chaudhry, Grade 9
Crescent Academy International

True Friends

What is a true friend?

A companion.
Someone to laugh and cry with.
You can trust each other.
They're always there.
True friends always encourage you.
They take a place in your heart.
You tell them everything.
They care about everything you say.
You don't know what you'd do without them.

That is what a true friend is.

Lindsay Luzod, Grade 7
St John Lutheran School

Each Day

Each day is like a star,
It teaches you how to act from afar.

But if you think too far from you,
You will discover yourself surprisingly blue.

Each day is a morning dove,
Waking us from up above.

Each day gazes upon us,
Like the sun off a yellow school bus.

Each day is up to me,
It is there for all to see.

Derek Roe, Grade 8
St Anthony of Padua School

Ireland

There is this place I have been told,
Where streets are paved with shimmering gold.

The rolling hills of green are like the ocean,
If you were sick this site is your potion.

Fences made of stone embrace this land,
This is where St. Patrick used to stand.

There is no dance such as big,
As Ireland's own, the Irish Jig.

This land of Ireland, there is no clone,
Just go and kiss the Blarney Stone.

Riley McCartney, Grade 8
St Anthony of Padua School

Hockey

Hockey, hockey, it's so cool
You use your hockey stick like it's your only tool.
Skating really fast when the puck hits your stick,
You take a shot and it goes so quick.
You're about to score
And you can hear the crowd roar.
A big player comes ready to hit you makes you want to cry,
But you're skating so fast that you pass him right by.
Hockey, hockey it's the best sport ever.
It's the only sport that you do not have to be very clever.
The sport is a wild chase.
When you're skating really fast and suddenly stop,
The cool wind from the ice will blow right in your face.
When your hockey team is winning the game,
The other team just goes down in shame.
Hockey, hockey it's the best sport ever, I will never ever quit.
Nope, never not one little bit!

Jake Lemasters, Grade 7
Jefferson Middle School

Skateboard

Four inches above pain I fly.
Seven plies of maple, four wheels of urethane.
If any one of those were to falter, I would surely lose skin.
Complete trust is put into my board; for once I am on it, it is in me.
It morphs into an extension of my legs.
The only thing that can take me down now is reality.
Reality sinks its teeth into my mind, creating a wound that fills with doubt.
I'm not supposed to go this fast, I'm not supposed to keep my balance on this demon drop.
This mammoth of a mountain that seems to be growing around me with every thought I have.
My legs begin to shake
My boards leaves my body and becomes a foreign object underneath me, bucking wildly.
Wait! I force my legs to steady; I fight with everything I have to beat the reality out of my mind.
I'm winning this battle now.
My board once again becomes a part of me.
I crouch, increasing speed.
I must beat my senses, never letting them catch up.
I fly out of the cloud of doubt and worry.
The hill is now behind me, along with everything else.
I have won.

Brian Bazydlo, Grade 8
Beach Middle School

Prayer Changes Things

My favorite thing to do is pray, each and every day. When things aren't going my way; I pray.
Pray that tomorrow will be a better day. It's not hard to say that tomorrow is not promised today.
So even though it doesn't show doesn't mean I'm not going through, just like you.
Remember to pray for me. And I'll pray for you. Prayer inspires me to have a dream.
Do you believe? With prayer, you can achieve. I believe in the best. And with prayer I'll always have success.
No matter who tries to put me down or who tries to make me frown.
I will always have pride. And know that prayer makes me feel this way deep inside.
Yes prayer changes things. For people like your siblings.
And even you, especially when you're going through.
When you think there's no one there to talk to; pray. To thank God for this day.
Things are not always fair. And most of your closest friends won't be there.
But the person that will always love you in spite of what you do. Will never stop loving you.
Do you believe prayer changes things? Because when you pray for the wrong you'll always come out strong.
Just remember when I'm going through pray for me. And I'll pray for you.

Lorreal Jones, Grade 8
Hally Magnet Middle School

Seasons

Spring, everything comes alive and awakens. Flowers bloom and animals come out of their long sleep. The breeze then tickles the bare branches of unbloomed trees. The sun warms Mother Earth with her brilliant rays. Clouds as fluffy as a cotton ball and white as a cotton tail. Then a soft May shower comes to moisten the grass and give the thirsty plants a drink of fresh rainwater.
Summer, the time of fun and peace, to relax and lay back. The grass as green as green can be. The trees laugh as the warm breeze blows through their leaves. The sunflowers look so bright and happy as their leaves dance in the wind. The sky as blue as the deep blue sea. At night the crickets sing and chatter the evening away. The fireflies light up the night with a little spark. As the fire bounces and jumps with happiness and as bright as can be.
Fall, the air crisp with the smell of dried up leaves as they drift to the ground and land so gracefully on the dry ground. The sun still bright and warm, the sky still blue with wispy clouds floating away. As animals prepare for the harsh weather ahead, they gather food and find a place to relax, to have a wonderful sleep.
Winter, a cold, windy and white wonderland season. As the air grows colder and the wind gets brisk and snowflakes float to the frostbit ground. As the sun shines onto the freshly fallen snow it shimmers in happiness and equality. The clouds silver lined in royalty and importance.

Sondra Fleeman, Grade 9
Grayling High School

Her Smile

Her smile was as bright as the sun.
She was under the bright blue sky.
Money, she had none.
She got money from passersby.
Her smile was enchanting.
She stood up in front of a crowd.
The people kept on ranting.
Everyone there was wowed.
She smiles so sweetly.
She finally stopped smiling.
Everyone rustled around loudly.
But still, her smile was as bright as the sun.

Stefanie Mooney, Grade 8
Central Middle School

Spot

I have a dog named Spot
Spot to me means a lot
We always like to play together,
We don't care about the weather
Spot especially likes those days
When we both play around and act all crazed
Countless times Spot saved the day
With his cute brown eyes
Spot is the best dog I ever saw,
Especially when he sips through a plastic purple straw
You might be amazed at the things Spot can do
But I am sorry to tell you none of this is true
Even if a dog like Spot roamed the land
Nothing like this could ever be done by a man's best friend.

Jennifer Hurdelbrink, Grade 7
Mattawan Middle School

From the Heart

Dancing comes from the heart
An experience you can't lose sight of
It only takes a dream to start
I know I've grown to love

Once you start it's just like riding a bike
You never forget
Everything about it is just right
The dancing vision is in your head now let it set

Being a dancer isn't just fun
It's not a game it takes commitment
Moving so gracefully touching the sun
Being twisted and turned and bent

Dancing comes from the heart
An experience you can't lose sight of
It only takes a dream to start
A dream I've grown to love

Jennelle Stricklen, Grade 7
Hally Magnet Middle School

My Heart

My Heart is beating so hard
That if I see you I just smile.
People tell me you are here and there
I look at you and see that you do care!

Sometimes I doubt you in doing anything
All that changed when I became a teen!
My sister loves you but not as much as me
I didn't know but now I see.

You used to sit me on your lap and talk to me
I sit down and tell you what I want to be.
You give me anything I want and need
You see me growing like a flower seed!

I don't see that person leaving
I don't care for people seeing.
They're just mad because they ain't got what I got
He told me never to smoke pot.

How come people don't like you
All that matters is that I do.
They think that person is my friend
But you see that person is my daddy 'til the end!!!

Betty Williams, Grade 9
Southfield High School

Left Eye

Left eye you did your thang while on Earth
Now it's time to go be with God so just rejoice.

You was born a star and you know it
but God called you home now it's really time to show it.

You reached your goals while on Earth
but go with God and have new birth.

Torri Livingston, Grade 7
Hally Magnet Middle School

The Rocking Chair

The girl sits and rocks in her rocking chair
day after day
She has no place to call home
The girl feels alone
She seems unhappy
Her hair is long and nappy
Her clothes are torn
Her heart is scorn
She has no shoes
This girl never moves
You want to help her
It's hard to resist
But you can't help her
Because she doesn't exist

Taylor Robinson, Grade 7
Hally Magnet Middle School

Friday

It's finally Friday, oh what a long week,
The weekend is for a lot more sleep.
I can't wait for the dance,
I'm in such a trance.
I'm so glad it's Friday,
Today is going my way,
Only two more hours,
And then a few fun hours.

Jenson Phillips, Grade 7
West Middle School

Used To

We used to be friends
We used to have fun
We used to be inseparable

We used to joke around
But soon it got outta hand
You made me hurt,
You made me cry.

It used to be fun 'n games
But now it's the end.
I put my trust in you,
But you threw it away.

I can't go on never knowing,
When you'll attack
First you're my friend, now you're not.
You don't know when to stop,
You just go on.

You don't understand,
It's not fun 'n games no more,
It's all used to.

Kelsey Green, Grade 7
Ruth Murdoch SDA Elementary School

School

You say it's a waste of
your time.
It might seem that way
right now,
but when
you reach college
you'll sure have some knowledge.
Now, maybe you think it was there
for a reason.
That reason is what you make it.
You could be a fool
or someone who
stays in
school.
Your choice?

Alex Stair, Grade 8
St John Vianney Catholic School

Faces

I've got no face beneath the mask
It started to melt off just yesteryear
But if I was to Search in a toy box,
Or my old drawers,
There it may lie in pieces;
An eye here,
An ear there,
And skin everywhere

But how do you go about reattaching a face?
With glue?
With tape?
No you would look like a freak show.

But how would reattach a face?
Do you throw on new pieces and hope they stick?
Do you take the old ones and warm them 'till they melt back on?
Or is it purely gone forever lost in a hall of drunken mirrors
An eye here,
An ear there,
And skin everywhere.

Stephany Sheppard, Grade 9
Portage Central High School

The Enemy

When we couldn't take out the one of their scouts we
Knew they would be here without a doubt,
When our lookout saw them she gave a shout,
For their numbers were so large she could not count,
They are like a disease for it's hard to make them go away,
Why are they here you might say, they're here for our food packed or thrown away,
Yes these are not soldiers though they march in line,
But ants who think our food is prime,
But soon they will learn it's time to leave.
Because Raid is our friend and a trusty one indeed,
For without it we would be the ones who would have to leave.

Clifford Allen, Grade 8
Ruth Murdoch SDA Elementary School

Coal Mining

Whose body is under there,
Sitting beneath the coal filled air,
Waiting to be rescued from this horrible nightmare.
Some have risen above the sky
While others sit and wonder why,
Why did this happen to them and all their coal mining friends?
They were just on a regular run when all of a sudden
All the laughter and fun slipped away and is still not back.
Twelve went down one alive wondering why he was the one not to die.
He feels the guilt deep inside and all the anger to arise,
When he finally hears a noise, a very gentle voice,
Saying we will be down to get you soon,
And so that is how the story goes
And all the pain and sorrow grows.

Lauren Miller, Grade 7
Columbia Middle School

Laura W. Bush

Laura W. Bush was born in November.
A lot of people admire her.
She was an only child.
When it came to learning she was self-styled.

At seventeen, Laura stole her mommy's car.
She did not take it far.
Laura's religion is Methodist.
She went to church and rarely missed.

She went back to school and became a librarian.
That was when her love of books began.
She became active in fundraisers.
Her husband is the United States master.

She married George W. Bush on Nov. 5, 1977.
She thought he was the best of men.
Her husband was really outgoing.
He told really good jokes; he was easygoing.

Laura had a set of twins.
When she saw those girls, she had a really good grin.
Laura decided to devote the East Wing Salon to poetry.
She was a well read celebrity.

Chelsey Christie, Grade 7
Lakeview Middle School

A King's Dream

Words cannot explain
the life and legacy of Dr. King,
of his dream, which reached peaks
no one imagined could be seen.
His powerful words of peace, equality, and freedom
brought light to the eyes of
those who could not see them.
A dream that gave us the hope,
and the strength to continue
and for this,
we will never forget you.

Long live the King,
Long live the Dream.

Makau O. Bell Jr., Grade 7
Gesu Elementary School

God

Roses are red violets are blue
God loves me and He loves you too.
If you read the Bible you'll change your life,
when it comes to a crime you won't have to use a knife.
If you go to church God would think that was very nice.
If you still listen to secular rap you need to give your life up
and throw your hands up and worship him
and don't go around tryin' to be like the rest of them.

DeShon Catchings, Grade 8
Erma Henderson Upper Campus

Fortitude

The Commander stood calm and sure-footed,
His decision already deep-rooted,
He looked across the gore-strewn field;
He said to his soldiers, "We cannot yield.
With approval or not our fates are sealed.
Tomorrow our bodies will be entombed in earth,
But Gentlemen, on this day we prove our worth."
And obediently they charged ahead,
All accepting of their morbid fate;
Not a single word was said,
As they charged ahead at a furious rate.
Alas, by noon each man was dead.
Heroes despite their lethal plight,
Embodied fortitude as they charged to fight.

Tim LeBlanc, Grade 9
St Thomas More Academy

Unforgiven

The apology of unfaulted things
The pain, how it stings
Like a ship, it sinks into my heart
These things, why won't they break apart?
His whispered words gently leave his lips
When his pride violently rips
Unnecessity of purpose
Sympathy to surface

Unfaulted they are
And yet so important
Scoldings of disgrace
He is ashamed to face
Blinded from their wrong
Now listen to his song
To the edge he was driven
They, forever, will be unforgiven

Tammy Leung, Grade 9
Troy High School

Spring

When it starts to rain most of the days
Plants and flowers start to grow
Spring is coming on its way
Beautiful scent start surrounding your nose
Bees come out and buzz around
Birds come too and sing sweet songs
During spring, you hear sweet sounds
You just want to hear no matter how long
The cool mist blows across the air
And blows through leaves and beautiful flowers
During the spring, you feel them everywhere
And the sun shines so bright through the hours
Big fluffy clouds float in the sky
As birds fly through them up so high

Hanna Chehab, Grade 7
Flynn Middle School

Savior

Long ago and far away
there was a special place.
A special place where born that day,
a boy with a little face.

This little boy was just a baby,
whose name had been Jesus.
Many people had said, "Maybe,
He has come to please us."

As Jesus grew and grew and grew,
He began to preach and teach.
As He was preaching, people knew
Jesus was good at speech.

No one knew what Jesus would do,
or that He came to save us.
I'm thankful. Are you?
So I say, "Thank you, Jesus."

Erin Martin, Grade 7
St Ann Elementary School

War

Soldiers running for their lives
Guns shooting off
Bullets killing
People dying for their country
Armies fighting over stupid things
Peace seems impossible
War always comes back

Tim Tippett, Grade 8
Central Middle School

Love

Love is a force
You cannot control.
Love is a flame
That burns within you.
Love is the binding
That keeps the world together.
Love is a quest
You can take.
Love is affection
That comes from the heart.
Love is destiny
You must fulfill.
Love is lost.
You must find it.
Love is a feeling
That can make you uneasy.
Love is beautiful;
It must be admired.
Love is a dream;
It will take you away.

Bhavdeep Singh, Grade 8
Boulan Park Middle School

Summer

It's a great feeling when you're at the beach
sandals off, toes in the sand
the people around you screaming and yelling
splashing the cold water on your feet
the coldness of the water sends a chill down your spine
then the waves start coming, then they drift away slowly
the sun beaming down on the boats makes the sand warm and gives it a glow
just then a gust of wind blows your mouth wide open
as you yawn you get the taste of the sea water in your mouth
what a taste, all salty and blue

Jordyn Cantlin, Grade 8
North Rockford Middle School

The Seasons

As the seasons turn 'round and 'round a brand new season is found.
Summer, fall, winter, and spring virtues of its own, each season brings.
The seasons are turning 'round and 'round summer is the first one found.
With summer comes pools and lakes it's amazing how much energy fun takes.
The seasons are turning 'round and 'round fall is the next season found.
With fall comes leaves, and Thanksgiving we give thanks for all that is living.
The seasons are turning 'round and 'round winter is another found.
With winter comes white, fluffy snow where it all comes from, I do not know.
The seasons are turning 'round and 'round spring is the last one found.
With spring comes flowers and rain all of this beauty, I cannot complain.
The seasons turn again and again the cycle will never end my friend.

Rachel Schumacher, Grade 8
St Gerard Elementary School

Lady in Distress

Dishonor is what she felt.
And disrespect is what made her heart melt.
Distrust in God is what she could feel,
Disgrace is what she felt for not doing His will.
Distress and discontent is what made her bitter.
She disregarded and disagreed with everyone who came near her.
Taking care of herself she did discontinue.
She was displeased with everything and there was nothing she could do.
But then she realized she was never dispelled from God's grace.
So she got her house in order, was dispelled from Earth, and went on to see His face.

T'Arica Crawford, Grade 7
Hally Magnet Middle School

I Wish

I wish you were here to guide me on my way.
I wish you were here to walk me down the aisle.
I wish that we could have spent more time together.
I wish we would have never fought.
I wish you could be here for my graduation day.
I wish you would have made better choices in your life.
I wish you were here to ground me.
I wish you could be here to become a grandparent.
I wish I wish I wish
Most of all I wish that I would have said I love you at least one more time.

Paige Cousins, Grade 9
Posen Consolidated High School

The Story of Sam and Jan

There once was a man named Sam,
He loved to eat Spam.
He loved that it came from cans,
Sam always scooped it out with his hands.
Sam only liked name brand,
Not that nasty generic ham.
Now Sam had a wife named Jan.
She very much hated Spam.
Every night when Same came home with a can,
She would snatch it right from his hands.
That is the story of Sam and Jan.
I couldn't tell you more about Spam,
Because I've run out of rhymes.

Glenn Hoyer, Grade 7
Grand Blanc Middle School

Finding a Pet

First we need eyes
Some warm, loving eyes
Then we need a pinch of playfulness
An always-ready playfulness
Next add some loyalty
An unbreakable loyalty
Add some good times
With a bit of frustration
Mix and blend until even
This will become a loving pet
To any person lucky enough to own him/her
This is a recipe for man's best friend

Kyle Wicklund, Grade 8
Central Middle School

The Holocaust

In the year 1942
Was the year of the death of Jews
They were sent to camps
Where there were insects and ants
Jews were beaten
Jews were starved
Jews ran around without scarves!
The Nazis were mad
And evil, too
The Jews didn't know what to do
Sometimes in the big, blue sky
There was smoke a mile high!
Nazis burned Jews
And Greeks, too
Until Hitler's rule ended
Followed by the war
Now the Jews are free
And Hitler is gone
But the time will be remembered
As the Holocaust

Kaitlin Bedra, Grade 7
Jefferson Middle School

The Seasons

There are four seasons altogether
With good and bad types of weather

Spring brings life to all plants
Also to those awful things called ants

Birds fly in from the south
Teeth are shown from the bears yawning mouth

The warmth from summer comes after
With children swimming and all their laughter

To fun zoos, parks, and beaches
While eating all sorts of fruit like peaches

It starts to get cold after all
For it is now time for fall

Beautiful colors paint everything around
Orange, red, and brown leaves abound

Frosty winter comes bringing white snow
But it is not all bad you know

With snowball fights
And longer nights

Wonderful seasons I cry
Looking up at the always blue sky

Stephanie Kotschevar, Grade 7
Centreville Jr High School

Who Am I?

Who am I?
I am sadness, rage, and glee.
I am climbing up a tree.
I am active and outside.
And my homework, well…I tried.
I am acing my hardest test.
I am trying to do my best.
I am peace, grace, and power.
I am singing in the shower.
I am broad horizons and greatly weighed down with change.
I work hard to reach my goals that are out of range.
Sometimes I'm afraid to take the next step,
But this is usually personally kept.
I am a smile in the morning and a grin at night.
I am not perfect, but I want to be right.
I am full of troubles, questions, and fears.
I am not ashamed to shed some tears.
People expect me to stay the same way,
But I can't help it; I change every day.
I am trying so hard to be
The person that's expected of me.

Devon Velding, Grade 8
St Anthony of Padua School

The Bird

One day I awoke to see,
A large bird flying free.

Who was flapping gently against a cool spring breeze,
Flying swiftly amongst the trees.

Slowly gliding as a kite
This was truly a glorious sight.

What a gift to get to gaze,
Upon this bird in its prime days.

Staring at it in the sky.
Oh, how, I wish I could fly!

Josh Laske, Grade 7
St Anthony of Padua School

You and I Are Best Friends

I am very self confident
I am also very extravagant
I am very friendly
And always be there true and respectfully
When you need someone to count on
I will be there until the pain is gone
We can be very trustworthy
When we need help we can be there definitely
I know you are not going anywhere
'Cause you said you will always be there
And I always knew you would
We will always be friends and it is all good
13 years we've been around
13 years we've been down
Through the elevations of life
We've never had a fight
We have been together from the start
And I love you with all my heart
We have seen the thick and thin
And now we know we are BEST FRIENDS to the end!!!

DeJenae Love, Grade 7
Hally Magnet Middle School

Getting Your Brother Mad

First blast your music
And sing very loud and make sure he can hear you
Next use some smelly body spray
That he does not like
After that leave things in his way
So he has to go around it or pick it up
Add some more singing and turn your music up even louder
Mix them all up really, really well
Make sure you do them in different orders every time
And last purposely forget to tell him who called to talk to him
Remember you do it because you love him so much

Emily Casanova, Grade 8
Central Middle School

1st Street Beach

Crashing and splashing go the waves
The lifeguard is running
Kids are diving, no plopping into the water
Dogs are barking
People are screaming to the dogs, "Go home!"
Seagulls are flying and shrieking in the air
I must go because the sun is going down

Zak Payne, Grade 7
Manistee Middle School

How to Make a Taco

My favorite kind of food is a taco.
If you touch mine I'll give you a sock-o.
How you make it is fairly easy.
Start with a tortilla and make it cheesy.
Then you add the beans and the meat.
This may take a while better have a seat.
This next step makes the taco taste like a dream.
Smother the taco in sour cream.
After that add my favorite vegetables.
Lettuce and tomato put color on all tables.
Last but not least, no need to scoff.
Add a packet of your favorite taco sauce.
That my dear friends
Is how this recipe ends.
Now go eat,
I'll leave you with this final farewell: bon appetite!

Jordan Barr, Grade 8
MacDonald Middle School

February's Frost

The trees freeze in February…
The ice melts during spring,
Flowers bloom beautifully…
While slowly comes the rain.

The summer sun dries up the puddles…
And out come the lemonade stands.
While all the thirsty people say,
"That was a quarter well spent."

The trees change colors
Yellow, orange, and red
Now the leaves are on the ground,
Instead of overhead.

Sweaters are pulled out from closets
And coats are worn every day.
It's starting to get chilly,
Kids await the month of May.

The 1st snow of the season falls in December…
Ice covers everything the month after,
And soon the trees will freeze in February.

Nichole Kulhanek, Grade 9
Airport Sr High School

Love Spell

Can't eat,
can't sleep,
all I can do,
is think about you.
Why me, what's wrong?
Do I really love you
or is it just another feeling
catching me and holding tightly?
Let me go, let me go, quit holding me so tightly,
please remove your LOVE SPELL from me.

Tyler Tosto, Grade 8
L'anse Creuse Middle School East

Fear Is in Your Mind

Fear is in your mind
And in time it will incline.
All you need to do is say,
All fears will go away.
And you realize that you fear,
Something that is nothing to fear.
Darkness, spiders even wasps' nest
Unless you're allergic,
Then you have nothing to fear of it.
All you have to say,
Is that all fears will go away.
And if you fear zombies, werewolves, and vampires
All you have to do is realize,
That they would have already gotten you,
Before your very eyes.
All you have to say,
Is that all fears will go away.
And soon you will realize what you fear does not exist,
Or it is ridiculous

Michael Blouse, Grade 9
Roseville Jr High School

Where Have All the Piggyback Rides Gone To?

Where have all the piggyback rides gone to?
They are gone, along with the memories
It seems like my childhood is out of view
As I take on responsibility

Gone are the action figures and the dolls
No longer does everyone hold my hand
I've learned to pick myself up when I fall
I'm growing mature and taking a stand

So long temper tantrums and grumpy pouts
I'm expected to take in the whole truth
And though I may sometimes fall into doubt
I must realize I've passed out of the youth

Time goes by quickly and changes occur
We learn to grow up and become mature

Rachael Kutschman, Grade 8
St John Lutheran School

Championship Tennis Match

Playing competitive tennis is fun,
And tension is a major component.
It is the reason rivalries begun,
Between one player and his opponent.

The tiebreaker of the State Title match:
I really want to win; I'm playing well.
I need to find a play that will unlatch,
And then the victory will be so swell.

Now it's 8-8, both two points from the win,
I hit an overhead right down the line.
The final excitement will now begin.
I know this last point will surely be mine!

It's an ace up the middle and I won!
My opponent is finally outdone!

Patrick Cole, Grade 8
Dearborn Heights Montessori Center

Football

As we pray in the locker room,
Everyone is ready to take on the other team,
As we win the toss we choose to receive,
Patrick runs the kick back to the 50 yd. line,
Our offense starts out,
Kevin snaps it to Spencer,
Spencer hands off to Ryan,
As he breaks through the line we block,
He keeps running until he makes it as far as possible,
Then we set up to do it all again.

Luke Milne, Grade 8
St John Vianney Catholic School

Family

People who love and care about you
Even if they're mad at you
That's family

People who will put down everything and help you
Even if that means stopping everything they're doing
That's family

People who will stay home with you even when you're sick
While all your friends are hanging out
That's family

People who stay by your side
Through thick and thin
That's family

People who will always be there for you
If that's not family, I don't know what is!

Brianna Blackmon, Grade 7
Jefferson Middle School

Skater

Hockey player
Tough, serious
Tripping, skating, concentrating
Stick, net, toe-pick dress
Turning, jumping, ice chipping
Dig, twirl
Figure skater
Ashley Tompkins, Grade 8
Central Middle School

Just Wondering

I want to walk up and say,
"Why do you treat us this way?"

I wish I were brave enough,
But I'm actually not that tough.

So I just stay away.
Andrea Hale, Grade 8
Portage Central Middle School

Summer

No sleet or snow
No cold or ice
Just a warm wind that blows
On a day that's nice
Kayla Lockwood, Grade 7
Camden Frontier Middle School

Broken Window

The day was frigid, bright
with a brilliant sun shining
through the broken window
of the old abandoned barn,
mice scurrying silently
under the broken table
into the strip of sunlight.
Conrad Blom, Grade 8
Cutlerville Christian School

Summer

Leaves cross the yard
The clouds are filling the sky
There are baseball games going on
Kids jumping in a pool
Like a lion pouncing on a deer
The grass is fresh
The birds are chirping
Along with the frogs creaking
The lawnmower is running
The animals scattering fast and strong
People are laughing
Children are playing
What a day
Nick McClure, Grade 7
Addison Middle School

I'll Never Forget…

I'll never forget that day when you first came into our home
I don't ever want to forget that day when your smile was like a pot of gold
You were just very tiny, but in a way you were big
It seemed like you could do anything, not even I could

I won't ever forget how it feels to be this happy
People would smile as they walked down the street
You were so little, but I can't say you were neat!

You are like my rainbow and I am like your gold,
You are my medicine when I have a cold,
You are like a hero, many times you've saved the day,
You are my sunshine on a cloudy day

I know this sounds silly to say this about my dogs
But I'll never forget when they entered my world
Bringing happiness to my family, and surely to my life!
Jessica Hurdelbrink, Grade 7
Mattawan Middle School

I Love Being a Kid

Those were the days when our own worries were when
Recess was too short and bullies would ruin tree forts.
Boys had cooties and girls had no booties.
Getting love letters with your tummy feeling light as a feather.
Scared to step on a crack cause you didn't want to break your mother's back.
But now we're getting older and carrying folders to a new class every day.
I'll be getting older in May, because it's my birthday.
Girls will have boyfriends and lov'em to the end.
When we were little play time was all we did. Don't cha love being a kid?
Amanda Zaborowski, Grade 7
West Middle School

Will You Remember Me?

Great Grandma…
As nice as feathers on a cozy bed
Who asks, "How are you?"
With a sweet smile
Who cares about her family and friends so much
She cooks food for the holidays and comes to visit
Enjoys orange juice, coffee and water
Who smells like a bouquet of roses
And tastes sweet as sugar
She is a mountain of joy
She tells me, "I love you!"
Whose softest voice sounds like the inside of a seashell
Who is the best cook in the world
Whose chocolate chip cookies melt in my mouth
She can't make chocolate chip cookies anymore
She can't race me around the block
I would talk to her, spend time with her and sit with her at dinner
And she is now watching over me
I was so sad when she passed away
Asking "Will you remember me?"

Zach Paul, Grade 8
Hillel Day School

Family

Sometimes I feel like breaking down
Because no one ever hears a sound!
They make me feel like I am hurt
Because they treat me like I am dirt
I think my family hates me
They always scream and yell
When my family yells it hurts
They make me feel unwell
I try everything I do
I try my very best
But it really hurts to know
They think I'm a speck of dust
I guess I'll just give up now
Nothing's ever good
Living with my family is worse than living in the hood
I love my mom
I love my dad
And everybody else
But it hurts so much inside
To hear them scream and yell
Tarah Oisten, Grade 9
Allegan High School

Just Because

Just because I'm gone
    Doesn't mean that I will forget you
    Doesn't mean that I don't still love you
    Still talk to me because I might answer
Just because I'm gone
    Doesn't mean that I'm still not looking over your shoulder
    Doesn't mean that I still won't pray for you
    Still think of our good memories because I miss you
Just because I'm gone
    Doesn't mean that you're still not my best friend
    It doesn't mean that we won't see each other again
Just because I'm gone — you'll live without me
Nicole Travarthen, Grade 8
Central Middle School

Don't Make Fun of Me

Don't make fun of me
Just because I wear glasses
Don't laugh at me
Don't call me names like four eyes
Don't be my friend
Just because I wear glasses
Doesn't make me a nerd
Doesn't mean you can make fun of me
I can still do what others do
Just because I wear glasses
I can't always be the best friend
They don't stop me from having fun
Just because I wear glasses — don't pick on me
Curtis Walls, Grade 8
St John Lutheran School

Grinning

Smile
Sparkle, bright
Laughing, whitening, shining
Teeth, dimples, sad, mad
Upsetting, depressing, frustrating
Upside down, pout
Frown
Zabrina Gonzalez, Grade 7
Montague Nellie B Chisholm Middle School

The Lone Girl

Her hair is silk
Her skin is snow
As she walks by people stare
She has nothing to give or share

She lives in an abandoned house
Her only friend is her pet mouse
Her time had ended in the cold winter's snow
No one knew why she was alone
Ashton Pawlowski, Grade 7
Montague Nellie B Chisholm Middle School

Winter Today

Yesterday it snowed, it's already melting
Go outside and play, before it's all gone

Shovel the driveway, before parents get home
Then go to your friend's house, and have some fun

The grass is showing, you don't want to think about it
A spell of heat, left over from fall

Cold at the bus stop, but warm after school
Turning down the thermostat, not so cold anymore

No snowmen or snow forts, in front of the houses
The snow is too dry, it won't pack at all

A nasty wet winter, so warm and sunny
Now you just wish, that spring season will come
Josh Winkelmann, Grade 8
North Rockford Middle School

Thanksgiving

I sat there looking around the table
And all my relatives are telling fables
We've got the kids playing and getting along
I'm happy that everyone is so strong
We laugh, sing, play, pray, and cry
And no one is shy
But the most important thing is that we're here together
On this wonderful day called Thanksgiving
And that we give thanks for what we have
Emma Tchamba, Grade 8
Ruth Murdoch SDA Elementary School

Thanksgiving

Thanksgiving is a time where you give thanks for everything that has happened throughout the year.
It's a time where you sit back, watch football and have a vegetarian beer.

Thanksgiving is a time where you feast and entertain.
It's a time where you do not leave your domain.

It's a time where you don't want to watch anyone touching your food.
Or else you'll yell out dude, you're rude! I'm not in the mood.

Last but not least, Thanksgiving is a time where you can play charades.
And carefully hide the way you tell your parents your bad grades.

Johnathan DeAugust, Grade 8
Ruth Murdoch SDA Elementary School

I Watched You Closely

I watched you from the day you were born, you were so cute and cuddly.
I watched you when you were young, you were so footloose and fancy-free.
I watched you as you grew into a teenager, you were so young and in love.
I watched you as you turned the big twenty-one, you were as careful as I noticed from above.
I watched you as you put out all those fires, you were as brave as can be.
I watched you closely and tried to keep up with you, you were way too fast for me.
I watched you as you searched for the love of your life, you soon met your future soulmate.
I watched as you tried to get her to notice you, you then went on your first date.
I watched you as you so bravely proposed, you were so jovial when she said yes.
I watched you as you made wedding plans, you ordered the tux and the dress.
I watched you as you walked down the aisle, you two were soon united as one.
I watched you as you kissed your beautiful bride, you then danced until the day was done.
Now watch me, the Lord; take my first break since the seventh day of creation,
You are now hers to have and to hold.
She will watch you forever, or at least until she needs a break too.

Elizabeth Warriner, Grade 8
St Gerard Elementary School

Frances Folsom Cleveland

Frances Folsom Cleveland was born in Buffalo. And into a fine young lady she would grow.
She was an only child and she was self-styled.

Grover Cleveland was administrator of her father's estate. She thought he was great.
Cleveland had been her father's partner. To her family he was not a stranger.

Their affection turned into romance. When she fell under Grover's trance.
She married President Cleveland in 1886. And she entered into the politics.

She was the youngest first lady in the nation's history. And her beauty was a certainty.
He was the first president that was married in the White House. And very proud of his beautiful spouse.

In 1888 the Clevelands left the White House after four years. They'd be back to Frances it was clear.
But they were back; in four years. By the public they were loved even greater.

They had five children. But Frances was still very feminine.
Cleveland died in 1908. Their life together had been great.

She remarried in 1913 to Professor Thomas Preston Jr. He was a friend who was a college professor.
She died in 1947 and she was buried next to Cleveland. Their life together had been grand.

Cullin Burns, Grade 7
Lakeview Middle School

Life the Desert

Life is the desert of love and pain
Every grain of sand is not the same
When you learn this, you begin to feel, from your head
To your heel, the heels of your shoes are the pain and love
That makes every grain of sand not the same

Charles W. Fritts, Grade 7
Hally Magnet Middle School

It

It lives in frustration
It lives in sorrow
It lives in dread
It lives in fear
It lives in torment
It lives in anger
It lives in hate
But through all this
It has a savior
Who helps it out
When it is down
He guides it from violence
When emotions take over
He brings back the peace and joy,
Fun and happiness
They even each other out to make things seem normal
But underneath it all things are sad for it
Sometimes I think I am like it

Josh Cornwell, Grade 9
Roseville Jr High School

Due-Day

'Twas the night before Due-Day and all through the house,
NCIS on at eight with my dad quiet as a mouse,
My dad was quiet quite out of care,
In hopes that this poem soon would be there,
When all of the sudden I had an idea,
To write about writing it, would that get me there?

Nine rolls around,
Hurray! I'm almost there,
Close to being done,
Oh sweet, sweet despair.

I glanced at our tree
Standing tall right there,
I looked at the ornaments,
My favorite one wasn't there.

It's a horse in a beautiful glass bell,
I saw many ornaments with little glass bells
I can't find my favorite, oh what will I do?
I looked again and there it was,
I found it, I can write,
So Merry Christmas to all and to all a good night.

Katie Garlinghouse, Grade 7
Sault Area Middle School

Willow Tree

The old willow tree was born from the seed
The seed that was planted for one's good deed
A very, very long time ago,
The great seed was buried in the light, deep snow
Through the weather, snow and the ice
The willow tree grew to be very nice
The little tree grew strong and tall
Making a natural home for all
The roots extended far, far beyond doubt
By clipping, snipping the branches about,
Caring people helped the tree out

The meek willow tree has now grown old
So many memories that cannot be told
The tree shall continue to grow older than old
Offering its leaves and all of its gold

Samantha Bondy, Grade 7
Columbia Middle School

War

Shouting, roaring, wailing, and crying
Needless killing and destruction.

Tongues of fire and deafening booms
Cities reduced to rubble.
Consuming, devouring,
Destroying all in its path:
People, crops, buildings, and lives.

Tearing families apart,
Breeding discrimination and fear.
Claiming to bring peace, but bringing nothing.

Profits from pain,
Sectarian fighters
Destroying their past.

Soldiers torturing,
Spreading propaganda and lies.
Corrupt leaders paying their country's destroyers,
Sponsoring genocide and hate:
WAR

Steven Simpkins, Grade 7
Grand Blanc Middle School

The Wonderful Spaghetti Pizza Combo

Spaghetti
Long, thin
Stringing, eating, dining
Meatballs, noodle, pepperoni, crust
Slicing, boxing, sharing
Cheesy, hot
Pizza

David Heykoop, Grade 7
Montague Nellie B Chisholm Middle School

Friends

Friends
Trustworthy, cool
Assist, guardianship, cherish
There for you
Friends
Jordan Allen, Grade 7
St Anthony of Padua School

Flight

Whoosh, snap!
Wings flapping,
A branch snapping.
Higher!
Higher!
The elegant bird takes off into the skies.
Flap!
Flap!
Flap!
Feathers flying,
Floating,
And flashing.
Even higher yet the graceful bird,
Is now but a dot in the sky.
It sees a target,
A tree,
A branch,
And just like that,
Silence again.
Travis DeWall, Grade 7
Hudsonville Christian Middle School

August 9th

Eight, Nine,
I'll never forget.
The only day I will ever regret.
I never said goodbye,
Never told you how I feel.
The day I lost you
Felt unreal.
Hearing the songs
And seeing people with their sisters
Makes me long for you again.
I'll never forget the day you went away.
Everyone says to stay strong,
But you are not here,
And they don't know how it feels.
Everything seems to be wrong.
I'll never forget you.
You are simply the best.
I'll forever be your little sister,
Forever your biggest fan,
Forever missing you,
Until we meet again.
Scarlet Urbin, Grade 9
Eppler Jr High School

Love

What does love mean to you?
Love is a strong feeling toward someone
Love of a crush or a friend
The love of a relative or place love of an animal

The love of a crush
A crush is when you admire him
A crush is when you look over at him
He smiles at you and you smile back you get chills up your spine

When you gently push him and he gently pushes you back
When you are walking and you are side by side shoulder to shoulder
When talks in a warm voice to only you and no one else

When you say you are mad at him but you really aren't
When you joke around and he doesn't take you seriously
When you give him a hug at the end of the day
And you just want to stay in his warm inviting arms

The love of many things
Love of something, place, relative, and a crush
Love of an animal or something you look up to
The love of many things helps you in life
Love many things as they love you
Kassie Lint, Grade 8
Richardson Elementary Middle School

Winter Storm

Rolling, growling gray cloud
Hungry for befuddled minds and timorous souls.
Silver droplets of blood pour from the monstrous beast
As he searches for a place to strike.

Anger strikes; the beast's strong arms chuck clear pellets of glass.
Laughing villainously as he strikes with his burning ropes of fire.
Dreadful, danger, destruction.
Screaming at every whip of his rope.

Lights of the world go out, mourning souls seek refuge,
As the beast devours them with one gulp.
He gets what he came for; he is satisfied,
Enough to cease his anger.

The frightening pellets of glass turn into light, fluffy crystals.
Gray skies turn into serene blue.
White cotton balls scattered every so often.
Turning the dark soil that once scattered the land into a blanket of glittering stars.

The sparkling crystals float gently into a piece of art,
Caramelizing arms of the mighty statues of the forest with glittering sugar.
Flying spirits come out of hiding and feed again on the blossoms of the needle statues.
Serene surroundings for now.

Ally Scheidel, Grade 7
Assumption BVM School

Quidditch

The sport of wizards, I've been told.
The sport where seekers catch a ball of gold.
The three chasers pass the quaffle to each other.
And the beaters they bat at the bludgers.
The ball of gold, a snitch it's called.
The bludgers make sure the chasers are stalled.
The quaffle is used to score the goals.
They score goals not in nets, but into holes.
Holes guarded by the keeper fifty feet high.
So the players fly high way up in the sky.
When the seeker catches the snitch
One hundered-fifty points he scores.
Therefore when watching Quidditch
You are never bored.

April Surinck, Grade 9
Roseville Jr High School

My Thoughts

My thought are ambitious,
My thoughts are wild and crazy,
My thoughts are sweet,
My thoughts are rude and crude,
My thoughts are happy,
My thoughts are sad and bitter,
My thoughts are beautiful and ugly,
My thoughts are peaceful,
My thoughts are loud and harsh,
My thoughts scare me,
My thoughts excite me,
My thoughts thrill me,
My thoughts are heartbreaking,
My thoughts are cold and deep,
My thoughts are personal,
My thoughts are special,
My thoughts are angry and disappointing,
My thoughts are what I am,
My thoughts are my own.

Alyssa Hendrick, Grade 7
Oakland Christian School

Paintball Gun

All week long I sit and wait
For my owner to take me to the course
Where we play every Sunday
My two best friends the hopper and tank
I am awoken and my red eye turns on
I am ready to defeat and win
Paint running out of my barrel at 264 fps
Balls coming out at 17 bps
Running I know it I see my next victim
Before I know it I have shot and he yells, "Out."
I am a paintball gun
This is my life

Paul Swedenborg, Grade 7
Manistee Middle School

I Remember

I remember the sandy beaches
    Swarming out in front of me

I remember the hot sand
    Under my feet as I ran to the water

I remember the sparkling, cool blue water
    Splashing onto the shore

I remember taking my first dive
    Into the freezing, deep blue water

I remember splashing around
    Until I could take the cold no longer

I remember floating on my back
    Happy as could be

I remember getting yelled at
    Because I was out too far

I remember the hot sun beating down on me
    As I laid on shore

Darci Wood, Grade 7
Manistee Middle School

Vehicles

Car
Blue, fast
Stopping, cleaning, racing
Engine, exhaust, transmission, horn
Crashing, speeding, turning
Slow, big
Truck

Victoria Swift, Grade 7
Montague Nellie B Chisholm Middle School

Cable

Cable, it's a wonderful thing,
It's even better than a diamond ring.
Hundreds of channels
With hundreds of stars,
It can reach from Earth to Mars
Never ending
Sights and sounds
That flows through all
Cities and towns.
So much to watch
It is very top notch.
There are so many things to choose from,
Sports, music, and more
I only wish I had it
So I can watch more than
Channels 2, 7, and 4.

Faith Trotter, Grade 8
Gesu Elementary School

The Tears I Cry

The world is running,
always in motion.
Let is stop!
For it weakens me.
I can weep the deep blue.
I can fall into darkness,
feel lost for all eternity.
Oh please, stop your running.
Miniature I might be today,
but tomorrow a mere memory.
If only the world would stay still.

Crystal Ajja, Grade 7
Flynn Middle School

This Night I Chose

My legs are crossed, my eyes are closed,
Thinking about this night I chose.
I empty my restless mind
To find a silence of some kind.

I hear a lone wolf howl
A sound so empty and hollow,
To find his lost pack,
Or someone to watch his back.

I hear a herd of horses
Their hooves trampling,
Voices rambling
In a tongue I may not cease to know.

I hear crickets call
Welcoming nightfall
Rubbing their limbs together,
Gathering like birds of a feather.

I bring in a deep breath,
And let it out slow.
Trying to rest,
Thinking about this night I chose.

Taylor Howard, Grade 8
Wayland Union Middle School

L-o-v-e

Love is   usually
Made up   of 2 people
that knew   each other
for a while and they can't
can't be without each other
When they think about their
soul mate they often get
chills down their spine
and a smile
on their
face

Brittany Pinkard, Grade 8
Hilbert Jr High School

When...

When I die, who will take my place?
When I die, will there still be a human race?
When I die, who will help the poor?
When I die, will there be any war?
When I die, I hope the world will be peaceful
When I die, I hope I was successful
When I die, I hope I'm more than dust in the wind
When I die, will I have sinned?
When I *live,* I hope to accomplish many things
When I live, I hope I don't go door to door selling silly things
When I live, I hope to solve civil cases
When I live, I hope I don't lose my money on those silly horse races
When I live, I hope I won't have many things to resent
When I live, I should just focus on the present

Zach Fellows, Grade 8
Perry Middle School

Behind This Smile

Behind this smile, all you will see,
is boundless sorrow, the real me.
I cry and I hope, I wish and I dream.
My cheerfulness so fake, you'll never hear me scream...
I fight this insanity that tends to run my mind.
I'm scared, I'm lost, I want to die, for I'm being left behind.
You all think you know me, but do you see me bleed?
Have you ever heard my thoughts, known what I think I need?
I don't think so, so you have no right,
to say "It'll be okay!" for I'm not in the light.
You can say it if you know me. But please don't be so sure.
I've been called an enigma, a puzzle. To me there is much more.
Behind the smile...

Michael Bailey, Grade 8
Valleywood Middle School

Why??

Why is it that when I like you, you don't like me.
Why is it that when I tell you that I love you, you don't say it back.
Why is it that when you walk by I wish you were closer to me,
but when you walk by me you drift farther away.
Why is it that when I finally give up on loving you, you realize you love me.

Katrina Garlick, Grade 8
Whitmore Lake Middle School

Football

The players are sweating
Bones are breaking
And they are on the field
It is the Rose Bowl with the stands packed to the fullest
With anxious patrons on both sides
The game is never dull at any moment
It is very cold outside only five degrees
The sky is very cloudy and the wind is brisk
At the end of the game players are hurt and lives have been at risk
The players are proud and shake hands, telling each other, "Good game."

Matt Hall, Grade 7
Jefferson Middle School

Graduation Day

I never thought this day would come
when we would grow apart.
We may not see each other again
but I'll always see you in my heart.
When I stand up to the podium stand
I look and see my friends.
I am wishing deep in my heart
This day will never end.
You haven't been just a buddy to me
You have always been my friend.
I'll miss you, but we will always be together in the end.
So thank you so much buddy, for always being my friend.

Kelsey Wagner, Grade 8
Lewiston Middle School

Two Sets of Eyes

No two men always agree,
Nor two women either you see.
This is because no two are alike,
Each has their own views,
Two people have two sets of eyes,
Looking at something in two different ways.

When one says yes,
Another will say no.
When a nation wants peace,
Another wants war,
Do two sides ever agree,
Or do they always continue to fight?

But then again,
Sometimes they do.
He can change her view,
She can change his.
Two people have two sets of eyes,
Looking at something in two different ways.

Patrick Furlo Jr., Grade 8
Clarkston Middle School

So Many Shoes

Shoes, shoes, so many shoes
Going to school, which ones to use?

Nike, Adidas, or your new pair of Vans
The choices are endless, in footwear land!

Blue, green, black or red
Shoes with heels, shoes with no tread?

Zippers, strings, hooks, or eyes
So many shoes with choice of ties!

So I wish you luck with the shoes you wear
Always keep in your closet, a second pair!

Josh Campbell, Grade 9
Cadillac Jr High School

Forgiveness

Do you have any compassion for people
We shall see if you have any heart at all
As for forgiveness at the big steeple
If God answers we shall have a big ball.

Do not be tempted by the devil's mind
But stay away from the sinners, they're low
And try to help people and to be kind
If you sinned God and you would know.

God will be patient and will forgive us
God loves us and will forgive if we ask
Ride to Heaven with people on a bus
To trust in God, that will be the only task.

Just ask God for forgiveness, don't be shy.
If you ask Him, you will rise to the sky.

Kevin Yee, Grade 8
St John Lutheran School

Popularity

Popularity gets you nowhere.
You will never see "popularity"
On a job resume

Popularity gets you nowhere.
In twenty years,
Your kids will never call you "popular" anyways.

Popularity gets you nowhere.
Your husband should like you
As you are
He won't care if you were "popular"

Popularity gets you nowhere.
It's just a phase in school,
That never gets you anywhere in the
Real World

Porsche Garrison, Grade 7
Paw Paw Middle School

Crushing

I glance across the room for the hundredth time,
to see your eyes looking back at mine.

I search for your face in the sea of all the others,
I have your picture in my mind but I want another.

My lonely heart longs to feel your strong embrace,
then you turn my way and my heart begins to race.

The world is melting away in this moment that we share,
should I break the silence or should I just stare?

Elaine Carlin, Grade 9
Lawton High School

The Field of Bright Flowers

There's a flower in the field
Swaying in the wind
Spreading the beauty that it reveals
Over and over again
In the field where it lies
The flower awakes
As the sun begins to rise
Over the horizon

Jandy Chang, Grade 7
Flynn Middle School

The Love Test

I love it when you kiss me,
I hate it when you don't.
I love it when you speak to me,
I hate it when you won't.

I love it when you're there for me,
It lets me know you care,
I hate the fact that when I feel down
You never seem to be there.

I hate it when you blow me off,
To be with your friends,
But I couldn't hate you that much,
Because I love you to the end.

I love it when you say you love me,
That's what I love the best,
But our hate conquered our love,
So we failed the love test.

Kyerra Moody, Grade 8
Hally Magnet Middle School

Angels Watching Overhead

Angels watching overhead
Midnight is here
Laying peacefully in my bed
My little kitten is near

Midnight is here
A soft purr fills the air
My little kitten is near
Angels watching everywhere

A soft purr fills the air
Cuddling with my teddy bear
Angels watching everywhere
Remembering who I care

Cuddling with my teddy bear
Angels watching overhead
Remembering who I care
Laying peacefully in my bed

Jennifer Kish, Grade 7
Grand Blanc Middle School

Softball

Softball is a really cool sport
It isn't played on a court.
Catch fly balls and get batters out
It makes the fans scream and shout.
I get up to bat and hit the ball
I hope I don't miss and fall.
Softball is very fun
I get to play it in the sun.
I run a lot, but that's okay
Even though I'll be hurting the next day.
The players wear mitts and betters gloves
Everything that makes softball loved.
Softball is super cool
It's too bad we don't play in the pool.
I cannot wait until our first game
I better work on my aim!

Cally O'Hagan, Grade 9
Cadillac Jr High School

Acting

I am nervous
Scared
take a deep breath
Hear the cue
Walk on stage
Bounding heart
Stops
And with the
first couple
words
Calm
I'm in my own
Little world
Me and my
Cast members
Our little
world
Walk off
Stage
Rush of
Excitement

Connor Thompson, Grade 8
St John Vianney Catholic School

Spring Is Here

When the flowers open,
And the grass grows,
You know it's time for spring to show.
When the birds chirp,
And the butterflies come,
You know that finally spring has sprung.
When the weather starts to get warm,
And the wind is a breeze,
You know that it is time for spring.

Kayla Ferguson, Grade 7
Jefferson Middle School

Music Is Poetry

Music is poetry —
In my point of view.
I play it every day,
Do you?

Music is poetry —
I'll say it again.
And I'll keep saying it,
Until the end.

Music is poetry —
To me, it is the best.
A way to express myself,
It is the best!

Music is my type of poetry —
Since I am not good with words.
Good thing I am almost done,
This seems absurd.

Oh well, now I'm finished!

David Perzyk, Grade 9
Roseville Jr High School

November

Football is here.
It's time to cheer.
The Lions are back
In their jerseys that are black.

Austin Fuller, Grade 7
St Ann Elementary School

The Lesson of Life

Life can be hard,
life can be rough,
life can even press your luck.
Don't worry about tomorrow,
'cause it will come.
Don't worry about yesterday,
'cause it is done.
Worry about today,
'cause it's all you can change.
Don't be down and lonely,
because you'll never know,
just what may happen.
So be up and happy,
make people wonder.
Life can be hard,
life can be rough,
life can even press your luck.
Just relax and press on,
and make people wonder,
because one day they just might
make you wonder.

Caryn Fogle, Grade 8
Hilbert Jr High School

Heartbroken

I look outside; it's a rainy day,
There's nothing I can say.
It feels as if I lost something,
Something that can't be restored.
Something that's so fragile, that can break.
My heart is broken, shattered on the floor.
She shall never know about my feelings,
But, one day maybe my heart will be put back
Piece by piece
By her.

Paul Kako, Grade 7
Flynn Middle School

A Question I Had to Ask*

On Monday I asked my teacher
Something I would never have asked in a million years
A curious question
Not a funny question
I asked it that morning to see what she would say
I didn't get an answer till the end of the day.
While she was marking
our arithmetic books I said,
"I've got a question to ask you."
"I guess, if you must."
I stopped for a second
Because I was so scared
I asked her the question
She stopped for a second
I was a little scared
She looked at me and said,
"What did you say?"
Then she fainted
in the middle of the room
But all I asked was,
"Were you ever skinny like me?"

Felicia Thelen-Holmes, Grade 7
Columbia Middle School
Patterned after "Were You Ever Fat Like Me?" by Kalli Dakos

I Hate Writing

I hate writing it's not very exciting
Or fun I'm done
With writing I'm going to start fighting
Against writing Why? 'Cause it's dumb
I don't want to try I want to eat pie
I don't want to think I want to drink
I don't want to type I just want to gripe
I'm not going to write I'm going to fight
Against this curse before it get worse
I'm going to stop before I pop or drop
If they won't let me stop I'm going to call a cop
I'll put them in jail where they'll tell their tale
Of how they should have let me stop writing

Lauren Olson, Grade 8
Ruth Murdoch SDA Elementary School

Loving and Hating You

I hate you for the things you do,
but I love you for how far we grew.
You're sweet, and you're kind,
you are always crossing my mind,
each and every day.
And if I could, I wouldn't change
anything to be another way.

Sometimes you are mean,
and you make me want to scream!
Even though we're never on the same page,
I love you, and that will never change!!

Logan Gross, Grade 7
Jefferson Middle School

Ode to Chocolate Milk

Chocolate milk,
Oh chocolate milk,
How wonderful are thee,
This powdered donut complements you nicely,
With your calcium-filled goodness,
I'll drink you then you'll be gone,
But a fly landed upon you,
Then you fell to the floor,
Then you soaked into the carpet,
Now you are no more.

Casady Haines, Grade 8
Mendon Middle/High School

Don't Fall in Love with a Guy

Did you ever like a guy
and always know he didn't like you?
Did you ever want to break down
and think…what good will it do?

Did you take a look in his heart
and wish you were there?
Did you ever take a good look in his eyes
and say a tiny prayer?

Did you ever watch him dancing
when the lights were turned down low?
And you whisper softly to yourself,
Oh my Lord, I like him so.

Do you ever seem to wonder where he is
and wonder if he is so true?
One moment you are very happy,
and the next you're very blue.

Don't fall in love my good friend,
You'll see it doesn't pay.
It causes broken hearts,
We know it happens every day.

Andrea Munger, Grade 8
Lewiston Middle School

Easter

Easter is here
There is no more fear
Jesus has risen
The champagne is fizzin'
All is calm
With all the palms
We should start reading Psalms

Matthew Vickery, Grade 7
St Ann Elementary School

Greatest Mom Ever!

My mom
She is funny
Smart and kind
I go to see her
Over spring and Christmas break
Also over summer vacation
During school I then
See her every other weekend
In the summer
We go swimming
If we are not swimming
We are at the park
Either riding bikes or walking
I love seeing new places
My mom lives in Ohio
Dad in Michigan
So every other weekend
I see a different place
My mom is awesome!

Seth Spencer, Grade 7
Addison Middle School

Why

Why do I have butterflies,
Why do I feel weak,
Whenever I think of you,
Or when I hear you speak?

Why do I dream,
Why do I hope,
That one day you just might notice me?

Why am I happy,
Why do I smile,
Whenever I see your face?

Why do I think of you,
Why do I dream of you,
Every time of day?

Why do I care,
Why do I love you,
When you don't even feel the same way?

Amanda Shaffner, Grade 8
Hilbert Jr High School

What Is Wrong

What is wrong with my face full of bumps
What is wrong with my ears they do not listen
What is wrong with my head it is too confused
What is wrong with my gut it is always hungry.
What is wrong with my voice it always squeaks and it is so loud

What is wrong with me I am only a teen oops! That one key word
TEEN.

Andrew Wilson, Grade 8
Concord Middle School

The Second Date

I didn't think it would end that way
On the night of that special day
It was my first date
I was in a hurry, and couldn't be late
You see, she finally said yes, the girl of my dreams
So I wanted to splurge, dinner, movie and maybe some ice cream
She was the perfect girl
Her hair, body, brains, and face were out of this world
I knew she was my queen and I was her king
She just didn't know my true thoughts, visions or my dreams
On that day we went out
I was so happy I wanted to boast, brag, and even shout
I just knew it was going to happen, I have thought about it every day after day
I had the walk, talk and I knew just what to say
So I leaned in close, as she stared into my brown eyes
I licked my lips and puckered up…but she turned away to my surprise
She said she was a good girl and good girls wait
So I swallowed my pride and thought to myself…well, there's always the second date.

Xavier Houston, Grade 7
Gesu Elementary School

What Is the Opposite of Opposite?

What is the opposite of opposite?
I don't believe I've found it
This difficult question needs some proper thinking
Is the answer being symmetrical?
If not there is a question…

What is the opposite of opposite?
You may find it to be very close
I have found it so I really must boast
Each and every person here
Has a promise for a new year
They are mostly just the same
And that's the answer to this game
The opposite of opposite cannot be found easy
For if you really thought about it, you would be very queasy

I have but one word to say to end this obnoxious guessing game…
It's all the same

Steven Gray, Grade 8
Central Middle School

Hidden Pains

Silver bangles
Rings and chains
They use the make-up
To hide the pains
Favorite colors of silver and black
Sometimes I wonder, "Do they ever look back?"
Ripped up clothes all torn in shreds
And what is that upon their heads?
They dye their heads red, purple and green
Sometimes the look makes you want to scream
The moms and dads want to disagree
When people think their kids are mean
Some people say "They can't be human!"
But I know they're just men and women
The kids all think it's really cool
The don't realize it's just a tool
A way to dissolve the pains they can't solve,
A way to hide from the world outside.

Adrieanna Hosea, Grade 7
Kuehn-Haven Middle School

Sports

Basketball
Shooting, dribble
Throwing, bouncing, fouling
Pass, free throws, lines, out
Spiking, bumping, setting
Serve, net
Volleyball

Taylor Way, Grade 7
Montague Nellie B Chisholm Middle School

Thinking of You

So I'm sitting here in the silence in the dark
And I'm thinking of you
I'm thinking of how much I love you
And how much you hurt me
I'm hearing you talk to me
And tears stream down my face
I'm seeing you ignore me
And confusion bubbles in my mind
I'm thinking of you
I'm thinking of my faults
And why I'm not up to your standards
I'm hearing you compliment everyone but me
And I roll my eyes
I'm seeing you just you
And I want to know what you're thinking
I'm hearing you
I'm thinking of how many guys would die to have me
And I laugh how fast you would feel jealousy
I'm hearing myself with my friends laughing, joking
And I see you alone…
You're thinking of me

Brittany Springstube, Grade 9
Roseville Jr High School

Friends

A friend is someone who you can always trust,
And keeps secrets like a lock on a diary,
It's someone who you can forgive no matter
how bad the problem may be,
A friend is someone who encourages you to
keep going even if it seems impossible,
It's someone who cares for you and wants
what's best for you,
Someone who likes you for who you are
Caring, kind, reliable, respectful are all indeed
what a friend is,
A friend is someone who you can ask for advice,
Someone who you can have fun with and be yourself,
And when you find a true friend,
You'll surely know what it's all about.

Jacquelyn Rought, Grade 7
Paw Paw Middle School

Spongebob Squarepants

A yellow square with holes
With big eyes, eye lashes and a long nose
I live in a pineapple, under the sea
I have many friends
Patrick, Gary, Sandy and Squidward
The Krusty Krabs is where you can find me,
Working as a fry cook
Serving up smiles
My #1 hobby is jelly fishing in jelly fish fields
Can you guess who I am?
Spongebob Squarepants.

Chelsea Bentley, Grade 7
Gesu Elementary School

When School Is Out

When school is out
And the last bell rings
And brightly shines the sun
Go out and have some fun

Don't hang around inside all day
Go ride a bike with a friend
Buy some ice cream on a hot summer day
Or go swimming by the bay

Go have fun while the time lasts
And just have a blast
Come on and go play
And have fun every day

You may cry some tears
But it's the best time of the year
And there is no doubt
When school is out

Kayla Ely, Grade 7
Grand Blanc Middle School

Barbara Pierce

Barbara Pierce was born in Rye. One day she would unify.
Born to Pauline and Marvin Pierce. On June 8, 1925 it was fierce.
Barbara has an exciting childhood. She had one sister and two brothers during her girlhood.
She met George at a dance she though he had a lot of knowledge. She went off to college.
She went to a boarding school as Ashley Hallin, South Carolina.
She went to Smith College, Massachusetts it is close to Virginia.
They married in January 6, 1945. She had a trouble loss in her life.
She had a wonderful marriage. They had over the years 5 children she carried.
Their daughter Robin died from leukemia it was not a smooth transition for her brother. Barbara was a sad mother.
She was at the White House from 1989 to 1993 with applause.
As wife of the president she selected the promotion of liberty as her special cause.
Barbara was an asset to her husband during the company for president.
She helped him in the race by persuading the American resident.
Barbara helped the homeless and people that have AIDS.
Helping the elderly and volunteering for schools were her crusades.
Barbara is 76 years old.
One word that describes her is bold.

Alex McLellan, Grade 7
Lakeview Middle School

The World Is Quiet Here

The dawn spreads its pink and golden wings and flies over the horizon. Tiny roses sparkle with the dew of a new morn. Sunlight dances on water like a ballerina on fairy wings. The grass ripples like a jade ocean in the earthy breeze. Butterflies dance to the crickets last lonely song. The air smells of the flowers that are like a rainbow in its grassy bed. The river flows its sleepy lullaby for the creatures of the night who bask in the golden sun. The world is quiet here.

The night swallows the last bird's song of morn. The stars dance in the sky like silvery fairies. The crickets play their lullaby for all the morn's creatures whose teary eyes need a rest. The gurgle of the stream fades into the eyes of night as the moon watches over his beloved creatures.

The World Is Quiet Here

Kaitlyn Church, Grade 7
Camden Frontier Middle School

12 and 0

The perfect season was a perfect start as they beat Kent State with a lot of heart.
If they beat Hawaii they'll go 2 and 0 which is what they did, look at them go.
Here comes the Irish of Notre Dame but it looks like today they lost their game
as MSU beats them to go 3 and 0 they beat Notre Dame their arch foe.
As we skip the next game because we know who won, we beat them so bad it was one and done.
So time for Michigan the biggest game they also lost to Notre Dame.
As they play Michigan like a star, they upset their team coached by Lloyd Carr.
So time for the Buckeyes of Ohio State the team that I really really hate,
luckily we beat them 20 to 8 and upset the team Ohio State.
Time for Northwestern they're out in the west but that doesn't mean that they are the best
as we blow them out 40 to nothing it looks like MSU is starting something.
7 and 0, 7 and 0, they're so close to 11 and 0.
Next they play the Indiana Hoosiers who some people call the Indiana Losers.
MSU wins 62 to 7 and I think MSU has gone to heaven.
Next Purdue a very tough game but everyone knows we're not the same.
We beat Purdue what a close game but everyone knows MSU is not lame.
It's time for MSU to go to work when they play Minnesota they'll go berserk
as they beat them 28 to 7 MSU is getting pretty close to eleven.
One more game till 11 and 0 luckily Penn State's ranked pretty low
MSU WINS BIG TEN CHAMPS! What a season for this fine team,
I can't say what happened in their bowl you'll just have to guess because everyone knows MSU is the best.

Sean Gardner, Grade 8
St Gerard Elementary School

To a Special Friend

Until the end of time,
You'll always be a friend of mine.

Our friendship to hold dear,
And to hold it very near.

To laugh, smile, cry, and care,
And precious moments we'll always share.

Our thoughts and feelings will be respected,
And our secrets and promises will be protected.

To be friends forever,
And go through life together.

Shelby Nichols, Grade 7
Sault Area Middle School

A Part of Me

It's been three months now that you left me.
My life without you is so empty.
Now that you're gone it's like a part of me is missin.
I'm waiting to get a way back to you so I'll listen.
I said that I love you and I always will.
I just wish I could see you to let you know how I feel.
Now without you I always feel lost.
I would still do anything for you no matter what the cost.
I just wish I could remember you being right by my side,
The way me and you used to take long walks outside.
You taught me everything that I now know how to do.
Now it's hard to see me without you.
I always ask God "what did I do to get the things I got now?"
I'll fix them all just teach me how.
I can't wait till I can talk to you at least,
Until I meet you in heaven…
Rest In Peace

Ashley Herfi, Grade 7
Flynn Middle School

Monster

A monster is a bull in my closet.
I got so frightened I began to sweat.

Even though I pray to Jesus,
I try to make no fuss.

My mommy put a night light in,
But to keep me safer I wish I had a twin.

I swear I heard a monster sneeze,
But I think it was my brother trying to tease.

When the door opened up,
I saw it was just a grown-up.

Olivia Quam, Grade 8
St Anthony of Padua School

Summer

Every day,
Off to the beach,
To splash in the cold
but good feeling water
Fresh squeezed lemonade
With 10 ice cubes and a mini umbrella
Birds chirping all day long
No homework to worry about,
No ruling and yelling teachers,
Nothing to do except to have loads of fun
But after 2 weeks you're pooped out and your brain
is going to waste,
it's dying
And you miss all your friends
And want to go back to the school to learn
But, sadly off to a new and huge journey.

Christiana Bonomo, Grade 8
St John Vianney Catholic School

Losing My Daddy

A hospital room filled with my family
My dad's on the bed my mom sitting near
Me and my sisters inch close to the bed
And Grandma and Grandpa sit near their son

Only forty-nine is already dying
That terrible demon called cancer was there
It looms in that body my own daddy's body
How could he die I was only nine years old
He'll never see me graduate he'll never see me grow
I was only a little girl not even a teen
He'll never see me at college
He'll never see me married

He's missing out on so much
If only he were here life seems it would be so much better
That day he died I felt like dying too
I wanted out of my nightmarish life

But now that he's gone
I feel like an outcast when people talk about their dads
Now all I have is a distant memory
'Cause what's a girl to do when she's lost her daddy?

Amanda Anderson, Grade 8
Oakland Christian School

Family

Family is very supporting and is always there for you.
Family is very fun to hang out with,
If they weren't here we wouldn't be where we are now.
Family is the best thing in the world.
Family is so great to have.
Having a family is such a privilege.
Family is awesome.

Logan Harvey, Grade 7
Camden Frontier Middle School

A Place to Be

I sit by the shore
Trying to calm my thoughts
I love the sound of the waves
Splish, splash, splish splash
The cold breeze
Makes me go brr
As the seagulls fly by
Shrieking and squealing
As I look down the shore
As I sit by the shore to calm my thoughts
Splish splash
Lacey Krolczyk, Grade 7
Manistee Middle School

The Real Me

I will never get
Why you feel this way about me
Should I change for you?
I just don't know what to do
I've been someone I'm not
But then I became me
You just don't like how I am
You don't like the real me
But you need to understand
That I'm just being myself
I don't want to change
I want to be me, not someone else
Please don't do this to me
I like being myself
But you don't like the real me
Shauna Zielaskowski, Grade 8
Posen Consolidated High School

My Parents

My parents are loving,
Like a Nana who is caring.

My parents are sweet,
Like a flower's sweet nectar in the park.

My parents are busy,
Like a swan preparing her nest.

Other parents should be like mine,
So the world can be a better place.
Amber Hauer, Grade 7
Flynn Middle School

Snowflakes

Snowflakes
Hundreds in flight
Float gently from the sky
Whirling and twirling where they are
Snowflakes
Alex Lebo, Grade 8
Central Middle School

Sorry

I wake up every morning feeling sorry for the people in this world.
I wonder why them and not me.
They lost everything they had, including themselves.
The victims in the hurricane only had their family, if that.
How would you feel if you lived on the streets
With nothing but the ground under you?
Spending your life trying to support you and your family.
It's a scary thought to believe, but it happens to many people.
So next time you see somebody like that, pray for them.
Hope that they find what they need.
I am so happy that God is with me all the days of my life.
I will always thank God that it's not me.
Nobody can take away what means so much to me.
Not even a hurricane.
Ashley Milano, Grade 7
North Rockford Middle School

My Love Is Forever*

That day I knew my life would change
That day I knew it would never be the same
That day I knew you would never come back
That day I knew my life would lack
You were my favorite person, you understood me
When this happened I knew it could never be
But the day I heard, I knew it was the end
For I knew my grief would just begin
I guess our time was short and I never told you how much "I loved you"
And I know you would say the same thing, too!
You're gone and my memory seems to fade
I now realize it's your love I will crave
I know people die for a special reason
But why did it have to be in my favorite season?
I love you, Uncle, that will never change!
And my love for you covers a wide range
I will end this poem with my love to you
As long as you know, my love is TRUE!
Courtney Morris, Grade 8
Hally Magnet Middle School
*Dedicated to my Uncle Mookie

Peace

I am peace,
You know me for my love.
I was born in the beginning of time.
And now only live in your wishes.
My best friends are love, caring, and sharing.
My enemy is war.
Because he makes me be forgotten and lost in space and time.
I fear you'll never find me.
People will have less and less kissing and more and more killing.
I would love if war is the last one killed and all the rest of killing is done,
Because I'm alive once again,
With love everywhere.
I dream of war to be dead forever, and me to be alive once again.
Erica Buschlen, Grade 8
Verona Mills School

The Four Seasons

Winter, summer, spring, and fall
Each with something to share
Winter being cold and blue
While spring is wet and rainy
Fall being bright with wonderful sights
Summer with hot, dry fabulous days
Each season can also be wonderful
Bringing you many things
Like wind, rain, snow, sun, and some fun
So no matter what time of year
You always know there will be four season
Winter, summer, spring, and fall

Chris Foster, Grade 7
Centreville Jr High School

The Truth About You

I found the truth about you
I found out why you cared.
I found out all the things you encountered
I found out that you were scared
But so was I.

So all the things you could see
Are probably already there.
So open your eyes and you'll see.
The true beauty in me.

Because I won't tell you what you'll see
So go ahead and see the true beauty in me.

Amber Seiler, Grade 8
Hilbert Jr High School

Elephant

My family is a strong elephant.
My mom the trunk
Strong and controlling
Always has the heavy load.
Joe, my step-dad, is the feet
Big and tall
He keeps our family running.
Megan, my sister, is the ears
Talkative and nosey
Always wants to be part of something.
Lambeau, my dog, is the tail
Muscular but a scardy cat
Is both strong and weak.
My cats, Abby, Winny, Bailey, and Sophie,
Are the mouth
Loud and sweet
They're never quiet.
And I am the eyes
Responsible and neat
Take the lead and helps hold the family together.
My family is a strong elephant.

Carly St. Clair, Grade 7
Paw Paw Middle School

Waiting for the Rain

For minutes, hours, days, and weeks,
I have been waiting for you.

I am beginning to doubt myself
And may not be able to hold out any more.

Because now waiting for you,
Is like waiting for rain in this drought.

But now that day has come.
The day that you tell me everything
I have wanted to know and hear.

The day we are no longer shy
To be around each other.

That was the day it rained.

It's too bad we had to wait for the rain.

Kierstin Dent, Grade 7
Gesu Elementary School

Grandfather

Why should I feel this way?
When someone I love just passed away?
Why can't I cry?
Why can't I feel the need I want to die?
Could it just go away?
But I have to face the fact that he just left the other day.
My grandfather I will miss.
I will never forget the moments we reminisced.
I will love him with all my heart,
and in my heart they won't tear us apart.
He will always be here each day,
but I hate the fact that he passed.

Antonio Cottrell, Grade 9
Southwestern High School

Halloween

Witches and goblins and ghosts! Oh my!
All come out one dark and scary night.
All the homes are decorated with lights,
Leaving skeletons and scarecrows
To haunt us through the night.

Pumpkins are carved into jack-o'-lanterns,
With scary faces lit with candles so neat.
Kids dressed in costumes run down the street.
Bags in hand they go door to door
Yelling out, "Trick-or-treat!"

This holiday gives everyone a fright:
It must be Halloween Night!

Riaa Dutta, Grade 8
Boulan Park Middle School

Soldiers

S upport our troops
O ver in Iraq
L oyal and brave
D oing what they think is right
I mminent dangers
E verywhere in Iraq
R anks of soldiers
S tanding brave and proud

Kayleigh White, Grade 7
Sault Area Middle School

Spring

Spring is when the flowers bloom
and the grass is green again.
Birds come back like a dear old friend.
Spring makes the world feel new.
The birds are busy with something to do.
Building nests for their young.
They sing songs the new life has begun.
The sun warms the earth.
There are signs of new birth.
Caterpillar becomes butterfly
and fly up to the sky.
Bees go from flower to flower.
And the world awaits a spring shower.
Spring is my favorite time of year
because my birthday is in April.

Elisa Harris, Grade 9
Roseville Jr High School

Money

Benjamin Franklin
Madison, Jackson,
And Washington too.

Are all out of my pocket
And out of my hand.
Minus a
$50, $100, and a $10,

Out of the store
And into my hands
A cell phone,
Some shoes
And some clothes to wear.

I got a little Versace,
Gucci, and Burberry too.
Some Air force ones,
Nikes, and Timberlands too.

Now eight bags in my hand
But sadly to say
No more money to spend.

Kassandre Tomlin, Grade 8
Hilbert Jr High School

My Mom and Me

My mom and me are like two peas in a pod.
We do everything together it is so cool that is true love right there.

My mom and me are great together that's our job!
Sometimes we may bump heads, sometimes.
We fight, we argue, we even might cry,
But that's what a mother and their daughters do, that's their job.
When I am feeling sad she always finds a way to cheer me up
Or when I need help she's there for me.
She's a friend you can count on!

When my mom tries to protect me from doing something that I know is wrong
And I think she's just trying to ruin my life. But I know that's what moms are for.
My mom is like an angel that God made just for me
And he will not ever take her away from me,
Because he knows how much I love her.
If He did, He would know how devastated I would be!

Sooner or later I'll be leaving to go to college
And we won't be close, but we'll find a way.
Just like I said, we are like two peas in a pod.
When you have strong love like this that distance will never matter
And our love will be even stronger.
I'll love you forever!

Hayley Scott, Grade 8
Gesu Elementary School

Nancy Reagan

Nancy Reagan was born on July 6, 1923 in New York.
Like most people she ate her food with a fork.
She was the wife of Ronald Reagan.
He was president and came up with a big plan.

When she was a baby she was adopted.
When she went to school she often read.
She grew up in Chicago.
She went with the big city flow.

Soon after graduation she became a professional actress.
In Hollywood movies she was a big success.
She landed a role on Broadway in the musical *Lute Song*.
Her brown hair was medium long.

Her first screen role was in *Shadow on the Wall*.
She met Ronald in 1949 he was handsome and tall.
He was president of the Screen Actors Guild.
She thought he had a good build.

Mrs. Reagan has a daughter, Patricia Ann, and a son, Ronald Prescott.
I hope she didn't have to scold them a lot.
She raised money to buy new china for the White House.
She made it look like a beautiful house.

Justin Taylor, Grade 7
Lakeview Middle School

Sea

Whoosh! Whoosh!
That is how the ocean sounds every night and every morning
Every afternoon, too, for that matter
A purring little kitten
Playing with ships, its balls of string

The salty sea dogs
Get tossed around
By the playful kitty sea
They scream "No more!!!"
The kitten rests
The sea again is a melody

In, out, in, out
Go the waves
The kitten is purring
Sleeping, snoring

The sea is at bay again.

Mackenzie Bush, Grade 7
Assumption BVM School

Transportation

Car
Fast, shiny
Speeding, steering, spinning
Wheels, metal, bolts, brakes
Fixing, riding, cleaning
Skinny, long
Bike

Joey Goloversic, Grade 7
Montague Nellie B Chisholm Middle School

Love

A dozen red hearts filled my mind;
A dozen filled hers too.
I finally met my perfect match;
My heart forever true.

I talked with her, I walked with her
And every single day,
When I stepped from one path to the next
She'd be in my mind always.

She filled my mind
And I filled hers
All other thoughts
Became a blur.

A dozen red hearts filled my mind;
A dozen filled hers too.
I finally met my perfect match;
My heart forever true.

Cody T. Harrell, Grade 7
Grand Blanc Middle School

Sad

When you're sad
And when you're down
You turn to me
With a frown
I know your reason
I know why
It's about
That cute guy
I know how you feel
I know your pain
You have your ways
I know you'll be fine
We will get through this bind
Just remember he wasn't worth your time

Paris Dipzinski, Grade 7
Grand Blanc Middle School

Labeled

You look down on these people with eyes of shame,
But they look at you with a heart of no blame.
People with so much care, limited by a chair,
Disabled you label them.

You pass them by without a glance.
You don't even give them a fair chance.
"They're not important," you say. Not worth your while.
But they just sit there with a smile.
Disabled you label them.

They can't walk and are labeled lame.
But when it comes to importance,
In God's eyes we're all the same.

Abby Buursma, Grade 8
Cutlerville Christian School

My Friend

He stands by the path, a glimpse of golden yellow
In the abundant corn field, he's the only one
All summer long, real tall and proud
Never bowing his head, only his feet touching ground
With a skinny stalk, so strong and green
He talks to birds, he's a friend indeed
He doesn't have hands, only long, rigid arms
At the top is a head, as round as can be
With small seed eyes, he smiles at me
His hair stands out, bright around his head

In the summer I see him, on my way to work
During winter he hides, as a seed in the Earth
His cycle repeating, never ever ceasing
Every day we talk, it's like magic you see
For he's real shy, only likes talking to me
And before I go on my way, we exchange a smile
That will be on my face, until there's no tomorrow

Amanda Lenard, Grade 8
Posen Consolidated High School

Leaving on a Jet Plane

I'm leaving on a jet plane
I know where I'm bound
I'm leaving on a jet plane
My life is turning around

I'm leaving on a jet plane
I've left my past behind
I'm leaving on a jet plane
I'm gonna find what there is to find

I'm leaving on a jet plane
I am climbing up the mountain
I'm leaving on a jet plane
Me, is where I keep all my confidence in

I'm leaving on a jet plane
I am really excited
I'm leaving on a jet plane
A new fire in me, ignited

Sarah Rydel, Grade 7
Flynn Middle School

He Is

The one I love
The one I hate
The one I have not yet
Learned to appreciate
He is my heart
He is my fears
He's been my enemy
Throughout my years
Sometimes I wonder
Is he my friend
Whether he's a boy
Whether he's a man
I cry and pray
Before I sleep at night
He is the only man
I will not fight
Trying to keep him a secret
Why should I bother
The man I speak of is my father

Emanuel Harris, Grade 9
Cass Technical High School

Summer

Children playing all day long
Playing tag, and basketball
Roller hockey, swimming pools
Ice cream and BBQs
No more school, and football too
Playing guitar, and video games
Staying up late, sleeping in
That is why summer is so fun

Corey Egelton, Grade 7
Jefferson Middle School

Seasons

Seasons are all well and good
But if I could I would
Change a few things
Winter is all cold and stings
I wish that all the birds would sing
Spring is rather nice
But there are too many mice
Summer is the hottest one
There is just too much sun
Fall is rather dull
Because all the leaves fall
Seasons, seasons, seasons
Which one do you like?

Julie Logan, Grade 7
Ruth Murdoch SDA Elementary School

I Am Who I Am

I am who I am,
I wonder who I will be.
I hear people talking about me,
I see them whispering right beside me.

I pretend there is no one judging me,
Yet I feel trapped.
I must watch where I go and what I do,
So they don't talk about me.
There is nothing I can do to stop it,
Besides just say to them,
I am who I am.

I understand hate is everywhere,
I say they will stop some day.
I dream about it all being over,
I try to ignore them all.
I hope it all soon stops.
But until they stop, I am proud to say,
I am who I am.

Catia Odisho, Grade 7
Flynn Middle School

Changes

You changed my life
Without a sight.
You make me smile
As if I just got a doll.
When I tear you always
Appear.
You always know when to ask me
The things at the right time.
Especially when you asked to
Be mine.
I've never been treated this way
And until this day you changed
Me in every way.

Danielle Rice, Grade 8
Clarenceville Middle School

Dreaming

When I look at you,
A smile always shines through,
Dreaming all day, dreaming of you,
I want you to know, I love you.

I put my arms around you,
I want to hold you tight.
I couldn't ask for more
Than being with you tonight.

It's getting late already,
Time to say goodbye,
But I can't pull myself away,
No matter how hard I try.

De'Von Glasscoe, Grade 8
MacDonald Middle School

Liquid Skies

I feel a drop from above,
The wind picks up,
To my surprise,
The skies are a flood.

Like a waterfall on land,
Rain teems down on my head,
And I let it all out,
Delight from every demand.

Thunder booms and lightning cracks,
The heavens have met where I stand,
Puddles spill at my feet,
But I enjoy every amazing leap.

Andrew Smith, Grade 8
Thunder Bay Jr High School

Pain

Pain is a thing that goes
on every day.
It could be because someone
has died in your family.
It could be because of
someone trying to abuse you.
Abuse is one of the worst
things to go through in life.
It could be verbal abuse or physical.
It is just another way of pain.
Pain is something people
are going to have to deal
with in their life, or they
will be scared for the rest
of their life.
Pain will happen today, tomorrow
and the next month. And even
the next ten years.

Deante McCullough, Grade 9
St Johns Schools

Sweet Peas

Sweet Peas are so pretty
The intricate design is breathtaking
The white petal with purple lining is so gorgeous
It shows God exists and sustains nature

Joyce Yoon, Grade 7
Ruth Murdoch SDA Elementary School

Ocean Tranquility

As I stroll along on the golden sand,
I shield the blinding sunlight with my hand.
Pearly white seagulls glide above me, up so high.
The sun glares like a diamond in the crystal-clear sky.

In the distance, waves gently swell.
Lying in the sand is a shimmering seashell.
Sunlight upon the water makes the ocean sparkle and shine;
I listen peacefully to the sound of the seagull's whine.

Cool, refreshing water reaches my feet,
As the sun gives off a radiant heat.
The sound of the waves' whispers echo in my ear,
And I look towards the sky, so blue and clear.

In these moments I feel absolute peace;
My worries and doubts temporarily cease.
And as I breathe in the crisp, salty air,
I cherish this peaceful day with care.

Shivani Kaushal, Grade 7
Grand Blanc Middle School

Kayaking

The summer breeze in my face
When we arrive at that special place.
"The beach! We're here," my sister says to me
I love the water and beautiful scenery.
Birds are flying way up high
Like white, puffy clouds above in the sky.
Fish are swimming 'round and 'round
But to the water they are bound.

We hurry to the dock to get all ready
Easy now, be very steady.
The boat starts to move front and back
Not tipping our craft keeps us on track.
Paddling from side to side
Makes me feel like my muscles are tied.
Boating is hard but very fun
My dad said to me, "Are you tired yet hon?"

In the waves, splashing about
We never ever want to get out.
We head back to shore
Where we started before
I wish we had time for much, much more!

Sarah Latimer, Grade 7
St Thomas More Academy

My Family

What is family?
My family is my inspiration
My help in time of need
A supportive source of pride
Patient and willing to listen
Always accepting, never judging
A kind of protection I won't find anywhere else
Loving, forgiving, understanding
A never failing love
With me no matter what my choices
Disciplining when I need it, kind yet firm
Willing to let go and have fun
Excited to see me and to be with me
Creating memories that last a lifetime
That is my family.

Suzanne Trigger, Grade 7
St John Lutheran School

A Friend Like You

Having a friend like you,
Is a dream come true.
On day one, two, or three,
You are always there for me.
We live, laugh, and cry,
I hope this friendship will never die.
We tell what's on our mind,
Looking for the treasure that is left to find.
All the fun times we've had together,
I'll remember them from now on and to forever.
You always make me smile,
Not for a little, but for a while.
Our friendship is so incredible,
I can't believe it's even possible.
I will love you until the end,
My wonderful dearest friend.

Valerie Begian, Grade 7
Trinity Lutheran School

Life

Just tell me what would
Life be without friends, to tell
You the truth nobody really know
Because everybody has a friend
And if they don't now, they
Will later in life, no matter what
They look like, how they act, etc.
So far those of you
Who think you don't have
Friends and you feel and think
Your life is horrible, you don't know
Exactly what you're talking about because trust
Me you will always have
Friends!!

Jordan Konior, Grade 7
Gesu Elementary School

Earliest Memory

Earliest memory
At the sink
Listening to the running water
Making me feel sleepy

Sleepy
Devin James Farthing, Grade 8
St John Lutheran School

God's Love

God is sitting high above
Showering the world in His love
Holding us with a strong grasp
Keeping us from the devil's rasp
All alone with his power
He can help us every hour
Comforting us when in despair
He is with us everywhere
Never failing to be around
One day He'll raise us from the ground
Sam Jar, Grade 7
Peace Lutheran Church & School

Behind Locked Doors

Behind locked doors,
Not knowing if the grass was greener.
Secluded and forgotten,
Left behind in the dark.
The key is found,
Should the doors be opened,
Or left to rust?
A fork in the road,
Without a map to guide.
Start a new beginning,
Or stay behind locked doors?
Claire Hamill, Grade 9
Grosse Pointe South High School

Life

Life is
Like a roller coaster
Full of ups and downs
Twists and turns
Hills and drops
It keeps you in…
Suspense
Never failing to change
Increasing to a point
Free falling,
Almost
Hitting rock bottom
What's next?
It keeps you in…
Suspense
Teeahnah Addison, Grade 8
Erma Henderson Upper Campus

Only if I Can Go Back and Change the Past

As I look in the past
I see so many problems
So much drama I caused
Only if I can go back and change the past
Lost friends and family trust
It's hard to gain back
Harder than a math problem
Only if I can go back and change the past
Lies and mistrust
Stealing things and breaking them
Betrayal and hate
Only if I can go back and change the past
Depressed and loneliness
Seeking for attention
What more could I ask for
Only if I can go back and change the past
Now I'm a much happier person
Seeking goals and achieving dreams
After realizing that being miserable isn't going to get you anywhere
I finally knew who I was
But still only if I can go back and change the past
Nicole Obeada, Grade 8
Richardson Elementary Middle School

Frozen Sugar

Frost and frozen, soft and sugary.
Not much fun if it melts away.
Build a snowman, play in it.
With the snowflakes hitting your face.
How long you'll be out, nobody knows.
At least until Jack Frost bites your nose.
You run inside to warm up.
There your mom is with hot chocolate.
Your fingers feel nippy, along with your toes.
You take a sip. The warmth rushes throughout your body.
The creamy whipped cream, the gooey marshmallows. That's better.
Finish off your mug, and you are off!
Back into the cold, the soft blanket of snow.
Grab your sled and you're off again.
Frosty and frozen, soft and sugary.
Kelsey Crawford, Grade 8
MacDonald Middle School

A Snow Touched Land

The sun is rising it's time for realizing,
the first snow has finally come…
you look out your window awaiting a brilliant show,
dancing lights play off the glass, you hope this time will never pass,
snow laced trees, dusted walks, everything is blanketed in crushed up chalk,
postcard perfect, it's all worth it,
the first snow has finally come…
snowballs, snowmen, this time will never end,
powdered play things, this is what winter brings,
the first snow has finally come.

Kylie Stephens, Grade 8
MacDonald Middle School

Listen

Thank you for always being there,
to listen and understand.
I appreciate all you do for me,
and how you show you care.

Thank you for making me feel whole again,
for putting my pieces back together.
You saved my life,
And I love you more than ever.

You may not understand,
why I do what I do.
But you never criticized,
you just helped me through.

I knew I could come to you when I was down,
'cause I knew you'd always be there
to pick me back up
and say listen, everything will be ok.

Ian Wallace, Grade 8
Gesu Elementary School

What Happened?

I don't understand how this world came to be,
with hate and frustration all being the key,
to unlock the worst in people's mind,
since the lock and key to war was already
broken way before it's time.
Hate keeps escaping and
frustration keeps on seeping through
confusion keeps the world in a constant spin,
although we try to stop it over and over again.
While racism waits and hides in the corner,
justice is tied up trying constantly to break free.
Kindness is crying and shaking back and forth
while peace, love, and hope hold each other close,
right and wrong can't remember their name,
what happened is all I have to say.

Danyelle Pouncil, Grade 8
Flint Southwestern Academy

Happiness

Happiness is:
Like a beautiful sunny day in early spring
The color yellow like my bike on a sunny day
Hot like taking a soak in a hot tub
Cold like air-conditioning on a hot day
Sounds like robins chirping in late spring
Tastes like ice cold lemonade on the Fourth of July
Smells like freshly cut grass on a summer morning
Looks like the sunset at dusk
Feels like the top of the water in an afternoon swim
Like my horse gliding through the sunshine

Derek Glauch, Grade 7
Manistee Middle School

The Word

The things I've seen take breath away,
I've gone miles and miles in just one day.

You would never believe the places I go,
The people I've seen with this light to show.

I've been through places exceedingly dark,
But on my heart I have an unfading mark.

I travel the world so all can see,
The work my God accomplishes in me.

To show everyone His eternal love,
That is my Heavenly gift from above.

Tony Oleck, Grade 8
St Anthony of Padua School

Cry of a Lone Wolf

His graceful stride was smoother than ice.
His paws were blacker than the dead of night.
His pelt was the silvery snow.
His eyes are as golden as the sun.

I step back trying not to make a sound.
He turned to look at me then lifted his head to the sky.
He let out one long mournful howl breaking the silence.
His howl was of a lone wolf.

Ashley Holladay, Grade 7
Montague Nellie B Chisholm Middle School

Disney

At Sea World we saw seals
Some of them rolled on wheels

MGM had wonderful movies
Only one was groovy

We went to Epcot, the place with the big ball
We even rode up its wall

I played "Who Wants to Be a Millionaire"
It must have been a million degrees in there

At Animal Kingdom there were many animals to see
We even saw a shrew with a flew

We touched stingrays in a tank
They felt as slippery as dead fish on a bank

At Magical Kingdom I rode Space Mountain
They even had a magical fountain

Florida was a total blast
But unfortunately that is in the past

Abby Timmerman, Grade 7
Montague Nellie B Chisholm Middle School

Summer's End

I close my eyes and wake up to the summer's day. I go outside and play all day. The sun goes down — the night has sprung — the stars come up and the fun is gone. The sun came up and the coast guard was great! We all love to celebrate! I blink for a second and look around, I soon noticed nothing is to be found. I sit in silence. Waiting from time to time. As I wait, I think. The summer has ended and there is no time for that last moment.

Jenna Hitsman, Grade 7
Mona Shores Middle School

Hurricane Katrina

Hurricane Katrina was and is the worst thing that happened to New Orleans because lots of people died. To live and breathe is what they all tried. Most of them drowned because the water was too high to swim even though they didn't think it so. But God still had His eyes on them. Some even died trying to get on a plane but to them the idea seemed insane. Some even died by the heat, the thought of having cold water seemed pretty neat. Even though that all happened, the sun will still shine, that's why we should keep them in mind.

Daysha Doss, Grade 7
Coolidge Middle School

Eliza McCardle Johnson

Eliza McCardle Johnson was born October 4, 1810. She was a fine specimen.
Born in Leesburg, Tennessee, to a small family.
Eliza's astrological sign was Libra. She would pray at the basilica.
Her religion was Methodist where God was the emphasis.
Eliza would be in a fix. Her father died in 1826.
Eliza McCardle Johnson had a good education. She went to academy school 'til graduation.
Eliza married Alex at sixteen. She was his queen.
They had five children, Martha, Charles, Mary, Robert, and Andrew Jr. They would not be poor.
Eliza McCardle Johnson thought family came first. She was far from the worst.
Eliza McCardle Johnson's husband was the 17th president. Alex Johnson made big accomplishments.
Eliza was in the White House in 1865-1869 in Washington, D.C.
Eliza was handicapped because of a mishap.
On January 15, 1876 Eliza McCardle Johnson died. It was her goodbye.

Alisha Johnson, Grade 7
Lakeview Middle School

The Girl of My Dreams

The girl of my dreams
Everyone can't see
This dream girl to me
Is a reality not yet seen
The girl of my dreams has
Mind body and soul
Everything needed to make a person whole
The girl of my dream
Means a lot to me
She is there when I'm down
And to make sure I don't physically and emotionally drown
She is there to support me as I do her
She is there for me through thick and thin
I and her together will always win
The girl of my dreams is a mystery to me
I'm hoping one day to find a real life version of her
I'm wondering if this is a promising chase or if this vision will be thrown back in my face
I know one day we will be together
The girl of my dreams everyone can't see
Because she is a true vision of beauty to me

Christopher Moore, Grade 8
Hally Magnet Middle School

My Old Book

I sit on an old and dusty wood bookshelf
Waiting to be opened.
Yes, I watch my owner come
She opens me and looks at my fabulous colorful pictures.
I flip all of my pages from 1-266.
Look I'm sitting on the dusty old bookshelf
Waiting to be opened again.

Carissa Leach, Grade 7
Manistee Middle School

Summer

Hip-hip hooray, the children scream and shout
We are all so excited, school just got out

Summer is that time of year, when we have fun, rain or shine
When we laugh and play, just about all the time

Flip-flops, towels, a day at the beach
A bucket and shovel, one for us each

Swimming, tanning, water balloon fights
Spending time with friends, on breezy summer nights

Bonfires, picnics, the Fourth of July
When everyone gets together, to watch fireworks fly

Playing games daily, like football or tag
Hide and go seek, capture the flag

But here comes August, pencils, rulers, pens
Shopping for school supplies, back to school again

I need to stop dreaming, the weather is weary
Because, for now, it's only February

Jenna Johnson, Grade 8
North Rockford Middle School

The Race

Standing at the starting line all tense and nervous,
    as your senses are impervious,
to how fast you really can go. Bang!

All of the sudden there is a stampede
of runners just trying to succeed.
While flying by like a freight of men,
    trying to go at their fastest rate.

Nearing the end of the race thinking your almost done
with this mind numbing chase,
You spring out on the last stretch,
    to try and catch up on those last men.

That is when you've found,
what place your bounded into.

Spencer Westhuis, Grade 9
West Ottawa High School

Summer Vacation

Summer vacation is a lot of fun,
it's when everyone gets to play in the sun.
Instead of school,
all the kids swim in the pool.
All the kids do what they like best,
instead of studying for a test.
Kids go out to play,
in the hot sun all day.
Everyone has fun on the beach,
and the teachers don't have to teach.

Dominic Grancitelli, Grade 7
Jefferson Middle School

A Winter's Day

Snowflakes fall on the ground at people's feet
Sitting down, now, at the table to eat
Sledding down the hill, for children is fun
Wrapped up, waiting for dinner to be done

Going to school all bundled up and warm
Watching the news for a really bad storm
Having big snowball fights with friends at noon
Wrapped in your big blanket watching cartoons

Laura Flowers, Grade 8
Grosse Pointe Academy

When the Clock Strikes Twelve

When the clock strikes twelve I shall learn how to fly
When the clock strikes twelve I will touch the sky
I shall go as high as a bird can fly
I shall do this every day and when the night goes by

When the clock strikes twelve I will stand on the sea
When the clock strikes twelve I shall be the queen
As the sun goes down all things will see me
Standing on the highest wave there will ever be

When the clock strikes twelve I will sing the longest song
When the clock strikes twelve I'll sing all night long
The whole world will know nothing'll go wrong
As I put a string in their ears of a happy song

I will glow as bright as the moonlight
Then all will see this glorious sight
And the children will laugh and say I was right
As they stare at the light that glows in the night

Sarah Townsel, Grade 7
Montague Nellie B Chisholm Middle School

Fears

You can't escape from your fears, only confront them.
You hide in hope of never having to face your fears.
If you run away from your fears you only get tired of running.

Tyler Maser, Grade 7
Manistee Middle School

I Am

I am a crazy kid who likes Mad TV.
I wonder if people think the same thing I do.
I hear ringing in my head.
I see a monkey.
I want 5,000,000 dollars.
I am a crazy kid who likes Mad TV.
I pretend to fight people.
I feel happy when I think of chocolate.
I touch and eat chocolate.
I worry about getting hit by a car.
I cry when I think about sad things.
I am a crazy kid who likes Mad TV.
I understand algebra.
I say I like sports.
I dream about my family.
I try to skateboard good.
I hope I will become a skater.
I am a crazy kid who likes Mad TV.
I remember how I got the scar on my head
I think my hair is cool.

Cody Underwood, Grade 7
Roseville Jr High School

The Nice Sky

The nice sky is all about the sun
that brings out the flowers
and the nice white clouds look so pretty.
Then when the morning comes,
there is a nice colorful sky
and I can tell you what they are:
orange, purple, black and yellow

Wayne Hayes, Grade 7
St Johns Schools

If I Was a Wolf

If I was a wolf
I'd run through the wood
hoping to catch a meal that tasted good.
Maybe moose,
caribou, or even a goose.
If I was a wolf I'd howl at the moon
and sleep in a den wanting to have fun again
and again.
Once I awoke from my deep night slumber
I would look for a piece of fallen lumber
as my throne
on which I could claim myself king of the forest.
If I was a wolf I'd clean my coat
as sleek as a brand new boat.
I'd hope to find the perfect mate,
whom I do not wish to hate.
If only I was a wolf, sadly I'm not.
I'm just a human, nothing gained
nothing got.

Austin Cascarelli, Grade 7
Columbia Middle School

The Woods

The sun shining through the trees
The birds calling out to each other
The wind softly rustling the leaves on the trees
The squirrels chasing each other from tree to tree
The butterflies fluttering through the air
The eagle soars high above
The woods are very peaceful

Amy Borntrager, Grade 8
Central Middle School

Excruciating Ice Cream

I got a bowl of ice cream
And my it was so cold
Before I even ate it
I could feel it through the bowl

I finally took a bite of it
And when I did oh dear
My whole head got bad frostbite
And off fell my left ear

My esophagus froze over
My stomach acid stopped its burn
My colon left my body and said,
"Maybe now you'll learn"

I know my body hates me
I do this every day
If I keep up this habit
I fear I'll soon decay

Christian Fulljames, Grade 7
Montague Nellie B Chisholm Middle School

Big House

My big house is taller than the sky.
My big house is wider than the world.
My big house has everything in the world.
People think their house is big but they haven't seen mine.

I have tons of things in my big house.
Whatever you want I have in my big house.
It takes you two years to reach one part of my big house.
To go through the whole thing takes you ten years.

My big house has one billion pools and one trillion hot tubs.
I go swimming every day before and after school.
I have my own skate park all to myself.
As many times as I have tried to make it.

I tried to get to the other end in a year.
It's very hard to reach the other end.
I have never been able to get through two sections.
My big house has things I do not even want.

Andrew Allyn, Grade 7
Montague Nellie B Chisholm Middle School

Do You Love Me?

I know you, you know me.
Everything I do, you can see.
So what if you spot me, doing something wrong.
Would you stop, and teach me as I go along.
Do you love me? Or do you not?
What if I leave? What do you got?
As I redo my mistake,
watch how proud I stand.
What I am trying to say is…
Thanks for giving me a hand.

Sarah Chehab, Grade 7
Flynn Middle School

Life

It's hard to tell whether life is
A reality or a dream
Life is something you should deem
Life is special in every way
For without it, you will have nothing
Everything is what it can bring
From happiness to sadness
And everything you can think of
Life can fly away like a dove
If you make a huge mistake that you cannot retake
Life is something you should care
Even though sometimes
There's something you cannot bare
What will happen will happen
And what has passed should stay passed
Whatever you have done long ago
Should be forgotten
And what you do now in life is what is important
Dream, do, go, and say all that you want
For you only have one life
And one chance to do them all…

Nhi Tranhuynh, Grade 7
Flynn Middle School

Baseball

Baseball is my favorite sport,
It doesn't matter if you're tall or short.

You have to be lightning fast,
Otherwise you will come in last.

It's respectable to be strong as an ox,
That's if you want to play for the White Sox.

Dust and dirt swoop through the air,
Which makes it hard to bear.

For me, I love this sport most of all,
Everybody should play baseball.

Alex Szymczak, Grade 7
St Anthony of Padua School

The Sickness

My grandpa got sick I thought, oh,
He will get over it quick
My grandma called my dad starts to cry
He says, Melissa, he's going to die
I knew who they were talking about
I gave them doubt
My dad sits me down he says he is going to die
I start to cry
I say "No he's not!"
Even thought I know he is
Time flies by like a bullet he's gone.
It soon becomes dawn
And he has already died
No more fly away
Gone, bye bye
But in my heart my grandpa didn't die
He's strong and still alive
I still say to this day it's all a lie

Alexis Tortorelli, Grade 7
Paw Paw Middle School

The Coming of the Morning

In the gray lit hour of twilight
Between the night and coming day
A mist rose from the dew cloaked ground
O'er all a quiet stillness lay.

The birds had not begun their song
And the stillness reigned o'er all.
These creatures waited for the time
In which they could release their call.

Then a rosy color touched
On the faces of the clouds.
The sun's first rays turned to gold
The silent earth's misty shrouds.

In all of His great majesty
The sun then rose and took His place.
To rule o'er the day to come
He did the tranquil night replace.

A great cacophony of song
Rose up in joy to greet his reign,
For every creature's spirit soared
Because the day had come again.

Timothy Lashley, Grade 9
Juniata Christian School

Cardinal

A dart of crimson flame
The cardinal slices through the autumn wind
Bursting with energy and vibrancy,
So unruly and untamed.

Laura VanEngen, Grade 8
Cutlerville Christian School

Notes About Nonsense

Flaming turkeys are very lame,
Flaming chickens are very strange.
Flaming lions are very tame,
I just shot at the archery range.

Flaming chickens are very strange,
Some dogs wear a chain.
I just shot at the archery range,
One *Batman* villain is named Bane.

Some dogs wear a chain,
Construction sites need a crane.
One *Batman* villain is named Bane,
One author is Mark Twain.

Constructions sites need a crane,
Flaming turkeys are very lame.
One author is Mark Twain,
Flaming lions are very tame.
Robert Shaker, Grade 7
Grand Blanc Middle School

Life

You write your story.
Life is like an empty book.
Make it worth reading.
Katie Copeland, Grade 7
Dearborn Heights Montessori Center

Homework Agony

My desk is
    no pile.
My desk is
    a landfill.

My pencil slashes
    against the paper.
My pencil breaks
    in agony.

Piles of books
    pile on me.
Pages flip
    back and forth.

Papers go back
    into folders.
Books close
    into bookbags.

The misery
    is done.
The fun
    begins!
Zach Neithercut, Grade 8
St John Vianney Catholic School

Hate

Your mind clouded…
As if someone painted a solid red mural in my head,
Because that's all I can see,
Blind to any object around you…
Dark thoughts swirl in your brain as if they were ripping you apart…
Piece by Piece…
Slowly at first it grows gaining size as my hatred swells into a monster
I couldn't muster enough strength to contain.
Vengeance;
The ringleader of it all
As my hate for the agitator grows
Shrewdly I start to think…
I start to unknowingly wish things I never would have said.
It's no coincidence.
It will catch up to you.
No use to cynically deny it
The more you repress
The stronger it gets.
There's only one way to beat hate and eliminate the darkness of your mind.
To release the falsified anger inside you
Hatred will resign…
Deniz Fidan, Grade 7
Holmes Middle School

A Woman

A woman so strong a woman so sweet,
The kindest person you would ever meet on the street.
A woman who cried and kept her feelings inside,
A black proud woman that wasn't ashamed to show her smile.
A person who didn't judge or question all of the above,
A woman who wanted to be equal and change her future around,
A black proud woman that came along and took control,
A person that had a goal.
She was told she could do anything,
She put her mind to just be true to what she wanted to do.
In 2005 I guess God said it's time for you to go
So you can spend time in my kingdom.
Diamond Dyess, Grade 8
Erma Henderson Upper Campus

I Am

I am a girl who loves art and music.
I like when other people like the same music as me.
I feel more people should draw and create things.
I hear many beautiful sounds from the songs I listen to.
I see paintings and sculptures made by famous artists.
I am a girl who loves art and music.
I wonder if I will always see things people miss.
I know I will always love the sound of music.
I care for the people who can make beautiful things with a pencil.
I wish I could show the world how beautiful things can be.
I am a girl who loves art and music.
Paige Elwen-Gonzales, Grade 7
Paw Paw Middle School

Oh How I Love

Oh how I love
To be her bud.
Oh how I love
To be his little man.
Even if it was just for one day.
Oh how I love
To see her so happy.
Oh how I love
To see the happiness in his eyes.
Oh how I love
To see the love in her eyes.
Oh how I love
My mom and dad.
I would die with them to stay with them.
I guess I didn't know how good it could be.
Oh I will always love my mom and dad.

Patrick G. Wilson, Grade 7
Manistee Middle School

My Mom

She's my best friend!
She's the one I can go to when I'm down.
She's the one who knows when something's wrong.
She's the one who watches shows with me.
She loves Gilmore Girls just as much as me!
She's the one who made me emotional.
She's the one who made me a book worm!
She's the one who made me, me.
She's my best friend!

Simone Frappier, Grade 7
Camden Frontier Middle School

Bad News

I have no feelings
For my best friend has died
It is hard to move on
When somebody so close moves on
I'm trying not to be greedy,
But it is hard
When someone who took care of you all your life dies.
This might sound crazy
But it's the truth
I found out about bad news on Christmas Eve
When I visited my father
After not seeing him for three years
We had a party
I got to see my family
They seemed to be so happy
But I felt unwanted
By my father and evil stepmother
At the end of the party
They gave me the bad news
I don't want you to feel bad for me
So you will just smile and leave me be.

Joshua Caswell, Grade 9
Manchester High School

Hockey

Hockey is a fast sport
That means don't come in last.
Played with six players on each side
The rink is fifty feet wide.
The furious motion
Might be the wrong potion for some.
It is hard hitting
Thus make sure equipment is fitting.
The game is sixty mad minutes
But don't become sad.
As your skate hits the ice
You might be rolling the dice.
The faster you go
The more you feel the cold air rush through your nose.
Hockey is fun if you win or lose
So do not drop your chin.
The harder you try
The more successful you will be.
Some say hockey is not an intrigue
But they have never been fatigued.

Dan Le Blanc, Grade 7
St Thomas More Academy

Fear

In a land full of hate
those who live there know their fate
ruled by the iron grip of doom
a dark figure that ever looms
fear ever present in their mind.
hope they will never find freedom is all but lost
to fight for it will pay a cost
sleepless nights, and haunted dreams
or endless wars,
and ruthless fiends
a dark shadow begins to fall
and evil voice starts to call
riding forth and evil hord
serving the voice of their evil lord
souls lined up at death's very gate
the sun falls, the hour grows late
but one thing they cannot kill
is a brave heart and an iron will

Cameron Barber, Grade 7
Oakland Christian School

Sports

Tennis
Hard, small
Hitting, falling, smashing
Net, racket, club, hole
Flying, going, rolling
Rigid, solid
Golf

Kyle Fahrlander, Grade 7
Montague Nellie B Chisholm Middle School

The School's Lunch

Lunch at our school isn't very good,
It doesn't taste like how it should.
The chicken nuggets don't look right,
They're better in a big food fight.
The milk is way way too expired,
It will be there when I'm retired.
The fruit is moldy, old, and dry,
On top there lays a dead black fly.
The mac and cheese tastes like plastic,
I'll pack my lunch and pass on it.
The salad is around six years old,
The lettuce looks like green green mold.
A dollar twenty-five we'll pay,
When applesauce tastes like clay.
The food is nasty, I don't tease,
Don't make me eat it, please oh please.
I hate our lunch, it's so so icky,
And trust me, I'm not that picky!

Mary Schlicher, Grade 8
Lewiston Middle School

Mom

Mom you love me
Mom you care for me
Mom you come to all my games
Mom you're nice to all my friends
Mom you are by my side all the time
Mom you're the hottest mom in town
Mom you're my best friend
Mom I love you

Lindsay Poikey, Grade 7
Camden Frontier Middle School

Forgive

I stand here today,
Looking right at you.
Please don't say sorry,
There's nothing you can do.
My life's going on,
I believe yours is too.
I've waited so long,
What's the big deal?
So many times I sought,
To say it before,
But that was then,
This is now.
Here I am,
So ready and prepared.
So many people are against you,
But I've moved on.
So now I stare right at you,
And I will try to say…
I do forgive you.

Krishlynn Buck, Grade 9
Muskegon High School

Seasons

Spring is the time for flowers
Spring is the time for baby showers

Summer is the time for swimming
Summer is the time for camping

Winter is the time for snowmen
Winter is the time for sledding

Autumn is the time for raking leaves
Autumn is the time for changing trees

Spring Lyons, Grade 7
Jefferson Middle School

You Mean All of This to Me

You're my first thought when I wake up,
and my last thought as I fall asleep.
I hope this will last,
as years and years pass.

Whenever I cry,
you won't say good-bye.
You hold me tight,
to make it all right.

Whenever we kiss or hug,
I know I'm in love.
I love you more and more each day,
I will never forget the month of May.

The first time I saw your eye,
I just knew you'd be my guy.
I think about you all the time,
I love that I can call you mine.

I love your smile, and your face,
there is no one who can take your place.
You're the guy I love to see,
you mean all of this to me!

Kelsey Young, Grade 7
Flynn Middle School

The Desert

Out on the scary desert,
The hot dry wind pursued us,
With the sun beating down on us,
The hot dry wind pursued us,
Wishing the sky would weep its water,
The hot dry wind pursued us,
Eventually the desert drove us mad,
The hot dry wind pursued us,
We could not survive there anymore,
The hot dry wind pursued us.

Nate Pedder, Grade 7
Flynn Middle School

Lightning

Who am I?
I will come and go,
I will shine, then will blacken.
I can only be viewed for a second,
My brother likes to roar.
Lightning

Harrison Frede, Grade 8
St Anthony of Padua School

A Pine in Spring

Sitting on the ground,
The sun shimmers
Like the morning dew
Through the pine branches
Who giggle in the bone-chilling wind.

The sky has become
An ocean of cerulean blue,
There are birds dancing
To their own song,
Earthworms
Digging tunnels through the soft soil,
Bees collecting nectar
From a nearby flower.

The wind
Stings like a jellyfish,
The air, is a cool and crisp
Winter-fresh breath mint.

Shane Wechsler, Grade 9
North Farmington High School

What If?

What if the day was never bright?
Always the same shade of the night.

What if the ocean was not wet?
As dry as the desert could ever get.

What if the night was always day?
Always seeing a yellow sunray.

What if a bird had no wings?
Walking just like most other things.

What if the Glaciers were not cold?
Being too hot would get quite old.

What if the rainforest was not hot?
If it were cold I would like it not.

But why should I care if it's not me?
I could be anything I want to be!

Trevor Torres, Grade 7
Flynn Middle School

Life Is Like a River

Life is like a river, flowing endlessly on, never stopping.
Life gets complicated, faster and important.
Life however ends, as a river
When it empties into an ocean or lake.

Stephen Schmidt, Grade 8
Hilbert Jr High School

Opposites

Monkey
Hairy, stinky
Swinging, climbing, eating
Banana, vines, clothes, cars
Running, swimming, driving
Exciting, smart
Human

Manuel Villeda, Grade 7
Montague Nellie B Chisholm Middle School

I Gaze

I look into his eyes
All I see is him and me
I can't stop looking at him
I just wish that one day he will do the same
I hope and pray
I love him with all of my heart
I can't stop thinking of him
One day just one day
He will say those four special words
I love you too

Kara Andre, Grade 7
West Middle School

I Am

I am a nice person who likes cheerleading
I wonder what I will turn out to do
I hear people talking
I see words
I want a million dollars
I am a nice person who likes cheerleading
I pretend to be famous
I feel happy
I touch things
I worry about my life
I cry when I think of my dad
I am a nice person who likes cheerleading
I understand that things will not always go my way
I say to take one day at a time
I dream that life will be problem free
I try my hardest to succeed
I hope to be a great student
I am a nice person who likes cheerleading
I am fun and understanding
I am a great friend

Breanne Kelly, Grade 7
Roseville Jr High School

The Kitten That Wore Mittens

All I ever wanted was a little kitten
With paws that looked like little mittens
I begged and begged with no reply
And without my kitten time flies
Then I had finally got him
I called him little Tim
And as days go by
How he has grown my my
Now he is grumpy and old
And meaner and uglier than mold
And now I think I don't want a kitten
With paws that look like mittens

Alycia Workman, Grade 7
Montague Nellie B Chisholm Middle School

If Only He Knew

I look at him across the room,
Of course he won't notice me,
I'm just another teenage girl fallen in love so tragically.

I look at him dancing with her,
Of course I don't have a date,
There's no one I'd ever like as much so I'm just going to wait.

I watch him on graduation day,
Of course I'm standing here,
As he runs off with her I almost shed a tear.

I listen as he marries her,
Of course I'm in the front row,
And as they kiss I don't think my hearts ever been this low.

I cry as he dies with her,
And as the priest reads his journal aloud,
I'm very shocked to hear him utter these sounds.

"I look at her across the room,
Of course she won't notice me,
I'm just another teenage boy fallen in love so tragically."

Morgan Gray, Grade 7
Wolfe Middle School

Snake

Snakes so slippery and sly
They'll sneak up behind you and make you die
Their venom is deadly it kills quite quick
You don't even have time to feel sick

Snakes start by wrapping around you
From your feet to your hips
From your hips to your head
There it will consume you,
And before you know it
You're on your deathbed.

Hannah Johnson, Grade 7
Columbia Middle School

Golf

I love to play this game,
That may someday bring me fame.

As I sink that 50 foot putt
I can feel it in my gut.

That something's going right,
So I try to win with all my might.

I can almost feel the win
While I look at the pin.

I hit my next drive,
On that very long par five.

The ball burned as hot as a griddle,
And it moved very little.

The ball is an owl in the night,
It is a very cool sight.

I watch my ball roll,
Right into the hole.

J.T. Lovell, Grade 8
St Anthony of Padua School

Paradise Possibilities

Life is full of possibilities,
With numerous choices to make,
Decisions that make you feel superior.
So don't be kept in the chamber of lies,
Just spread your golden wings and fly,
Because life isn't everlasting,
So live your life like
You're already in paradise.

Kaitlyn Coffey, Grade 7
Columbia Middle School

Beautiful Beach

The sun is an oven,
Warm on your face,
The taste of salt coats your lips,
Children are laughing,
Sounding like the gulls,
Singing their happy songs,
The tide splashes in,
And floats back out,
Into the cool wet sea,
The sandcastles stand like mini forts,
Ready to fight off the enemies,
Sand squishes between your toes,
Wet and cool like mud,
To me this day,
Seems too perfect to be true.

Sarah Stanton, Grade 7
Addison Middle School

Airsoft

Airsoft is a sport, its fun in every way
Little yellow BB's flying in your way.
As the gun shots fill the air, it's loud against your ear, but soft from far away.
Excitement fills your eyes but fear is about when the beginning has come.
We dress in dark green camouflage, which hides us deep within the forest.
The first shot is fired — bodies scurry all over the field.
Then they fire back at us and people start to get shot.
Usually a little ouch indicates an out.
As the day goes by time runs out
This means we better get them fast.
Its all come down to this moment of truth
Who is the best player — me or that adult?
That is what I ask myself.
He seems pretty good but I can get him out?
I pop up and shoot — he screams "Ouch!"
I yell with joy, "YES!"
That was that — the day was at an end.
All that was left to remember the moment where I had beat them all.
But then the next day came and it stared all over again.

Kolbi Hess, Grade 8
Beach Middle School

A Tree's Fate

A tree hatches from it's seed — a new life begins
It clings to its parent, seeking protection from the world
As the wind blows, it stand firm in its spot, showing its strength.

Snow falls, but the tree doesn't even flinch
The tree helps us out in many ways
From tree houses to shade
But all stories don't have a happy ending…

A lumberjack walks into the forest, ax in hand.
He walks up the tree, a gleam in his eye.
The tree tries to back up, knowing that it will soon die, but its roots keep it there.
The ax swings towards the tree, but it cannot scream.

Kate Eichman, Grade 7
Peace Lutheran Church & School

Grandpa

I never even knew what you looked like,
I hardly ever saw you
But then you became ill,
And everything changed
I thought it would be fun, for you to always be around
I would see you all the time.
Seven years passed and you started forgetting my name.
You always loved me, no matter what
Whether you called me Liz or Liza, I knew you were talking to me.
We shared laughter and good times,
We enjoyed holidays and much much more
Your last taste of hot chocolate was with me and Mor.
Even though we don't share here anymore,
I pray to God that we will meet again in heaven.

Liza DiAntonio, Grade 8
Oakland Christian School

Chicken Part II

She ruined a majority of the chances,
I could have had with you.
Now you are confused,
Of what you should possibly do.
Oh, how I ache for the day,
When I reveal what my feelings are for.
We'd bicker, who loves each other the most,
Though you'd swear you love me more.
Now all the jolly laughter that we've shared,
Has officially gone to waste.
Because of one hateful person; to the bond,
Applied a venomous paste.
Now, when I look into those "Emo" glasses of yours,
I wonder what the next man will think of me.
I sometimes feel used, like a deer caught in headlights.
Both of us now are scattered, from what I can see.
I have a strange prospect of the matter now,
To our hearts; if we jeopardize to listen.
Both of us will dominate this lack of integrity,
Though I dread we are both far too chicken.

Paige Nicke, Grade 8
L'anse Creuse Middle School East

Spring

The best season of the year is spring.
Please listen to my linguistic string,
About the season spring.

Very warm
Little storm.
Trees transform
Art form.
Flowers bloom.
Caterpillars start to consume.
Sun shine.
Peace divine.
Peaceful.
Blissful.
Cheerful
Bountiful.

I really like spring as you see.
It's the better season out of the other three.

James Williams, Grade 7
Ruth Murdoch SDA Elementary School

My Room

My floor unseen under the mounds of clothes
The light scent of deodorant left on the shirts
The books sprawled here and there and everywhere
The book light above my bed still warm from use
The bed a mess with sheets bundled up in a ball
My mom almost fainting, surprised at the gargantuan mess
This room is my only sanctuary

Luke Anderson, Grade 8
Central Middle School

Dreaming

Today, it was so windy and cold,
But spring is here is what I have been told.

Where's the sun to warm our backs?
I want to wear shorts instead of slacks.

I long for an occasional shower,
That will hopefully grow a beautiful flower.

I want to walk with cooing doves
And not have to wear my winter gloves.

When will spring arrive for me?
Soon is what I do believe.

Emily Schaible, Grade 8
Beach Middle School

Falling Down

Do you ever feel like you're inside-out?
When you have no doubt
that the world doesn't know what you're about.
Do you ever feel alone?
Even when you're not on your own,
even when you're on the phone
talking and laughing
but wishing someone ACTUALLY cared.
Do you ever feel scared?
Like no one will be there
when
you
fall
down
and
down

until you'll hit the ground.
Wishing
Someone
Out there
cared.

Emilie Pichot, Grade 7
Ruth Murdoch SDA Elementary School

Hitchhiker

The hitchhiker, a good old man,
Who gets a ride by sticking out his hand
But most cars just drive by,
Some people might say hi,
The mean type could go by.
Will the meaner type stop right there
And give him an evil glare?
But up the road there's a man of love and care
So he decided to pick you up there.

Andrew Smith, Grade 7
Guardian Lutheran School

Rosalynn Carter

Rosalynn Carter was the first child in her family, so far it was a family of three.
When her father died, she cried and cried.

She was the wife of Jimmy Carter, she also worked as a dressmaker.
She had one child with Jimmy, their daughter's name was Amy.

She became first lady in 1962. Rosalynn helped Jimmy's campaigns come through.
She needed glasses for seeing near and far away. So she got contacts and that is the way she wanted it to stay.

She was the head of the campaign, and she had a nice brain.
Rosalynn and Jimmy moved into the White House in 1976. Naturally she was interested in politics.

"Steel Magnolia Blossom" was her nickname then came the fame.
She attended meetings with Mr. Carter. She then got smarter and smarter.

She was very pretty and she lived in the city.

Brandi King, Grade 7
Lakeview Middle School

From the Earth's Perspective

I see planets from afar, my Moon surrounded by the stars,
Other objects are all askew, but the mighty Sun blocks my view.
As I grope away the Sun's wrath, I must orbit and follow her path,
As her mighty light blinds, I try to veer, but her scornful laugh is one to jeer.
I rotate, spin around and around, to try to maim out her awful sound,
Now I struggle day to day, only trying to get away.

My Moon is mine for he follows me so, never too high, never too low,
Sometimes I face him as I slowly turn, only to let the Sun make my face burn.
A citadel she powers, others look little, while she's big and strong, right in the middle
We orbit around her, it's her decree, but without us, what would she be?
Although she looks warming from a view, she's freezing cold on the inside too,
The Sun plays with my people's lives, she can make it too hot to survive.

My Moon is brave, for once a year, he blocks the sun, so my face won't sear,
I thank him as I face his way; we celebrate as we banter and play.
I think hard, as I turn from Moon's sight, my people would die without the sun's light,
And without the Sun, where would we go? We would all be amassed without orbit's flow.
She's protecting us from losing our place, and the light she whips isn't meant for my face,
It's meant for my people, so they can survive, so my people can eat, stay strong and alive.

I fought her orbit, I fought her rule; I thought that she was being cruel,
But she mothers the planets, my sisters and brothers; we're all a big family with the Sun as our Mother.

Kari Kiddle, Grade 8
Pathfinder School

Untitled

Simply irresistible like the plump, acid taste of freshly picked plums,
juice being crushed, gushing out like brain knowledge flows,
as the moments are devoted to the books with its time spent to our sovereign Lord.
Learning never quite grasping the message to our incomplete intellectual minds,
the message is bone-chilling like a falling snowflake landing on a freshly-bloomed rose,
all just to wonder who will pass the gate of eternal love.

Amanda Rika Deemter, Grade 8
Cutlerville Christian School

Remember

Do you remember, I do
The day it was hot
And the ocean was boiling
We sat on the sand
The seashell you were toiling

We sat and we talked
Like there was nothing to do
But deep in my mind I was thinking of you
The way you are sweet, kind, and gentle
Your beauty makes me go mental
There is not a moment that you are rude
It seems you are always in a good mood

But sadly this day soon will end
But never the goodness you always seem to trend
Kevin Farmer, Grade 8
Gesu Elementary School

My Dream

I had a dream last night, and I love what it meant.
Everyone should dream of this, so this is how it went.

I was at a magic fountain, I thought wishing was the case,
As I threw in the nickel, I went another place.

I was in my own world, a place where I was queen,
No one was ever evil, and no one was ever mean.

Everyone had X-ray vision, and only saw the inside,
Their outside didn't matter, so no one ever cried.

There were no such words as skinny, ugly, weird, or fat,
Models were pretty inside, and it didn't stop at that.

Everyone was giving, so no one was in debt,
And everyone got a hug whenever they met.

Soon I was awakened, oh that place I'll miss,
It would be a miracle if my real world were like this.
Erin Bobbitt, Grade 7
Gesu Elementary School

Friend?

A good friend will stand up for you,
Even though they know you are wrong.
When you wake them up at night to talk,
They ask, "What took you so long?"
When a friend sees you cry,
They will cry with you until there's not a tear left,
Because they wouldn't ask you why.
But the best way to describe a friend,
Is they are the one standing next to you in the end.
Melissa Stewart, Grade 9
Cadillac Jr High School

My Life Is a Shame

My life is a shame, full of pain.
I'm glad I'm here instead of there.

My life is a shame put into a game.
I'm like the dog who gets into fog
wherever it goes.

My life is a shame, and there's no way out;
like a pig with no snout, I can't smell the roses,
instead I'm in many poses.

My life is a shame, full of gain;
not good nor bad but far worse than that.

My life is a shame, but I'm tame
So I gain no pain from this shame game.
Lauren Fox, Grade 8
Otsego Middle School

The Window

In the morning I wake up and open the blinds
I look outside to see the most beautiful view

The frost lines the window like a frame on a photo
The clouds are rolling by, way up high, in the sky

The trees stand like bare skeletons swaying side to side
Because of the wind that you can hear whistling

The sun casts a shadow that makes everything look dead
But truly everything is just waking up, just like me
Gabrielle Doman, Grade 7
Assumption BVM School

What If

What happens if I don't have money do I become poor?
What happens if people don't want to live in America anymore?
Will our greatest foundations be lost and never found
What happens when we're under attack
And our troops aren't around
Will we be unprotected?
Will everyone run around and things become hectic
What if our leaders don't come through?
Will Bush run out on us too
Is this poem so wrong because it is so right?
That people are afraid of the truth
Spite all I feel this way
No matter what the government say
Because I'll preach what I know
But on the real though
People don't want to know
I have questions need answers
I want the truth
If not then we're all doomed.
Kibri McMurray, Grade 7
Ludington Magnet Middle School

Triumphant Win

The smell of sulfur
In the air
The sounds of gunfire
Is far from rare

But there it flies
Our flag of glory
Against the blood red skies
We see it once again arise

We hear a cheer
Our men advance
The doom of the enemy
Now comes near

For loved ones! For God!
The chant that has formed
We surround our enemies
In one massive swarm

They raise the white flag
Our victory had come
Under excellent leaders
The war is now won!

Alicia Oakley, Grade 8
Ruth Murdoch SDA Elementary School

Echo

A quiet country road,
all is quiet here, and I am alone.
I feel I must move on,
or else could I be here for all of time?

I feel a quiet beat,
a million people, on this lonely street?
Am I all alone,
or is this an illusion?

Is real really real?
How can I express this thing I feel?
Swept up by the crowd,
an echo of another time and place.

Nick Daniel, Grade 8
St John Vianney Catholic School

Tigers

Tigers roar as loud as they can
They jump through rings of
Fire and back down to the
Ground again
They're black and orange
And big cats too
If you try to find them
They're at the zoo.

Ashlea Kuster, Grade 7
Camden Frontier Middle School

Donn*

God, why did you choose such an early day to end Donn's life?
He left behind family, friends and a grieving wife.
When Donn died, we all felt sad and cried.
Donn, why did God take you?
He knew we'd feel bad.
God, why did you choose such an early day to end Donn's life?
He had been filled with such strife; he had so much to live for with his wife.
Now, we his family and friends weep and it's harder every night to sleep.
Why did God take you, Donn?
We miss you and can't help asking "Why?" but now we say "Goodbye."

Joyce Cutliff, Grade 7
Jefferson Middle School
*Dedicated to my friend Donn Richard Nielson who died on March 2nd 2006.

Love

No one gets me I'm all alone
my heart beats cold you're my heavy load

My shoulders are weak I'm falling apart
no one left I'm in the dark

You're almost there reaching out for my hand
but you tricked me and let go I fall back to the sand

I know what's right and where I should be
but I'm still here it's like you're holding onto me

The emotional pain it's all too much
everything explodes in one big rush

Finally it closes but you walk right back in
I wonder if you even know you're dragging a knife across my skin

The Earth is cold it's shutting me out
I'm left alone that's what love is about

Katelyn Blair, Grade 8
Mio AuSable Middle/High School

When

When I used to pretend it would go away…I would sit in my room and cry all day.
I cried dawn till dusk…dusk till dawn.
When I cried I thought…maybe they would change.
I could hear the words at night…
Until I turned my music up so loud…the words just seemed to drown.
The words scared me…I thought they'd never end.
When I knew they were going to be home…the words repeated in my head.
The tears ran down my cheek…like the blood shed of Jesus Christ our Lord.
I used to be scared…whenever they were near.
The thought of the names and words…still ring inside my head.
So whenever you can't stand another word…
Or another name just turn up your music…
And the words seem…to melt away

Amber Fritz, Grade 7
Perry Middle School

Days of Our Lives

The morning starts with sun-kissed dew,
Nothing's wrong and everything is new.

The afternoon is full of laughter and fun,
Kids are out playing and enjoying the bright warm sun.

The evening is filled with serenity and peace,
It's when the playing, laughing, and fun must cease.

Now we have to say good-bye to one more day of our lives.

Tessa Margaritis, Grade 8
Ruth Murdoch SDA Elementary School

The Not So Simple Life

Friends are like stars
They come and go
But the ones that stay are the ones that glow.
True friends are like a four leaf clover
Hard to find but lucky to have.
Best friends are meant to be together
And stay together
Without giving up on each other.
My friends are crazy
But I love them more than anything.
Girls just wanna have fun.
We follow our heart
But nothing's better than letting go.
Life isn't as easy as it seems
Life is like trying to catch a falling star.
We have to take control.
Then you'll see all the things you do,
Affect every one around you.
Underneath this smile,
It's dangerous to know…
Life is unstoppable.

Mindy Diep, Grade 7
Flynn Middle School

The Perfect Brother

My older brother loves to smother me and my little sis
His skills athletic are not pathetic a basket he doesn't miss

He's much more fun than anyone and I just don't know why
Maybe the reason is just as pleasin' as he is as sly

He's a go-getter and a trendsetter every single day
He always goes and never slows no matter what gets in the way

He's very slim and very trim but eating all the time
My love for him is above all things and will be for my lifetime

Though fight we might in spite, we always work it out
He might not get what he wants but never does he pout
This name I say not in shame Tommy is great no doubt!

Shelby Saelens, Grade 8
St Thomas More Academy

Never

It would always last forever
They were meant to be together
Never would it end
When they were in the park under the moonlit sky
As she leaned over
And whispered in his ear
Our love will never die
As she drifted away into the starry night
Forever and always

Mallory Fischer, Grade 8
Immanuel-St James Lutheran School

Man's Best Friend

Jiggy and Coco are crazy dogs
They can also be just like two logs.
They like to run around and play.
Other times they sleep all day.
When there's food they're always around.
They even eat stuff off the ground.
I like to watch them play tug o' war.
They flop and roll all over the floor.
They always look so happy and glad,
Unless they're in trouble for being bad.
Most of the time they can be fun.
But other times I wish they were done.
They always make a lot of noise.
And sometimes they chew up my favorite toys.
Even though they're a pain in the rear,
I'm very glad we have them here.
Dogs are called man's best friend.
They'll stick with you to the very end.
If they weren't with us here.
Life would be very boring I fear.

Zach Birt, Grade 9
St Thomas More Academy

Dreams

There are dreams to tell the world about
And dreams to keep a secret
Dreams to wish for,
Dreams to long for
And dreams you can only hope for,
But secrets are secrets
And wishes are wishes
And hopes you can only hope for
But a dream is a dream
No matter what
So let it stay a
D
R
E
A
M.

Julia Archer, Grade 7
Gull Lake Middle School

Gone But Still Around*

I've heard your name,
ten thousand times over,
but you've never heard mine.
I will always hear yours,
you will never hear mine.
I will always see your face,
you will never see mine.
I know the color of your eyes,
but you will never hold mine.
I know the way you walk,
but you will never watch me.
I know the expressions on your face,
but you will never read mine.
I will always watch you.

Sharon Downer, Grade 8
Immaculate Heart of Mary School
*In honor of our deceased ancestors.

Seasons

When the Earth
is cold and white,
all other color
drained from sight,
winter is here.

When the Earth
is alive and green,
shaking off
its white crystal gleam,
spring is here.

When the Earth
is hot and dry,
and big, lazy clouds
drift through blue sky,
summer is here.

When the Earth
leaves its warm, dull phase,
to become cool,
bathed in colors ablaze,
fall is here.

Rebecca Feuka, Grade 8
Perry Middle School

The Many Ways to Laugh

The many ways to laugh —
Clear
Loud
Short and sweet
To breathe through your teeth
To hiss like a snake
Long and loud
Whisper like

Jacqie Maynard, Grade 8
Central Middle School

Just Because

Just because I am a foster child
    Don't laugh at me if I cry
    Don't think I don't have parents
Just because I am a foster child
    It doesn't mean that I don't have people that love me
    It doesn't mean that you can talk about me behind my back
    It doesn't mean that I am scared
Just because I am a foster child
    I know it's wrong for you to say bad things about other people
    I still don't always make the wrong decisions
Just because I am a foster child — please don't ask me about it

Catherine McNeil, Grade 8
Central Middle School

A Leader for Every Culture

Rosa Parks was a leader for every culture in the world
that has been segregated from any other culture why?
Because she put her life in jeopardy just to let everybody know
that she was tired of being segregated from the white culture
and from the stores she wanted to shop at
and the park she wanted to sit at.
October 24, 2005 we lost the person that set us free from segregation
and from being second
so we all honor her for her strength and integrity
and ability to show no fear and take a stand
not just for her own culture but for every culture
that has been segregated from their rights to be free
and to live their life the way they want to
is free and to the fullest.

Malcolm Hunter, Grade 8
Erma Henderson Upper Campus

The True Power of Work

Work, work, work
What do you think of
When you hear the word work?
Do you feel a sudden empowerment?
Which can result to the intensity of your soul
Or could it just be your body without willingness to do so
Whether we know it or not
Work is placed all around us every day all day
And even as we speak work is being set aside
Even to be more recognized
But have we come to a conclusion that throughout all our lives
It has come to take over,
From the deep overwhelming power to boss us (workers) around
From just a silly leveled and yet unknown, popularized word
And the fact that too much influence, too much stability
Over your overall state of well-being, increases the chance of homicides
In our natural, busy, working city
With work indulging our mentality place much of your knowledge,
Or what you have acknowledged through meaningless working conditions
In the form of a life process; or as a mere image in our mind as when it
Can be absorb through some people's eyes, as just a game because, all we do is work.

Ashirell Nash, Grade 9
Cass Technical High School

Now You're Gone

I figure that you're dead.
I try not to cry when that runs through my head.

You're gone now.
I loved you with all my heart.
Back at the beginning,
I wish that I could start.

I would remember the moments we had,
cherish the time we shared.
Every kiss and touch would be in my mind,
each I love you spared.

Now you're gone,
and no one will know the things we did.
I will always remember you,
you let my life be lived.

Kayla Courter, Grade 9
Carsonville Port Sanilac High School

What Is Heaven?

A day of peace
Endless ice cream
A cold winter day sitting next to a fire
Watching TV after a long day of school
A day at the park
Jumping into a pool on a hot summer day
A cold piece of cherry pie
This is what I think of Heaven.

Joseph Bumstead, Grade 7
St John Lutheran School

Influential

A knot of confusion;
A decision to make.
And a path that could go
Two very different directions.
Both ways seem tempting;
But do I follow the path of others,
Do I let the influences of society decide my life?
Or will I be able to stand up for myself,
And live my life the way I want to.
Do what makes me happy,
And not worry about living up to everyone else's expectations.
It takes courage, confidence, and defiance
To even begin to live for yourself.
You only get one chance,
One life.
Take advantage of it,
Cherish it, and embrace every moment of it.
You never know when your last day might be.
So live your life for you,
And no one else.

Natalie Kusza, Grade 8
Brandon Middle School

A Missed Memory

My most missed memory is my dog.
When he ran out into the fog.

As I followed him I realized it was too late.
A car had already decided his fate.

And now I wish I could rewind
And travel back through place and time.

An explosion of energy brown and white
With expressive brown eyes and a huge appetite.

I realized I had lost a great friend,
A dog who would have followed me to the end.

Mary MacKenzie, Grade 7
Guardian Lutheran School

Life

We're born, we live, eat, breathe, sleep, die
Expectations are high
What more can we do to please you?
Role models, who are they? Can't people be themselves?
Pictures on the shelves
Remembering the time
People do crimes wasting their lives
Can you hear the cries of the new baby?
Not knowing what's ahead means they can't dread
After families and marriages and people become old
They say I lived a good life
And then they die remembering their times

Christina Young, Grade 8
Central Middle School

Meg

Meg is kind and really great fun
My inspiration in rain or sun
She is athletic in every way
Volleyball and soccer every day
Hilarious and clumsy like a kitten all the time
Similar to a clown reciting a silly rhyme
Hangs out with me whenever I call
Homework, dinner, movies, and all
Sometimes she's weird and a little bit lazy
Other times she's active and somewhat crazy
She has some names for people like me
"Bung-bung," "Babe," and even "Honey"
And now let's get back to her life's good points
She's funny and sweet and never disappoints
Her personality is great and so is her form
Her face is tan, gentle, and warm
With beautiful, curly, sun-kissed hair
And colorful, stylish, clothes to wear
Meg's a good friend and always will be
And a super great idol she is to me

Marissa Prain, Grade 8
St Thomas More Academy

Page 153

Stab in the Heart

Permit me to tell you about death,
    For I have seen them go
    So young and full of life
    Not to move again,
    Or look you in the eye

Yet the death I remember most,
    Felt like a stab in the heart
    Knowing I won't hear your giggle,
    Or see your smile,
    Until we meet again
          Lindsey Thibodeau, Grade 8
          Grosse Pointe Academy

I Don't Understand

I don't understand,
    Why the space never ends
    Why animals walk on four legs
    Why we walk on two
    Why the sky is blue

But most important,
    What will the world come to
    Why people are racist
    Why we fight over stupid things
    Why there is war?

What I do understand is,
    Why the grass grows
    How a light shines
    Why cars move
    How I wrote this poem.
          Mark Tatoris, Grade 8
          St John Lutheran School

Please Help Me

Why do I have to run,
Every day we run, and run
And run and run.

Please help me,

I'm going to die.
Why does running have to tire me?

Please help me.

I know it is good for me it must be.
But one more day of running,
And I'm definitely going to die.

So for my sake please,
Please help me.
    Jennifer LaFontaine, Grade 7
    Columbia Middle School

A Silent Swear

He stood
Shoulders arched
Face impassive
His rifle lay solemnly
Across his chest
It moved slowly
Until the tip
Was
At his shoulder
Once
Again
He turned, feet in
Step
With the others
Left, right, left, right
He marched
Waving good-bye
To the land
He once knew
Into the land
Unknown
    Amber Price, Grade 8
    Hally Magnet Middle School

I Will Fight

Gunfire across the field
Bomb exploding in my ear.
Screams of anger, death, and hate.

I sit down
My heart pounding faster
Than I can breathe.

Tears in my eyes.
Rage in my scream.
Sorry for all my wrong.

Bullet strikes me.
I sigh and shed a tear with relief.
I have no pain or fear.
I die, but it is not in vain;
It is not in vain.
    Sean Shannon, Grade 8
    St Gerard Elementary School

Peace

Peace is the quiet serenity of noise
Try it with the best grace and poise
Truth and happiness
And the world's quiet bliss
No wars or diseases
For peace only pleases
The tranquility inside of us
    Jenan Mardini, Grade 8
    Crescent Academy International

Day Dreams

Jumping from cloud to cloud
Soaring through the air
As light as a feather
Soaking up the sun
Shooting through the stars
Laying in the snow
Swimming in the ocean
It's your dream
Imagine it the way you want it
    Morganne Bayliss, Grade 8
    Oakland Christian School

O What a Tragedy

I took one step
My eyes could not believe
The pain which lies before me
My face fills with fear
My eyes water with tears
O what a tragedy

The widows at home
Mourn the loss
Of their beloveds never coming
To hold them close
To kiss them goodbye
O what a tragedy

The children cry
For they do not want to say
Goodbye to their daddy
O what a tragedy

The battlefields
Filled with brave men
Who risked their life
For what they believe
O what a tragedy
    Melissa Hull, Grade 8
    Oakland Christian School

Red Poppies

A woman so glad
she ran through a garden
Full of red-blooded poppies.
I wonder
why she is glad
as she ran through red poppies.
She ran and ran,
in her white gown with her young child.
I wonder
why she likes to run
through the gardens
of red-blooded poppies.
    Ashlyn Kouba, Grade 7
    Columbia Middle School

What We Had in Dr. Cason*

Dr. Cason was a principal
That we've learned to love and know
But she was not an ordinary one
When I was thinking
Of what I had in her
I started to realize how much she cared
Then her strong mentality I began to understand
So many times people took her for granted
But some people don't think about her love and care
Or how when we needed her she was always there
Hally is so blessed to have had a treasure so rare
She dealt with many things
That Hally didn't know or see
But yet people can say
What's right and what's wrong
If some of us were her we'd be a terrible sight
She'd been leading for so long and I have no regrets
She never failed her students
So I indeed thank God for a principal like this
And it could be none other than Dr. Cason!

Britney Tillman, Grade 8
Hally Magnet Middle School
*R.I.P. Dr. Cason

Don't Label Me

Just because I'm "smart"
   It doesn't mean I'm a geek
   It doesn't mean I know everything
   It doesn't mean I don't have to try

Just because I'm "smart"
   It doesn't mean I'm a social outcast
   It doesn't mean I get all A's
   It doesn't mean you can push me around

Just because I'm "smart"
   It doesn't mean I'm only good at being smart
   It doesn't mean I have to look the part
   I can succeed

Just because I'm "smart" — don't label me

Dominique DiPiazza, Grade 8
St John Lutheran School

Who Am I?

I am the sun that shines so brightly.
I am the mighty tiger of the jungle.
I am the minuscule mouse the squeaks in the night.
I am the colossal redwood that waves in the grand forest.
I am the insignificant blade of grass.
I am the inspiration for the greatest masterpieces of art.
I have touched all existence.
I am life.
I am God.

Aaron Langlois, Grade 8
St Anthony of Padua School

I Wish

I wish I could let loose the tears,
let go of all my fears,
get rid of all this hate,
and maybe it will lift this weight,
I wish I didn't have to put up with their fake smiles,
as I walk up and down the aisles,
at least I know I have two true friends,
who will be there will me till the very end,
I wish I could let go of the pain I feel inside,
but all I do is run and hide,
'cause I know I wouldn't gain a thing,
sometimes I wish I could just let go…

Angela Beach, Grade 8
Posen Consolidated High School

Mad Max

He runs on his wheel
When we're trying to sleep
But during the day
He won't make a peep.

A little pink nose
He sticks in the air
Just try to resist
His "pick me up" stare.

He stands on his hind legs
And looks so forlorn
With a fuzzy white belly
So cozy and warm.

Max is a comic unlike any other
And we're doubly blessed — he has a twin brother.

Twice the antics, the squeaking
The nocturnal noise
Have you guessed what we have?
A pair of mouse boys!

Michaela LeBlanc, Grade 7
St Thomas More Academy

Imagine

I wait by the river in the black night
Hearing rain's rhythm dance
Slip and tingle in my red hair
I sing through a garden of love
Full of sound and a dizzy rose, peach blossom scent
I hear birds fly across the sunset
Singing music of the heavens
Seas soothe me
At the sky's paradise
I hear a voice in the wind
Finally calling me home

Alisha Jackson, Grade 7
Hally Magnet Middle School

Friends

Running recklessly with resilience
Blabbering while watching television
When it rains we stay in
Just to be even more bored
Hanging out all day
Watching the sunset
Before the sunrise
Sharing super secret secrets
Visiting each other's houses
Staying over, awake all night
Forcefully beating video games
Always wanting to win
Having as much fun as humanly possible
Until was burst with excitement
Enduring the biggest fight
We will never be mad
We will always be close
Even if we move away
We will always be friends
Until the end of our life
And even still

Jason Porritt, Grade 8
Richardson Elementary Middle School

Teardrops

I lost someone very dear to my heart,
Now my life is falling apart.
I try not to show any emotion, but it
Takes pride and devotion.
I try to be strong but these feelings
Won't go away, I want to
Understand why God took him away.
My *Best Friend!* I try to
Act like it's not a problem, but
Teardrops just start falling. I just
Don't understand why, why did
He have to die.

Nyesha Knight, Grade 7
Flynn Middle School

Spiders

Small, yicky, slimy
Completely totally grimy

Black, white and red
They live under your bed

Tiny heads, eight legs
They all lay bunches of eggs

Itchy bites
Scary nights

There's nothing worse than spiders.

Matt Bohn, Grade 8
St Gerard Elementary School

I Am

I am small and thin,
I am not happy with whom I've been,
I am not happy with how I look,
I am not able to read a long book.
I am not with a rich happy family,
I am a torn soul but still not happy,
I am sad most of the time, but still act happy.
I am strong but still feel weak.
I am misunderstood but still pretty good.
I am not your normal boy,
I am not living at one address,
I am young but still depressed.
I am excited for next year,
I can't wait to get out of this school right here.
I am going to be happy there you see,
I am going to have more friends.
I am a person who hates who I am,
I am a person who wants his parents together again
I am a person who won't forget his dad walking out the front door,
I am still mad at my mom for getting that divorce.
This is who I am. Now might you all understand?

John Gregory, Grade 8
St Anthony of Padua School

Life

Life is a new born baby.
Life is a seed ready to grow.
Life is the sun rising above the clouds.

Life is when someone you really care about dies
or like you won or lose in a basketball game.
Life is growing out of the baby stuff that you like when you were little.
Life is about meeting new people.
Life is about accomplishing your goals.

Life is about making your own choices.
Life is about hard work and determination.
Life is about having ideas and sharing them.
Life is about sacrifices.
Life is about doing what you want to and becoming your own person.
That's life.

Christopher Braswell, Grade 7
Gesu Elementary School

The Great Outdoors

The great outdoors has many animals that live and roam around there.
The great outdoors is full of green trees.
The great outdoors is a way to relax from the hustle and bustle of the city.
But now in the great outdoors the animals are hunted.
But now in the great outdoors the trees are being chopped down.
But now in the great outdoors there is no relaxing.

Casey C. Wagner, Grade 8
St Gerard Elementary School

Depression

I cannot begin to explain,
How depression is a slaughtering pain.

Depression is a dark empty place,
I can see it grimacing on the person's face.

I wish I could wipe the agony and bitterness they face,
And put confidence like joy in their place.

"So, I pray to our God," I say,
"Don't let your sadness take your life away."
Kristi Carpentier, Grade 8
St Anthony of Padua School

A Spirit That Lives

The early fall morning
The cold breeze
Light a candle and pray on your knees

There's a magic in the sound of their name,
Here come the Irish of Notre Dame

The crowd cheers, you chug your beers
Shake up the thunder,
Because there's a magic in the sound of their name,
Here come the Irish of Notre Dame

There's always next year don't fall to your fate
At least next year you'll beat Michigan State
Alex Mueller, Grade 8
St Gerard Elementary School

The War of the Worlds*

The aliens attack,
When you turn your back.
They've been planning this for years,
After they figured out our fears.
You think it's over,
But again they take over.
The cries aren't calm;
Especially when they have you in their palm.
They get more excited,
When we get less delighted.
We hear a lie,
That we've got to try.
Please make them stop!
All of a sudden they go "pop!"
They disappear,
Beneath our tears.
We yell "Hooray!"
And say "Olé!"
It's finally over.
Veronica Makin, Grade 7
Grand Blanc Middle School
Based on the movie.

Honor

Blood of the sword
Tears of the blade
It will be withdrawing
And tears will be shed
The blood of tears will fade
Warm to the heart
Cold as the mind
It will be the last breath
Never forget your enemies
It's your destiny
But a destiny can change
Whatever it may be
Somewhere it will be your time
Time to time, place to place
The sun will rise up and the moon will shine
Shed tears and blood will come
As the moments will come
The memories will be a lifetime
It may be the heart of the honor
But the mind of the fire
Will always bring perfection.
Mustafa Al-Asadi, Grade 8
Star International Academy

Below the Surface

As I stride on the sand, a new step I take,
I long for a swim, this decision I make.
A great powerful wave that crashes on the shore,
When I go swimming I'm just wishing for more.
When I dive in there is a great rush,
But within my body there is a still hush.
The water is rich like a chocolate bar,
I am wondering, can I swim that far?
I put my head up, out of the wave,
One breath is it; time I must save.
I dunk myself under, back under the surf,
My fingers are blue, as blue as a Smurf.
But I keep swimming as far as I can go,
For when I am in the water, there is no woe.
The water's calling me forward to dive into the deep,
I feel as though I am in a deep sleep.
Here I go down into the sand,
I know I am not in a foreign land.
For my secret lies within the wave,
Down in the depths, the water I crave.
Teresa M. Dettloff, Grade 8
St Anthony of Padua School

The Beam of Light

When you're sad, don't sit, don't cry.
Because when the Lord closes a door,
He always opens a window.
Yes, it may be dark, but just watch,
For the beam of light.
Sarah Smith, Grade 7
Flynn Middle School

Pink

Pink looks like fluffy cotton candy on a summer day at the fair.
Pink is the taste of ice-cold pink lemonade on a hot sunny day.
Pink smells like sweet pea scented perfume.
Pink makes me fell relaxed even when I am worried.
It would be like I'm on a beach or swimming with a blue beagle nosed dolphin.
Pink sounds like a wonderfully beautiful wave crashing along the seashore of an ocean.
It's quiet but beautiful.
A pink place is a beautiful sunset setting across a rolling light blue sky.
It could also be a place where couples meet and share the love they have for each other.
Pink is where small fragile flowers bloom at the start of spring.
Pink can also be the place where love begins and pink and red roses are given to the girls
by their young sweet new love.
Pink is graceful like a swan swimming through a blue shimmering pond with the sun
shining upon it like a stage light shining on a performer on stage.
Pink is also a hidden but yet seen strip in a rainbow shooting across the sky after a rainfall.
Pink is an awesome color.
Pink is my favorite color.

Candice Weidmayer, Grade 9
Manchester High School

War-torn Girl

Iraq. A country in the Mid-east and has cold weather the least.
I could have sworn, there wasn't a war…but then it happened.
A little girl, with hair like a cinnamon swirl.
She had a happy life, but then it felt like a knife.
Off goes a bomb and…she has lost her mom.
She once was glad, but now sad.
She didn't want to stay so she came to say, "I'm going away."
So she closed her mouth, and went south,
To float on a boat and sailed way…way away.
And that night she looked up at a star and fell far…far into slumber.
The next thing she knew, she was in a strange place when a woman with a beautiful face asked her,
"Where are you from? Why have you come" The girl had none to say, what had she done?
Her country may have been in a mess but that didn't mean her people were any less.
So she packed a sack and walked all the way back
Back to her home where she belonged and she was greeted in song.

Eric Regalbuto, Grade 8
MacDonald Middle School

I Remember…

I remember my first birthday Barney came to see me
I remember my grandma's funeral I was eight in the third grade
I remember going to Great Wolf Lodge the wolf was trying to get me
I remember eating my first gummy worm it was so delicious sweet too
I remember my first time playing basketball I tried to shoot the ball into the hoop but it didn't make it
I remember the good times and the bad times
I remember having my boyfriend named Ryan what a charming knight he was
I remember going to the beach with ice cream in my hand as it fell on the ground
I remember playing soccer on a rainy day I fell in a mud puddle
I remember raking the leaves in the backyard it took me forever
I remember building a snowman last winter I named him Frosty
I remember my dog when I took him for a walk he wouldn't budge
I remember riding my bike for the first time it was so much FUN!
I remember the past it was great!

Brittany Dutton, Grade 7
Manistee Middle School

True Friends

Friends are people you can always count on,
A shoulder to lean on when times are tough.
Friends leave, but in your heart, they're never gone.
And good friends, you can never have enough.

When loved ones pass away, your friend is there.
Inseparable, through thickness and thin,
About the little things your friends will care.
True friends give you that warm feeling within.

Showering you with lots of hugs and love,
Sharing great memories and the best of times,
Friends are like God's gift from heaven above.
When you love your friends a mountain you'd climb!

Near and far, friends are always in your heart.
Loyal and true friends can't be torn apart.
Emily Michelle August, Grade 8
St John Lutheran School

Awkward

In the luxurious abode of a family friend,
Some minor business I had to attend,
For when mingling, I started to talk to someone,
But looked down to discover my shoelace was undone,
I bent down to weave the lace over and through,
When behind me a looming, dark shadow grew,
A voice then asked me, "What are you going to do?"
I said, "What else can I do, simply retie my shoe."
His reply was, "Want to go for a drink?"
Almost losing my balance, I tried to think,
"Maybe," I said, "It is getting late."
The voice replied, "I think those shoes look just great."
I said, "Thanks, they're new, yet quite inexpensive."
Then realized I was being a bit apprehensive,
I asked the silhouette, "So what brings you here?"
He said, "It's kind of noisy, hold on one sec dear."
I rose up and turned to where the shadow had grown,
A man, with his eyebrow raised, on his cellular phone.
William Kim, Grade 9
Grosse Pointe South High School

When I Look

When I look to your heart,
When I look to your eyes,
When I look to your soul,
When I look to you,
I see my life,
I see my soul,
I see who we are,
When we are together we can see the world.
When I close my eyes I can still see your face,
When I close my eyes I can still see us together.
When I close my eyes I can still hear your heart beating.
Karol Dailey, Grade 9
Muskegon High School

The Nest

As I lay in bed and put the day to a rest,
I am full of sorrow for the next.
I listened to the birds singing their song,
They have sung it happy for so very long.
Now they sing the long song of loss,
For their chicks never got to pick through moss
Trying to find their favorite treat,
For I took the eggs to eat.
I thought they tasted great,
Even though I closed their life's gate.
Starr Emerson, Grade 7
Columbia Middle School

Winter

the winter season is the best of all
it certainly beats the season fall
I like skating, snowboarding and skiing
but I would say that the best thing is sightseeing
when the snow is on the ground and in the air
I can just roll in the snow without a care
then make some snowmen and igloos
it's a lot of fun till you get wet shoes
now that the snow is gone and winter is over
it just feels weird to not need a snow blower
Brandon Beach, Grade 9
Posen Consolidated High School

How Could I

How could I let the devil walk through the Heavens above?
How could I fall once more, and still he doesn't defeat me?
How could I think he loves me?
When I'm in trouble, he abandons me.
How could I dream of beautiful dreams,
When I'm hanging upside down?
How could I say there's no light at the end of the tunnel,
When I don't look?
How could I think of such things?
It was just my imagination.
Jovon Curry, Grade 9
Thomas More School

Television

Television is the best invention yet.
I use mine daily, I never forget.
It shows you pictures on the screen
they can be huge or barely be seen.
They can be flat, wide, plasma, or even the theatre screen.

You can play games and watch movies too
it does all of this just for you.
You can even have satellite or crappy cable
watch it from the couch or at the kitchen table.
I'm so glad that this poem isn't just a fable.
Robby Klein, Grade 8
Posen Consolidated High School

Worms
On Earth
In a forest
Up a tree
On a branch
By a leaf
Above the ground
Below the sky
There was a bird
Thomas L. Lemke, Grade 7
Columbia Middle School

Wind
Soft and gentle,
mild and calm.
It is so beautiful
like singing a song.
It can pick up leaves
and blow them away
or sweep through
my hair and blow across my face.
Now when I sit down
on a warm summer day
it's always there
to sweep me away
Krista Laviolette, Grade 7
St Mary Queen of Angels School

I Wonder Why
I wonder why people tease
I wonder why when people tease
people argue
I wonder why when people argue
people fight
I wonder why when people fight
people battle
I wonder why when people battle
people have wars
I wonder why when people have wars
people die
I wonder why we had to tease.
Jessica Spaun, Grade 7
Walled Lake Middle School

What Is a Star?
What is a star?
A home for many wishes
So radiant and bright
Pinpoints of power
Glistening to the eye
Gracefully moving across the sky
A path to lead the way
An imagination of strength
Forceful circles of gas
This is a star
Kathryn Ziegler, Grade 7
St John Lutheran School

Dreams Are Real
I have a dream,
You have a dream
You close your eyes
And a big bright beam,
Shines through the door.
You just feel like you're going to war.
You just wish this thing would stop, and the next thing you know…
POP!
You realize this thing is not a dream!
This is true…This is me…This is you…
Dreaming
Something
Real.
Wyman Stewart, Grade 7
Ludington Magnet Middle School

The Music
The music in my head is constant,
It separates me from the world,
Gives me time to think of my life,
It calms me when I am upset,
It makes me feel good about myself,
And sometimes it encourages me to do what I thought I couldn't,
I love music no matter what type it is,
The hip-hop makes me excited,
Rock and roll, gets me in tune with my soul,
Country, it reminds me of love,
The blues helps me soothe
Music itself is beautiful,
And it is a great part in my life,
I will always love…The Music.
Chauna Gibson, Grade 8
Guardian Lutheran School

Hunting
I am warm and snuggled like a bear in my bed.
I hear the clock strike five A.M. but don't want to budge.
The cabin is like ice until my dad tends the fire.
I know if I don't get up there will be no deer
So only then do I kick into gear.
Into my clothes I fly like a bird.
With layers and layers I jump out the door.
I climb up the tree as fast as a squirrel.
The safety harness swings around the tree.
I hear it click without a doubt of getting hurt.
Then from the low horizon sun I see it.
The biggest buck ever born into this world.
He comes with the rustling of the leaves and the blowing of the wind.
Then the bow rises and fires with one slow swift motion.
Off the arrow flies straight through the air and right on target.
The deer is hit and didn't even know what happened.
Down the deer falls with a thud.
As a product I have a bloody arrow and a dead deer.
That is the satisfaction of a hunter.
Ryan Segard, Grade 7
North Rockford Middle School

Entwined

A young girl playing tag with a friend runs
Across a field in which rabbits hop, hop
Over a river where fish swim, swim, swim
To a dry bay where flies buzz, buzz, buzz, buzz
On the large street is loud, loud, loud, loud, loud
As a siren beep, beep, beep, beep, beep, beeps
A long tone goes, goes, goes, goes, goes, goes, goes
Somewhere peace, peace, peace, peace, peace, peace, peaceful

Emily Williams, Grade 8
Grosse Pointe Academy

I Am

I am irritated and bored
I am wondering when school ends
I am hearing the class bell
I am seeing an unprepared test
I am thinking of summer break
I am irritated and bored
I am pretending I am out of school
I am feeling the weight of school work lifting
I am just touching summer freedom
I am worried about having a longer school year
I am only crying in dreams of others
I am irritated and bored
I am to understand others
I am to say that school's too short
I am dreaming of an empty space
I am to try to be good at everything
I am hoping to leave school early
I am irritated and bored
I am too excel at everything I try
I am to do things I don't want to

Devin Daugherty, Grade 7
Roseville Jr High School

Remember

Do you remember the times you were young?
Folding socks with your mom,
Watching Barney with your dad.
When going to the grocery store was a big trip,
Sitting in the front was prohibited.
Talking to strangers was scary,
And the dark was eerie.
Holding a stuffed animal made you feel safe,
Eating all your vegetables to get a piece of cake.
Your bedtime was at seven,
Kneeling by your bedside while saying a prayer to Heaven.
Can't go to sleep without Mom and Dad kissing you,
Telling them you love them before they do.
Remember these times,
Hold them dear to your heart.
Because this is how you grew up,
This is the start.

Devyn Trester, Grade 8
Beach Middle School

I Love You

I got your back you got mine
I'll help you out anytime.
To see you hurt to see you cry
Makes me weep and wanna die.
And if you agree to never fight
It wouldn't matter who's wrong or right.
If a broken heart needs a mend
I'll be right there to the end,
If your cheeks are wet from drops of tears,
Don't you worry, let go of your fears.
Hand in hand love is sent,
We'll be friends 'till the end.

Kimethia Tally, Grade 9
Southwestern High School

Sports

Sports are fun,
Just like the sun.

Basketball is fast,
Just don't get a cast.

In baseball you sit,
Just waiting to hit.

In volleyball you fall,
While hitting the ball.

In track you run,
And start with the gun.

In soccer you kick,
Just don't make a pick.

In cheerleading you stunt,
And cheer about the punt.

In football you tackle,
The crowd starts to cackle.

Aubrey Boerema, Grade 7
Montague Nellie B Chisholm Middle School

Goodbye*

When I was four my father died
I can remember that I cried and cried
My father was drunk and hit a tree
It also killed my Uncle Joey
For twenty-two hours he fought his death
Right to his very last breath
My dad was gone to be no more
I never got to say goodbye and for that my heart tore
And still today 9 years ago the tree still bares the mark
And whenever I see it I feel empty and dark

George Brown, Grade 7
Manistee Middle School
*In loving memory of my father and Uncle Joey

Rainbows
Rainbows
Radiant, remarkable
Glow, gleam, twinkle
They replace the clouds
A pot of gold
Marie Rappuhn, Grade 7
St Anthony of Padua School

Mr. President
Every day
I think to myself
Just take me away take me away
There is no life, no love, no laughter
Just sorrow, hate and awful disaster
Because of one man
So many have died
We put our lives
Our love
And hope
All in the hands
Of one simple man
It's all up to him
Who goes?
Who stays?
The one simple country
That needs us to pray
Has taken away
Mother and father
So here I am alone
Waiting just waiting till I see them again
Jen Bouchey, Grade 7
Gull Lake Middle School

What's Inside
What is this inside,
my body so deep
a deep, warm feeling
sometimes I want to weep

It feels like the sun
warm and cozy inside
but then there it is
now you just want to hide

You think it's true
and sometimes real
but it never comes out
the way you feel

Then you notice
this thing inside
that thing you feel
is love, joy, and pride
Brianna Long, Grade 8
Gesu Elementary School

Slow Down
I am walking a narrow path
Not looking at what I have passed
I see everyone staring
But I don't know why
I look around to see where we are going
I see the graveyard beside me
I am scared
I am frightened
Why are we going so fast now?
Who has died?
Do I know them?
Life is a mystery because
I am walking a narrow path
Not looking at what I have passed
Lisa Gojcevic, Grade 7
Flynn Middle School

A Recipe
A recipe for us to be
A recipe for us NOT to be
I loved you more
So why'd you leave?

It was a recipe for disaster
A dried out train wreck
I fell even faster
Since you threw away the best

A recipe for us to be
A recipe not meant to be
A broken heart left behind
Still I wonder why it had to be mine
Desirae Brewer, Grade 9
Melvindale High School

Detroit Pistons
D efense is their game and
E verywhere they go people know
T heir names
R ip, Chauncey, Tay, and Wallace X2
O thers like Dyess and Evans
I t's just to name a few
T he race is nearing to the end and the

P layoffs are just about to begin
I t's time to
S tand tall and defend the ball
T he Detroit Pistons are
O n the way to an
N BA Championship, and no one will
S tand in their way

GO PISTONS!!!
Chevon Anderson, Grade 8
Hally Magnet Middle School

My Aunt Vicki
As I sit here, watching TV I realize
how lucky I am to have such a
great aunt! My Aunt Vicki!
As she takes me horseback riding,
to lunch and we talk
Aunt Vicki
I feel like I can talk to her about
anything at all
Aunt Vicki
Friends, boyfriends, parents,
siblings, anything, anything at all
and she wouldn't tell a soul!
Aunt Vicki
She gives me jewelry, like
necklaces, bracelets, and earrings.
I get that from my friends but
when it comes from my aunt it's
really special.
That's *my* Aunt Vicki, I love her
and I couldn't ask for a
better aunt.
Michele Pedder, Grade 7
Flynn Middle School

I Am…
I am who I am,
You can't change me.
I can control my own life.
Don't try to fix me,
'Cuz I have my own mind.
I have my own personality.
I am my own person.
This is who I am.
Megan Adams, Grade 7
Flynn Middle School

Nightmares
You wake up one morning,
and feel really nauseous,
Maybe even cautious,
For there's sweat in your hair,
and check also where,
but will not dare.
For fear is creeping upon you,
in its most unnoticed form.
For you're entirely a swarmed.
Trying for your pulse,
You feel delirious,
and it will seem mysterious.
For it has come to reality.
Even if you try to grasp air,
you know you had a terrible
Nightmare.
Henry Chen, Grade 8
Central Middle School

Sparkie

There is always someone,
Waiting at the door for me.
White and fluffy as a snowflake,
He makes me feel warm, inside my heart.
His wet nose,
and black eyes stand out,
In his friendly face,
He loves to chase,
Also his very long tail,
And he's always ready to play
With his toys
After a meal, he is still ready to eat!
He enjoys his bean bag pillow,
Sleeping on his back, with his four paws in the air.
When he is awake,
He gets excited about going outside,
Acting like a track star.
He think he is superman when riding in a car
With the window down
Who is he?
Man's best friend!

Edward Marable, Grade 8
Gesu Elementary School

Bad Days

Don't ever come to me and say,
That you had an imperfect day.
I'll say it once, and I'll keep repeating,
Every day is enjoyable if you're still breathing.

Colin Burns, Grade 7
St Anthony of Padua School

Why?

Why dream of better things?
Why should I feel this way?
Why should I care?
Why do I cry when you're not here?
Why do people laugh when they see me?
Why is love such a powerful word?
Why when you say it I fold?
Why do I smile when you look at me?
Why do tears strain my face when I cry?
Why do I run after you, when you're gone?
Why do I sing the same old song?
Why doesn't anyone hear what I am saying?
Why do people act like they don't care?
Why do I share my feeling with you?
Why doesn't anyone answer me?
Why do I keep on going?
Why is it, that I hear your cry?
Why in winter do flowers die?
Why don't you hear my heart beat?
Why is the question, but not an answer.
So why keep asking WHY?

James Eaves, Grade 8
Hally Magnet Middle School

Bad News

I can't think straight,
Life is a mess.
Sure I love life,
But it's full of stress.
Murders here, robberies there,
Abuse and violence everywhere.
You can't just sit down and watch the news,
Without a kidnapping bringing you the blues.
Gangsters and thugs robbing folks,
And at the same time thinking it's all a joke.
Street fights gone wrong bring people to pain,
They can't walk without crutches and canes.
Small kids involved in child abuse,
You can see their eyes watered saying,
"What did I do?"
Teens drinking and driving thinking it's o.k.,
Until someone dies and won't see another day.
Just when I thought it was over,
And my dreams have come true,
I'm called to the office to hear,
"We have some BAD NEWS!"

Jalisa Jamison, Grade 8
North Pointe Academy

Dreams

What's that down the street?
Are you going to keep running?
Or are you going to face it?
So what are you going to do?
If you run you will be a deer running from a cheetah
you know you will be caught.
If you stay you are a possum just sitting there
as brave as ever.
It listens,
It talks,
It follows you until you listen.
It's your dream.

Austin Ames, Grade 7
Grand Blanc Middle School

Skiing

Gliding through the snow
The reflection of sun reflecting off the snow
Powder in my face
I feel like I'm flying in the cold winter air
Cheeks red
Nose is running
My eyes are watery
I'm feeling the cold air rushing through my veins
Snow in my coat
Cold as could be
Nose running red 'cause
I just hit a tree

Max Howland, Grade 7
Gull Lake Middle School

Midnight Run

Stirred into a run
Two brown horses side by side
Run as though possessed
Midnight marvels of nature
Gleaming bright in the moonlight

Felicity Tyll, Grade 7
Tyllfield Preserve School

Flying Free

I jumped off
of the grass, and
I went higher and higher,
until my house was just a dot
beneath me.

I flew,
with my arms outstretched;
the wind brushing my face.
I felt free,
like I could do anything.

I soared,
all around the world,
when I realized
that not being able to fly free
is like being trapped in a cage.

A thought came to me.
Everyone deserves to fly
but not everybody can take wing,
so I set off to help
someone fly.

Ben Levin, Grade 9
Berkley High School

Together Forever

You are the arms
I run to, to hold
together we will never
let our love grow cold,
you are so special to me,
our love is like
a never ending waterfall,
so don't sit back
and let it fall,
all our problems
will come to pass
and I see us last,
I have never felt this way
about anyone else,
I wish love no other
as long as we are…

Together Forever!
Mike Robinson, Grade 8
Central Middle School

My Oma

My oma is my great grandmother,
And I would not have wished for any other.

She was sixteen years of age
When she came here from Germany to meet life's new page.

She'd tell us some stories of her young life,
While I leaned up against her and Dad cleaned her knife.

She slowly began to drift away from us,
And faded away without a fuss.

Tears represent the past of my friend
But I'm not the only one who wishes her life didn't come to an end.

Jamie Boelstler, Grade 7
Roseville Jr High School

Death

What is the holocaust?
The holocaust to me is the word "death."
Death is something that most people fear.
Fear is what the Jews felt when they heard or thought about the Nazis.
Nazis who were German soldiers, which loved to torture Jews.
Jews were beat, starved, and worked to death.
Death to me is the word holocaust.

Alyssa Adams, Grade 7
Jefferson Middle School

"Sissy" — Life Ain't the Same*

When someone you love dies life ain't the same.
As some people live life like it's a game.
When that one person dies you think of the good times and good years
as you sit back and try to fight the tears.

When you wake up in the morning and can't see their face
tears trickle down your cold lonely face.
You try to forget but she's still in your mind
but you look at her picture time after time.

You look at her pictures that are in albums and frames
and think of her favorite game.
I would kick the ball and she would chase after it
and she would bring it back covered in slobber and spit.

Her name was Sissy and that was her favorite game,
she died on March 30, now as you know life just ain't the same.
You don't know what I'll do to spend 10 minutes with her,
rub her, pet her, and brush her hair.
That was my dog and Sissy was her name.
Since she died my life ain't the same.

Richard Easterly, Grade 7
Roseville Jr High School
*In loving memory of Sissy Easterly

If I Were a Preposition

If I were a preposition
I would fly over the moon
Away from the sun
I won't be back to Earth 'til I'm done
Toward Mars
And count upon the stars
Lie on a cloud
And listen to the silent sound
Ride on an airplane
And fly to Maine
Fly over all those states
See all of the pretty sizes and shapes
Go to Miami
Have all the celebrities wave to me
Fly to L.A.
Walk by all the people and say "hey!"
Walk to Rodeo Drive
After I shop and get some stuff, I will feel so alive
Go to New York, and shop some more
And go into the Cartier store

Tyresa Stevenson, Grade 7
Hally Magnet Middle School

Jungle Animals

Giraffe
Long, tall
Munching, running, gathering
Spots, tongue, jungle, tail
Seeing, doing, looking
Cute, huggable
Monkey

Chelsey Zeller, Grade 7
Montague Nellie B Chisholm Middle School

Friends and Family

F riends can always be
R emembered
I n good ways or
E ven bad.
N one are the same, they're all
D ifferent, yet they may still
S hare the same

qu **A** lities
the **N** in the
en **D** they can be just like

F amily,
A lways there for you
M aking sure you are safe.
Fam **I** ly members are unique just
L ike friends.
When **Y** ou think about it everyone's there for you.

Rebekah Cameron, Grade 7
Manistee Middle School

Friendship

They are the ones who help you in good times and bad,
They are the ones who cheer you up when you are sad.
They are the ones who will always love you,
even if you're feeling blue.
They are the ones who write you like good pen pals,
And they are the ones who paint your nails.
Good slumber parties come and go,
Your friends will never leave you, no.
They are the ones who have your back,
Love and kindness they never lack.
They are the ones who are your friends.

Shelby Myers, Grade 7
St Mary Queen of Angels School

Spring Is Near, Spring Is Here

Spring is near, spring is here
Flowers blooming everywhere.
Children playing in the sea
With fish and other things.
Mothers baking apple pies
While birds fly in the sky.
The night has come but the fun has begun.
Roasting marshmallows over an open fire.
Singing campfire songs
As stars sparkle in the sky.
Lighting off fireworks and sparklers.
Then the kids go to bed with joy in their hearts
To wake up the next morning to have even more fun.
They wake up to play basketball, volleyball
And other summer sports.
As they are playing they see something
A leaf fall off the old oak tree.
It was yellow, orange or was it green?
It does not matter; it was the first day of fall
All they're fun is gone because spring was gone.
Spring is here, spring is gone.

Jacob Plocharczyk, Grade 7
Jefferson Middle School

Closed Eyes

When I'm here it is just me.
But when I close my eyes I can be anywhere I want to be.
I can be on Everest at the very top.
I can run through golden fields without a stop.
I can dine with the very best of royalty.
I can be with the pirates on the rolling sea.
I can be in Scotland sitting on the hills.
I can fetch the water with Jack and Jill.
I can hang with the monkeys in the tall green trees.
I can swim under the ocean with the mermaids three.
I can sleep on a cloud in the sky so blue.
I can live the life of whatever I choose.
You can do it if you try.
All you have to do is close your eyes.

Mary Novak, Grade 9
Grosse Pointe South High School

Things Are Not What They Seem

The house is cold.
An eerie chill sweeps the house.
Tension creeps about the halls.
The rooms are quiet,
all but the room upstairs.
A faint cry slithers down the stairs,
it flows into the bedrooms of her children.
Things are not what they seem.

Michelle Keller, Grade 9
George A Dondero High School

Wind

The wind is like invisible waves
It keeps people cool on very warm days.
It blows wickedly and wildly through my hair
While I'm on the Ferris wheel at the county fair.
The wind is like a very big race which it wins always.

Alex Ostrowski, Grade 8
St Anthony of Padua School

Young Love

I like her but I don't know how to tell her.
All I think about is her all day.
I like her but I don't know how to tell her.
Why does friendship have to get in the way?

Of course I've liked a girl before,
But it's never been so real.
I need to know if she likes me back.
I need to know, what does she feel?

Brandon McCutchen, Grade 8
Helen Keller Middle School

Food

Oh food oh food
You taste so good
You nourish so many
And you smell so good

You make me want to have a feast
You also made me obese
Your ingredients are like a story
They talk to you

Whether you're chocolate or cheese
Some even make me sneeze
You're always delicious
In your own way

So pick up your forks
Pick up your spoons
You better have room
For the great tasting food.

Lucas Hanson, Grade 7
Montague Nellie B Chisholm Middle School

Needs

Needs are for everyone,
needs can be serious or fun.
Needs are for people who are sick or dying,
needs are for people who are hurt or crying.
Needs for antics and shenanigans,
needs for foods and medicines.
Yes, there are all kinds of needs as you can see,
lots of people have needs even you and me.

Nathan Orleskie, Grade 8
St Gerard Elementary School

Heavenly Hugs

I feel your arms wrap around me like a big, fuzzy teddy bear.
You guide me along the beach, leaving only one set of prints.
You carry me.

You hold my hand as I learn to walk.
Never alone, you always guide me.
When I stumble and fall, you pick me up.
In my daily battles, you never give me
more than I can take.
You are my friend, my guide,
the love of my life.

You live in me through all my pain.
I will fear no evil for you are with me.
You are with the brokenhearted,
giving hugs from heaven above.
Your unfailing love and mercy,
let it show through me to everyone around.

I lift my eyes up to the hills.
Where does my help come from?
My help comes from you, maker of heaven and earth.
Oh Father above, tell me one more goodnight story,
Give me one more heavenly hug.

Diana Friend, Grade 8
Frost Middle School

I Wish

The sky was dark.
And filled with stars.
Leaning against the tree bark.
Staring up at Mars.

Sitting alone with you.
With no one else around.
Oh, it seemed so true.
On the comforting ground.

I wish this moment would never end.
This is how I would like it to be.
This is how every moment, I wish I could spend.
Leaning against this comfortable tree.

Sam Altman, Grade 9
Posen Consolidated High School

Living the Dream

L et fear control you,
I n all of it, take refuge.
V indictive pleasure in your heart,
I nsanity will rip you apart.
N othing left if you seek revenge but
G oing nowhere without an edge.

T heories flying through your head,
H ope destroying your sense of dread, now
E vil cannot seduce your heart.

D eath and dreams control your fate,
R elinquish control before it's too late.
E ven with all of your imperfections,
A ll will go well with a sense of direction. Just
M ake it all right, before it's too late.

Luke Bruski, Grade 8
Posen Consolidated High School

Mistakes

As humans we make mistakes
Sometimes they are small
Sometimes they are big
Mistakes are natural
Everybody makes mistakes
Mistakes may effect your life forever
Mistakes can change the way you plan your life
Mistakes may effect your family and friends
But all the mistakes you have made
Can be fixed and you can overcome

Jabari Turner, Grade 8
Gesu Elementary School

Cinderella

As the river runs by
I sit and sigh.
The carriage wheel rolling round
I'm headed toward the castle where I'm bound.
In slippers of glass I still ask
Will fulfill my task.
Out the door I will fly
Telling myself that I will try!
Through the doors I walked
All the people danced and talked.
Then there was dead silence
All I wanted was compliance!
Down the stairs I went
You should have seen the looks they sent.
Some just stared; others just weren't prepared.
The Prince walked up to me.
I then though is this what it's cracked up to be.
Then we danced all night; this felt so right.
But then the clock struck its chime
So I looked at the Prince one last time.

Brittany Hyde, Grade 7
Hopkins Middle School

The Perfect School

A shining hall where voices call sweetly to each other.
Where each and every person there is treated like a brother.
Where teasing stops, and rude words drop right out of the air.
Where a friendly person would never stop to stare.
Where kind words rule. The perfect school.

Hannah Ritsema, Grade 8
Oakland Christian School

I Am

I am a person that loves music.
I wonder how many stars are in the sky.
I hear guitars.
I see my life in 20 years.
I want a Gibson guitar.
I am a person who loves music.
I pretend to be a rock star
I feel excited.
I touch a smooth surface
I worry about what will happen in the near future.
I cry when I lose someone I care about.
I am a person who loves music.
I understand the world isn't the safest place.
I say you don't know what you have 'til it's gone.
I dream of succeeding my dream.
I try to get better at the guitar
I hope I will become successful.
I am a person who loves music.
My favorite band is Green Day.
My hobby is playing guitar.

Sarah Pickett, Grade 7
Roseville Jr High School

Butterflies

Beautifully created creatures,
With their dignified features.

Astounding to watch and amazing to view,
With their charming colors, with a pleasant hue.

When their wings spread out wide,
Their dazzling designs cannot hide.

As they soar through the sky,
Their wings flutter oh so high.

Green, yellow, purple, and blue,
Each one is unique, but looks brand new.

Each one differs, yet they blend,
There is a message that they send.

Everyone is different; just be yourself they say,
When we do the world will accomplish more each day.

Hannah Faber, Grade 8
St Anthony of Padua School

Tears of the World

There is a girl who sits near the window looking upon the world, who is she?
Is she the one they're all talking about, is she the lost one?
Is this the child, the angel among the demons?
Why does no one see her, why does no one hear her cries?
Has she been completely forgotten, lost in history, stuck in the past, or never truly heard?
No, her smile still lives throughout the world,
and the tears of her tortures fall like the rain quenching the thirst for freedom of others.
Her eyes, still looking upon us every day, when the sun comes to play, so does she.
No, she is not altogether forgotten, she is only hard to find, but always there.

Alicia Rigoni, Grade 9
Kingsford High School

Edith Kermit Roosevelt

Edith was born in Connecticut 1861. Edith would never become a nun.
She was born to Charles and Gertrude. She always had a good attitude.
One brother was all she had, one mother and a dad.
In her childhood she moved to New York, she never used a pitchfork.
She had a lot of friends in her childhood. Being nice was her livelihood.
In New York she received her education. She did not have an occupation.
Ladylike manners is what she learned. This would help her in return.
When Edith was older, Roosevelt she would marry. Five children she would carry.
She had four boys and one girl. She loved curls.
Edith was the first lady from 1901-1909. This would be the time she would shine.
She took care of their children and supported her husband. She was always understandable.
She died on September 30, 1948. She never was overweight.
She died at the age of 87. She loved her life when she was eleven.

William LayPort, Grade 7
Lakeview Middle School

Fishing

As the oars sink in the water, I hear frogs on the shoreline. It's silent and the only thing I can hear is a bird chirp off in the distance and a duck quack as it dives under the surface of the water. The sweet grass smiles down at the insects and water lilies float on the murky shore. The wind is as gentle as a lamb and the tree's leaves are butterfly wings in the hot summer air.

Zach Clifton, Grade 7
Addison Middle School

Christmas Morning

I woke up that morning. Got out of bed. I saw my presents, but they were red.
We unwrapped our presents with joy and glee. After that we drank some tea.
I was so glad God came to Earth, and I was so happy Mary had His birth.
I picked up the phone and called my friend. I told him what I got start to end.
I got a new skateboard and a new bike. The kid I talked to was named Mike.
Mike got a bike and 95 dollars, and the new game NBA Ballers.
He had to go and same with me. I hung up the phone and went back to the tree.
I looked at the tree. I just stared and stared, then thought what God Himself shared.
He died on the cross for our salvation, and we should thank Him for creation.
He was born in a manger so humble and meek. Jesus' birth was very unique.
Even wise men still seek Him today, but He cannot be found in a manger with hay.
He is found in the spirit of Christmas with love. The symbol of His peace is the white dove.
The real meaning of Christmas is giving and sharing. That is a good sign of caring.
The wise men traveled from far away just to see Jesus in a manger of hay.
Jesus grew up preaching the good news, walking around His neighborhood.
We go to church and learn good news. We have to share it and not refuse.
The real meaning of Christmas is not to just get gifts. When you are humble, your faith lifts.

Nick Watkins, Grade 7
St Ann Elementary School

Goodbye

There was a young girl with dirt on her face.
She sat by the fire full of disgrace.
She started to cry but didn't give in.
She wiped her tears and started to grin.
She packed up her stuff in a little red sack.
And then she yelled, "I'll never come back."
So she left for the train.
In the pouring rain.

Andrew Harper, Grade 7
Columbia Middle School

I Am

I am a boy that likes to make friends.
I like the relationships and quality of my friends.
I feel the pain of people who have no friends.
I hear people who argue with their friends.
I see the loving and caring hearts of my friends.
I am a boy who likes to make friends.

I wonder who needs a good friend by his or her side.
I know that my friends are goodhearted and caring.
I care about the health and safety of my friends.
I wish everybody had a good friend or two.
I am a boy who makes friends.

Kayne Goodwin, Grade 7
Paw Paw Middle School

Betty Ford

This first lady's first name is Betty.
She probably made her husband, Gerald, spaghetti.
When she married, her last name was Ford.
She was the president's wife and was never bored.

She showed talent as a dancer.
She fought with breast cancer.
People said, "She's a gutsy lady."
They admired her bravery.

She once drank alcohol but now she does not.
Her addiction taught her a lesson she never forgot.
Everyone liked her so they wore buttons.
She taught others to get medical attention.

She was popular, others wanted to be just like her.
She made the Betty Ford Treatment Center.
Now she lives in Palm Springs.
In her lifetime she has done many amazing things.

She was in the White House from 1974 to 1977
And raised funds for handicapped children.
She was a champion of the National Endowment for the Arts.
And to promote better care for the elderly she did her part.

Brandon Arntz, Grade 7
Lakeview Middle School

Springtime Is Here!!!

Smell the flowers, they smell fresh
Pet the bunnies on the grass
Make a shout that school's out
Scream a cheer, springtime is here

Easter's coming, let's eat candy
'Cause everybody knows it comes in handy
Kids run around with their friends
Until they know school's back again

People play outside in the pool
Some may sunbathe 'cause it's cool
Some go fishing unless they have bait
Some have parties, that seems great

So hang with friends, yell a cheer
Do what you want 'cause…
Springtime is here!!!

Rebecca McClain, Grade 7
Roseville Jr High School

Life

A girl small and frail with skin as white as milk
Smiling and gurgling
Like a babbling brook
Stumbling steps turn into strong strides
As her words begin to make sense
She gets rid of her crib replaced by a bed
First day of school she gets on the bus
A brave smile on her face
A huge transition is about to happen
She grows and grows
Until she finally stops
Her graduation day has finally passed
She moves out her room is empty
Like a barren wasteland
And you're hurt
She's driving down the road she's turning to the right
You hear the screech of brakes
And know nothing will ever be the same
She is gone, nothing left except the pain in your heart
The tears in your eyes
And a piece of gray marble.

Anjelica Schnittker, Grade 8
Richardson Elementary Middle School

Summer Fun

Beach
Warm, sandy
Swimming, building, sunbathing
Dunes, fish, chemicals, jumping
Cleaning, diving, dunking
Slide, floating
Pool

Clark Gillish, Grade 7
Montague Nellie B Chisholm Middle School

Running for True Love

The wind in your hair
The morning dew under your feet
Your body is feeling the tare
As you're catching up to the heat

Running is fulfilling
As fulfilling as love
It makes you feel like your living
As your heart flutters away like a dove

Faster you push toward your destination
Wanting this more than ever before
You reach the point of hesitation
And yet your body is wanting more

Heather Ramacker, Grade 9
Cadillac Jr High School

Dog/Puppy

Dog
Mean, hairy
Barking, biting, growling
Walking the dog
Playing, petting, caring
Playful, cuddly
Puppy

Craig Fox, Grade 8
St John Lutheran School

Chilly

C old
H ypothermia
I ce
L ips are chapped
L iquid nitrogen
Y ucky

Jared Heys, Grade 7
Assumption BVM School

A Horrible Storm

The wind blowing,
Lightning flashing,
Thunder booming,
A horrible storm.
All through the night,
Rain pouring down,
People are frightened,
A horrible storm.
The storm has calmed,
The rain has stopped,
The sun is out,
The thunder is quiet,
The lightning is gone,
People aren't frightened
The raging storm is tamed

Ethan Thomas Durocher, Grade 7
Flynn Middle School

Summer Days

Today the sky is gray, but through my eyes I see a sunny day.
On this day I plead with God to let it stay, but also thank God for making it this way.
The grass is green, the sky is blue, and this beautiful day reminds me of you.
You're the one who loves me and is always there.
I love you just the way you are, my personal star.
You glow and glow in the pitch black sky,
Your eyes reveal the light that shines,
From Heaven above you're a symbol of God's love.
Why should God send someone as wonderful as you?
You inspire me to do the best that I can do.
I just want to be like the beautiful YOU!

Rachel K. Martin, Grade 8
Ruth Murdoch SDA Elementary School

Blah, Blah, Blah!

Blah, Blah, Blah!
You're still talking, and your mouth is going crazy,
All these words you're saying, it makes my head hazy!
People tell you to stop, and please just take a rest,
But when you keep talking like that,
Well, to them you're just a pest!
We do everything we can,
To make you understand,
That you can't keep on doing this,
Because we're not big fans!
You talk all day and talk all night,
Just the sight of your mouth moving, is not a pretty sight!
The cacophony is too much; you really are a talker,
We should pick you up, carry you to school, and stuff you in a locker!

Givan Hinds, Grade 7
Ruth Murdoch SDA Elementary School

Your "So Called" Best Friend

What is a best friend?
Someone who is supposed to be there until the end
You are not ever there when I need you most
I miss you so much, you don't even know
I keep thinking, where did my best friend go?
You don't even care about me anymore
I have never thought of ending our friendship before
Now I think I might
I can't stand feeling like this for one more night
I'm crying as I'm watching our friendship die
I can't help but think it was a big lie
I love your dorky little giggle and your voice
I really don't want to end our friendship I think I have no choice
I'm crying just thinking of it
I think I would go insane without you
I don't know what else I should do
Without you, I'm not the same
I'm not bubbly and crazy
I'm depressed and lazy
I wish I could go back in time
Back when I was your best friend, and you were mine

Deanna Elsey, Grade 7
Flynn Middle School

Waves

Waves clashing up against the boat
with people sliding off the deck
the only thing on their mind will it float

Bigger, bigger waves defeat the boats
people, people everywhere trying to stay afloat
just as soon as the sun comes out
one wave takes them all.

Zeke Gregory, Grade 8
Mendon Middle/High School

My Hero

He has arms strong as a tree,
Knock down evils at the count of three.
His heart is warm as the sun,
Shine on Earth like father to the son.
His eyes are full of justice and peace,
Protect and guard people from wicked gaze.
He was athletic, a chivalrous sportsman,
Favoring horse riding as an superb amusement.

He has weakness just like others,
Strikes of sadness please to bother.
Misfortune occurred like a crash of thunder,
As the horse halted instantly as he collapsed like a diver.
Immobilized and grieved as he was,
Strong, cheerful voices help him rise.
Build and assemble many new programs,
To help and support others with same problems.

Optimistic and adorable as he was,
The hero's day soon came to a close.
The stories and legends that he left,
Soon remain a tail of gift.

My hero is superman, Christopher Reeve.

Danfeng Ni, Grade 9
Roseville Jr High School

The Flamingo

Beady eyes, black beak
Long legs, webbed feet
One foot he stands
In the water, on the land
Proud bird, now fly
Bright pink in the sky
Stops his flapping, comes back down
Once he lands, he looks around
Ruffles his feathers, joins the crowd
Their graceful necks stretch out and bow
They spread their wings and then take flight
Hundreds of birds, what a marvelous sight!
In the sun their silky feathers gleam
Flying in colonies over the stream.

Tina Geelhoed, Grade 8
Cutlerville Christian School

Aunt Dorothy

This summer my aunt Dorothy passed away
No "I'll miss you" or "good-byes" I could say
She was my favorite aunt I guess
I felt God was putting me to the test
I loved my aunt Dorothy so
Why He took her, I don't know
When I think of her I get depressed
When I think about all her pain and stress
I wish that I could bring her back
Because giving her love was where I sometimes lack
She was so sick
She was the one God picked
I miss her so
I hope to go
Where she is

Brittney Short, Grade 8
Oakland Christian School

Twilight Goddess

Twilight Goddess, why do you cry?
Those silent tears of sorrow
The tears you shed for his lies
Twilight Goddess, why do you cry?
The tears keep falling from the midnight sky
Her heart will soon turn cold and hallow
Twilight Goddess, why do you cry?
Those silent tears of sorrow.

Brooke Foote, Grade 9
Onsted Middle School

My Stand

Come to my lemonade stand,
Where everything is fresh!
It only takes a quarter
To cool your warm flesh!
With just a glass of lemonade
Your thirst will be quenched,
And you won't need any shade.
Tart, sweet, tangy,
However you'd like,
I'll set up down the street,
Walk, run, or grab your bike!
Just picked lemons are what I'm all about,
And with the right amount of sugar,
These lemons won't make you pout!
The freezing ice will cool your sweaty face
And with plenty to go around,
There is no need to race.
Come here now,
This lemonade isn't bland,
And it's only here,
At my lemonade stand!

Lauren Baywol, Grade 7
Grand Blanc Middle School

Rivers

Winding down mountains
coming large and sometimes small
Rapidly running
Zane Neitzka, Grade 8
Mar Lee School

Thinking and Talking

Thinking,
alone, peaceful,
sitting, studying, reading,
books, library, football, microphone,
running, screaming, laughing,
friendly, exciting,
talking.
Kurt Kwiatkowski, Grade 9
Onsted High School

Aunt Patti's House

At Aunt Patti's house
My feet dangling from the ground
Hugging Auntie Patti
Sad, lonely, worthless
My parents yelling and in a fight

Heartbroken!
Casandra Ebertsch, Grade 8
Central Middle School

United States

What Is My Country?
A safe place
The home of many friends
Freedom for all
A place of religion
Welcoming all people
A land of many wars
Helping hands to others
The home of the brave
A great nation
That Is My Country!
Tyler Alcantara, Grade 7
St John Lutheran School

The Life

As I thought in the woods,
My mind came to wander,
Am I really alone,
No, I cannot believe this,
Of course I am alone,
Then my eyes said things,
Things my mind didn't,
A wondrous thing,
A powerful thing,
Life
Zachary Crumb, Grade 8
Central Middle School

The Night Before Christmas

"No more Christmas," Santa said this one New Year
No more presents those kids want so dear
There will be no Christmas anymore once and for all
For Christmas hasn't been Christmas for ever at all.

Each letter that's sent to me is read by my elves
Nothing is reasonable for Santa to make
I hammer away making yo-yos and red wagons
You think they'd be pleased.

Of course they're not happy or pleasant at all.
They all tell Santa "That's not what I wanted at all."
They threaten my elves and me with hateful letters that they write
This is why Christmas will never be the same even tonight.

Now you know why there will be no more Christmas
Forever and ever 'till the day that I die.
Andrew Gibbs, Grade 7
Ruth Murdoch SDA Elementary School

The Classroom

The bulletin board overflowing with papers and colorful projects
The background sound of students murmuring while the teacher speaks
The smell of aged books that fill the shelves
The powerful sound of the teacher's voice filling the room
The polished, stable desks
The appalling blue carpet beneath my feet
The classroom is a place to learn

Victoria Duff, Grade 8
Central Middle School

These Eyes Don't Cry No More

I'm waiting for the tears.
I feel the sorrow, pain and happiness.
But these eyes don't cry no more.
Damn these eyes.
Damn I can't show my feelings.
Damn I can't show pain, happiness or sorrow I've been through.
Damn each time I think about him.
'Bout how we broke up.
Damn every time I think 'bout sadness, death or other horrible things.
I wanna cry but these eyes don't cry no more.
Every strong feeling of pain, sorrow or happiness makes me wanna cry.
But I can't show my emotions.
These eyes won't let me cry no more.
Look at me. Look at my eyes.
You see no tears. But I feel pain.
These eyes just don't wanna cry no more.
No cryin. No tears. All emotions.
My eyes don't cry no more.

Cheyenne Peters, Grade 7
Glenn W Levey Middle School

The Winter War

Where now is the bloody field
Where soldiers fought with no yield
The beaten path is now red
From all the soldiers that are now dead

The violence has all stopped
The battle has now ceased
The bombs now no longer drop
They all feel an eerie peace

The battle is over all is still
Death and hatred have a strong will
In the snow an army lies
Thanks to hate they have all died

They do not quiver
They do not cry
They do not feel
They all have died

The snow is falling on the ground
Over all the dead that will never be found
The cry of soldiers is heard no more
And so ends the winter war

Austin Elrod, Grade 7
Columbia Middle School

Martha Washington

Martha Washington was born June 2, 1731.
Her important life had just begun.
She was the oldest of eight.
So she could stay out late.

She received an education.
That's something not available to everyone.
She married Daniel Custis when she was 19.
He died in 1757 a short marriage was not foreseen.

She had two kids named Frances and Daniel
Alone they would dwell.
She married George Washington in 1759
A soldier's wife was not her design.

She cared for sick soldiers and made them clothing.
They were very fitting.
She moved to the Mount Vernon plantation
Because they were laying the White House foundation.

After George W. died Martha burned their private stuff.
That was very rough.
Martha Washington died on May 22, 1802.
Because of a severe fever she was through.

Scotty Loper, Grade 7
Lakeview Middle School

I Promise

I promise to be the best I can be.
I promise to always be myself.
I promise to always follow the rules.
I promise to work hard.
I promise to be as helpful as I can be.
I promise I will always be there for you.
I promise to love you 'til the day I die.
I promise I will never cry just for the fun of it.
I promise to never lie to your face.
I promise never to hurt you.
I promise to always tell the truth.
I promise you will always be the one.
I promise to live life to the fullest.
I promise to follow my dreams.
I promise to never play games with your heart.
I promise never to give into peer pressure.
I promise I will always be true to myself.
I promise to always believe in myself.
I promise not to tell anyone your secrets.
I promise I'll never make you cry.
I promise to always be loyal.

Megan Campbell, Grade 9
Roseville Jr High School

Older Sisters

She is the one who gives you advice and style.
The girl who tells jokes and makes you smile.
You grow up as playmates in princess dresses,
You fight and fight until the other one fesses.
Sometimes you quarrel and other times you laugh,
But she watches out for you like a mother cow and her calf.
If you were abandoned in Timbuktu
She would travel by land, sea, or air to find you.
The deepest secrets are told to each other,
Whenever you play house, you're daughter, she's mother.
It is a kind of love that will not go away.
No matter the hour, the time, or the day.

Olivia Schomer, Grade 7
Oakland Christian School

Friends

Friends are people you can count on
Whenever you are down
Friends are people you can trust
Whenever you are lonely
Laughing
Playing
Just hanging out
Friends are people you share secrets with
Even if you're scared
So if you have a frown
Or you just may be down
Friends are people you can go to
Whenever you are down

Andrew Parrish, Grade 7
Flynn Middle School

The Treasure

Long, long ago,
Was a treasure somewhere.
It was buried very low,
But I didn't care.
First, I went to a jungle,
Then to a snowy place.
I found a man in a bundle
Of a blanket with a little face.
He told me where it was
He said, "In a metal snowman…
Just tell him the daily buzz."
But when I saw it, there was only a can.
And in that can was it,
The treasure of power,
As big as a zit,
What it was, was a golden flower.

Miles Kamaloski, Grade 7
St Ann Elementary School

Heaven

What is Heaven?
A perfect paradise
A place of good time
A blessed home
Joyfulness and goodness
A place of equality
A gracious home
A gift
A world of happiness
A time to remember
Filled with memories
That is what Heaven is.

Kelsey Farthing, Grade 7
St John Lutheran School

The Good Side

Gone down the drain,
Never gonna be the same,
I've decided to change,
To act and to be different,
Not to be inconsiderate,
To be fair and to be nice,
Not to get down and not to get in fights,
To give it all my might,

To be thoughtful and to be good,
In all the things I do,
To hear the "wows,"
And not the "boos,"
To be brave,
Not to be scared, and to be saved,
To be smart,
To have all the soul and all the heart.

Dale Ciarkowski, Grade 8
Posen Consolidated High School

My Favorite Place

My house
Every morning
Every night
Day in and day out
Always comforting
Always welcome
Always loud
Right after school
Homework time
The stove sizzling
People talking
My sister yelling
Mom cooking
Dad working
Food on the table
Sleeping in my bed
Talking to my family
Hanging out with my friends
Playing games
Every day…
Happy to be home!

Nicholas Kennedy, Grade 7
Flynn Middle School

Life

Life is like a puzzle,
Challenging to piece together,
Always requiring patience and time,
Stressful, annoying,
And yet so rewarding when it ends.

Brittany Berry, Grade 8
Carman-Ainsworth Middle School

I Am Me

What do people expect from me?
Everything they want,
I don't see.
The only person I want to be is me.
I don't want to be a groupie,
I don't want to be a jock.
I don't want to be popular,
I don't like to mock.
And I wear what I want,
Not what is in.
You might not like it,
but it's not a sin.
Say what you want,
It won't bug me.
I express the way I want to be.
Not the way you want me.
I'm not here to please you,
Whether you like it or not.
I am me.

Emily Schnoblen, Grade 7
Flynn Middle School

The World

Where things rise and fall.
Is it really for us all?
Where people die,
And children cry.
Different things happen,
Rules are often broken.
Where is the love?
Is God really up above?
People believe,
People deceive.
Different skin colors are compared,
And beware!
There is always some sort of trend
But truly, the world never ends.

Alex Schrotenboer, Grade 7
North Rockford Middle School

Mini Sticks

On one summer day
I challenged my brother to play
A game of mini sticks
Because I thought of a few new tricks.

He walked into his room
So I had to assume
He accepted my challenge.
Now I could get my revenge.

We set up the nets
And we placed our bets
Then I shot, I score!
I've never done that before.

We played for an hour.
I got the power.
He shoots he scores,
Now it is tied 4 to 4.

I shot it from the side,
He about died
Because it went in
And I yelled "I win!"

Megan Baker, Grade 7
Addison Middle School

Stranded

Crooked but dainty the flower stands,
crying out for some attention,
feeling its roots stuck in the dirt and
wanting to walk away.
Tangled in despair it pleads,
"Help me! Help me!
Lead me away."

Danielle Naber, Grade 8
Cutlerville Christian School

Daddy

Daddy where are you?
Are you in prison or on the run again?
I don't know,
but I do know one thing.
You're not where you're supposed to be,
because you're not with me.
All I wanted was a chance,
to go to the daddy daughter dance.
But I can't
because you're not here.
Me and mommy planned it out so perfectly,
it was supposed to be you, her, and me.
So let me ask again,
daddy where are you?
I don't know,
But I do know one thing.
You're not where you're supposed to be,
because you're not with me.

Kerry Malik, Grade 7
Roseville Jr High School

Not Knowing

Pain and fear held up in your heart,
Not knowing when to be scared,
Or even when to cry,
Emotions hit you deep down inside,
That can't come out until you die,
Wherever you go, you know what to expect,
Hurt and a soul that can't be correct,
The feeling of a shadow on your back,
Following you everywhere,
And there's no control, of ever looking back,
Thirteen tears on a rose,
Too close to you, that you got to let it go,
Love is true a long as you mean it.

Kyla Small, Grade 7
Jefferson Middle School

Something's Missing

Something's missing
Something I need
Something I want
Something to make my world complete
My mom tells me this something
Is my dad!

She tells me he left
When he found out she was pregnant
She told me he didn't want me
But then that something came into my life!

My mom met a guy
They got married
And I finally had that something that was missing!

Chrystal Keen, Grade 7
Hopkins Middle School

Best Friends

Boyfriends and girlfriends come and go,
but best friends stay forever.
Through the snow, the rain, the sunny days and nights.

Shoulders to cry on,
People to help you up when you fall.
To stand by your side through thick and thin.
Your best friends.

Yes, they argue, disagree sometimes,
but best friends you'll always be.
Who knows your secrets? The people you have a special
connection with that you have with no one else, who you can
call on and they have your back?
Your best friends.

Boyfriends and girlfriends come and go,
but best friends stay forever.
Those are the people you are with most of the time.
The people you know will help you in a bind.
Those are the people that are your best friends.

Boyfriends and girlfriends come and go
But best friends, best friends stay forever.

Nia Bailey, Grade 8
Gesu Elementary School

Elizabeth Truman

Elizabeth Truman was born on February 13, 1885.
On a cold morning Bess arrived.
She had many strong opinions.
And no hesitation about stating them.

Her nickname was Bess.
When Harry asked her to marry him she said, "Yes."
They were married in June 1919.
She liked to keep the White House clean.

When she dressed up she wore pearls.
Which looked nice with her golden curls.
Her daughter was born on 1924 her name is Margaret.
Bess played piano; she probably played *Minuet.*

Bess traveled with Harry as he campaigned.
They probably traveled through sunshine and rain.
After Roosevelt died Truman took over the president's seat.
In four years later he had a repeat.

She was the new first lady in 1945-1953.
She came from a fine family.
She went through two miscarriages.
She pushed Margaret in a baby carriage.

Tre Pretzel, Grade 7
Lakeview Middle School

Red, White, and Blue

Each color has a message,
One that's brave and true,
Other nations fear the flag
With the red, white, and blue.

The red stands for the battles,
That took so many lives,
The men that kept our nation free
The men that died with pride.

The white stands for our freedom
That remains pure, untouched by man,
Some have tried to take it away,
But God had His own plan.

The blue stands for the oceans
That frame our perfect land,
Land full of freedom and delight,
Blessed by God's own hand.

Briana Torrey, Grade 8
Juniata Christian School

Love

Love is a complicated subject.
So many tricks,
So many ways to show you care.
One true love,
A husband or wife.
And the most difficult words to say are:
I LOVE YOU

Sasha Rudow, Grade 7
Flynn Middle School

Letter to a New Child

No one will ever understand,
A new life, a blank sheet at hand.

Everything parents do,
Should be to influence you.

They should treat you in a loving way,
Cherish you through night and day.

Right now you are really small,
Someday you will be strong and tall.

Although you will want to stay,
You will have to go away.

Leave the Earth and all your friends,
It's sad that a short life ends.

Your soul will no longer roam,
But come to know heaven as home.

Ryan Rooney, Grade 8
St Anthony of Padua School

The Job

I came home from school, I knew that it was time.
I was not getting paid, a nickel or a dime.
It was very silent in the cold and dreary house.
I went to go put on my freshly cleaned working blouse.
I went toward the room like a criminal to her death,
I knew the room was going to be a horrible mess.
I bravely went and prepared my tools for war.
I had to clean this room down to the very core. I had to do it; I opened the door,
Oh my word, this job is the worst.
Did I do something wrong? Am I cursed?
I cleaned the bathtub, the fumes made me sick.
The junk in this place was foreign and thick.
Now was the task,
The worst for the last,
The toilet, which is the worst job of all.
The shock of this all made me want to fall.
The battle was trying, hard, and rough.
The intensity of it all was very tough.
Did I do it? Could it be so?
Wow how fast that job did go.
I did it! The battle has been won! Cleaning the bathroom is finally done.

Lydia Bowling, Grade 8
Oakland Christian School

The Empty House

This empty house has no sound.
There is no creaking of doors and no squeaking of chairs.
The long grass ruffles outside but no rumbling of a lawnmower to cut it.
No clutter of pots and pans during dinner.
There is one sound, though, of a lone mouse scattering for food.

Ian Gregorski, Grade 7
Manistee Middle School

The Detroit Pistons

The best team in the league,
They show you the game you need to see.
They may be down in the first half,
But in the second — they will come back and the visitors won't laugh.
They're starting 5: the Wallace's, Hamilton, Billups, and Prince,
Helped them to the playoffs and they have been the best since.
Ben in his braids or sometimes 'fro,
His defense is always a great show.
Rasheed is the center on the team,
He continues to make the Pistons gleam.
Rip wears a brace because he broke his nose,
But that is often how the game of basketball goes.
Chauncey is a great player; he often makes a "three,"
It is just what the fans want to see.
Tayshaun is truly the "Prince of the Palace,"
And he rules everywhere from Detroit to Dallas.
My friend Kayla and I are going to watch the Pistons play Sunday,
We are hoping it will be a very fun day.
The sun won't shine in Phoenix anymore
Once the pistons walk through the door!

KaliAnna Keenoy, Grade 7
Addison Middle School

Ravens

The ravens fly
Over me every day;
Casting shadows down upon me,
While gliding in the limitless gray sky.
"Caw" they screech
Perched upon the power lines.
Waiting, waiting,
The ravens fly into the midnight sky.

The ravens fly
Landing in my yard;
Their beady eyes,
Send a chill down my spine.
They have a menacing look to them!
For that I respect them,
Yet, I fear them for the exact same reason.
In the end,
The ravens fly,
Taking me along with them.

Rachel Mahon, Grade 7
Grand Blanc Middle School

Jack

Jack was a remarkable kid
He went to the lake every day
I always wondered why he went to the lake
And why he hung his clothes on a hickory limb
He swam strong and fierce like a shark
He was very dignified and rather plump, as well
He wondered why he was always proud of how he swam so well
He never asked what people thought of him
That's why he was remarkable.

Lynsey Morea, Grade 7
Columbia Middle School

The Island

Boundless floods from the unknown,
The Titan woods shaped like a cone,
Forms that are unable to be discovered,
Why does anyone want to find it, I wondered?
Like Mountain Dew, there are dews that drip,
The mountains are falling like a broken hip,
And the tall mountains fell into the ocean,
Without a shore it's like an explosion,
Why the sea aspires, I don't know,
The sky is on fire, so it won't snow,
The sky surging over an outspread lake,
The lonely waters will never be awake,
The Water Cycle does not apply,
The chilly water is still with not a fly,
And the flowers like the lolling lily,
Grow in the snowy area that is quite hilly.

Taylor Zaszczurynski, Grade 7
Columbia Middle School

Ouch

I ran into a tree.
And got stung by a bee.
When I went inside to my mommy and cried.
She wiped my face 'til it was dry.

I went back outside
And was playing around.
When all of a sudden I fell on the ground.
I looked around my side to suddenly see.
The same old bee from the same old tree.
All of a sudden I felt a big prick.
Then the tears came so quick.
I thought in my head oh no not again
I sprinted inside and tripped in the den.

Drew Morris, Grade 7
Grand Blanc Middle School

Mushrooms

Frodo, Sam, and Pippin took a shortcut
Surely Farmer Maggot will send his mutt
After them for coming onto his land
Too bad he does not have quicksand

Farm Maggot has mushrooms which you don't want to take.
The mushrooms are surely delicious in a cake
You can put the mushrooms in a pot
To make them very hot

Frodo, Sam, and Pippin enjoyed the talk they had
When it was time to leave they were very sad
They did not want to leave this delicious food
And when they left they all were in a bad mood

When they got to Brandybuck
They were in such a muck
Until they got a basket
As big as a casket.

Heather Anderson, Grade 7
St Ann Elementary School

Reggie Bush

Quick, untouchable, exciting
Running, catching, scoring, leaping, throwing
Stiff arming, flipping

Michael Conant, Grade 7
Camden Frontier Middle School

Dedication

Dedication people need it to strive on it to succeed.
Dedication people use it every day to excel.
People use dedication in sports and everything else.
Dedication it makes the day go much faster.
And dedication if nobody had it,
We would not be living in the world we live in today

John Carey, Grade 8
Hilbert Jr High School

Generosity

I see a girl with big blue eyes staring straight ahead.
As though the world would stop at her one command.
Her long blond hair cascading down her shoulders as though a big waterfall.
She has a great poise about her, from her cute button nose to her little pink toes. She acts as though she doesn't care about anyone but herself.
But stirs within her body lies a more considering person who thinks of anyone but herself. Anyone can be hateful but it takes up more time, helping people takes but a moment of your time, one day she will finally come out of her shell and recognize who she really is.

Amanda Baumler, Grade 9
Kingsford High School

Where Were You?

One day I asked God some questions of mine
Misunderstanding is what I was going through at this time
I asked Him "Where were You when things were misunderstood?
When a lot of misfortune was going on in suburb and 'hood
Where were You when people made mistakes?
Like when people misthink that it is Your fault that things ain't straight
Where were You when people went to Vietnam and Iraq?
To fight for America to feel like a champ
Where were You when people have goals that can't be reached?
Or when people have enemies that they can't defeat
Were You here or were You there?
When people was full of despair
Where were You when people lost fathers and mamas?
When folks went through so much drama
Where were You when my grandmother was sick?
When *I* had problems that couldn't be fixed
Were You anywhere around
When babies were born without sight or sound?"
I sat there hoping He'll give me an answer without being misinformed
He said "Going through all of those situations, I was in everyone's heart from the time I was born"

Amber Wright, Grade 7
Hally Magnet Middle School

Far Away

Far, far away where my brother will stay, in California on a warm winter's day. Here in Michigan the snow is falling down. And the weather is cold just like I had told. Two different times, in two different places, I hope I can meet a lot of new faces. The sun's shining there and the clouds are coming in here. In California, it never will snow, as well we all really know. I love California and I hope you do too because it's a wonderful state for just me and you!

Cyndi Tobin, Grade 7
St Mary Queen of Angels School

Should I Tell Him

"I can feel the man's pain inside his eyes, should I help him should I ask if he wants help."
This man is desperate for love, he might've told his friends that no one cared.
"Should I tell him that I care, that I feel a spiritual woman in his house who looks over him when he sleeps, when he eats, when he showers, when he plants flowers, when he walks and when he talks."
"Should I tell him that a beautiful woman that is caring and loving for him, she cares for this man deeply."
"Should I tell him that she cries at night in the morning and the afternoon."
Of all the 365 days of their lives, they will never stop crying.
"Should I tell him that she planned to take him away soon, to be with him. He's only 84 and she's 86."
"Should I tell him that she's in Heaven as an angel just waiting for him."
"Should I tell him that he's already gone with her…"

Kathern Stark, Grade 9
Kelloggsville High School

Hockey

Hockey hockey pass me the puck.
Watch the stick as I duck.
Goalie goalie don't let them score.
This game is a bore.
Puck puck as it sails.
The other team is on my tail
Skate skate with all my might I hope my skates are tight.
Cheer cheer we won the game.
The other team is very lame.

Jarred Hall, Grade 7
Jefferson Middle School

Old Man Jiglo

I got up early one morning and went on a walk
I met Old Man Jiglo and we began to talk
The cold wind blew
It whistled a tune and the old man sang along

Ta dumb, te dee, ta dumb, to doo
They whistled a song they did the two
The wind calmed
He stopped his tune

We both sat down on an old cracked bench
Old Man Jiglo began to quench
When he was done he put the canteen back into his pocket
We continued our walk as morn turned to day

The sun was bright the day was hot
The old man pulled out a pencil and paper and began to jot
He wrote about sunshine, he wrote about friends
He wrote about life until the end

Brianne Lambrix, Grade 7
Montague Nellie B Chisholm Middle School

Gone

As I stand beneath the willow tree
I look at the grass covered grave
Thinking to myself I say
Why did you have to go?
You have family here
And many places yet to see
Great grandchildren to meet and hold
As if they're your own
When you left us
It seemed you left the whole world
When really you abandoned me your little girl
Yet I still think to myself
You're gone from me
But went up to God
God pulled you from us
God took you out of your position
And as this tear makes its way down my face
I remember you're gone to a better place.

Meri Laverty, Grade 8
Centreville Jr High School

Hanging Out at the Farm

Pig
Muddy, pink
Running, eating, snorting
Water, puddles, grass, fields
Mooing, pooping, milking
White, black
Cow

Ashley Twiss, Grade 7
Montague Nellie B Chisholm Middle School

The King

No crown of jewels upon His head,
But a crown of thorns forced on instead.

No easy road did He take,
But a bumpy one for all our sake.

None of the troubles kept Him from the next dawn,
For like a bird He would soar on.

Coming to us from the midst of creation,
Now to all people, an inspiration.

A man of power, will, and might,
A man of strength day and night.

Who is this man that came to us?
The one and only, King Jesus.

Brittany Berry, Grade 8
St Anthony of Padua School

My Cousin Amina

When my cousin died my heart was broken
I heard voices being spoken
In the middle of the night
I wasn't feeling so right
Just thinking about her every time
I didn't feel like spending a dime
She was the best
Of all the rest
Suffered a lot
My heart began to rot
Just thinking about her makes me want to cry
I couldn't even lie
It was like she was by my side making me feel all right
I could see her in the bright sun light
Talking to me while I'm bending my knee
Imagining her and me
Knowing we will be together forever
But that will be never
She is gone now to a better place I will never forget her
And she will never forget me when my cousin died

Nada Faouzi, Grade 8
Lowrey Middle School

Conquering My Fear

Racing down the slope
Faster and faster
Nearing closer
The jump seems to race toward me
Rising up the jump
I say a quick prayer
And off I go
Soaring through the air
The snow whips around my face
Everything below me seems so tiny
The ground getting closer and closer
Then I hit it
I glide down the rest of the hill
Finally, conquering my fear
I have successfully ski-jumped

Corlene Laing, Grade 7
North Rockford Middle School

Pass Along a Smile

Pass along a smile,
pass along a grin,
pass it at least a mile,
pass it along to win,
pass It along to the next person you see
pass it along
pass it to me
when the whole world is smiling
when the whole world is glad
we can just take a moment
to forget all the bad
we'll all be grinning
from ear to ear
it might never happen again
so we can all give a cheer
for once in a lifetime
event that happens
when you pass a smile
the chain never ends

Kaitlin Hirschman, Grade 8
Posen Consolidated High School

Freedom

What is Freedom?
  Freedom is living without fear.
  Making your own decisions
  Being yourself
  Freedom is for all people
  A gift from God
  Believing in what you think is right
  Freedom is peaceful
  Depending on yourself and God
  Believing in what you think is right
  Freedom is America.
That is Freedom!

Taylor Vergin, Grade 7
St John Lutheran School

1st Win

We had lost every game before hand
Wc thought we would lose this one, too.
Some of us were serious athletes others were just along for the ride.

As we sat and watched the 7th graders,
We cheered and booed, and yelled, as crazed fans do.
At first they were winning, but defeat was their fate in the end.

Emily and I were having a great time,
Sitting above the crowd, pencils were our microphones.
Commentating the little kids' game, as 8th graders who were thinking big.

Conversing with Mia and Coach,
Mia rapping like a gangster, until her heart's content.
Laughing and chatting during their game, but soon it would be our turn.

During our game there was tension, worrying about the turnout.
We were playing our hardest,
And agreeing with the referees.

It was close at the end but we won against the Spartans!
Our team jumped up with joy,
And screamed with our first win.

Megan Lamrock, Grade 8
Richardson Elementary Middle School

Twilight

In my dreams I am the twilight,
A secret place in between.
I cannot be classified as night or day,
As one or the other,
Yet I am.

My colors blend, become more dark or light,
Depending on my mood;
Sometimes I am bright, near normal daylight,
Sometimes I have more sprightly shadow, the reason unknown,
Yet I do.

There is the sun, there is the moon,
And there are their domains.
But there is one place, on fragile moment,
A crystalline moment where time will stop and no one will know,
Yet I will.

I will not be defined, I am of both worlds.
I will not be contained by others' whims.
I will fly across the horizon and do all that I can,
Other may not approve of me being this way,
Yet I am.

Sarah Pauling, Grade 8
Peace Lutheran Church & School

Loved Ones

Our life together was like heaven above
And ended like a heart with no love
The angels took her and flew her away
The only thing I wanted was for her to stay
The loss of this loved one I'm still dealing
These are my words that help the healing…

Loved ones come and loved ones go
The reason for this no one knows
Just as you start to love them to death
Their heart stops after one last breath
No matter how much you beg or cry
They don't come back and you don't know why
When they leave they take a piece of your heart
The piece that they had from the very start
The piece that is gone is filled with pain
Pain that could make you go insane
You'll always hurt I can guarantee this
Because your loved ones will always be missed

Catrina Comstock, Grade 9
Cadillac Jr High School

Shooting Star

S hining over us
H oping my wish will come true
O nly one chance to see it
O nly one chance to wish on it
T onight the sky is clear
I wish
N ice night to be looking at stars
G oing through the pitch black sky

S hining the brightest among all the others
T earing through the night
A iming downwards towards us
R acing down until it's no where to be found

Marie Cross, Grade 7
West Middle School

The Tree House

I walked down a forest trail alone
Miles away from any train car horn or phone
In their places were the songs of birds
My pants were all covered in burs
I stumbled upon an old sturdy tree house
As I climbed up the ladder I heard the scamper of a mouse
In it I found a chair and a navy blue hat
When I looked out onto the trail I saw a large bobcat
I decided to stay up there so I sat down and fell asleep
I awoke when I heard a mouse peep
I realized that I was covered in dew
To my surprise it was a day anew

Tyler Hubbell, Grade 7
Columbia Middle School

Friends

Are we friends or are we not?
If you are then help me now.
So please don't say you're not.
I need a friend to dedicate all
My love and my white doves.
Please take care of my loyalty friends
For I will not be near.
So if you hear a whisper
You know it will be me whispering in your ear.
I wish that you are a part of me
So I don't have to disappear.
So you tell me
Are we friends or are we not?
For if you're not I won't be there
To help you in your needs.
I can't help to think us both
Are going to perish in the
Darkness for eternity and never
Come back to the light and you will die.
So are we friends or are we not?

Sarah Wood, Grade 7
Flynn Middle School

Fire

Fire
Hot, burn
Heating, melting, hating
Forest, house, freezer, glass
Cracking, smashing, dashing
Cold, wonderful
Ice

Benny Van Heest, Grade 7
Montague Nellie B Chisholm Middle School

What Is Space?

What is space?
So many questions,
Is it the universe?
Is it the emptiness between my brother's ears?
Is it created by God?
Or imagined by man?
Is it for us to explore?
Or is it forbidding?
Did seventeen Americans have to die there?
Or in the attempt to get there,
Is it worth their deaths?
Or is it all in vain?
Will this end like the Tower of Babel?
Or will it have a happy ending?
So many questions
How many answers?
Will we ever know the answers?
Or will we always look up at night and wonder
What is Space?

Carly Vaitkevicius, Grade 7
North Rockford Middle School

The Door

I am…

Feeling mad, upset, and sad all at once
That's what I feel
When I'm in pain
When I look inside myself
All I see is fog
No light no door
Just fog

I am,

Trying to find anything
Anything to give me light
Or anything to help me out
The fog is going away
But I still don't see a door
I'm stuck all alone
No one to help me
I see a cloud
Right above me
As I stand looking up
The cloud rains down on me.

Erica Bender, Grade 8
Wayland Union Middle School

Eagle

Soaring above the clouds
A free spirit
Swift as the wind
Silent as the night
Brave and bold
As a lion
Graceful as a dolphin
And noble as a horse
Dipping and diving
In the air
So high up
As to touch the sky
And reach the stars
Eagle

Isabel Stafford, Grade 7
Ruth Murdoch SDA Elementary School

Love

Love is a gift
Love is sharing everything with someone
Once you find your love
It's like a gift from above
When you love you're sharing and caring
A person to share your life with
A person to love
And once again…
Love is a gift from above

Brielle Hicks, Grade 7
Flynn Middle School

Curious Questions

Have you ever wondered if dreams come true?

Do you question how trees are once bare,
But yet fill their branches?

Have you ever wondered why the sky is blue,
But is filled with invisible air?

Have you thought how each and every snowflake has its own personality,
But seem to look all the same?

Have you ever wondered how animals work together like a family,
But how a family of people can not?

Do you question how your brain can hold so much memory and information,
But yet is so small to even imagine it?

Do you wonder why we cry,
But laugh at the same time?

Do you question your life?

Krista Krautner, Grade 7
Flynn Middle School

If Only You Knew

I wish you knew my feeling for you, but I'll never speak a word
I've tried to send you a sign, but the message is still unheard

I think of you each day and night, you're stuck inside my head
I'll never tell you my obsession, for your reaction I often dread

I've wanted to tell you for so long, lately I have tried
I can't put it any other way, it will only make me cry

My love for you will never end, even when you're gone
Even when memories are forgotten, it will always carry on

I hope someday you'll know the truth, and hopefully it will include…
Everything I feel right now…

I wish you only knew

Julie Black, Grade 8
Flynn Middle School

Winter

I'm inside by the cozy, glowing fire.
It's almost eerily quiet,
I only hear the popping of wood and snow sliding down off the roof.
Outside, I see millions of snowflakes falling from the sky,
It's breathtaking.
I think it is amazing that each one is different.
They are drifting slowly down in various directions,
They look like they would be as soft as down,
To me, this is one of the best ingredients of winter.

Adrienne Lira, Grade 8
MacDonald Middle School

On My Wedding Day
I turn and face you
Gazing into your crystal blue eyes
I just melt into their depth
You take me away
I seem to lose all control
Soaring as you guide me
On this long and treacherous journey ahead
Love and passion
Can you feel it rising?
I give you my hand
As you slide on the silver band
You look up at me with a tear in your eyes
I break down right then and there crying
As we say our final I do's'
And you say
There is without a doubt in my mind
That I
Truly do
Love you

Amy Sannes, Grade 8
Beach Middle School

Love
Love is a blossoming flower,
A blossoming flower is a rainbow of love,
Rainbows of light fill me with passion

A wink or a smile only lasts forever
So if you love me let me know,
Because if you don't then let me go!

Erin Westrate, Grade 7
Montague Nellie B Chisholm Middle School

Too Short Her Life…Long Live the Memories
She arrived unexpectedly to my delight
My own little kitten my smile so bright
My favorite Christmas, I'll never forget
Precious kitten in stocking that's how we met.
How quickly she grew to a tall slender cat
Hiding and pouncing, sometimes a brat
My sister her favorite target it seemed
When she jumped out of hiding how Kelsee would scream
She'd chase small dog Sadie all over the house
She also loved the catnip sewn up in her toy mouse
You could usually find her in some sunny spot
Sun bathing on steps when it was hot
This Christmas she started coming around
With whole family she could be easily found
While I expected to see her for many a year
Time ended so quickly for my kitty so dear
She fought a hard battle those last few days
Even though it was hard for her in so many ways
My Calico kitten the pick of the litter
She was a great cat I'll never forget her

Ashlyn Brinklow, Grade 8
Beach Middle School

Daddy's Girl
There she sat on the warm beach sand
The most beautiful girl, her life in my hands

Her little curls of blond shining in the sun
Her little tiny fingers building sand castles and having fun

As I look into her eyes I see all of the memories
Traveling the world to different mountains, plains, and seas

Every time she stumbled, tripped, or fell I caught her
The most beautiful girl in the world, my daughter.

Katie Kirwin, Grade 7
Montague Nellie B Chisholm Middle School

Angel's Vision
The sunset is beauty
An angel's vision
Red,
Yellow,
Orange,
Setting the world on fire
Saying the day is over
Black,
Blue,
White,
Fills the sky
Moon,
Stars,
Dreams,
Creep upon us

Carly Moore, Grade 8
St John Vianney Catholic School

Be Free
Here I am on this rickety old ship,
Rocking back, and forth
I get queasy.
After my journey is done,
I am sold on the street, just like cattle,
My mom and me are separated,
In addition, I am forced to work in the fields
I get paid nothing and have to listen to everything,
My "Master" says, if I do not listen I am whipped.
Day after day, I get more tired.
Every day working nonstop and I do not even get a good meal.
Finally, a war broke concerning us slaves.
Now I am free running, and running
After many months of working,
I finally get to see my mom again.
I am very happy that I am free now,
I get to learn, read, and write,
Something I would have never learned when I was a slave.

Robert Gazo, Grade 7
Flynn Middle School

Life

Parties and school
Fights and fools
Attitudes and fits
Clothes and kicks
Break ups and
Hook ups
Don't forget
The drama and lies
So why do they
Call these the best
Years of our lives?
Dalia Abdow, Grade 7
Flynn Middle School

An Odd Day

We went outside to play basketball.
Our game lasted until four.
After we went to the mall,
We bought a wildflower.

We saw a baby crawl
Right under the Eiffel Tower.
She followed a trail of gum balls
That led to a flower.

Her mother finally caught her
At a dinner plate.
I found a ball all covered in fur.
The fur was wound on straight.

When we got home,
We found a gift in the yard.
In the box we found a drum.
Next to the drum was a card.
Erin Kennard, Grade 7
St Ann Elementary School

What Is Death?

What is Death?
Crying rivers
A cold feeling inside
A friend lost and memories to remember
Quiet and motionlessness
Losing a part of yourself
An ending of life
Grief
A last breath
God's comfort and peace
Tear stains on your face
An extinction of that person
Caring person all around
Gone
This is Death.
Christina Busquaert, Grade 7
St John Lutheran School

The Twisting Path

Down the twisting path,
You're singing and laughing.
Down the twisting path,
You see nothing.

Down the twisting path,
There are sudden bright lights.
Down the twisting path,
The lights are a fright.

Down the twisting path,
Their car crashed.
Down the twisting path,
They were bashed.

On the twisting path,
A car crash.
Rebekah Quinn, Grade 7
Oakland Christian School

Breathe

Inhale your first,
Inhale your last.
The first breath you take,
It will soon be your past.
It may not seem fair,
But it will always be there.
Sometimes it may be hard to see,
So take a deep breath,
And just breathe
Shannon Dooley, Grade 7
Flynn Middle School

The Dream

"Watch out there's a crocodile"
Said somebody above
I looked up and saw it
Skimming across the water
Where was I, in Africa?
Yes! That's where I was
Near a Pharaoh's tomb?
The croc was getting closer
I couldn't even move
My voice was gone, taken away
I was being held down by the phantoms
It was getting closer and closer
Oh no! This is it! I thought
It was an inch away from my head
It opened its mouth to chomp me down
"Ahhhh!"
I woke up.
All this time it was just a dream
Taking place on the Nile.
Mackenzie Jordon, Grade 7
Columbia Middle School

Fall Day

Fall is a season
One of four
It is very colorful
When you open your front door
Some of the colors
That can be seen
Are red, orange, yellow, and green
Leaves on the trees
And on the ground
When you look they are all around
During fall there is a strong wind
So I asked myself why
Does it sound like a violin?
Maybe because it's blowing fast
I don't know
But all I want is for fall to last
Victoria McBean, Grade 7
Columbia Middle School

Best Friends

We're there for each other,
We make each other cry,
We criticize,
We joke,
We push each other's buttons,
We stick up for one another,
We trust,
We act like four-year-olds,
We dance like fools,
We sing too loud,
We fight over childish things,
We yell,
We get over it,
We stay up all night talking about boys,
We laugh so hard it hurts,
We cause havoc,
We love each other.
Who are we?
Best friends.
Stefanie Younce, Grade 9
Eppler Jr High School

Summertime

Summer is a time of fun
But just until the day is done
Flip-flops and Tank-tops
The day stops
Volleyball and swimming
Both give a small time of winning
But just until the day is done
Music and laughter
Just until the day is done
The day is done
Katie Frey, Grade 7
Guardian Lutheran School

Life

Life can be tricky
throwing curves at you.
Having you make decisions
that will affect you no matter what.
Having good times and bad,
making friends and losing family.
Having fun and getting hurt,
doing things you like and things you hate.
Starting school or finishing it,
making a lot of money or just enough,
having luck or just not your day.
Being kind to people
and them being in return,
finding someone you love
spending the rest of your life with.
Doing things that you thought weren't possible,
going up in life and sometimes down,
but whatever curves you get
just remember this,
you aren't the only one
who has this type of life.

Cheryl Romel, Grade 8
Posen Consolidated High School

Question

Which way does the little bird go?
What does the little bird know?
What is his secret?
Will he tell the rose?
Where is this place where he flies?
How does he know which way to go?
Is there a tree to rest in?
Is there a worm to eat?
How does the little bird know which way to go?

Ciara Thompson, Grade 7
Columbia Middle School

A Knife in the Dark

The hobbits and Strider left from Bree.
They bought a pony and were filled with glee.
They bought the pony from Bill Ferny.
The hobbits were eager to start their journey.

The hobbits and Strider went through a marsh.
The flies and midges were very harsh.
They were very annoyed and got bitten a ton,
But finally they escaped the swamp one by one.

Frodo was stabbed with an evil knife.
The wound he got could end his life.
He was hurt so bad, he couldn't walk.
He slept a lot and could barely talk.

Kyle Thomason, Grade 7
St Ann Elementary School

If I Were a Preposition I Would Go

I would go over the grass.
To the sea, everywhere underneath.
Me and Piglet together at last swimming with seabass.
At the rec chillin.
Never listening.
In the Bronx.
No one in my face.
Screaming and kicking, never in Africa.
Under the sun.
Having some fun.
Running with lions.
Laughing with hyenas.
Back home into my bed.
Back to school the next morning.

Mya Wims, Grade 7
Hally Magnet Middle School

No Other Grandma Like You

You have always been there for
The holidays…
Hands outstretched with
Open arms…
You are very loving and caring
And the best grandma anyone could ever ask for
I wish everyone has a grandma like you
For you make everyone happy around you
You are very wise and very kind
Your heart is of an angel
The warmth you share is like
The sun shining down on us in the spring
Everyone wants to be around you
Like as if you are a magnet of energy
That pulls everyone close to you
Your eyes are so beautiful
They're like the sun beaming on a wide open lake
You love to cuddle and watch movies
And baby-sit little kids for some laughter
You will always be the best grandma
And you will always be in my heart.

Brianna LaNore, Grade 8
Richardson Elementary Middle School

Lip Gloss

Lip gloss is shiny and sleek
It goes on your lips not your cheek
It tastes so good in all ways
It will stay on for most of the day
It tastes so good it will ever go way
There are many flavors that I can choose
Peach, pineapple or even Pink Lemonade
Lemon, lime, and much much more
That's all I can remember
So go to the store and
Buy some more!

Candi Lee, Grade 7
Flynn Middle School

Football

Football
Touchdowns, contact
Big hits, skill
The game winning plays
Team
Robby Moore, Grade 7
Camden Frontier Middle School

You and Me

In my mind
I think of you.
Your soul entwined with mine.
With every breath
I'll be with you.
So beautifully sublime.

In the air
I'll dance with you.
My hands clasped with yours.
And in your ear I'll whisper
Of this love that I adore.

In the night
I dream of you.
And look into your eyes.
I know I'll never leave you
And I'd never want to try.

In my heart
I know it's true.
Together we shall be.
As we fly above the stars
Forever you and me.
Elizabeth Williams, Grade 8
Abbott Middle School

Goodbye

A whisper in the wind
A sparkle in the sky
a thousand words can't show me
How to say goodbye
A laugh that makes
me cry
A smile that makes
me laugh
We will be friends
Forever, until the end
Your eyes are
deep like the ocean
You heart is
so kind
I still can't find the
right words to say
goodbye
Demi Robinson, Grade 7
Flynn Middle School

Jeremy

Not a word was spoken
No chance to say good-bye
Along with my family I was also one to cry
He was my dad's best friend — inseparable were they
A friendship we thought you could never take away
As we were mesmerized by the news that day
Our minds were mentally shattered
Suddenly, our lives seemed as if they hadn't mattered
All ideas, thoughts, and words were of him and his family now
We all seemed to know, but couldn't help to ask how?
Indiana: a horrid tornado struck
Nothing was saved except his beat up Chrysler truck
The gory images flashed in my mind and began to be something that I started to hate
For now they were in front of me as we were driving through the state
No one knew the strength or wrath of what a tornado could do
They all were taken, Jeremy, Cheryl, and the children too
They weren't just best friends anymore, they were family to me
He's gone now, can't you see
Not a word was spoken
No chance to say good-bye
For sure they're in a better place now, we just don't understand why
Jamie Vadio, Grade 7
Roseville Jr High School

Friendships Never End

Inseparable, they were once said,
Best friends 'til the end.
Over and over, replayed in their heads.

Needing support,
During the tough,
Just being there,
Through the rough.
Whispers, loud mouths,
Nudges, smiles
Special meanings, different ways,
Guidance, in every phrase.

Just like when we were in kindergarten, you have to let go of my hand,
And enter the world, all alone.
But I will always be here,
When you come home, through the door,
Waiting by the phone.

We are not like butterflies, moths no way,
We are special, in an entirely different way.
We are what they call lucky,
Lucky because I have you, and you have me,
Best friends, who are meant to be.

Jennifer Doebler, Grade 9
Roseville Jr High School

I Am

I am
Sinner, Life, Child
I care strongly about Christianity
God is important to me.
Home is important to me.
Health is important to me.
Education is a great thing.
Problems are horrible things but you always
Have someone to take them to.
God is forgiving our sins.
More people are believing.
The devil is being defeated.
I am

Forest Vanderlip, Grade 7
St John Lutheran School

The Candy

I saw some candy
On the beach.
It was very sandy,
And on top was a leech.

I was filled with hunger
In fact I was starving.
Then there was a little boy who was younger.
He looked like a darling.

He was wearing a swimsuit of blue
And short brown hair.
I think he was about two.
He looked cute like a bear.

He was heading for my candy
Then his mother called him.
She also called his sister, Mandy,
And his brother Tim.

The candy was mine.
I ate it with a loud munch.
It was quite fine,
And that was my lunch.

Mary Feister, Grade 7
St Ann Elementary School

The South

The accents captivating to foreigners
The movement too slow for Northerners to comprehend
The fried foods for breakfast, lunch, and supper
The certain "Southern hospitality" we've learned to love
The south is like a big family reunion
Where the primary drink is sweet tea
While country reigns over all other music
Where the hot, sweet air is thick enough to cut with a knife
The south makes everyone feel at home

Jessica Nelson, Grade 8
Central Middle School

Get to Know Me

Just because I'm a teenager,
    Doesn't mean I'm irresponsible
    Doesn't mean I do drugs
    Doesn't mean I stopped going to church

Just because I'm a teenager
    Doesn't give you the right to talk about me
    Doesn't give you the right to stereotype me
    Doesn't mean I don't do my homework

Just because I'm a teenager
    I can still clean my room
    I can wake up before noon

Just because I'm a teenager…please get to know me.

Taylor Linebach, Grade 8
St John Lutheran School

Raptors of the Sky

In the skies a predator lurks
It's as vicious as a raptor
Gleaming talons of death
To those that it tails
It hunts
It's medium height and broad head
It has red tail feathers
Gleaming white chest and brown feathers
Streaks of brown feathers and black
They say it came from raptors
With its speed and deadly beak and razor sharp talons
It hunts for one thing and only one thing that's food
The raptor I speak of is a red tail hawk
Who rules the skies with its wings of white color
Animals fear it
May you never have to meet the raptors of the sky

Brent Williams, Grade 7
Addison Middle School

Walking a Lonely Trail

Walking along the wooded trail
The rain dripping off my fragile face
I think I'm lost, there's nowhere to go
Another step and I think I'll fall off
I can't scream, my mouth aches
Aches with pains and sorrow
I tensely bite my thirsty lips
Dry like the trails bark
The wind blows harder
Whipping my face with its punishing hands
Why can't I escape?
I dread leaving
But I'm scared to stay

Dina Mullins, Grade 8
Beach Middle School

Silent Love

I stare at you praying and hoping that you love me.
But deep inside locked away at the bottom of my heart I know that you don't.
Today I realized that I might never be able to be held in your arms and look into your eyes.
I realized that I will never be able to be called yours.
I realized that you will fall in love with someone else…someone better than me.
I realized that you might never call out to me and tell me how much you love me and care about me.
I try so hard not to think of this.
And that someday you will care about me and love me…
But until then I will wait in silent love.

Autumn Pilarski, Grade 8
Posen Consolidated High School

Life

Life is a funny thing. You can't describe life any easy way. But nevertheless I will give it a try.
Life is love, life is power, life is glory. Once you've lived your life you have done it all, the unthinkable.
Life is hard, life is easy, life can suck, life can rock. It all depends on how you live it.
Life is the world, a thing to do. Everyone has a life, even you.
Life is the rage that fuels you. It is all you want. Without life you are nothing, a meaningless mass.
Life is sweet, life is boring, life is meaningful. Life is nothing more than what you make of it.
Every life is unique, a true work of art. Your life is what you choose it to be.
So…how will you live your life?

Dave McCann, Grade 9
Roseville Jr High School

Broken Heart

A broken heart is a terrible thing.
It's like you don't even have one because it's been broken so many times.
Or maybe you're lucky and you haven't had one yet but you will, someday everyone has one.
Who cares how many times you've had a broken heart. The question is does it heal?
Does it heal like a little scratch that leaves no mark, or like a scab that keeps trying to heal
But keeps opening and soon becomes a scar?
You have to decide, but what you think may not be what your heart thinks.

Kayla Smith, Grade 7
Leslie Middle School

I Never Thought My Worst Enemy Would Be You!

A friend is what you refer yourself to be to me,
But when I look at you I see my worst enemy!

All the times you stabbed me in my back, and called me out of my name.
I could tell you weren't my friend then because I was the one you blamed!

And I can't forget about the time when you told my deepest, darkest secret.
How could I, you promised me you would keep it!

All of the ups and downs we've been through,
I never thought my worst enemy would be YOU!

I used to look at you as my other half.
But when I reminisce on all of of the good times, I realize that was long ago, long ago in the past.

I never would have thought all of these things would be true.
But I guess that's because I never thought my worst enemy would be YOU!

Lexus Lenton, Grade 8
Hally Magnet Middle School

My Inner Dragon

I've always loved my inner dragon.
I can hear the scales rattling,
From my scaly body, strong as diamond itself,
And the wind blowing through my wings.

And see the fire blazing bright through the misty air,
And I see cloud after cloud as I battle,
From the air to protect others from destruction.

And smell the smell of my enemy,
Burnt to a crisp 'til destroyed,
And harming nor hurting no more,
And I smell the smell of VICTORY!

And I taste fire, a taste like none other,
The eerie taste of burnt toast blacked 'til it's gone,
And I taste strength, power, and FIRE.

And I feel the heat of the fire,
Burning with intensity inside me as its blaze,
Licks the inside of my dragon muzzle,
With power, strength, and satisfaction.

That's why I've always loved my inner dragon.

Allison Wier, Grade 7
Belding Middle School

Peg

Sometimes, I feel so alone
When I think about her.
She is gone,
Now all I have are memories of what were.

It breaks my heart,
And I can hardly bear it,
To watch them rip her house apart,
When it's hard for me to even go in it.

Sometimes I lay awake at night,
Wishing I could change the past.
Crying, crying, crying,
Being with her was such a blast.

She made such a difference
She was so loved by everyone.
She changed my whole life,
Now she has gone off into the sun.

And I cried,
When she left.
And I also died,
When she took her final breath.

Kyle Yamin, Grade 9
Roseville Jr High School

The Sticky Rice Ball

For dinner my mom made sticky rice balls
I had one on my plate, but my cat made it fall
Once it left the table there was no stop,
It gathered up everything, even the mop!

It kept rolling and rolling till it went out the door
It even tore the carpet right off the floor
It rolled down the street, gathering a few cars
I was enthralled that it went so extensively far

Once it reached the end of the state,
We decided it was already much too late
It had already accumulated larger than a mall
There was no stopping the ominous rice ball

After a long time, it still wasn't caught
I felt terrible that this was all my fault
When finally the tanks stopped it at 4:55
I couldn't believe I was still alive

Katy Holmberg, Grade 7
Montague Nellie B Chisholm Middle School

Escape

We walk through lakes of many tears
We wonder all about our years
We learn from all of our mistakes
We figure out what each day takes
We cry our tears, we watch the rain
We meet new emotions, especially pain
We say that tomorrow "it will all be okay"
But we'll be miserable any way
Unless we find that simple thing
That little escape that makes us sing
Discover what gives your wings to time
That is yours, and poetry's mine.

Alexandra Schurkamp, Grade 7
White Pines Middle School

Dreams

Little twinkling stars
You may see them from afar.
As you lie in your bed
Thoughts come to your head.
You close your eyes and dream
And think about whipped cream.

A dream is light and fluffy
Sometimes makes you stuffy.
As you dream you forget about everything
And make a new start about anything
But all dreams come to an end
When the sun rises and lights your bed.
And sometimes the thought is still in your head
Little twinkling stars.

Elaine Kamvazaana, Grade 7
Ruth Murdoch SDA Elementary School

Love

You may experience this feeling,
And I envy you if you do.
When I see two people,
So happy with each other,
It makes me depressed.
I wish I could have somebody,
To have and to hold.
I'm always told that my time will come,
But what if I die,
A lonely one?

Nicole Purol, Grade 9
Posen Consolidated High School

For the Land of the Free

What is Freedom?
Freedom is my country
Freedom is my land
Freedom is my emotions
Freedom is my flag
It is dying for my country
It is my hopes and dreams
My inspiration
For the land of the free
Of this I am proud
That is true freedom!

Erin Smith, Grade 7
St John Lutheran School

Death

Death
When people are sad
They lost a loved one
They have a funeral
It seems like the end of the world
You cry and cry
But at the end
God is always there
He is comforting you when you are sad
He is watching you at all times
He loves you all the time

Brianna Tinker, Grade 7
St John Lutheran School

The Wanderer

Why do you wander?
Why do you stop?
Why do you sit alone on that rock?
Why do you wander as a rootless tree?
It seems like you want to break free.

Why was the sky forgetting you?
Is it because you're feeling blue?
Don't feel so sad as you can see,
You're only as perfect as you can be.

Lauren Ford, Grade 7
Columbia Middle School

Deck 9

On a Disney Cruise is the place to be
Singing karaoke at Studio Sea
Hanging out at the teen club, Aloft, on Deck 9
Seeing the cruise ship shine
Watching the waves churn in the Atlantic
The food is fantastic!
A suite on Deck 8
Where I'd always come in late
Swimming in the decorative pools
Following the simple rules
Magic happening everywhere
There is plenty of fun to share
Making new friends
Having good times with them until the cruise ends
Playing any sport on the beautiful court
The fun could not fall short
Wonderful shows, parties, and much more happening every night
Everything was just right
Leaving the ship makes you want to cry
But knowing that you had fun, you just sigh

Brook Fraley, Grade 9
Manchester High School

Flower

Finally my time has come, when I open up and bloom.
In the day, I am vibrant and free, and in the night, I watch the stars.
Summer comes and I am watered by a yellow pail.
The days are bright, and full of blue skies and white clouds.
The fresh green grass grows around me.
I know one day I will wilt but for now I will live my life to the fullest.

Paige Doubler, Grade 7
Jefferson Middle School

Pirates

I saw some pirates on a ship they sailed the seven seas
Suddenly their ship did flip but they managed to save five keys

To an island they did swim in hope to find shelter there
But one of the men broke a limb and they had to treat him with care

Stranded on an island they were until they found the cave
Inside the cave was just a blur so they sent forth their most brave

In the cave they did find a chest with five locks
Only something so divine could be in that great box

In the locks the keys did fit they turned in the holes just fine
Gold was found inside of it and, Wow did it shine

That night the pirates went to bed their gold very near
They had sweet dreams in their head when suddenly they all disappeared

No one knows what happened that night but their story is still being told
Of how the pirates vanished from sight along with their big box of gold

Kim Alberts, Grade 7
St Ann Elementary School

Friends

Friends are always there for you,
Confidants will care through and through.

They are the sun on my face
In gloomy times we do embrace.

As crazy as we get,
I will never forget.

If a battery were to dance,
It doesn't stand a chance.

Our friendship is unbreakable as a boulder,
As we stand shoulder to shoulder.

Kelly Morrissey, Grade 8
St Anthony of Padua School

Winter

Winter,
Snowflakes fall,
Layers of frost on the ground,
The bare trees dance in the breeze.
Winter,
Sheets of glossy ice lay upon the streets,
The wind zips through the air,
Everything is covered with thick layers of snow.

Winter,
Children sledding,
Making snowmen,
Bundling to keep warm.
Winter,
Streets filled with the light of the Christmas decorations,
Shoppers running, doing their last minute shopping,
Cars fill the streets to get with their relatives for the holiday.

Winter,
Children's laughter breaks the silence,
Christmas spirit is spread throughout the streets,
Everyone's kindness makes everyone's day.

Winter.

Jessica VanZee, Grade 8
North Rockford Middle School

Wind!!!

The wind can be a gentle breeze
A perfect way to start your morning
It may come in a whirling form
Which might turn into a storm
Still, God made the wind for us to enjoy
Now that I've told you what I think about wind
Just read this again
And tell me what you think

Joses Ngugi, Grade 7
Ruth Murdoch SDA Elementary School

Love

Love is like a rose.
The petals soft and sweet, the thorns sharp and harsh.

Love is like a dog.
Its fur so soft and silky, its bark so suddenly loud.

Love is like the sun.
Its rays that warm my skin, its rays that also burn me.

Love is like the night.
A time we sleep in peace, yet also a time we fear.

Love is like a bird.
Its song so pure and clear, but soon the bird will fly away.

Love is like the spring.
The days so new and sunny, the nights still dark and cold.

Love is like hot cocoa.
The taste can warm your soul, yet still can scald your tongue.

Love is like many a thing,
With its good, and also its bad. Do not rush, do not push.
Wait for it. Wait for love.

Aubriana Spenski, Grade 8
St Gerard Elementary School

How I Wish Things Were

Once I went on a trip
To the land of little prince Edward
With my father Robert.

Things were great except one thing was missing
A person whose love is unceasing and never forgotten.

Don't get me wrong,
She is in my life forever,
But whenever I'm with my father there is no mother.
And when there is no father there is a mother.

This is not how I wish things were
I wish when there is a mother there is also a father.

So when there are trips to the land of little prince Edward
There would be a mother whose love is undaunting
And a father who is gruff when things go wrong
Yet still gentle all the same.

That is how I wish things were;

So if you have a father and a mother together,
Love and appreciate all you have.

Leslie Harrison, Grade 8
Juniata Christian School

School

Today was the best day of school
Although people would say it's the worst
Everyone had to do everything last
And I got to do everything first.

Everyone said it's unfair
But of course I thought it was
After a while I got tired of it
Just like almost everyone does.

Today started to get really boring.
Even though at the beginning I thought it was the best
I don't want to be here anymore
I don't want to finish the rest.

Today I learned to be nice
Even if I don't want to be
Today I go home feeling bad
Because all I thought about was me.

Brooke Douglas, Grade 7
Montague Nellie B Chisholm Middle School

Who Am I

I am a bum perched on the street.
I am an incredible famous athlete.
I play lead guitar in a savage rock band.
I am a king and I own all sorts of land.
I am a canvas ready for painting.
My life is yours Lord; ready for the taking.

Tyler Gerke, Grade 8
St. Anthony of Padua School

Reality

Together for the first time
It feels so right
But yet so wrong
You make me smile
I make you smile
All the while my mind goes wild
As it feels so wild
Your touch
Smile
Eyes
Look
Smell…kiss
Are all insinuating the fever in my mind
It takes me further
And further and further
Until there is no more
And there we stand happy but yet so sad
Knowing that we will not see each other's
loving faces in the morning
'Cause the miles and miles that separate you
and me are not a dream, but…reality

Brittany Woods, Grade 7
Gesu Elementary School

Detroit Pistons

There were 15 seconds and Tay dished to Sheed
And he made the three pointer with some contact.
He ran to the bench because he started to bleed
He made the free-throw then their coach cracked.

He called a time-out 'cause they were down by 2
With 8 seconds left, man they got to play harder.
"All right guys we need…Hey I'm talking to you too
Dwayne you're going out but you got to be smarter."

They dribble, shoot and everyone's out of their seat
They miss the shot and the whole crowd yells so loud.
That's it, it's over, the Pistons beat the Heat
The Pistons are tired, happy and most of all proud.

That's the Pistons, going to work every night
They're all so talented, watching them is a delight.

Mohamed Khalife, Grade 7
Dearborn Heights Montessori Center

What Happened to Me?

I remember when I was young
Swinging on a swing
Yelling to my mom and dad
Look at me
I was so carefree
Never cared about anything
Pigtails was my hairstyle
A smile was always plastered on my face
Then came the horrid Junior High
Makeup was mandatory
Boyfriends was all the talk
As I turned a young teen
I thought I knew everything
I changed the way I dressed and acted
Just to be with the right crowd
As I sit and remember that girl on the swing
I start to dearly miss her
What ever happened to me
That young girl on a swing yelling look at me

Emily Stafford, Grade 8
Centreville Jr High School

I Have a Dream…

He had a dream,
Of a nation without division,
A nation where his children,
Could play with children,
Where blacks and whites together,
Weren't just pictures,
A place where love would overcome color,
He had a dream.

Michaela Pavlat, Grade 7
Sault Area Middle School

Spring

Forests of dancing branches,
The docile floor
The sky above

The hibiscus plant with the new buds,
the leaves curled around my fingers.

And with the world starting to awake again,

It's like falling in love,
To believe in yourself.

Joshua Gibson, Grade 7
Gesu Elementary School

A Garden Walk

As I tiptoe through the tulips, the lake's breeze at my back,
I am seized by their simple beauty:
Long, flowing, emerald green stems, the beautiful cups
With feathered-soft petals of different pastel colors,
Their poise, the elegant poise of a beautiful flower.
I finish my descent, tiptoeing through the rest,
And I move on to the roses.

I step carefully through the roses,
Flinching when the sharp thorns prick me.
I feel a drip down my leg, blood.
The roses, too, are beautiful:
The long green stems, the deep maroon petals,
And the thorns, sharp, pricking my skin as I walk.
I stop suddenly and inhale the deep fragrant scent,
My nose tingling from the smell.

All too soon comes the call of my mother.
Lunch. I glance once more at the beautiful flowers
And make my way toward the cottage,
Once again the lake's breeze at my back.

Courtney Dubay, Grade 8
Boulan Park Middle School

I Rise

You may drive me crazy into the ground,
But like the sun I rise.
You may talk about me like a dog,
But like the moon I rise.
You may put me in the ground in the grave,
But like my spirit I rise.
You may throw sticks and stones at my bones,
But like God I rise.
You may be hateful to me,
But like me I'm grateful and I rise,
I rise.
I rise.

Angelic Drake, Grade 8
Central Middle School

you said to me*

In your hands you hold the key
the key to my heart
the key to my soul
the key to my mind.

In my heart I hold you, I hold your love
the love you gave to me, when you did love me

In your hands you hold the key
the key to my heart
the key to my soul
the key to my mind.

In my head I hold your words, the words you gave me
the words I thought were true
"I love you Johna" you said to me
but now you can't even look at me
"I love you Johna" you said to me

In your hands you hold the key
the key to my heart
the key to my soul
the key to my mind.

Johna Walker, Grade 9
Carman Ainsworth High School
*Dedicated to Taylor Curtice

Change

Change is good sometimes change is best.
But change can be bad never change who you are
for you change who the world is.

Ronald Cook, Grade 8
Erma Henderson Upper Campus

The Brain

Whose brain is wider than the sky,
When the sky is infinite?
If the brain is so large,
How many of them can there be?
Where will you put them?
If the brain is deeper than the sea what is it as deep as?
Is it deeper than outer space?
For if it is then what shall it be as deep as?
Surely we do not know what lies beyond the vast areas of space
So how shall we know?
If the brain is the weight of God then how much does it weigh?
For we do not know the weight of God.
Will we ever know?
Will we ever discover?
Is it like trying to weigh sound, or shadows, or thoughts.
Is there a weight that we do not know of?
That is uncomprehendable to manly measure?
Only the brain itself knows of these things.
Only the brain itself will know.

Blake Hohlbein, Grade 7
Columbia Middle School

Church

A place where I can stay and pray,
Each and every single day.

No matter the weather or the time,
I am welcomed on the dime.

A place full of blissfulness and peace,
My relationship with God will increase.

I can tell God my trouble
Because he helps me on the double.

God loves us all no matter what,
Even if we are in a rut.

Nick Putz, Grade 8
St Anthony of Padua School

Anguish

Drowning in my sorrows
Standing alone.
Waiting for the water to fill to the top.
Fill up so I can drown and die slowly
All by myself
Alone in my anguish
My great suffering
I can't feel my heart; not one single beat.
The raindrops from the sky
They fall on my head.
Make my heart bleed.
No room to spread my faithful wings.
And fly away to the Heaven in the sky.
To feel happiness once more
With no one to hold,
In my anguish crying
ALONE!

KayLyn Patrow, Grade 8
Thunder Bay Jr High School

Springtime

The brown grass starts to turn green.
The big bumblebees turn quite mean.

Perennial flowers start to bud,
Poking their little heads above the mud.

Birds make their elaborate nests,
It's almost like a great contest.

Rain washes the dirt from the road,
Snow, cars, and puddles, oh what a load.

The warmer air against my skin is here.
Soon, summer will be very near.

Brianne Roth, Grade 7
St Anthony of Padua School

Invisible

Waiting at an open field
Just for a glimpse,
Walking by
Just to see your sun-kissed face,
I wait for you by the weathered bench
But you just
Walk by like I'm
Some invisible guy,
Surrounded
By what seems to be
Twenty of your friends,
I try to talk to you all the time
But again it's like I'm
Invisible,
I try to talk
But soon blown off
By you to go with
Your friends,
It's hard to tell if you'll ever notice me
The Invisible Man

Jeff Sprague, Grade 7
Detroit Country Day Middle School

Valentine's Day

Valentine's Day is special
Chocolates full of love
Someone put rose petals in their tub
Candles and flowers
Around the shower
Manicures and bubble baths
Smooth music and romance
You will listen to it as you dance
Kisses, hugs, and smiles
You are so glad this day came
You could make her happy for a while
With a kiss, a hug, and loving smiles
Try to treat her as if she is a queen
Valentine's Day only lasts a while

Oviera Westbrooks, Grade 8
Hally Magnet Middle School

Summer

Summer is my favorite of all seasons
And these are some of the reasons
The sun shines bright all day long
It makes me want to sing a song
There are so many things to do
Basketball, softball, and swimming too
In the heat of the day
One can lie in a hammock and sway
All too soon summer is gone
As the color green leaves your lawn.

Emily Kroll, Grade 8
Posen Consolidated High School

My Warming Life

I make your life much easier
With me it's complete
I pop your buttery popcorn
With my burning heat
As I work my magic
I see a munchkin peeking
Looking at my package
Waiting for my screeching
Look me in the eye
For I send blinding rays
BEEEEPPP
Here's your stupid popcorn
OOHHH
If I had just one day!!

Allyssa Bujak, Grade 7
Manistee Middle School

A Starry Night

A star
F rom up high
A soaring light
L azily in the sky
L eaning sideways
S ometimes I wonder
when I will be a star
admired from afar

Imani Mixon, Grade 8
Grosse Pointe Academy

Schyler

Mane long and thick,
Eyes big and round,
Tail like a river,
Flow down to the ground.

You are the gentle,
Safety on the line,
You protect me,
Like an angel divine.

When I ask you,
You give me control,
We are not two,
But a partnering whole.

Time spent with you,
Love your company,
Enjoying me too,
You whinny to greet me.

Schyler, oh Schyler,
With you I'm not judged,
Schyler, oh Schyler,
My pony beloved.

Erika Poli, Grade 8
MacDonald Middle School

Shattered

Everything I did
I though you were there
I found out you really never cared
You were the one I loved
And you slipped away so fast
When I closed my eyes
I dreamt about our past
And remember how you turned away so fast
I felt like a broken glass
And those pieces of that glass was my life
Shattered

Taylier Ranella, Grade 7
Peace Lutheran Church & School

The Ride of My Life

Do you think I should really go on this still?
Do you think I should really take this dare?
I guess it's too late; I'm almost up the hill.
I guess it's too late; I'm almost half way there.

I can feel the wind blow through my hair.
I can see the Earth's surface from afar.
Being up at the top is quite a scare.
I can reach up and almost touch a star.

I plunge toward the ground in an abrupt rush.
I can't open my eyes yet I'm having a blast!
I think this roller coaster is my new crush.
Is it possible to be going this fast?

I met this challenge with as much vigor as two enemies in strife
It wasn't at all terrible; in fact, it was the ride of my life.

Erica Salehi, Grade 8
Dearborn Heights Montessori Center

Cats

Cats
Cuddly, warm
Jumping, meowing, sleeping
House, shelter, cat food, heat
Walking, purring, pouncing
Fluffy, drowsy
Tails

Amber Forbes, Grade 7
Montague Nellie B Chisholm Middle School

Wildlife

Fish
Yellow, orange
Swimming, looking, dying
Fins, kiss, wings, feet
Flying, soaring, sleeping
Fast, blue
Bird

Taryn Bates, Grade 7
Montague Nellie B Chisholm Middle School

Remember the Holocaust

For many years,
the Jews were faced with many fears.

To concentration camps — they were sent,
nobody else knew where they went.

They were always trying to find a way,
to survive another day.

The Jews always tried,
to find someplace to hide.

Sometimes you want to ask, "why?"
It's enough to make you cry.

Remember the Holocaust so the world can see,
the horrors it brought to you and me.

Chelsea Murray, Grade 7
Jefferson Middle School

Yummy

Ice cream
Flavorful, cold
Dripping, licking, freezing
Cones, sandwich, pan, cheese
Cutting, thawing, filling
Thick, soft
Cheesecake

Harvey F. Cummings III, Grade 7
Montague Nellie B Chisholm Middle School

Bird Gift

Why do the robins sing aloud
They don't draw a very big crowd

The sound is not very bright
But you can hear it in the night

By the end of the day the sound fades away
Bringing about a brand new day

In the garden there is a lot of morning dew
As I sit and wonder just what to do

In the morning I watch the sun come up
The birds have taught me to never give up

Throughout my life I'll be able to say
I've watched many birds fly away

While life still goes on in a garden I'll find
Many a bird that stayed behind

Krystal Yost, Grade 7
Columbia Middle School

Puppies

P is for puppies
Cute as a teddy bear
Their paws and teeth
They use to play
Quick are their paws
As they run you down
Danielle Abney, Grade 7
Camden Frontier Middle School

Spring

Spring
What will it bring

Green things growing
Rivers flowing

Children's shouts of joy
Spring is here oh boy

April showers
Bring May flowers

Roses, daffodils, poppies too
Lilies, violets, and pollen ahchoo

Plants growing in the ground
and popping up when spring sounds

Butterflies humming
Bees a' buzzing

I know what spring will bring
So hurry up winter, so spring can ring
Christopher Egger, Grade 7
Mar Lee School

To Be Black

To be black is to be strong even though
the journey is hard and long

To be black is to ignore the stares
and act as if you really do not care

To be black is to be wise even in
your own eyes

To be black is the color you should love
You were made from the man above

To be black is something great;
it is something to appreciate

To be black is me
and I love what I see
Kris Knott, Grade 7
Coolidge Middle School

Lucy Hayes

Lucy Hayes was born in 1831.
Everyone said she was fun.
She married in 1852,
Never guessing what she could do.

They lived happily in Cincinnati.
When she divorced she cried to her daddy.
She married Rutherford B. Hayes, she loved to party.
She was bright and was called a smarty.

Over twenty years Lucy bore eight children, of whom five grew up,
They're mom was so nice that she got them a pup.
She won the affectionate name of "Mother Lucy."
When she was first lady she was loved by many.

Her parents were Maria Cook and Dr. James Well.
She was known as "Lemonade Lucy" as well.
She was the first president's wife to have a college degree.
Everyone said that she showed bravery.

She died in 1889.
She was buried in Fremont.
She saw no more sunshine.
That was the end of her lifeline.

Gregory Jeffery, Grade 7
Lakeview Middle School

Memory

In my memory
I remember things only temporarily

My grandma is one
Who I have loved and whose work is never done

She died and I cried
And there was nothing I could do all I thought were the feelings that I hide

When she died I couldn't think
I saw nothing and couldn't sleep a wink.

I only thought of her
No one else just to wonder

I can't understand why
She had to leave why she had to die

I miss her so much
She was my guide
my crutch my memory

Zachary Smith, Grade 8
Gesu Elementary School

Running

Sweat streaming down my face,
Feet pacing quickly against the paved road,
The wind is pounding on my chest,
I'm suddenly out of breath,
My lungs feel as if they're going to collapse,
My mind tells me to stop,
But my heart tells me to keep at it,
My arms pump as I sprint across the distance,
My heart seems as if it will pop out of my chest,
My pulse is as fast as the speed of lightning,
I cross the starting point,
I feel like I have just finished the Olympics,
Very tired!
Slowly I creep up to my bedroom,
Crawl into my bed,
And enter dreamland,
Where the race begins,
And I start all over again.

Brie Stevick, Grade 7
Addison Middle School

Sunshine

I cannot believe it. So sudden you're gone.
But I still know that your spirit lives on.
So many great times full of laughter and cheer.
Man o' man I still wish you were here.
I just cannot wait until it is my time.
My soul will meet yours in everlasting sunshine.
Sitting and relaxing remembering when…
Also reading this poem I wrote for you in pen.

Daniel Mammah, Grade 7
Chippewa Middle School

Swimming

I walk up to the block.
Focused, focused on the object:
To get first place.

I dive off the block.
The adrenaline kicks in.
My heart is pulsing, pulsing.
The water calms me.

I swim the lap,
The turn is coming.

I'm now done.
I look up at the clock.
I can't see because my goggles are fogged.
My heart is racing, racing.

First place.

Kelli Dryer, Grade 7
Grand Blanc Middle School

The Scared Kitten

The kitten walked down the hall
He wanted to play with his new ball
As he walked he heard a sound
It was coming from underground

It was a scary noise
The kitten lost his poise
He ran across the floor
Through the kitchen and out the door

The kitten walked around the house
All he saw was a mouse
His owner called for him
His name was Tim

Tim must have heard it too
He picked the kitten up and flew
They were back in the house in a flash
A minute later we heard a big crash

Ashley Spring, Grade 7
Montague Nellie B Chisholm Middle School

Seasons

Summer
Hot, dry
Swimming, hiking, biking
Fun, water, bright, white
Driving, shoveling, shopping
Cold, boring
Winter

Corey Sumerix, Grade 7
Montague Nellie B Chisholm Middle School

Make a Wish

Some people just don't know
How far life can take them as they go
Make a wish and you'll see it come true
All you have to do is believe in you
Follow the rainbow wherever it goes
Will you come back? No one knows
Keep your head up high
And always touch the sky
Keep a positive mind
And you'll always be fine
Never know when you'll get to the end
Sooner or later you'll meet some new friends
Whether you'll act, sing, or dance
But with your life you've to take a chance
Reach with the stars or the moon
Trust me someday you'll get there soon
Definitely have courage and confidence
Ask why? Well it just makes sense
Remember to always love
Family and friends 'cause they you trust

Alexis Mundy, Grade 7
Hally Magnet Middle School

Anna Eleanor Roosevelt

Anna was born in New York City on October 11, 1884 with a rich lifestyle in store.
Her mom and dad were dead by the time she was ten. How sad she must have been.
At 15, her aunts sent her to a European school to get an education. A French speaking lady was head of the operation.
Eleanor had learned French from her nanny, how uncanny!
To everyone's amazement she became a popular student.
To make her New York society debut, she returned to the United States in 1902.
Her distant cousin, Franklin Delano Roosevelt, made her a proposal that was heartfelt.
In 1905, she was filled with pride, uncle Theodore Roosevelt gave away the bride.
In 1910 Senator Roosevelt moved to Washington,
Washington was a thrill a minute for her, she became quite a socializer.
Before long five children they had. That made them very glad.
Her husband came down with polio. It felt like a deathblow.
Her husband became president in 1932. They now moved to Pennsylvania Avenue.
He was president for twelve years. That was the end of his political career.
President Truman sent her to the United Nations as a delegate. She was a great advocate.
She died from tuberculosis and sadly was missed.

Matt Agosto, Grade 7
Lakeview Middle School

Today

The key to this story is not the presence, but the past which lay forgotten, like a red bicycle of his dreams.
He may have been crushed under the presence of the elephant of life.
The rules, regulations, and laws of the past pass by without hesitation.
And there he is once again staring at the stone cold chicken noodle soup of his life forgotten.
When it hits him, the key to this problem is right in front of him like an open umbrella, just waiting to be closed.
The shadows fade as he gets away: it's a new day…a new future, no past, just the presence of life.

Clancey D'Isa, Grade 8
MacDonald Middle School

Super Bowl XL

S is for the super stars who play for Super Bowl fame;
U is for the unparalleled anticipation of this major football game.
P is for the players who will give one hundred and ten percent;
E is for the excitement which is the reason thousands of fans, last year, went.
R is for the running backs who are agile, quick, and ready to take a hit;

B is for the bling-bling, also known as rings, that the winning team will get.
O is for the offense which cannot afford to breakdown or flop;
W is for the winner who, at the end, will come out on top.
L is for the losing team, who blew the opportunity they had,
   And who will be flying home so terribly disappointed and sad.

X is for the x-tra pleasure the Super Bowl Forty brings;
   In the form of Super Bowl parties, half-time shows, and other little things.
L is for all the laughter we get from the commercials, especially the ones about beer;
   And for the long, long time we have to wait 'til the Super Bowl comes 'round next year.

Matthew Kudwa, Grade 9
St Thomas More Academy

Love

Love can be good. Love can be bad. You can see in the eye but it has to be a good look. Sometimes you fall in love.
I love people like my mom. Love can come back like recycling, bad love can kill. Love can be like freedom it is hard
to choose love because it is like a football game it can hit you hard. Can you love someone for the love or the fun.
Can you love for the nice things, because age is a little thing. Love big like a home.

Darnell Hannett, Grade 7
Three Oaks Public School Academy

The Sunken Ship Disaster

The ship sank
The family feel apart
Black holes in everyone's heart
My dad, the crew leader, lost and hopeless
But still glowing lightly
My mom, the body of the ship, broken and hurt,
But yet still loving and caring at heart.
My sister, the ship lifeguard, stands in the cold
Scared and hopeless, but still sharing her warm bright heart
My grandma, the ship builder, stands in shock
And not knowing how,
But still sharing her smiles the brightest as always
And I, the water who sank the ship
Stood still hoping the family wouldn't fall apart
The ship sank.

Samantha Evans, Grade 7
Paw Paw Middle School

Spring

Buzz…Buzz…here I am flying…
Spring is back and so am I…
Looking for a flower to drink nectar from,
I fly low and high all over the sky,
Over the hill I see…a flower
Thousands of flowers growing waving
Back and forth…what's that I hear?
Something…Buzz…I look back
And I see my whole hive is here
We fly as fast as we can to the flowers,
Finally we're back spring is here
It's warm flowers are growing
And all the animals are back!

David Hertzsch, Grade 7
Jefferson Middle School

I Am

I am tall and funny.
I wonder if I'll ever have a girlfriend.
I hear a gorilla.
I see a magic elf.
I want a car.
I am tall and funny.
I pretend to fly.
I feel the smooth skin of a dolphin.
I touch the tears of an angel.
I cry when I hurt.
I am tall and funny.
I understand the problems of starving children.
I say what I think.
I dream about riding a cloud.
I try to help people.
I hope to be famous.
I am tall and funny.
I worry about my family.

Michael Nocita, Grade 7
Roseville Jr High School

My Heart Beats

My heart beats as a drum.
My heart beats as a new born foal's would.
My heart beats like a waterfall, that never stops.
My heart beats to the rhythm of a bird's wings,
flapping in the cold wind and rain.
My heart beats and beats until it can't anymore.
My heart beats until that day comes.
And when that day comes,
I shan't be afraid,
but let peace flood my soul and very being.
My heart may not beat anymore,
yet my soul and spirit live on forever.
My heart beats,
but I shan't be afraid when death knocks,
on my door.
My heart beats,
but I will let it in and lay upon my bed,
and wait to be taken to another place.
The place way up in the sky,
where I will finally,
be at rest.

Shawnna Freridge, Grade 7
Gull Lake Middle School

Seasons

Spring
Warm, pools
Swimming, dripping, watering
Towel, swimsuits, football, leaves
Raking, falling, dying
Dry, cold
Fall

Derrik Brightwell, Grade 7
Montague Nellie B Chisholm Middle School

Junior High

Walking down the crowded halls,
Turning to your friends' calls.
Hurrying before the bell will ring,
Trying to remember what to bring.
You walk to your locker and grab your lock,
Quickly glancing at the clock.
You turn it right, then left, then right,
You get your things using all your might,
You will not lose this 3 minute fight.
You slam your locker closed and then,
Your books drop, pencils then your pens.
You hope you will escape this awful sting,
But then you hear the bell ring.
I'm late, I'm late is what you cry,
You lost the battle, but you won't die,
A typical day in junior high.

Simone Weithers, Grade 7
Ruth Murdoch SDA Elementary School

Old Tree

I was walking down the road
And something caught my eye
It was an extremely old tree
It was standing very still
As silent as can be

I was about to move on
Because I thought it was dead
Then I saw a pretty bird
Land on its branches

It started building a nest
And before my very eyes
I saw the tree was *beautiful*
And it wasn't really dead
It was a home for the bird

From that day on
I realized one thing
That everything is *beautiful*
In its own special way
Brooke Malone, Grade 7
North Rockford Middle School

Children Are There to Be Heard

We all have things to say
Whether you want to listen or not
You can try and stick us in the corner
Or make us think the way you do
But the truth is
We know what we believe.

You can tell us to be quiet
But our heads are filled with thoughts
You may not think them important
But whether you accept the truth or not
We each have our own opinions
We each have our own views.

So just listen and you might discover
The things we have to say
Are filled with truth and light
And if you give us a chance
You just might discover
Why children are there to be heard.
Asya L. Simons, Grade 8
Seneca Middle School

Puppies

Puppies
Slobbery and cute
Barking loudly
Like a siren
I only wish I had one.
John Denny, Grade 7
Grand Blanc Middle School

The Boy

He's always there, he's always been there for you, for everybody, but he's different, people don't understand, they never will, because they're afraid, afraid of something that nobody knows about.
Nick Gray, Grade 8
Ruth Murdoch SDA Elementary School

Betty Beatrice Beluga*

Betty the Beluga, so sparkly and white,
She swims through the sea in the day and the night.
She eats schooling fish, lobster, clam, and crab,
She dives down three hundred meters, oh she is so fab!
She lives in the Arctic, and she is sixteen feet long,
Betty weighs three thousand pounds and sonar is her song.
Betty swims in a herd, she'll swim there her whole life,
Together they cut through the water like a great big knife.
Once a year, Betty's herd migrates to the south,
She'll clean herself of algae at the St. Laurence River's mouth.
But then Betty went missing, no one knew where she went,
Then the humans found her, to the shore she had been sent.
Betty was a happy whale, and what had happened was a tragedy all the same,
A boat had hit the poor beluga, and those boaters became filled with shame.
There used to be several thousand belugas, but now there are very few,
Now most of the time you only see belugas in a zoo!
We must protect our sweet belugas, for if we do not try,
The belugas that we know and love — they just might DIE!

In memory of Betty Beatrice Beluga.
Nicole McLeod, Grade 7
Roseville Jr High School

Hillary Clinton

Hillary was born in Chicago, Illinois on October 26, 1947.
No one knew who she would become back then.
She has a brother Hugh.
In the city she barely ever heard a cow go moo.

As a child she enjoyed skating.
In college she did a lot of debating.
Hillary met Bill Clinton in college.
It later became marriage.

In 1980 Chelsea was born.
She is also a true born.
In 1977 she joined the Rose Law Firm in Little Rock.
She had the biggest house on the block.

For eight years she served in the White House as first lady.
She wasn't very shady.
In the public school system in Arkansas Mrs. Clinton played a leading role.
In front of the White House there was always a flag pole.

In 2000 a female senator was elected to represent New York in the USA.
When Hillary got elected her husband said, "Hooray."
Hillary's husband isn't president anymore.
Both of them we still adore.
Bree Rothman, Grade 7
Lakeview Middle School

Minutes

Time races.
People come,
People go,
I miss being alone.

Hours pass by.
Gifts are left,
Food is brought,
Time is taken away.

I need me.
Not you,
Not anyone else,
Just me

I'm ready to burst.
I see it coming.
I see the black car,
Coming to take you away.

I lied.
I need you more than anything.
I can't let you go.
I need to be alone with you one last time.

Hannah Jordan, Grade 8
Grandville Middle School

The Death of a Friend

Watching wrestling laughing and cheering
Eating TV dinners
The time spent together

Exercising, spending money
Talking
Shoveling

The cookies disappearing
Bills running high tempers flaring
The friendship growing

Life support
Crying and waiting, the emergency room
All quiet but a small heartbeat

Guns shooting, trumpets crying
The blanket of flowers
Tears blazing

Best friends forever
Many things realized
My grandfather
Victor Vifquin, died May 2001 81 years old

Coty Nolff, Grade 8
Richardson Elementary Middle School

Raven

Raven was so beautiful and loved,
But something happened when she was very young.

One night when she was put to bed,
It became a night we came to dread.

While she lay asleep all tucked into bed,
She didn't wake to be with us again.

Now she is in a better place,
Where God is looking at her beautiful face.

She knows just how much she is missed and loved,
As she looks down on us from above.

We all went through so much grief,
But we will never know her great feat.

She went through so much in her short life,
Until God chose to end her great strife.

She will always be missed and loved,
As she looks down on us from above.

Kara Peruchietti, Grade 8
St Gerard Elementary School

Rain Everywhere!

Rain, rain everywhere.
I like to splash in my rain gear.
The sun is fun but rain is a game.
Now the day is over, time to go to bed.
What will tomorrow bring…?
Tomorrow, tomorrow, tomorrow, tomorrow, is here!
It's raining, it's raining, the skies aren't clear!

Laurinda Krause, Grade 7
Manistee Middle School

My Pet's Name!

I got my new pet today,
At Marty's Pet Supply.
but something seems to be missing,
And I just don't know why.
So I asked my mom and dad
To see what they would say,
They looked at me and said,
Your pet just needs a NAME!
So I went to my room and thought,
George, Larry, Jim Carrie, no those feel so lame.
How about Hurricane, Tsunami, Monsoon, Tornado
No those seem untamed.
Missouri, Texas, Georgia, Kentucky,
All those seem so yucky.
Wait a minute I know,
I'll just call him Lucky.

Gabby Hamilton, Grade 7
Ruth Murdoch SDA Elementary School

Hate

What is Hate?
    An action
    An evil spirit
    A joy to the hurtful
    The effortless road
    Hurting of the helpful
    An emblem of the wicked
    Lucifer's instrument
That is Hate.

Timothy Smith, Grade 7
St John Lutheran School

Imagination

Why shouldn't we fly
Away from this world
With tragic beginnings
And horrific endings?

Why not just leave
And find a new spot
A new heart and soul
A new way of life?

It'd be a better place
To do what we wish
Our dreams never failing
Our fears never scaring

I know of this place
Where the sadness ends
And the joy just begins
This place of mine
Imagination

Beth Nowinski, Grade 9
Troy High School

True Love

It may just start with a flirt
But if your love isn't true
In the end it will hurt

If your love is pure
And not just a crush
It will never end
There is no rush

If you love someone wait
And let them find you
You never know
Your dream may come true

But don't wait too long
Go and find them
Soon enough they could be gone.

Jaclyn Young, Grade 8
Hilbert Jr High School

The Key to My Heart

The key to my heart is a thing only I know.
It is a bond between my soul and my love.
Is it the sound of my family laughing?
Or is the feel of my grandma's hug?

Everywhere I look could hold my future.
Only my heart can tell me which way to go.
Life is like a river, it twists and turns every which way it goes.
Let your heart take you down that river, for it holds the key.

When I was looking for the key it made me think, of ever so many things.
Could it be the feel of my heart beating at a ballet recital?
The sound of the orchestra singing around me?
Or is it the sound of my horse and I galloping?

As the years and life go by
So does love itself.
Now I can tell you.
Always trust your heart and its love.

This key holds my life, my love, my trust.
My life is my key.
My family helped me find it.
Only love itself holds the key to my heart.

Claire Haglund, Grade 8
Helen Keller Middle School

A Loved One's Death

The death of someone close. It came as a shock.
I knew he was sick, but no one's ever ready for their best friend to die.
NO ONE
A cold March day, a day like any other day.
I went to school and came home, but soon realizing my dad was not there.
When he got home the confusion, the tears rolled down his cheeks.
SOMETHING WASN'T RIGHT
The confusion came with his words "he's gone."
Words have never hurt so bad.
Why, why to him?
IT'S JUST NOT FAIR
The person, when I was little, wouldn't take a nap unless I was
by his side on his hospital bed.
SITTING, SITTING IN COMPLETE ANGER
Now I know he wanted to go.
It's been two years now since his death,
But it's still hard not to see him every day.
DAY AFTER DAY
No one's ever ready for their best friend to die
Especially if it's
THE DEATH OF A LOVED ONE

Angela Lalone, Grade 8
Richardson Elementary Middle School

Poker

You can win it all
Or lose it all
In the blink of an eye
You can become a superstar
If you play your cards right

They look you in the eye
You give them a cold stare back
You hope they can't see right through you
Then you lay down your cards
And you win

Tyson Klecha, Grade 9
Posen Consolidated High School

Night Fright

Night is the thing that hides under your bed
Monsters, ghouls and some without a head
Fright is the graveyard in your dreams
Aliens with big laser beams
Night fright is anything you're scared about
There are scary animals and monsters without a doubt.

William Donegan, Grade 7
Hopkins Middle School

Lonely Paradise

I close my eyes and all I see
Are you and I on an island of paradise.
The soft days, the starry nights,
The sand, the trees
Your hand in mine, then I wake up
And reality hits me.
It's not real, you aren't, this paradise isn't,
All it is, is a hopeless dream,
A hopeless thought, you're off with someone else.
And I'm here in cold snowy Detroit,
Waiting…Just waiting…

Stephanie Mladenoski, Grade 9
Sterling Heights High School

Tears

Tears slide down her cheeks
As she stands next to his grave
Coming down harder each time
The priest says her brother's name

Killed by a drunk driver
Who ran through a red light
That didn't see the little boy
Standing in plain sight

She sees her mother crying
And all she feels is shame
For she was the drunk driver
And she's the one to blame

Krista Lytle, Grade 7
Manistee Middle School

Meadow

A warm midsummer's breeze,
And the low, constant rumble of local bees,
Are all that move about with haste,
In this meadow, this tranquil place.

The willows sway to the wind's light caress,
Their beauty makes it all too easy to impress,
All that come to gaze upon this heavenly scenery,
Find delightful color and sounds filled with mystery.

And the river that curves restrainedly past,
Gently lodges the most exquisite bass,
An occasional deer will saunter into the rushes,
Drink, pose, then sprint off towards the bushes.

In this sanctuary's lofty blue firmament,
Birds of great color and form call these skies permanent,
Their many angelic hymns vibrate in the crystal air,
Wings glistening as they soar under the sun's soothing glare.

All these plants, bugs, and creatures,
Frame one considerably beautiful picture,
Where all can come to laugh and play,
Making this meadow a marvelous place to stay.

Ruth Robb, Grade 9
Concord Academy-Antrim

Life and Tears

FAKE
A four-letter word for back stabber
A hypocritical liar
A two-faced gossiper
That only wants more friends.

DRAMA
The life of a teenage girl
Rumors and gossip being spread
Something that is hard to avoid
And full of lies and emotions.

PEER PRESSURE
The part of life that is not easy
The start of popularity
What you always give into
But you know you shouldn't

LIFE
A roller coaster of hardships
A time to reach for dreams
A place to show strength and individuality
A time for tears and forgiveness.
Live it well.

Blake Sponaugle, Grade 8
Richardson Elementary Middle School

Hockey's Ultimate Goal

The glistening of the ice
The sounds of the fans
The players mentally ready
Encouraged by roars, up in the stands

The smells from the vendors
Blades and sticks all in motion
The puck is dropped
Both teams with one notion

The time clock ticks down
Voices become hoarse
My team smells victory
The other's remorse

A quest for the Stanley Cup
Throughout an entire season
A chance to be champions
Why play for another reason?
Joseph Trackwell, Grade 9
Roseville Jr High School

Friends

Friends
People you can trust
Loving
An inspiration
Always listen
Help when you're in trouble
Are always there
Never give up
Caring
Always make you laugh
Encouraging
Meghan Feldman, Grade 7
St John Lutheran School

My Grandma's Role

There's nothing like a Grandma,
To bring family and love.

To shower her grandchildren,
With blessings from above.

Like petals of a gentle rose,
Her kindness unfolds.

Warm hugs and fresh baked cookies,
And fun stories to be told.

God created Grandma,
Especially for me!!!
Samantha McLeod, Grade 7
Roseville Jr High School

I Love You All*

I love you all who showed up here
To help my family with their biggest fear

I love you all who showed up here
To pay your last respect as I lay here

I love you all who showed up here
So you can tell me your biggest fear

Your secret is safe here
'Cause I have passed and cannot hear

My time is coming up fast
So I have to say it's been a blast
And I love you all who showed up here
Darryl Paavo, Grade 9
Jeffers Jr/Sr High School
*In loving memory of my father
Darryl Donn Paavo 1949-1998

What If

Is a tree a tree
If it has no leaves?
What are snow blossoms
If there is no snow?
Will the birds still lay eggs
If they have no nest?
Can the limbs flow toward the sky
If there is no wind?
What is the season
If it is not fall?
Is the earth earth
If it has no color at all?
Brandon Douglas, Grade 7
Columbia Middle School

The Journey

What journey did we go on?
I'm not sure
Did we go for a reason
Like going for a vacation,
Or was it to meet someone new.
Did we all decide? I know I didn't.
How long will this journey last?
How long will they ignore me?
They said they told me,
But I didn't have a clue
They didn't like repeating.
Now I know as the memory floats
The journey was just a vacation
I was a very young one.
Now I will never forget that day.
Brooke Finch, Grade 7
Columbia Middle School

Dirty Socks

D ownstairs doing laundry
I n the basement
R agged clothes
T orn up in pieces
Y esterday's smell

S ulking with friends
O range stains
C ramped in a corner
K icked around
S oaked
Tor Vinson, Grade 7
Gesu Elementary School

Sunset at Sunrise

On a beach over the horizon
Sits a couple on the sand
Watching the sun
As it sets or rises
They look at the ocean
They get up and
Walk away
Leaving two pairs of feet
Trailing across
The ground like
A couple of doves
Swirling, swirling around one another
They hold each other's hands
And are silent
As they look deep within
The other's eyes they know
They found "The One"
Jaide Mickel, Grade 7
Addison Middle School

What My True Feelings Are

I get to hide in the corner,
As always, a shadow I am.
No one gets to care that I am alive,
No one needs to know the secrets I hide.
Do you know how bad I feel?
Like my heart is ripped in two.
My soul so empty.
How is it possible that I feel this way,
Without you?
When I'm around you,
I feel happy.
When I talk to you, I have fun,
Even if you don't say anything.
No matter how bad things are,
I will always hide,
What my true feelings are.
Kelcee McKellar, Grade 8
Otsego Middle School

Fire in the Eyes of a Stranger

The floor remains cool,
but you can feel the heat
of the flames below as they
engulf your one life memory

fire seems to crawl everywhere.
You close your eyes to block
the heat's intensity, as you attempt
not to relive the pain.

Smoke fills your lungs
and you take in your last
gasp of air, hoping that
it doesn't last long

life hasn't been fair to you
and you can feel your box
close in as your system shuts down
and the flames cover your body.

Blue ice fills your mind,
as you take in the last view
of your life and let it diminish, thinking
of the things that you could never achieve.

Lisa Greif, Grade 9
Saginaw Arts And Science Academy

Let Us Dance

Let us dance like no one's watching,
Let us dance like no one cares,
Let us dance as if there were no tomorrow
Let us dance with teddy bears.

Let us dance to forget our troubles,
Let us dance even if we die,
Let us dance to invent a passion,
Let us dance for you and I.

Let us dance for what we believe in,
Let us dance to escape from pain,
Let us dance to bring someone joy,
Let us dance in the rain.

Let us dance for world peace,
Let us dance, or give it a try,
Let us dance even if you're clumsy,
A broken winged bird who learned how to fly.

Let us dance to take away the stress,
Let us dance on the streets too,
Let us dance to discover ourselves,
I don't care who you think you are, just let me dance with you.

Danielle E. Schmidt, Grade 7
Harbor Lights School

Super Sized

people see the wrong side
the one easiest to see
but I guess I can't blame them
the one to blame is me

you think I sit at home all day
eating Twinkies and Milkyways
It's not true I try to eat right
though I'm still not what you'd call light

I've been pretty strong for all I'm concerned
I'm tall curly haired and really quick to learn
I really am quite smart I get all A's and B's
but it doesn't make up for it, from what I can see

I've been lucky enough to have found a few awesome friends
but my awe of the other girl I know will never end
I gaze at some and see what will never be
the skinny and thin version of a sweet and loving me

Emily Irene Schmitt, Grade 7
Grandville Middle School

Best Friends

Of all the friends I've ever met,
You're the one I won't forget,
You've been there for me through thick and thin,
You deserve more than just a pin.
Not even words can explain,
The times you've helped me through my pain,
You are the greatest person ever,
And we will be friends, friends forever.

Nicole Hindaia, Grade 7
Flynn Middle School

Over There

They go over there to fight for freedom
While we're all at home wishing to beat them
It all started with September 11th people say
But it goes much further back in the day

Things around here just haven't been right
Ever since they started to fight
Soldiers dying over there
As bad news spreads throughout the air

Soldiers dying
And families crying
Wishing we could have the troops back
That we went over to Iraq

Death is knocking at our door you see
Loved ones dying overseas
Trying to protect our country
Just so we can be free

Virginia Gowell, Grade 7
Montague Nellie B Chisholm Middle School

Flashing Lightning

Lightning flashes
With loud cracks of thunder
Lighting the dark clouds
With an abundant glow
Lightning flickers like
A bright light bulb
With every brilliant flash
Thunder booms out
Strong and hard
The thunder is
A shotgun
Blasting through the night sky
If you listen to thunder
You get the
Feeling of spring
Just sit and listen
You will find
That your troubles and worries
Will leave you
Until the storm ends

Kurtis Mangus, Grade 7
Addison Middle School

No Title

I am sitting here
With no thought
Wondering
Where is it?
What is it?
A poem
Then it came
A poem is that absent thought
That is instantly filled with life
The song
Of my emotions
It comes from the heart
Those memories, so sweet
With no classification
With
No title

Victoria E. Johnson, Grade 7
Hally Magnet Middle School

One Spring Day

The
water
glistens on
the golden brown
leaves as the sun shines
on the little kids playing
continuously and the dog
barks loudly off into the
light blue crystal
clear sky

Ethan Heyne, Grade 8
Cutlerville Christian School

Truth Is I'm Falling

The truth is I'm falling in love with you
I don't know how to handle it,
I don't trust it,
I don't know how you feel
I don't know if it's real
The truth is I'm falling in love with you
It seems to have just snuck up on me
It seemed to have just took me by surprise
I opened my eyes and the truth is
I'm falling in love with you
I'm scared
I don't know what to do
Though the truth is
I'm falling in love with you
I can't hide my feelings, which all together are tied up
I can't run because
I'm falling in love with someone the truth is that someone
Is you

Diamond Sharpe, Grade 7
Gesu Elementary School

Running

Feet hitting the cold, hard, blacktop
Hundreds of spectators
Mouths moving and arms going everywhere
But, all that's heard is the thump,
thump,
hump,
thump of your racing heart
Legs are so sore and tired but they just can't stop
Developed strong through training and now this race
They're not going to give out now
Around the corner
There it is, the letter spelling it out, FINISH LINE
Acceleration
Giving 110% these last seconds
The last few strides, rushing through the finish
Slow down but just can't stop
Your head turns, and the roaring crowd is heard for the first time.

Emily Joseph, Grade 8
North Rockford Middle School

Life

L is for love. Life is full of love.
it comes in many sizes, and all different ways,
love can sometimes feel like a maze.
I is for inspiration. Your world is filled with inspiration.
Sometimes it's a teacher or a friend,
but whoever it comes from it stays with you forever.
F is for family. Family is always there for you when you're down,
family is there when no one else is around.
E is for everyone. Everyone is full of life, we all live it differently.
Some give, some take, my lesson from this poem
is your life is no mistake.

Megan Frederick, Grade 8
Hilbert Jr High School

Alone

Young, restless and confused
I am
These surroundings don't
Make sense to me

A deep roar is what I hear
In the distance as I stand there alone
With no purpose

I need to make a decision
Do I stay or progress,
Leaves around me are whirling in distress

I feel as if maybe
Some one is with me,
But speak they do not
Why do I feel this way?
On such a disturbing and confusing day

I must not let
My secret be known
For I am already standing here alone
Baylea Fejes, Grade 7
Columbia Middle School

Little Jimmy's Crazy Beach Day

Little Jimmy went to the beach
One bright and sunny day
He had to dress kinda warm
For that windy day in May.

He pulled out his shovel
He pulled out his pail
The clouds turned gray
As it began to hail.

But Little Jimmy did not care
He stayed at the beach
And played with his toy bear
Until the day was complete.

Little Jimmy saw his friend Kim
When he got ready to leave
The sun smiled down on them
And the two smiled back.
Mariah Korson, Grade 7
Montague Nellie B Chisholm Middle School

Happiness

Happiness is as bright as the sun.
It sounds like giggles of little girls.
It tastes like fresh lemonade on a hot summer day.
It looks like a baby rabbit,
And it makes me feel like everything is ok.
Emily Keister, Grade 7
Paw Paw Middle School

Victory

What is victory?
    A symbol of hard work and determination
    Inspiration to keep going
    A game winning shot
    A dream come true
    Celebration and happiness
    Victory over death
    Short term happiness or eternal joy
    Relief it is over
That is victory!
Evan Cory, Grade 7
St John Lutheran School

The Outsider

Alone,

I glance at the chalkboard
and see my thoughts portrayed on it.

Alone,

though surrounded by hundreds of students
who never notice me.

But,
In the innermost part of my being
the Lord comforts me.
The One who sees what they don't.
A true Friend.

Alone, but not alone.

Suddenly,
surrounded by friends.
Acceptance never felt.
No longer unwanted,
but wanted.
Not an outsider anymore.
Andrew Christensen, Grade 7
North Rockford Middle School

S Is for Sun

S is for sun that comes out in the day.
S is for sun that takes the pain away!
S is for sun that shines so bright.
S is for sun that brings out the light.
S is for sun that is so warm and nice.
S is for sun that gives the world some spice!
S is for sun that is so glimmering.
S is for sun but when it's done it leaves you shivering!
S is for sun that is so hot.
S is for sun that is always moving from spot to spot.
Kelly Westfall, Grade 7
Camden Frontier Middle School

A Crazy Family

When you have a big family it's like having a zoo in your house
All the different types of personalities combine together and the house is like a battlefield
There is always a war going on
Having a family should be like buying a pair of shoes
Trying them on for size and if you don't like them you can put them back
But that's not how it goes
Family is there if you want them or not
You're born with them
They make fun of you when you do stupid things
But you know deep inside that they only do it because they love you
Sometimes it's hard to see that
They are the ones who pick you up when you fall and can't get up
They get you out of trouble
Even if you hate them sometimes
You can't change them
Every family is different and never perfect
That's why I love them
'Cause I'm a part of the madness
I belong to only one crazy zoo
That is my family

Kim Kue, Grade 9
Roseville Jr High School

Lucreta Garfield

Lucreta was born in Hiram, Ohio on April 19, 1832. This was her big debut.
A farmer was her dad, this did not make her sad.
She liked to explore, while traveling outdoors
Lucreta loved to read. This made her smart indeed.
She attended Western Reserve Electric Institute in 1850. It was a hoot.
She went to school with James. Later her husband he became.
She became a teacher. And not a preacher.
She taught school. This means she was not a fool.
Lucreta married James in November 1858 this was a day she could not wait.
They had 7 children. Eliza, Harry, James, Mary, Darwin, Abram, Edward. They would be good citizens.
James was elected president in 1880. Lucreta became the first lady.
March 14, 1918 is when she passed. Her husband she outlast.

Brandon McIntyre, Grade 7
Lakeview Middle School

Defining Me

Does the radiance of my brown sugar skin surprise you
Does the click in my heels over step you
Does the sway of my hips knock you off my path to success
Does my intelligence offend you
Does the thickness of my hair get you all tangled in my thoughts
Does my broad nose steal all your spotlight
Does the curves of my body represent the ups and downs
Do my people amaze you
Does my name emphasize who I really am or who you judge me to be
Does it bother you that my people were once Kings and Queens
Everything from my head to my toes represent the struggle and the glory of my ancestors
So you can sit and count on my day of downfall, but you'll be counting for forevermore.

Diamond Johnson, Grade 8
Hally Magnet Middle School

Grandparents

Grandparents are wonderful,
They spoil you with love.
They give you toys and cookies,
And are gifts from up above.

Grandparents are super,
They tuck you into bed.
They give you good night kisses,
And make the best homemade bread.

Grandparents are wise,
They've been here for ages.
They know the important facts of life,
And they write letters with a million pages.

Grandparents are heroes,
They have had many glories.
They've fought many wars,
And tell you the "Back when I was your age" stories.

Grandparents are wonderful,
They spoil you with love.
They give you toys and cookies,
And are gifts from up above.

Emily Halliday, Grade 7
North Rockford Middle School

Awkward

Every time I pass you in the halls,
I could feel the blood rush to my cheeks.

When we accidentally bump into each other,
You apologize and I can hardly speak.

My mind drifts off to thoughts of you,
I say I'm going to tell but I postpone it to next week.

They say this either clueless or mocking,
As soon as I tell them they say, "pa-lease"

I am afraid of what others will think,
But the most important opinions are by me.

Adults believe they know what it is like,
You know, to be a kid these days.

When they say this,
My mind fills with rage.

Being a kid these days can be summed up
Into one word:
Awkward.

Shelby Robinson, Grade 7
Gesu Elementary School

Spirit

Life is too short to sit back and wait for the call,
You have to get out in the game, play, give it your all,
Burdens may weigh down the broad shoulders you've got,
But you can't sit around and let your soul rot,
You've gotta pick up the pieces and move on in the game,
Show them you're strong, that you know the next phase,
Deaths, births, tears of joy and sorrow,
Remind us that there may or may not be a tomorrow,
But hold your head high and keep up the pace,
Come on. You've gotta put on that game face,
You can shout, scream, do what you please,
But don't stand around and wait for life to leave,
I guess what I'm trying to say is to live life to the fullest,
Never back down, you've got potential, you're the strongest.

Amanda Porter, Grade 7
Sault Area Middle School

Love

Love is something you give
It's not something you can just take away
You have to earn it don't waste it
Learn how to use it love the right way
Sometimes love blinds you
Don't think it's the end of the world
Just because the other person
Doesn't like you back. Watch your words
They are very hurtful. They stay in a person
Forever, be very careful.
Sometimes love makes you do crazy things.
Don't let it ruin your life, it's not worth it
Try not to love the wrong person
Love is very tricky
Don't try to kill yourself over a person.
There are lots of people out there.
Sometimes you don't even need love from
Somebody else. Just be careful and know
How to use it. Say I love you when you mean it.
Don't play with people's feelings. Use the golden rule.
Don't just love for looks. It won't last long.

Janeth Rodriguez, Grade 7
Paw Paw Middle School

Big Brother

He helps me with sports
Like basketball and bowling
Helps me with my homework
If my parents don't get it
He is always there for me
If he can't help then he will try
He could still spend some more time with me
My mom always bugs him
To come down here
He is always busy with work
I will love him forever

Travis Payne, Grade 7
Addison Middle School

Water Lily
Water lily, water lily
As fragrant as a rose.
When I smell you,
You tickle my nose.
Water lily, water lily,
As blue as can be.
When you're in the water,
I sometimes cannot see.
Water lily, water lily,
Spreading in the night.
So when it's morning,
I can see it in the light.
Water lily, water lily,
Where are you found?
I wish you could stay
All year around!
Stephanie Kilbourn, Grade 7
Mar Lee School

Friends
Friends are loyal
People you can trust
Friends will be there
When you feel like you are dust
When you are in a load of trouble
You can always call on them
Even when you're not that great
They think you are a gem
When you're feeling under the weather
They'll try and cheer you up
When you have friends like mine
You're always feeling up!
Jo-Jo McIntyre, Grade 7
Ruth Murdoch SDA Elementary School

Rivers
Rushing white waters
Flow over the rocks and earth
Never stop flowing
Joe Carlson, Grade 8
St John Vianney Catholic School

Here Alone
I'm standing here alone
Wondering why you hurt me
Why you said those things you said

I wait here hoping to hear your voice,
Saying how sorry you are
Saying that I mean so much to you

No no I'm here alone
Sad and lonely
Alone
Molly Piecuch, Grade 8
St Gerard Elementary School

Rachel Jackson
Rachel went to Tennessee,
She grew up in the country with lots of trees.
Rachel worked with her mother,
Her family did go to Tennessee it was only her mother and her brother.

Rachel was 18 when she married Louis Robards.
Robards was Rachel's guard.
Their marriage was a disaster.
They were sad after.

Louis and Rachel were planning to get a divorce,
But Louis would not,
Louis sued Rachel for adultery,
They did not like each other a lot.

Later on, Rachel said I do,
To Andrew.
Rachel met him when they were walking,
And they started talking.

Rachel was in love,
Andrew went above,
Then he became our commander in chief.
Democracy was his belief.

Mariha Roger, Grade 7
Lakeview Middle School

You
Your blue eyes…
When I look into your blue eyes I see clear ocean waters…
I see love, a kind of love I have never seen before.
I see gentleness that everyone wants and needs.
I see happiness that makes my world melt.
I see care, which will be needed for the hard times.
Your smile…
Oh what to say about that smile that melts my heart.
That smile that makes me feel ok.
That smile that helps me think positive when in a bad mood.
That smile that helps my heart beat.
That smile that I need to see forever.
Now that voice of yours…
That voice of yours makes me smile…
Not just a smile though, it's a smile that comes from the heart.
That voice I could listen to like, a favorite song.
That voice I could fall asleep to.
The voice isn't just heard in the ears, but in the heart too.
When that voice speaks out to me, I feel my heart reaching out for the voice…
I feel my heart trying to run out of my body and run away…
Run away to the heart of the voice.
Laura Dedvukaic, Grade 7
Flynn Middle School

Basketball

There was once a girl
Who dribbled down the court
As she said,
Basketball was her favorite sport
There are cheers here and there
There are cheers everywhere
I shoot that three
I hear the crowd shout my name
I look at the scoreboard
We won the game!

Linda Nikprelaj, Grade 7
Flynn Middle School

Spring

As I sat in the meadow
A flower looked at me
It was so innocent
Just like a bee

I heard the birds chirp
As they flew on by
The colors of rainbow
As bright as the sky

I looked at the trees
They stood so bold
Buds popping up
Recovering from cold

All the little critters
Came out to play
No one in sight
Not even a stray

For spring is so beautiful
With all of its flowers
Birdsongs all day
Holding God's power

Amber Cumings, Grade 7
Montague Nellie B Chisholm Middle School

My Wonderland

The wonderful place I imagine,
can only be in a dream.
With white talking rabbits and a Cheshire cat,
are only as real as they seem.
I've dreamt of talking caterpillars,
a tea party with the Mad Hatter.
Playing croquet with the queen herself,
doesn't really seem to matter.
Don't you wish you could escape,
even if you think you can't.
Journeying to a faraway place,
in Alice In Wonderland.

Amanda Stephan, Grade 7
Gaylord Middle School

It Could Be You

She sits in the rain with her hands on her head
She isn't moving but she isn't dead
She isn't that old five at the most
And her skin is so pale she looks like a ghost
The people around they seem not to care
They sit at their windows they sit and stare
Then one little girl steps into the rain
And some people question "Is this girl sane?"
She walks to the girl and extends a hand
The other little girl lifts her eyes from the land
A small grin a smile that says thanks
That comes from within so how is it
That only one girl helped that small child
That only one girl pulled her in from the rain
So strong and wild is that what has happened?
What our world has become?
That when someone needs help only one girl will come?
That people are so selfish they really don't care
And there's no guarantee that they will be there
So help out be one of the few
Just think of it this way: it could be you

Johanna Hardy, Grade 8
St Gerard Elementary School

Christmas

The trees covered in snow
The branches hanging down low
The bright twinkling lights on each house
The sparkling Christmas trees in the window
The beautifully wrapped present under the tree
The feeling in everyone's heart
The gathering of family and friends
The Christmas season is here

Katie Lemire, Grade 8
Central Middle School

Summer

I love the smell of the ocean breeze
That sweeps through my face
As I walk on the beach.

The sun shining bright
Not a cloud to be seen
The sky as blue as the ocean.

I can feel my skin getting tanned from the intense heat,
I can feel the hot sand going through my toes,
And I can smell the smoke from a local barbecue stand.

This is what I love the most
Just having fun while it's summer
Because when fall starts…school starts.

Heather dela Cruz, Grade 8
MacDonald Middle School

The First Snowfall

You walk outside
And take a sniff of the air
It smells like winter fresh gum
It looks like a blanket on your bed
Snowfall is cold
You feel the flakes hit your face
For the first time of the year
You make a snowman
Snowfall is a wave
White and cold
Always flowing fast

Cody Robidoux, Grade 7
Addison Middle School

Just to Win

I will not fold
Or give up the gold
Just to win
I will succeed
And I will proceed
Just to win
I will not cheat
To accomplish my feat
Just to win
I will not give up
To win the cup
Just to win
Yea I'll be mean
With me and my team
Just to win
I won't stop
Till I'm on top
Just to win
Watch what I'll do
Just to win

Scott Taylor, Grade 7
Flynn Middle School

Spring

Now that winter has come and gone,
Flowers bloom,
Birds and bees are seen at dawn
And take away our gloom.
Now we hear birds sing
This is beautiful spring.

Snow has melted,
Colors appear,
Rain has pelted
Everything is clear.
Now we hear birds sing
This is beautiful spring.

Gavin O'Gara, Grade 7
Flynn Middle School

We Love You

My dad, I wish he was still here
It's sadness that I fear

It happened October 8, 1997
Which is the day he went to heaven

He was trying to take us to school
There was a drunk lady acting a fool

We loved him so much
He had that special touch

Amber Hurd, Grade 7
Hally Magnet Middle School

When

When will you wait?
When will you see?
When may I speak?
When will you listen?
When is there time
I miss you
So wait for me
Look for me
Hear me speak
Listen to my words
Take some time
And let me guide you.

Whitney Mae Ewing, Grade 8
Otsego Middle School

Thanks Mom

You're always there
No matter if I'm right
Or if I'm wrong
You always take a stand
When I'm blue
You're always there
Right at my side
Catching every tear
Listening to every complaint
I know I may mess up
But no matter what
You're always there
At times it may seem I don't care
But what's most important to me
Is that you're there
I look for your guidance
And your beauty
To me you're perfect
Because no matter what
You're always there
And I thank you Mom.

Megan Messing, Grade 9
Roseville Jr High School

Who I Am

I am
Family, Friends, Pets
I care about God and other people.
Humor is important to me.
Kindness is important to me.
Love is important to me.
Forgiveness is a good thing.
Money is a bad thing, but
It can be used to help other people.
The world is falling into darkness.
Only forgiveness can bring back light.
We need to find our true friends.
This is who I am.

Paul Hoerner, Grade 7
St John Lutheran School

Life Still Continues

Life still continues
When you get bullied or
When you fail a test.

The clock is still ticking
When you lose a game or
When you're upset.

Life is like a clock
When someone dies
So don't weep, for
The clock is still ticking and
Life still goes on.

Nicky Cheung, Grade 7
Grand Blanc Middle School

Love of a Rose

My heart is a fragile rose
With not water but blood on its petals.

My life is in fast forward
But my mind in rewind.

I wish I knew what to do
When I am around you.
When I am around you I want to die,
But I want to live to see you forever.

I am lost in your eyes
I am lost in your smile
I am lost in your heart
I will always be lost
When I am around you.
I am a rose with not water
But blood on its petals.

Heather Foster, Grade 8
Holt Jr High School

Join Hands

S top the madness and listen
T o each other. Join hands.
O vercome the powerless and help other
P eople. Join hands.

T oday I look at every white and black.
H elp them join hands for the
E ntire world needs to Stop the Madness.

M ean people all over the world,
A ngry at each other for anonymous reasons.
D o you see why we should join hands?
N ot to harm people, but the help them for all
E ternity. We will say, Join hands.
S o, now I'm saying
S top the Madness.

When I say, "Stop the;"
You say, "MADNESS."

Stop the
Madness
Stop the
Madness

Christopher Ledford, Grade 9
Thomas More School

Dancing with Your Mind

When I move my feet
I flow with the wind.
Moving to the beat and feeling my soul.
It is slow
Deep and tuned in with my movements.

When I move
I glide with the beat
Slide with my feet.
Move to the groove
And hear the sounds as they go.

The movements are coming alive
The steps are turning into beats.
It is not the same you see.
You have to listen
And once you feel the rhythm,
It all comes so natural.

You must flow
As though you have no soul.
You must go deep and move with the beat.
So when you dance you must go slow
And move with the flow.

Ronni McGee, Grade 7
Gesu Elementary School

My Cottage

My cottage on Long Lake a nice far away home.
My cottage fun tubing, great swimming, cool skiing.
My cottage full of friends and great times and good food.
My cottage bonfires delicious hobo pies.
My cottage good pizza sweet ice cream good coffee.
My cottage delicious candy. A pretty church.
My cottage fun boat rides a speed boat paddle boats.
My cottage fun birthdays the cool fourth of July
My cottage in Orleans. Chocolate s'mores, wake boarding.
My cottage beautiful sunsets, nice walks, cool breeze.
My cottage on Long Lake a nice far away home.

Elisabeth Holberg, Grade 8
St Gerard Elementary School

Flowers

Flowers
Vivid, gorgeous
Beautifying, living, blossoming
Like the sun they lighten everything around you
Flowers

Samantha Linck, Grade 7
St Anthony of Padua School

The Basketball Game

Nervous, but ready to begin the game
Oh I'm so ready to win my fame
My coach says, we're a good team
It gives us players some self-esteem
We're bouncing the ball heading to the net
The game is going we're not done yet
The crowds' cheers go higher and higher
Winning the game is our only desire
We're getting closer no one can wait
This feeling to everyone is oh so great
Only ten seconds left of the game
SWISH! Into the net we won our fame

Sarah Abdmahmoud, Grade 8
MacDonald Middle School

Christmas, the Best Day of the Year

When the snow starts falling from the sky,
See the excitement in the little children's eye.
With decorations including little toy soldiers drumming,
All the children know Christmas is coming.
As they wearily crawl into bed,
They think about Christmas just ahead.
Knowing they've been good girls and boys,
Hoping Santa will bring many fun toys.
They close their eyes, dreaming until they wake,
Not knowing Santa is downstairs, eating some cake.
The day is finally here and the children wake early,
Their eyes glow, as they look at the ribbon so curly.
With a huge grin from ear to ear,
Surely, the best day of the year.

Kimmy Leverenz, Grade 9
Grosse Pointe South High School

An Ode to Poetry

Poetry does a lot of things
it helps me speak
and express my creativity.
I can tell people of my feelings
without me saying too much
or hurting anyone dearly.
Poetry stops the violence
of my little broken heart
but sometimes I do wonder
'did that violence ever start?'
Because sometimes when I'm alone
and soaking in my thoughts
I write a beautiful poem
and then I don't feel lost.

Rebecca Harvey, Grade 8
Grandville Middle School

I Wish

All winter long
I sit here hoping
That spring would emerge
So I could go fishing

The wind is cold
But the ice is too thin
If I walked out
I'd surely fall through

As the days grow longer
This urge gets bigger
I want to fish
O, how I want to

Nick Chene, Grade 7
Peace Lutheran Church & School

Glass

The translucent child
Of sediments superheated
Always moving, slowly though
Like a river in the winter.
And never safe from the
Danger of shattering
Crash! Boom! Bang!
All over in an instant,
The life of this constant traveler;
Walking, flowing, running
Even used as a barrier from its parent
By its parent, a joint effort its birth was.
Carrying fluid within fluid;
Gateway to art, to crystals;
Colored sometimes,
But mostly clear:
Is the child
Of nature and man

Josh Meadows, Grade 8
University Liggett School

L.C. Walker Arena

Eighteen players dressed on each side
The crowd babbling at the players in the penalty box
SMACK! A big shot from the right winter Robin Bouchard
Booming, banging, and chanting in the arena from the fans
Rerrrahhh, eeannt the goal horn goes off chalk one up for the home team
Smashing and banging up against the boards from both teams
Clapping from the fans when a big hit knocks a visitor player down
But when the refs make a bad call the fans boo
Yelling at the refs with potty mouth talk is what some fans do
Throwing stuff on the ice when a fan does not like the call
But security does not put up with that so out they go
The goalie smacks his stick five times to tell his team the power play is over
These are things you hear and witness when a hockey game is at
L.C. Walker Arena in Muskegon, Michigan.

T.J. Dorn, Grade 7
Manistee Middle School

Life Is a Box of Chocolates

Life is a box of chocolates —
you never know what you are going to get next.
Maybe you'll pick a cherry filled sweet
that's packed with laughter, happiness, and is a delicious treat.
Or you'll bite into milk chocolate that is very creamy
and find the true love of your life that you would say is dreamy.
Next, you'll find you've bitten into a lemon filled candy, smooth as pearls
that twists your life life like a peppermint's swirls.
Before you know it, you have bitten into a fudge, rich in flavor
this will take a dark path in your life — an experience you won't want to savor.
But, before you even taste your pick,
you must choose your fate, that can be a trick.

Megan Chesley, Grade 7
Grand Blanc Middle School

Imagine!

Imagine that you saved a life,
from a firing, hot flame.
Imagine that you stopped a crook,
from stealing, and then giving the blame.
Imagine that you escorted some people,
across a mighty blue sea.
Imagine that you taught a kid,
how to read and win a spelling bee.
Imagine that you proved someone innocent,
and freed them from jail.
Imagine that you were someone's courage,
you helped them succeed and not fail.
Imagine that you were someone's hero,
that they looked up to you.
Imagine that you can be anything,
with the right amount of courage and self-esteem all this can come true!
If you look forward and at the common good,
you can make a difference.
Imagine the world is a great place to live,
we are all counting on you!

Jackie Close, Grade 7
Flynn Middle School

Never Give Up

Giving up is the question
You ask yourself when things get tough
You think of what might happen
If you decided to give up
Never give up

Giving up is not the answer
Your dreams they will come true
Just follow through and you shall succeed
With everything that you will do
Never give up

Your life may come crumbling down
Your life may forever die
Your soul may never live again
Your soul may continuously cry, if you give up
Never give up

Giving up is the question
You decide, to do what's right
It's your choice to live your dream
Giving up is not the answer
Never give up

Vinson LaCross, Grade 9
Roseville Jr High School

Basketball

Preparing for a basketball game
It's hard not to complain.
You have to think to play good and hard
And play with all of your might.
Even when you don't have that much height.
Dribble the ball with skill and drive it to the hole.
Keep your head up and don't lose control.
Even when the other team starts to win
Don't lose your focus.
As the final minute approaches, the final
Seconds you take a three and as soon as
It leaves your hands you know it's over.
Swish!

Andrew Kern, Grade 7
Oakland Christian School

Diamonds

Diamonds sparkle like the stars in the sky.
They are like frosting on your body.
Diamonds are so expensive,
But yet they have so much meaning to them.
Loved ones get diamonds,
To show their love for one another.
They are a symbol of promise, trust, and commitment.
They come in many different shapes and sizes.
Some say the bigger the better,
But when you're in love it does not matter.

Jenice Stricker, Grade 9
Posen Consolidated High School

Amazon Adventure

In the Amazon a very far land,
There was a treasure sitting close at hand,
It sparkled and shone bright just like the sun,
To own it would certainly bring much fun.

Two planes took off to find this precious stone,
One went with permission; the other, none,
One crew was jolly, a crusty old team,
The other was grumpy and just plain mean.

They snaked up the old Amazon River,
What they saw next made them jump and quiver,
On the mountain below was a temple,
Getting there would not be very simple.

The villains got up there first to the gold,
The jolly team was thought to be out cold,
One crusty climber triumphantly stood,
With cunning and smarts he stopped them for good.

The jolly old folks left wealthy and glad,
The villains were downtrodden and quite mad,
For off the bad men went dragged to the jail,
So ends this exciting Amazon tale.

Trevor Zimmerman, Grade 8
Ruth Murdoch SDA Elementary School

Happiness

In this world, I always searched for happiness.
Everybody wanted happiness, like me.
Happiness is a weakness for a person.
Nobody can buy it,
Neither sell it.

It always makes me happy when I look around.
The singing of birds,
always cool my mind.
The dancing of trees,
always fill my heart with joy.

When my eyes see our wonderful nature,
Filled with trees, flowers and birds,
Makes me jealous, how happy they are.
When I see the little stars at night,
And the shiny sun at day,
I am always happy for their grateful gifts.

When I see my parents smile,
It makes me happy.
When I hear my sisters laugh,
that's a big laugh for me.
Sometimes I think I am always lucky for my happiness.

Jomy Jose, Grade 9
Roseville Jr High School

My Soul Is Mine, Forevermore

My heart is cold, the day is done, maybe forever, they have won.
My soul is here, but not my heart, my longing for my home will ever part.
My mind is wandering, thinking ahead, in the shadows the rats watch, looking for the dead.
When they find one, a splash is heard, we will be fed now, but not much, maybe a curd.
Thud, splash the anchor falls, loud voices and shouts are heard through the walls.
Clinking of metal, boon of trade, our fates are sealed this very day.
Some will fight, some will flee, when he is caught we hear his plea.
Master, Master, is this really our purpose, to slave in fields, and be dubbed worthless?
I am human, but treated slave; this was not a choice I made.
Who will help, come what may, and stop those monsters in the bay?
I now have a Christian name, in their brutal attempt to tame.
English, we are now forced to learn, each girl and boy in their turn.
Work in the fields, earn your food, return to your shacks built so crude.
Pain and hurt if you do not work, in the shadows the overseer lurks.
Trust is gone forevermore; Africa has closed its door.
There is but one thing they have not taken, my hope, and longing for lost land are not shaken.
My fight for freedom will prevail; my love and faith are not for sale!

Haley Tasiemski, Grade 8
L'anse Creuse Middle School East

Suddenly

My life is crumbling
The walls are caving in
And I'm starting to find it hard to breath.

So much pressure coming in every direction
From friends from family
And suddenly I'm finding it hard to breath.

I try to go to a place in time when all this sadness was filled with happy
memories and the sweet innocence of being a child
But then I come back, come back to all of this
And suddenly I'm finding it hard to breathe.

But then I got to you, you're the only person in my life that really understands me.
You never let me down; you were always there for me.
When I cried you always lent me your shoulder.
When life felt like it was too much to handle you always told me how it
could get much worse and to keep my chin up.
Then I would start to find it easier to breath.

You would take me away from all the stress and bring me to a place when all was bright.
I'm never afraid to be myself around you.
This is why when I'm with you
I'm suddenly finding it easier to breath.

Kallie Launius, Grade 8
Richardson Elementary Middle School

Those Letters

My love has shot up since my mamma first left. I want to be able to remember her first words and steps. I can't think of the days when her love first changed and rearranged me. My life is totally burned with passion to complete the journey she started me on. I'm ready to set off, go crazy, break down and cry, because of those letters: L-I-N-D-A.
Those letters spell the bond between mother and child. Those letters I look at every day of my life. Just to keep my life in one piece…together. Those letters thankfully remind me of you L-I-N-D-A.

Leslie Summerville, Grade 7
Glenn W Levey Middle School

Just Because I'm Special

Just because I'm special…
   I'm not a champion
   I'm not a pro athlete
   I'm not a super star

Just because I'm special…
   It doesn't mean I know everything
   It doesn't mean I'm the best in all I do
   It doesn't mean I'm perfect

Just because I'm special…
   It doesn't mean I was created sinless
   I didn't sacrifice my life for others

Just because I'm special…accept me for who I am!

Michael Hiddings, Grade 8
St John Lutheran School

Soccer

Soccer is a very fun sport to play,
I always play soccer during the fall.
It's the most fun to play during the day.
I love to run down the field with the ball.

Practice can be extremely hard at times,
When your coach gets mad and makes you run far.
Your legs are covered in some dirt and grime.
And you want some lemonade in your car.

But, there's no feeling like a burst of speed,
You pass the defenders and can see the goal.
Your teammates are yelling, and you take heed,
As you aim and fire with all your might.

You score and you're completely ecstatic,
But you know that you're melodramatic.

Keith Alangaden, Grade 7
Dearborn Heights Montessori Center

Ancestors

Ancestors,
What did they say,
We will be the ancestors some day,
Hopefully not today,
Are our ancestors still here in some way,
Are they the rivers, forests, lakes, and oceans,
We may not realize but they help us every day,
Making so many motions,
To help us go our way,
Without our ancestors we would be stuck,
With no forests, lakes, or rivers,
We would surely be out of luck.

William Wheeler, Grade 7
Columbia Middle School

Veteran's Day

November 11th.
A day of remembrance,
a day of grieving,
and a day of celebration.

The day proudly set aside for you,
the wonderful and brave soldiers of these
United States.

You've stood up for us in
every war, preserving our freedom
every second of duty.

The fallen and the standing,
we owe a great debt
of gratitude.

You have sacrificed much
For liberty,
For safety,
For us.

Lindsey Ruther, Grade 8
Boulan Park Middle School

Understand

My parents don't understand,
They think we are in the palm of their hand.
We are looking for fun,
But do work that's undone.
If our folks would just understand,
We do not want to be in the palm of their hand.

Chris Muñoz, Grade 8
St John Vianney Catholic School

Mom

There is no better name than Mom
Four you are courageous, beautiful, and strong
With you I am free
Like a bird in the wind you always guide over me
My heart beats with the sound of your voice
With your guidance I can always make a good choice
You are like the sign of God
a beautiful white dove
Who smothers me every day with all of her love
For you have much will
There are so many words to explain how I feel
I have tried my best but here is the rest
My mother I love you so
You are my mom the one I love
You are the wind in my hair
The air I breathe
You are courageous, beautiful, and strong
For you are my mom
you live within me

Jhanay Williams, Grade 8
Gesu Elementary School

I Ate a Pea

I ate a pea I did, I did
I ate a pea the size of a boat
When I ate the pea I choked and choked,
I swallowed it with a gallon of milk
The pea slid down my throat, into my tubes
Then it plopped into my stomach
I felt my stomach get bigger and bigger…
Then my mom said, "Stop whining and actually taste one,"
"You might like it," scolded Mom
I slowly put the pea in my mouth…
I chewed…and I chewed…and then I said…
"Hey that pea wasn't half bad."

Kate Heaton, Grade 7
Montague Nellie B Chisholm Middle School

Friendship Is Where the Heart Is

What is life without a friend
They make you laugh
When you never thought you'd smile again
They pick you up when you are down
They have your back no matter what goes around
They love you for you
And that's all we need
Without a friend
No life will be complete.

Kayla Bridge, Grade 7
West Middle School

At the Buzzer

Hearts racing, we run onto the floor
We are pumped up, ready for more
The music starts, it's our turn to Rock!
At the buzzer
The routine is flawless, we've practiced a hundred times
But now we're in front of the crowd, putting it all on the line!
Our smiles are bright and we yell with all our might
At the buzzer

Our stunts fly high, cause we aren't shy
To show our stuff and send the flyers to the sky
It's just enough to get the crowd all pumped up
At the buzzer
Our time is almost up but we aren't worried
We have done our jobs, got the crowd happy in a hurry
30 seconds left, and our routines almost done
We feel like our team's already won!
At the buzzer

Time is up and we run off the court
But the spirit it everything but short
For us cheerleaders it's all 2 minutes work
At the buzzer

Bryanna Godell, Grade 9
Cadillac Jr High School

Land of the Free

America is my country, the greatest land on Earth;
This is where I live, the land of my birth.
Many who came before me sacrificed their life;
So I could have an opportunity without strife.
Freedom comes at a heavy price;
We've fought for our prize more than thrice.
Our country has a virtuous past;
Our heroes' deeds always last.
For justice we've fought on our wars;
For our victory our country roars.
As the world can see;
I live here and I am free.

Mike Raths, Grade 9
St Thomas More Academy

Racing

The adrenaline is rushing through my veins,
As I go for the pass I keep switching lanes.
As my car starts to turn, I'm losing control,
My front end is sliding into a pole.
The car is stalling,
My position is falling.
Back of the pack for me,
That's not exactly where I want to be.
I got it started back up,
I feel like giving up.
Towards the end of the race,
I better pick up the pace.
I have gotten first place,
You should have seen my dad's face.
I won the metal,
Because I'm queen of the pedal.

Krista VanHaitsma, Grade 9
Cadillac Jr High School

Power Towers

Two towers stand proud and strong
But what would happen is so wrong
Out of nowhere
We heard a buzzing in the air
The first plane came and hit the tower
It hit with such strong force and power
We realized our nation was under attack
And we were all so taken aback
We all asked ourselves why
Why did so many people have to die
How could one man be so cruel
And lead his people to do this under his rule
We held many memorials for those who were killed
Some people were mad, confused, and even strong willed
And now all that's left is ground zero
To forever honor all the heroes
Two towers stood proud and strong
And what happened was so wrong

Sarah Van Acker, Grade 8
St Gerard Elementary School

Heart and Life

Your heart is like a feeble string,
When you're happy it will sing.
When you're mad, or you are sad;
Just look to Jesus; He will make you glad.
In the everyday life we live,
We should always remember to give and give.
For if we cannot give
We do not deserve to live in a
Country as good as this.

Jennifer Knowlton, Grade 9
Prairie Baptist School

The Chair

There lies the cat, quiet and peaceful
Silently in his chair.
She comes and sits beside him
Loving yet disruptive.
He leaves, his space invaded.

The cat not defeated
He lies like a lion, waiting for prey
Ready to retake his chair.
She leaves for some reason,
And the cat quickly retakes his chair.
She returns and angrily sees the cat in the chair.

She sits on the couch, laptop in hand
The cat has won
She is out of his chair.
She waits for the cat to leave again
But the cat is more patient, so she is defeated
Leaving the cat to his chair.
There lies the cat, quiet and peaceful.

David Kramer, Grade 9
Troy High School

Friendships

Friends are always there,
They always care,
They're never unfair,
They help through sad, bad, and ugly days.
They're like a ray,
A ray of hope.
They have the other end of your rope!
They'll never let go.
Through thick and thin,
good and bad,
They'll never give up on you.
If you support them too!
Friend, buddy, amigo whatever you call them,
They are your supporters, encouragers, and shoulders
to cry on.
Right or wrong
Friendships can stay strong!

Jazmyn Thomas, Grade 8
Central Middle School

The Clock

Every day I walk down the hall,
But all I see is a big white wall.

To my surprise the very next day,
I saw something from far away.

This object was circular and filled with numbers.
It looked like something that I've seen in my slumber.

When I walked up to this device,
It didn't seem like merchandise.

From here it, sort of, looked like a rock,
But when I looked closer it was a clock.

Taylor Sielawa, Grade 8
St Anthony of Padua School

I Am

I am
Honor, Faith, Respect
I care very much about my family and the love they give me
Trust is important to me
Fairness is important to me
Confidence is important to me
Voting is a fair thing
Self-consciousness is a bad thing, but can help you
to correct your mistakes
Technology is too complex
Sunsets and sunrises are soothing
People are too self-absorbed
This is me

Katelynn Barszczowski, Grade 7
St John Lutheran School

My First Summer Playing Ball

I remember when our team won its first game
It felt like we had just won the World Series

I remember when we lost our first game
It felt like Christmas morning with no presents

I remember when I first struck out
I was the worst person to be around

I remember when I made a stellar defensive play
I felt like Derek Jeter

I remember going to try out for baseball
I had a million butterflies in my stomach

I remember buying my first glove
It was the best in the world

James Hainstock, Grade 7
Manistee Middle School

The Morning
The morning sun,
Bright and beautiful
Climbing the sky
Like it could fly

Waking every beast
With its natural warmth
Pushing the darkness away
And welcoming the new day
Fritz Miot, Grade 8
Ruth Murdoch SDA Elementary School

Animals
Animals run free
Through the wilderness and beach.
They swim in the water.
David Barnes, Grade 7
St Ann Elementary School

Blue Moon
Marbled look of pillars high
Dummies dressed in gypsy cloth
Blue Moon stands high in the sky
Beasts with giant maws and froth

Dummies dressed in gypsy cloth
Knives and swords displayed all wrong
Beasts with giant maws and froth
Magic surrounds us all along

Knives and swords displayed all wrong
Books of magics
Magic surrounds us all along
Books of tragics

Books of magics
Marbled look of pillars high
Books of tragics
Blue Moon stands high in the sky
Amanda Papandreou, Grade 7
Grand Blanc Middle School

My Mother
M is for Mother
so wonderfully sweet
she listens to everything I need
having her for a mother is a great treat
she does awesome and amazing deeds

M is for Mother
so awesome and great
she is my friend
and full of love at an amazing rate
yet the rules she doesn't bend
Melannie Vincent, Grade 7
Camden Frontier Middle School

Sunrise Success
You smile as you see the bright sunrise over the ocean
As the sun's radiant rays hit the ocean with fierce power
In a vibrant disarray, the colors are a rainbow red,
Blue, orange, purple, and pink
The sky is reflecting that image on the clear blue ocean
The picture is distorted as the waves roll on the shore
Hitting like boulders on a mountain
The world around you is awaking
Crabs shuffle on the brown sand seagulls cry as
They go to retrieve their food for the day
You don't move not wanting to disturb the creatures around you
Salt rolls off the waves invigorating your sense of smell
You feel secure in the world you have created
There is no pain just life
As the sun is getting to its peak you get up and walk away
Travis Bales, Grade 7
Addison Middle School

Love
Lovely light brown eyes I see
Overwhelming kindness and beautiful
person to me
Vivid view of your love being together
Everlasting love we share forever
Love is true happiness in the persons and things you most enjoy
Malea Hunter, Grade 7
Hally Magnet Middle School

The Old Mansion
The mansion in the woods is very old,
I wonder why they let it go; open the door; go down the stairs
You will find the cellar where, the roof is a floor, and the ghosts moan
And the bushes around are overgrown.

In the mowing field that is long ruined grows an old tree, its branches broken,
My heart is in pain to see that tree, now all that has vanished are the leaves.

While walking up the stairs, I heard a scream,
Was it the wind? Or a daydream,
I hear him shout and screech and yell
Was it to me; was he trying to tell me of something unsaid,
Was I about to become dead?

Suddenly the sun went down, figures appear before me,
Will they leave or will they destroy me?
The figures walked on, so slow and sad, could it be possible that they were bad?

Are they human or are they ghosts?
What had happened to these friendly hosts?
Singing and singing, songs of pain, dancing and dancing, in the rain.
These are my friends, no matter how dead,
The spirits are not made up from my head.
Do not judge by hair; do not judge by skin; only judge by what's within.
Cassidy Creech, Grade 7
Columbia Middle School

Just Listen

My mom, why won't she understand,
that I am soon to be a man.
She treats me like I am a fetus,
if I'm so mature, then I don't need to fuss.

She cannot comprehend my thoughts,
my life is tied up in a knot.
I know it's right, but I don't want to work,
"Mom! I'm a boy my shirt needs some dirt."

I sometimes don't know if she's friend or foe,
She doesn't understand…I love her though.

Anthony Stevenson, Grade 8
St John Vianney Catholic School

One Day

Friends are like picture,
You wanna keep them forever.

Friends are like toys,
You wanna play with them all day.

Friends are like your favorite lip gloss,
You never wanna waste 'em.

Friends are like stuffed animals,
You never wanna let go of 'em.

But in the future when you are older,
You'll learn that you will keep good pictures.

But one day you will have to let go of
Your toys, stuffed animals, and your favorite lip gloss.

Because you never know when your friends are gonna change,
Or want payback for something that happened in the past.

Charlene Haisha, Grade 7
Flynn Middle School

Being the Best Sister

First you add a couple of good times,
Bad times, and ugly times.
Next you could add in a couple of fights,
Some arguments you could add as well.
Add a dash of laughter and cheer.
Then you may consider a spoonful of mischief or two.
What you really need is a loving heart.
Lastly, you will probably need a brother or a sister.
Mix all of these ingredients until nice and creamy.
This shall make you the best sister.
To love and to hold closely.
Remember a sister loves and cares at all times.

Caitlyn Hautamaki, Grade 8
Central Middle School

A Strange Boy

Long ago, there was a strange boy
Who thought school was cool.
To him going to school was a joy
And getting good grades was a rule.

If he didn't get good grades
And be kind to others,
His dad would put his hair in braids,
And do the same to his brothers.

During recess, he just did work
While other kids had fun and played.
He didn't want to be called a jerk
So he had his love of school fade.

Now that his love for school was finally gone,
He realized school didn't mean the same.
His new interests were not wrong.
He started working on his ball game.

Josh Thomas, Grade 7
St Ann Elementary School

Drunk

I went to a party remembering what you said.
I know that I knew this and that is all I said.
But somehow I'm lying here on a hospital bed.
I know not what I've done.

Help me Mommy help me why did I drink and drive.
I'm sorry I did not listen, I'm sorry for all the lies.
I'm sorry if I don't get to say my final goodbyes.
If I make it up to Heaven I'll make sure to wait for you.
I'm sorry Mommy one last time I love you in all I do.

Dominique Hall, Grade 7
Grand Blanc Middle School

Patches

She sleeps upon the couch, peaceful in sleep
Without foul worries or extremities
As I watch her slumber, she is a keep
Sleeping in here; to which we hold the keys

She has grown old in her years, now that she
Is not such a yarn-chasing imp she was
I hope she has not some infirmity
Then I would lose my cat, and weep because

This cat of mine is always there, when I
Need comfort from a close friend; peacefully
She would come to where I am and help mend
My problems, though she does unconsciously

She is my pet; solid friend, one that must
Stay with me always and rest, purring 'till dusk

Erin Fitzpatrick, Grade 8
Dearborn Heights Montessori Center

When She Goes Away

My sis will go away to school,
About the time we close the pool.

We'll stow her things into the car,
And drive her there, it's not too far.

And when it's time to say good bye,
I hope my mother doesn't cry.

Our house will seem like winter trees,
Whose branches yearn for fallen leaves.

I'm not like many bro's you know,
I hate to see my sister go.
Nick Burciaga, Grade 7
St Anthony of Padua School

Fear

The icy chill runs up my spine
My mouth goes dry
I want to cry.

I try to hear
But my heart is pounding in my ears
The world is spinning beneath my feet
My brain is telling me to breathe
But my lungs won't listen to my thoughts.

I try to scream
But my voice is gone
I try to move
But I'm frozen still.

Panic washes through my soul
I fall to the ground
"Please someone help me,"
I try to call.
Alyssa Peterson, Grade 9
Byron Center High School

What Is Death?

Tears on Earth
Happiness in Heaven
Sorrow of loss
Praise of joy
Lost in fog
Found by God
Songs of sadness
Songs of praise
Broken into many pieces
Put back together by God
That is what death is.
Brittany Bennett, Grade 7
St John Lutheran School

I Am

I am weird and I like turtles
I wonder how turtles turn their heads
I hear an elephant quaking
I see whales walking
I want $1,000,000,000.00
I am very hyper
I pretend I am a sea monkey
I feel spiders on me
I touch my pen
I worry about dying
I cry for dogs
I am James Bond
I understand smoking is bad
I say you are my buddy
I dream about ducks with a fish's head
I try to make people laugh
I hope to be someone when I get older
I am funky and unusual
You are my buddy and my family
You are my family in my own little world
Brooke Schmanski, Grade 7
Roseville Jr High School

Blue Sky

I sat and watched the sun rise.
Watching birds go by chirping
with all their might.
Flying through the big blue sky.
The sky is so delightful.
There are clouds floating in the sky.
They look like a pillow
The scent of nature
Wiping through the air.
I can't control the feeling
of flying through the air
The great feeling of being free
to fly like a bird through the sky
The big blue sky is always above me.
Kyrsten Widrig, Grade 7
Columbia Middle School

Jell-O

What is in the word Jell-O
Sometimes green and even yellow
Colloid is its state of matter
It can also make people fatter
Many eat it for the jiggle
Some like to make it wiggle
The sugar particles are well knit
So no matter how you like it
Go ahead and take a bite
You may like it, yes you might
Tina Mulka, Grade 9
Posen Consolidated High School

Flashlight Shone

Slowly, silently, like a moon
He walks in the night
This way and that looking for her
Yellow moon and yellow stars
One by one the officers look
You can see a glimpse of her
Beneath a bridge she is hiding
She is as white as a ghost when,
The flashlight finds her
Boom, she is gone
She has ran and very far she has
The flashlight could not find her
Once again, the flashlight
Has put them down
The fish don't move
In the silver stream at all
Hollie Whitmire, Grade 7
Grand Blanc Middle School

I Will

Can't I be me?
Can't I be silly?
Can't I be serious?
Can't I do what I want to?
Can't I stand out of the crowd?
Can't I be loud?

I will be me.
I will be silly.
I will be serious.
I will do what I want to.
I will stand out of the crowd.
I will be loud.

I won't be like you.
I won't follow the crowd.
I won't do what is cool.
I won't do what is wrong.
I won't be mean.
I won't be fake.

I will never do drugs.
Margaret Hall, Grade 7
Guardian Lutheran School

Dawn to Dusk

Dawn
Aurora, daybreak, sunrise, morn.
With dawn's first light, the dark is torn.
Dusk
Evening, twilight, nightfall, eve.
Dusk lasts minutes after sunlight leaves.
Amber Elder, Grade 8
Mancelona Middle School

Seasons

Seasons are a scrapbook for you to look through,
They tend to change right before you.

A wonderful season could be winter,
But when it gets chilly, your hands start to splinter.

Another vast season could be spring,
the wind whistles and the pretty birds sing.

A lovely season is autumn or fall,
It's an excellent season to go to the mall.

And then there is the season called summer.
When it's scorching hot, it can be a bummer.

These seasons are as different as dry eyes and tears
That make up plenty of joyous years.

Rebecca Veneklase, Grade 7
St Anthony of Padua School

Cold Toe

I had a toe that was always cold
Some even said it looked old
My toe would freeze over with ice
It even scared the mice

I would wrap a hot pad around that toe
But, would it unfreeze? No no!
Even in the summer in boiling water
That toe would stay frozen no matter

Finally on a winter night
My toe gave me quite a fright
I hit that toe again and off it broke
The noise was so loud the whole neighborhood woke

So now no toe for me
But, oh golly gee
I'd rather have no toe
Than a cold toe.

Lilly Luttrull, Grade 7
Montague Nellie B Chisholm Middle School

Winter

Winter is some people's favorite season
But I dislike it for a certain reason
I have to stay inside because it's cold
I get so bored and cramped that I think I will mold
Everywhere is covered in snow
It looks beautiful, but the temperature is too low
If it is too cold, I'll get sick and sneeze
Close that window, you're letting in a breeze
This ends my wintry wail
Soon, I'll be making a new tale

Elihu Michel, Grade 8
Ruth Murdoch SDA Elementary School

Flowers

Sitting on the hills of green,
Flowers! Flowers! Is all I see!
Red, blue, white, and even green,
Impossible not to be seen.

Sitting on the hills of green,
Flowers and ice cream sounds good to me.
There are so many things to be seen,
Open your eyes and don't be mean.

Sitting on the hills of green,
Water flowing down the stream.
All the flowers equal fifteen,
And all of them scream, "We're a team!"

Sitting on the hills of green,
Daffodils singing in the scene.
Swaying together it makes it seem,
That I'm really not in a dream.

Sitting on the hills of green,
The smell of flowers are so clean.
I know that I am just a teen,
But I am truly the flower queen!

Kathy Johnson, Grade 7
Flynn Middle School

The Protector of the Night

There is a man in the shadows
The hider from the light
The man you will never know
The protector of the night

Since you never see him
Because he always hides
He is in the light so dim
The protector of the night

No one knows where he goes
When it is daylight time
They say he hides behind a door that's closed
The protector of the night

People wonder where he's gone
Some say that he died
Others say that he still lives on
The protector of the night

But as for me I believe
In this life and when he is left behind
He will always be
The protector of the night

Chandra Doers, Grade 8
Kingsford Middle School

My Best Friend

My friend
Is the best friend
He can dance, sing,
Study, work, play
And do many great things.

My best friend can be
Bad sometimes.
If you look inside him,
He is the perfect friend.
He can be a nice, caring person.
When you look at him,
There is a person
    My best friend
Chassity Taylor, Grade 7
Gesu Elementary School

A Change in Life

Today is the day,
the day that I give
my life over to God.
This is also the day that
I change my outlook on
    the world.
This is the day that I
really find out who
I am and also realize
that I am going to do
something with my life.
The day that I put all things
aside and figure out why I am on
    this Earth.
Today I will define my purpose.
That day is today.
Today I will give my life over to God.
Jasmine Lattimore, Grade 8
Erma Henderson Upper Campus

Journey

I went on a journey
To a faraway place
And left not trace
I was a lost cause
And when I was gone
I felt like a pawn
On a game board that wasn't my lawn.
So listen to this poem
Don't stray away from your home
To a faraway place
Just stay at home base
And don't go and chase
No don't go and race
To a place that isn't called
    HOME.
Hannah Kurowski, Grade 8
St Gerard Elementary School

Veteran's Day

Soldiers will fight for us, soldiers will die for us.
We stand to this day with hope and we pray.
God blessed us with these soldiers, that's why I love Veteran's Day.
Soldiers, soldiers will stand for us, and help the little kids, and die for us.
That's why I'm thankful for this day!
Tarrayce Taylor, Grade 7
Coolidge Middle School

A Moment in Time

My fragile heart, all broken and sore
When I think about you, makes me miss you more and more.
As I think about the past,
I begin to reminisce the moments I hoped would last.
Our days together always made me smile
So many great memories that could last for miles.
Why did you have to slip away?
I wanted you by me, forever to stay.
I miss you every second that you're not here
Losing you was the most I had feared.
I'm sorry for all the unintentional wrongs
Maybe my actions were why you were gone?

A heart on my sleeve is what I wore
Never to be hurt, you promised and swore.
I thought you were my one and only
In the end, I'd never thought I'd feel this lonely.
The sad and unfortunate has come true,
No matter how hard I try, I just can't forget about you.
I couldn't understand why we didn't last longer
But my friends believe that my life without you has made me stronger.
Kimmie Chew, Grade 9
Roseville Jr High School

Feelings That I Hide

Deep inside I hide
My love for you
Each day it grows and grows
Like the way the weeds grow in the hot summer glaze
When I see you
My soul flies
High in the sky
Gliding with the angels
And their sweet beautiful cries
When I hear your voice
I get chills down my spine
My whole body tingles with lust and love
When I look into those green eyes
My whole body lights ablaze
Unstoppable in your purple haze
When you hold me, my body rises into space
And I can dance with all the stars and ride the comets
Then…then you leave and I return to this pitiful place called home
And finally I realize that you may never know of these…
Feelings That I Hide.
Jamila Secord, Grade 9
Cass Technical High School

Violence

Violence is not the solution
Kids think fights would solve problems
Problems never get solved when you fight.
Kids think beating someone will solve the problem
Fighting is a lose lose situation.
Violence is not the solution.

Kids think fighting is the way to be cool.
Being cool is not the reason to fight.
Violence is not the solution.
It is OK to watch fighting on TV
As long as you don't bring it into your world.
Violence is not the solution.

Kids that chose the violence pathway
As an adult they will be spending time in jail.
Violence is not the solution.
Kids can solve problems by walking away.
Also they can talk them selves out of it.
They can get an adult involved in it.

Violence is not the solution.
Kids should stay active with after school activities
Violence is not the solution.

Jinesh Patel, Grade 9
Roseville Jr High School

What If

What if a dog talked,
What if a pole walked,
What if a person balked,
What if a tree stalked,

What if a chair would dance,
What if a book would prance,
What if hair looked like pants,
What if a desk could glance,

What if clocks could fish,
What if TV's could wish,
What if walls could dish,
What if your name was Knish,

What if doors can read books,
What if humans all had hooks,
What if aliens became our cooks,
What if angels became crooks,

What if floors had to take classes,
What if cats had to wear glasses,
What if shirts cooked with molasses,
What if lads became lasses.

Crystal Rabe, Grade 7
Montague Nellie B Chisholm Middle School

Loving Wonderful Goats

Goats are sweet
Small goats, big goats
Goats love to eat
They love to make you smile

Running, playing
Best friends forever
Little bleats they love saying
Love them till the end

Eating everything
Messes everywhere
Babies born in spring
Mothers wanna scream!

Goats bleat, kitties purr
Fuzzy noses, hard hooves
Petting the goats' wiry fur
Goats forever!

Anna Teichthesen, Grade 7
Montague Nellie B Chisholm Middle School

Is This Love

I just want to know is this love
Because if it's not
Why are we together?
My love for you is words that I can't even say
I'm just wondering how is your love for me
I just want to know
Is this love?
Is it real?
That is all I want to know
But remember
My love for you is words that I can't describe

Secret Harris, Grade 7
Hally Magnet Middle School

Now He

He used to be just another
guy in another class of mine,
but now he's the one that
seems to make my heart flutter.

He used to be someone
who I found slightly annoying,
yet now he can make me smile
and feel like I'm special to someone.

He once was just another cute guy
who I thought wouldn't see me,
except now he's the first to give me attention
and I just hope he doesn't make me cry.

Crystal Wazny, Grade 9
Heritage High School

Writer's Block

Blank, blank, blank, blank
Nothing.
Empty thought tank
Nothing.
How do you write when your mind won't think?
In a cloud of white it seems to sink.
Try after try
Why, why, why
…Can't I think?
…Can't I rhyme?
…Can't I write?
What do you do when you're forced to write,
But nothing comes out, against your might?
Gazing thoughtlessly…
Failing endlessly.
Waiting for the words to crawl,
Across the page in my scrawl
Into something I can call
A poem.

Kelsey Clampitt, Grade 8
MacDonald Middle School

Index